Contents

KU-539-099

Published by CGP

Editors:
David Broadbent
Rachel Grocott

Contributors:
David Barnes
Evangeline Bell
Rene Cochlin
Robert Gibson
Heather Gregson
Kim Hodges
John O'Malley
John Pritchard
Katherine Reed
Edward Robinson
Andy Walker

Coordinated by Paddy Gannon

With thanks to Lucy Loveluck and Glenn Rogers for the proofreading.
With thanks to Laura Jakubowski for the copyright research.

ISBN: 978 1 84146 375 9

Website: www.cgpbooks.co.uk
Clipart source: CorelDRAW® and VECTOR
Printed by Elanders Ltd, Newcastle upon Tyne.

Based on the classic CGP style created by Richard Parsons.

What the Examiners Want

GCSE History — it's more than just names and dates.
To get those top marks you need to LEARN these three simple skills.....

1) Get those *facts* right

You need to know your facts and you've got to be able to explain them clearly to the examiners. It's the most important skill — it shows you understand.

1) | RECALL | means remembering the facts <u>accurately</u>.

2) | SELECT | means picking out the <u>relevant</u> facts for your answer.

3) | ORGANISE | means putting the facts you've chosen into the best <u>order</u> for answering the question.

4) | DEPLOY | means actually doing it right — using the <u>right facts</u> in the <u>right order</u> to answer a question.

2) *Explain* yourself

Getting the facts down just isn't enough. You need to look at each fact in detail and then explain to the examiners what it means — this is something you need to practise.

1) | DESCRIBE | means giving the <u>right facts</u> for the topic or period in the question — nothing else.

2) | ANALYSE | means writing about the facts in <u>detail</u>, showing you <u>understand</u> them.

3) | EXPLAIN | means telling the examiners what the facts <u>mean</u>.

3) Make up your *mind*

Finally, you've got to use the facts you know to look at source material. This is any piece of information about a historical period, e.g. books, newspapers, photos etc.

1) | COMPREHEND | means <u>understanding</u> what the source is saying about the period.

2) | ANALYSE | means looking in <u>detail</u> at what the source is telling you about the period.

3) | EVALUATE | means working out if the source gives <u>relevant</u> information, and if it helps you to answer the questions — if you know a source is giving false information SAY SO.

4) | INTERPRET | means explaining the <u>meaning</u> of the source and what <u>opinion</u> of the topic it gives.

Remember...

— learn the FACTS first, and get them clear in your head. That'll make answering questions and looking at sources a whole lot easier. It's all up to you...

How to Study History

Not just facts but how to **use** them

For GCSE you won't get many questions on the facts themselves — the Examiners want to see you <u>using</u> the facts to answer questions. There are <u>four key ideas</u> that'll help you use your facts — the four 'C's: Cause, Consequence, Change, Continuity.

Cause and consequence

1) <u>Cause</u> means the <u>reason</u> something happened — e.g. the causes of the First World War. Any time you have a fact in History, think about <u>what</u> caused it and <u>why</u> it happened. There are always reasons why an event takes place and it's your job to work them out.

2) <u>Consequence</u> means what happened <u>because</u> of an action — it's the <u>result</u> of an event, e.g. a consequence of the Second World War was that the USA and USSR became superpowers because the big powers in Europe were now too weak.

3) These two ideas fit together — think of them like a row of dominoes. The <u>first</u> domino is the <u>cause</u> which <u>starts</u> the others falling, the <u>last</u> one is knocked down as a <u>consequence</u> or <u>effect</u> of all the others falling over.

Change and continuity

1) <u>Change</u> is when something happens to make things <u>different</u> — there can be <u>quick</u> changes, e.g. the assassination of Archduke Franz Ferdinand led to the outbreak of the First World War; or there can be <u>slow</u> changes, e.g. the tensions between Britain and Germany in the early 1900s were a long-term factor leading to the start of the First World War.

2) <u>Continuity</u> is the <u>opposite</u> of change — it means when things stay the <u>same</u>, e.g. the Romanov dynasty ruled Russia for 300 years.

3) These ideas are opposites — think of <u>continuity</u> as a <u>flat line</u> going along until there is a sudden <u>change</u> and the line becomes a <u>zigzag</u>:

Examiners want your **opinions**

1) They want to see you use these ideas in your answers — <u>link facts</u> together and tell the Examiners <u>why</u> something happened and what the <u>results</u> were. <u>Explain</u> if there was a change and if so, what things changed from and what they changed to.

2) You could also be asked to give an <u>opinion</u> — e.g. the most important reason for some event, or how successful someone was. You need to be able to include all the <u>facts</u> and the <u>reasons</u>, and say which <u>you think</u> are the most important, and which are the least important and <u>why</u>.

Opinions are great, but you need to back them up

— you'll only do well if your opinions are supported by relevant examples, and if you analyse all the facts thoroughly and explore your conclusions in detail.

Handling Sources

There are **two** main kinds of **sources**

1) Primary sources — this is evidence <u>from</u> the period you're studying, e.g. a newspaper report on the First World War from 4th September 1914.

2) Secondary sources — this is evidence <u>about</u> a historical period, e.g. a 1989 book entitled 'Origins of the First World War'.

Sources may be <u>visual extracts</u>, e.g. photographs & maps; or <u>written extracts</u>, e.g. diaries, newspapers etc.

If you want to **do well** look at sources **carefully**

1) You've got to find <u>evidence</u> from the sources which is <u>relevant</u> to the question.

2) Show you <u>understand</u> the source, and use the facts you already know about the period to <u>explain</u> what the source is saying, and <u>how</u> it says it.

3) Say whether the sources give <u>enough</u> information about the topic or if there are gaps or <u>inconsistencies</u> — say if they're telling the <u>truth</u>, or deliberately lying, or perhaps just wrong.

4) Say how <u>reliable</u> or useful the sources are for answering the question.

5) Make <u>conclusions</u> based on the sources as historical evidence.

Don't confuse facts and opinions — always think about <u>who</u> is writing, <u>why</u> they are writing and <u>what</u> they are trying to say.

Top tips for answering source questions

Do

1) Use the source material — not just what you know already.

2) If a question says use three sources A, B and C, you must use all three.

3) Check what the sources tell you — look out for what a source says, who wrote it and when they wrote it.

4) Compare what a source says with the other sources given to see if they have different versions of the same story.

5) Make sure you use the facts you already know about the period to judge how useful the sources are, and to help you answer the questions accurately.

Don't

1) Don't add facts you already know if the question ONLY asks about the source.

2) Don't judge a source because of the type of source it is — don't automatically decide that any eyewitness account is accurate or any newspaper article is a propaganda piece.

3) Don't take sources at face value — look at what a source really means. Sometimes the real meaning can be hidden — e.g. a history book about the Russian Revolution that comes from Stalin's time won't mention Trotsky. So unless you know about Trotsky, you won't realise that the source has been written to exaggerate the importance of Stalin.

Sources are the backbone of history

Evaluating sources is an <u>important skill</u> for historians — and one you have to demonstrate in the exam. Make sure you read every source <u>carefully</u> and don't judge them at face value.

Exam Essay Skills

Planning your exam time

1) Exam questions have a <u>mark scheme</u> beside them, with how many marks each one is worth.

2) Look at this first and <u>work out</u> which questions carry <u>most marks</u> — make sure you spend <u>most time</u> on these questions.

3) There are at least one or two questions in an exam which require <u>essay length</u> answers.

> *<u>Learn the Rule</u> — the <u>more marks</u> a question is worth, the <u>longer</u> your answer should be, so make sure you leave time to write enough.*

The **three key areas** of essay writing

1) *Planning* your essays carefully

<u>Sort out</u> what you want to say before you start writing — think about how to answer the question, what the <u>key words</u> are, and if any ideas of <u>cause and consequence</u>, or <u>change and continuity</u> will be useful. Scribble a list of your main points and put them in order.

2) *Giving the* **right content**

Don't just chuck in everything you know. You've got to be <u>relevant</u> and <u>accurate</u> — e.g. if you're writing about the rise of the Nazi Party, don't include stories about a London camel called George who moved rubble during the Blitz. <u>Stick to the facts</u>.

3) *Clear* writing style

First use the <u>key words</u> from the question to explain what the essay is about. Then <u>explain</u> and <u>analyse</u> the question. Each paragraph deals with a separate point in detail. Use <u>facts</u> to support your ideas. <u>Answer</u> the question by giving your opinion. Avoid long, complicated sentences — make it easy for the examiner to see how much you know.

> *Give a full answer to the question — cover both sides of any argument. Check your work before the end of the exam and correct any errors.*

If something goes **wrong**

1) If you <u>learn</u> these skills and <u>practise</u> them you won't have to worry in the exam. Just relax and answer each question carefully, following the guidelines here.

2) If you make a mistake — <u>DON'T panic</u>. If it's just a <u>fact</u> you've got wrong, then go back and <u>cross it out</u> neatly. If there's room, write the <u>correct fact</u> above the mistake — if not then put an asterisk symbol (*) beside the mistake and find a space in the margin (see p.6).

3) If you realise in an essay that your <u>argument</u> is wrong, then <u>DON'T cross it all out</u>. Work out where you went wrong and then <u>add</u> another paragraph to the end, <u>explaining</u> why your first argument was wrong, and giving the <u>right argument</u> instead — you will <u>gain marks</u> for <u>recognising</u> your mistake and for correcting it. Better still, <u>plan</u> the essay carefully first.

If you fail to plan, you plan to fail

Planning may seem like a tedious waste of your precious exam time, but you won't be saying that when you get halfway through your essay and realise it's 500 words of total rubbish. Think about it.

Spelling, Punctuation and Grammar

You get marks in your exams for having good <u>SPaG</u> (spelling, punctuation and grammar). This stuff might not be particularly thrilling but if you can get it right, it's <u>easy marks</u>.

Remember to Check what you've Written

1) Leave <u>5 minutes</u> at the end of the exam to <u>check your work</u>.

2) 5 minutes <u>isn't</u> long, so there <u>won't</u> be time to check <u>everything</u> thoroughly. Look for the <u>most obvious</u> spelling, punctuation and grammar <u>mistakes</u>.

3) <u>Start</u> by checking your answers to the questions which award <u>SPaG marks</u>. There'll be instructions on the exam paper telling you which these are. <u>Only</u> check the rest of your answers if you've got <u>time</u>.

Check for common Spelling Mistakes

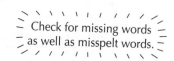
Check for missing words as well as misspelt words.

When you're writing under pressure, it's <u>easy</u> to let <u>spelling mistakes</u> creep in, but there are a few things you can watch out for:

1) Look out for words which <u>sound the same</u> but <u>mean different things</u> and are <u>spelt differently</u>. Make sure you've used the correct one. For example, 'their', 'they're' and 'there':

Woodrow Wilson thought colonies should have a say in <u>their</u> own future.	East Germany and West Germany were divided for 45 years, but now <u>they're</u> one country again.	Under Tsar Nicholas II <u>there</u> were food shortages, demonstrations and strikes.

2) <u>Don't</u> use text speak, and always write words out <u>in full</u>. For example, use '<u>and</u>' instead of '<u>&</u>' or '<u>+</u>'. <u>Don't</u> use '<u>etc.</u>' when you could give <u>more examples</u> or a <u>better explanation</u>.

3) Make sure you've used the appropriate <u>technical terms</u> (like 'collectivisation' or 'détente'). If they're <u>spelt correctly</u>, it'll really <u>impress</u> the <u>examiner</u>.

Make sure your Grammar and Punctuation are Correct

1) Check you've used <u>capital letters</u>, <u>full stops</u> and <u>question marks</u> correctly (see p.8).

2) Make sure your writing <u>isn't too chatty</u> and doesn't use <u>slang words</u>. It should be <u>formal</u>.

3) Watch out for sentences where your writing switches between <u>different tenses</u>. You should usually stick to <u>one tense</u> throughout your answer (don't worry if you quote from a source that's in a different tense).

4) Check that you've started a <u>new paragraph</u> every time you make a new point. It's important that your answer <u>isn't</u> just <u>one long block</u> of text (see p.8).

5) Watch out for tricksy little <u>grammar mistakes</u>:
   - Remember — '<u>it's</u>' (with an apostrophe) is short for '<u>it is</u>' or '<u>it has</u>'. '<u>Its</u>' (without an apostrophe) means '<u>belonging to it</u>'.
   - It's always '<u>should have</u>', not 'should of' (the same goes for 'could have' and 'would have' too).

   If you know that you <u>often</u> confuse two words, like 'it's' and 'its', <u>watch out</u> for them when you're checking your work in the exam.

Check, check, check, goose, check, check, check...

Blimey, there's a lot of stuff to check... which is why it's really important to practise it all <u>before</u> the exam. That way it'll be second nature, so you'll do it all automatically and make <u>fewer errors</u> in the first place.

Spelling, Punctuation and Grammar

Making a mistake in your exam is <u>not</u> the end of the world, so don't panic if you find one.
If you just cross it out <u>neatly</u> and correct the mistake, you <u>won't</u> lose any marks at all — excellent.

Make your corrections *Neatly*

1) If the mistake is just <u>one word</u> or a <u>short phrase</u>, cross it out <u>neatly</u> and write the correct word <u>above</u> it.

> Communist party members loyal to Stalin ~~recieved~~ ^{received} privileges such as holidays.

2) If you've <u>forgotten</u> to start a <u>new paragraph</u>, use a <u>double strike</u>
(like this '//') to show where the new paragraph should <u>begin</u>:

See p.8 for more on paragraphs.

> Collectivisation helped peasants work together and provided large-scale organisation for food production. **//** However, the new system was not very successful at first. Many people died of starvation after a bad harvest caused a serious famine, which was made worse by the kulaks, who had started to destroy crops and animals in protest.

Use an *Asterisk* to add *Extra Information*

1) If you've <u>missed something out</u>, think about whether you have space to write the missing bit <u>above</u> the line you've already written. If you <u>can</u>, use a '∧' to show <u>exactly where</u> it should go.

> Civil rights issues became a particular focus in 1955, with the Montgomery bus boycott. Rosa Parks was arrested for refusing to give up her bus seat for a white man. Martin Luther King reacted by organising a _∧^{bus} boycott with other black ministers. The success of their peaceful protest was inspirational to everyone who opposed segregation.

2) If the bit you've missed out <u>won't</u> fit above the line, use an <u>asterisk</u> (like this '*')
to show the examiner <u>where</u> the missing bit should go.

3) Write the <u>missing words</u> at the <u>end</u> of your answer with another asterisk next to them.

> The Treaty of Versailles was very harsh on Germany. A lot of land*was confiscated and Germany was forced by Article 231 to accept the blame for the war.
>   *including Alsace and Lorraine

Cross Out anything you *Don't* want to be *Marked*

1) If you've <u>written something</u> that you <u>don't</u> want the examiner to mark, <u>cross it out neatly</u>.

2) Cross out any <u>notes</u>. If you don't <u>finish</u> your answer <u>in time</u>, don't cross out your <u>plan</u> —
the examiner might look at it to see what you were <u>going to write</u>.

3) Don't <u>scribble things out</u> without thinking — it'll make your answers look <u>messy</u>.

When making correction, neatness is the name of _∧^{the} game

Examiners love it if your answer is <u>neat</u> and <u>tidy</u> — it makes it easy for them to read. This means they can spend more time giving you lots of <u>marks</u> for the great stuff you've written. So neatness is win-win.

Spelling, Punctuation and Grammar

Some words are darn tricky to spell. The only way to be sure you'll get them right is to <u>learn</u> them <u>off by heart</u>. This page has some of the <u>most common</u> ones you'll need to know for your history exams.

Learn these *Useful Words*

The underlined words are useful in a lot of <u>answers</u>, so you need to know <u>how</u> to <u>spell</u> them.

> There are convincing <u>arguments</u> for and against General Haig's tactics in World War One.

> The Nazis were <u>successful</u> at controlling people through fear and propaganda.

> Chamberlain signed the Munich Agreement <u>because</u> he <u>believed</u> Hitler would keep his promises.

> Fidel Castro <u>attempted</u> to overthrow Batista.

> The Wall Street Crash <u>affected</u> companies across the world.

> American banks were <u>encouraged</u> to lend money to lots of <u>businesses</u> in the 1920s.

> There are many <u>differences</u> between the New Economic Policy and War Communism.

Spell *Technical Words* Correctly

There are a lot of <u>technical words</u> in History. You need to be able to <u>spell</u> them <u>correctly</u>. <u>Learn</u> these examples to start you off. The <u>coloured letters</u> are the tricky bits to watch out for.

agriculture	constitution	evidence	parliament
alliance	defence	fascism	rebellion
biased	democracy	foreign	reliability
conflict	diplomacy	league	resistance
controversial	effective	military	source

> You'll also have to learn how to spell the names and technical terms from the options you're studying. So for Germany you'll need to be comfortable with names like 'Stresemann' and terms such as 'the Luftwaffe'. Go back through the options you've studied and make a list of all the tricky names and words you'll need — then get them learnt.

Learn this page and make spelling errors history...

Mnemonics can help you remember how to spell tricky words. For example, you can remember 'biased' with the phrase '<u>B</u>ecause <u>I</u> <u>A</u>dore <u>S</u>ugary, <u>E</u>nglish <u>D</u>oughnuts' or '<u>B</u>leary <u>I</u>nsomniacs <u>A</u>void <u>S</u>leep <u>E</u>very <u>D</u>ay'.

Spelling, Punctuation and Grammar

This page is full of tips for good <u>punctuation</u> and <u>grammar</u> to help you avoid making any silly mistakes.

You need to **Punctuate Properly**...

1) Always use a <u>capital letter</u> at the start of a <u>sentence</u>.
   Use capital letters for <u>names</u> of <u>particular people</u>, <u>places</u> and <u>things</u>.

2) <u>Full stops</u> go at the end of <u>sentences</u>, e.g. 'Archduke Franz Ferdinand was killed in June 1914<u>.</u>'
   <u>Question marks</u> go at the end of <u>questions</u>, e.g. 'How successful was the New Deal<u>?</u>'

3) Use <u>commas</u> when you use <u>more than one adjective</u>, or to separate items in a <u>list</u>:

   > Hitler envisioned a <u>highly militarised<u>,</u></u>
   > <u>racially superior</u> German nation.

   > Lenin's April Theses promised
   > <u>peace<u>,</u></u> <u>bread<u>,</u></u> <u>land</u> and freedom.

4) <u>Commas</u> can also <u>join two points</u> into one sentence with a connective(such as '<u>and</u>', '<u>or</u>', '<u>so</u>' or '<u>but</u>'):

   > Old Communist leaders opposed change<u>,</u>
   > <u>so</u> they decided to get rid of Gorbachev.

   > Hoover tried to help big business<u>,</u> <u>but</u> he
   > didn't do enough to help ordinary people.

5) <u>Commas</u> can also be used to separate <u>extra information</u> in a sentence:

   > Gorbachev<u>, who became General Secretary
   > of the Communist Party in 1985,</u> was more
   > open to the West than previous leaders.

   > David Lloyd George<u>, leader
   > of the Liberal Party,</u> pushed for
   > social reforms to help the poor.

   When you use commas like this, the sentence should still make sense when the extra bit is taken out.

...and use **Grammar Correctly**

1) <u>Don't change tenses</u> in your writing by mistake:

   > Some business people were angry that the New Deal allowed trade unions into the workplace.

   <u>Both</u> verbs are in the <u>past tense</u> — which is correct. Writing '<u>allows</u>' instead of '<u>allowed</u>' would be wrong.

2) <u>Don't</u> use <u>double negatives</u>. You should only use a negative <u>once</u> in a sentence:

   > It was called the Cold War because there wasn't any direct fighting.

   Don't put 'no' here.

3) Write your longer answers in <u>paragraphs</u>. A paragraph is a <u>group of sentences</u> which talk about the <u>same thing</u> or <u>follow on</u> from each other. You need to start a <u>new paragraph</u> when you start making a <u>new point</u>. You show a <u>new paragraph</u> by starting a <u>new line</u> and leaving a <u>gap</u> (an <u>indent</u>) before you start writing:

   This gap shows a new paragraph.

   > From 1933 Hitler started a programme of public works, such as the building
   > of huge new motorways. This gave jobs to thousands of people.
   >   Even though there was increased employment, the Nazis altered the
   > statistics so that things looked better than they were. Wages were also poor.

When you <u>plan</u> long answers, remember to start a <u>new paragraph</u> for each of your main points.

Phew, now you're fully SPaG-ed and ready to go...

Having good SPaG is a great way to get <u>marks</u> in the exam, and having bad SPaG is a great way to lose marks. Which is why it's dead <u>important</u> to learn all the stuff on this page (and all the other pages too).

Worked Example 1

To be extra helpful, we've put together these two worked examples for you to take a look at. They should give you an idea of how much you need to write, and the level of detail you need to go into. Pay attention to how many marks each question is worth, and make sure you read and understand the comments that are written in red.

Source A: Nazi Party tactics during the November 1932 election campaign.

The behaviour of the Nazis became more violent. On one occasion 167 Nazis beat up 57 members of the German Communist Party in the Reichstag. They were then physically thrown out of the building. Stormtroopers also carried out terrible acts of violence against Socialists and Communists. In one incident in Silesia, a young Communist had his eyes poked out with a billiard cue and was then stabbed to death in front of his mother. Incidents such as these worried many Germans, and in the elections that took place in November 1932 the support for the Nazi Party fell. The German Communist Party made substantial gains in the election, winning 100 seats. Hitler used this to create a sense of panic by claiming that Germany was on the verge of a Bolshevik Revolution and only the NSDAP could prevent this happening.

Source B: Marinus van der Lubbe and the Reichstag Fire of 1933.

I can only repeat that I set fire to the Reichstag all by myself. There is nothing complicated about this fire. It has quite a simple explanation. What was made of it may be complicated, but the fire itself was very simple.

Marinus van der Lubbe — at his trial in November 1933

Source C: Goering and the Reichstag Fire.

At a luncheon on the birthday of Hitler in 1942 the conversation turned to the topic of the Reichstag building and its artistic value. I heard with my own ears when Goering interrupted the conversation and shouted: "The only one who really knows about the Reichstag is I, because I set it on fire!". With that he slapped his thigh with the flat of his hand.

From evidence provided by a German general at the Nuremburg War Crimes Trial in 1946

Source D: The Hitler Youth Movement.

Hitler Youth Military Band in 1942.

Worked Example 1

1 Study **Sources A to D** and then answer **all** parts of Question 1.

(a) Study **Source A** only. Explain what you can learn from the source about Nazi Party tactics during the November 1932 election campaign.

(5 marks)

(b) Study **Sources B and C.** Use your knowledge to explain if the sources agree on the cause of the Reichstag fire in 1933.

(7 marks)

(c) Use **Sources B and C and your own knowledge**. How useful are sources B and C in explaining why Hitler was able to establish a dictatorship between 1933 and 1934?

(10 marks)

(d) How useful is **Source D** for learning about Hitler's policies for young people? Explain your answer using **Source D and your own knowledge**.

(8 marks)

(e) **Use your own knowledge** to explain how Hitler and the Nazis were able to control the lives of German people between 1933 and 1939.

(15 marks)

1 a)   The source shows how the behaviour of the Nazis in the run-up to the election became much more violent. It shows how the Nazis carried out physical attacks on Communists and how in one incident a young Communist was blinded and then murdered. The source also shows that the tactics adopted by the Nazis may have backfired on them. Support for the Nazis fell in the November election, while the Communists won 100 seats. Hitler was concerned by the drop in support for the Nazis and tried to turn it to his advantage by playing on fears of a Communist revolution. This shows that Hitler could skilfully manipulate political events to persuade people, as well as use violence to intimidate them.

Top Tip. The first question is designed to warm you up and will be around 3-5 marks. It's also important not to write too much here — remember it's only worth 5 marks.

1 b)   In Source B, the Dutch Communist Marinus van der Lubbe states that he set fire to the Reichstag himself. In Source C, however, blame for the Reichstag fire is placed on one of the leading Nazis, Goering. The two sources do not agree on the cause of the fire and both need to be treated with some caution. Marinus van der Lubbe may have been tortured or intimidated into giving a confession. We now know he had learning difficulties and so he may not have understood just how much trouble he was in. He gives the impression that he has explained his role in the event many times — he could perhaps have been coached to say these things. In Source C, which is based on testimony from a war crimes trial, the General giving evidence may have wanted to make Goering look as bad as possible in order to shift any blame away from

Worked Example 1

himself, and to make himself look as cooperative as possible. Also, Goering is supposed to have made the claim at a birthday lunch for Hitler where the atmosphere might have been relaxed. It is possible that Goering was boasting or joking about his involvement in the Reichstag fire. The sources do not agree, but there are strong reasons to suspect that both are unreliable. To get a full picture of events you would need to consult a wider range of sources than B and C alone.

Top Tip. *It's a comparison question so make sure that you write about both sources. The question also asks you to bring in your own knowledge, so don't just rely on the sources for the 7 marks.*

1 c)   Both sources B and C deal with the Reichstag fire of 1933. The Reichstag fire was used by the Nazis to increase fears of a Communist revolution in Germany and to promote themselves as the only group powerful enough to prevent this. The fire was used as a major issue in the election of 1933 and was also used to justify the severe measures passed by the Nazis after the March election. The fire is therefore an important event when explaining how Hitler and the Nazis were able to establish a dictatorship.

The sources disagree about who actually started the fire. Source B is the confession of the main suspect: the Communist, van der Lubbe. Source C was produced much later and suggests that the fire was actually started by the Nazis themselves. Source B would suggest that the Nazis simply used events in order to strengthen their support and establish a dictatorship. Source C suggests that they took active steps to frame the Communists, and gain support. However, the two sources alone do not provide enough information as to who may have actually started the fire.

The fear of Communism, which the Reichstag fire helped to create, was a major reason why the Nazis were able to get the Enabling Act passed. This Act gave Hitler the powers of a dictator and was agreed by the Reichstag during a meeting that saw Communist and Socialist members forcibly prevented from attending. However, there were certainly other factors that allowed the Nazis to create a dictatorship between 1933 and 1934 – the two sources tell us nothing about these other factors. For example, they do not cover the Nazi use of propaganda and violence, the impact of the economic depression, or the way in which other parties, groups and institutions in Germany were prepared to work with the Nazis in this period.

Top Tip. *You'll often be asked to comment on the usefulness of a source or sources. Remember, all historical sources are useful to some degree; it's just that some are more useful than others. With this type of question, be ready to write about why the source is useful, but also be prepared to comment on its limitations.*

Worked Example 1

1 d) The photograph in Source D is very useful for anyone learning about Hitler's policies for young people. Hitler set up the Hitler Youth in 1926 and used the movement to influence as many young Germans as possible to accept Nazi ideas. The picture is particularly useful in the way that it shows how the Hitler Youth stressed the importance of military skills and organisation. The boys are wearing <u>uniforms,</u> carrying <u>flags</u> similar to those that would have been used by the SS, and are arranged in a <u>formal military style.</u> After 1933 all German boys were expected to join the Hitler Youth movement. In 1936 all non-Nazi youth organisations were banned and in 1939 membership of the Hitler Youth was made compulsory.

Different groups existed for different ages, and specific groups were set up for girls. Hitler's ideas for German girls were less military than those shown in the picture and tended to concentrate on activities that promoted good health and domestic skills. The source is not as useful for learning about Hitler's policies for girls, though it can be used as a starting point from which to study the way in which the Nazis attempted to organise and indoctrinate young Germans into accepting Nazi ideas.

The picture does not, however, show those young Germans who were prepared to resist the Nazis. Organisations like the 'Edelweiss Pirates' and the 'White Rose' group resisted all attempts to brainwash them into being Nazis and some young people were drawn into active resistance against the regime that ended with many being executed as traitors.

Top Tip. *If you're asked about the usefulness of a picture, make sure you mention some details from it.*

1 e) Hitler was able to control the lives of German people between 1933 and 1939 by using a range of methods that made the most of the total power secured in 1933 with the passing of the Enabling Act.

Top Tips: *This is worth 15 marks so treat it like a mini-essay. PLAN your response. The plan of this answer is clear – control of and coercion of political parties and those who did not conform, propaganda, control of political systems, and reasons for people to willingly accept Nazi control.*

After 1933 all political parties other than the Nazis were banned. Communist and Socialist leaders who stayed in Germany were arrested and those who could, went into exile elsewhere in Europe. The Nazis set up a series of concentration camps for all their political opponents and these were soon used to imprison other groups in society who did not fit in with Hitler's vision of a pure German race – these included Jews, gypsies and homosexuals. <u>These attacks on the civil liberties of some Germans helped</u> <u>Hitler control the German people, as non-conformity was punished with imprisonment.</u> Control was strengthened by the use of the secret police and civilian informants to

Worked Example 1

catch dissenters. This soon developed into a system where people could be arrested and questioned without any real cause.

Look how the answer is structured into paragraphs — examiners like to see this neat and planned approach.

Propaganda was also a key factor in the Nazi control of Germany. The Party controlled all public information and nothing could be broadcast on radio, shown in cinemas or printed in newspapers unless it had been approved. Nazi propaganda was also spread at large rallies and meetings and through well-organised events such as the 1936 Olympic Games. The school system, youth groups and all other cultural activities were linked to the Nazi propaganda machine, and designed to indoctrinate people with Nazi ideas, making them less likely to resist Nazi control.

Hitler's control of the German people was also strengthened by his political reorganisation of Germany. Local government was reshaped into provinces known as 'Gaue', each controlled by a loyal Nazi Party member. Hitler and other leading Nazis controlled the workings of the German state at the national level and the Reichstag quickly ceased to have any real function in the Third Reich. At the very top of this system was the Führer, Adolf Hitler, but Nazi political control spread throughout German society. Positions in the civil service, law, education and government were open only to loyal members of the Party. People who were not committed Nazis were unable to obtain influential positions.

The Nazis did not only use coercion and political domination to control the German people. Most Germans appear to have accepted being controlled by the Nazi regime. For many people Nazi Germany was a substantial improvement on the later Weimar years. They had jobs, more money, more effective law and order, and a feeling of national pride that had been denied them since the Treaty of Versailles. Many people saw Hitler and the Nazis as a good thing. Many of the worst aspects of Nazism, such as the murder of disabled people, and the true fate of many who were sent to concentration camps, remained unknown to the majority of Germans. Hitler's control over every aspect of life may have seemed an acceptable price to pay for work and stability.

In conclusion, the Nazis used the political control they gained from the Enabling Act, and the coercion of those who resisted, to control the German people. However, this would not have been possible if the increased prosperity and stability the Nazis achieved, and strict control of public information, had not made most Germans willing to accept Nazi control.

Keep a focus on the question. Look at the underlined sentences: these are GOLDEN SENTENCES that bring the essay back to the central point of the question — control of the German people. Each paragraph should have at least ONE golden sentence, usually at the start or end.

Worked Example 2

Source A: A speech to Congress by President Truman (12th March, 1947).

The second way of life [Communism] is based upon the will of a minority forcibly imposed upon the majority. It relies upon terror and oppression, a controlled press and radio, fixed elections, and the suppression of personal freedom. I believe that it must be the policy of the United States to support free peoples who are resisting attempted subjugation by armed minorities or by outside pressures.

Source B: The elections in Poland in 1947.

The elections finally took place in January 1947. By then, the Communists had locked up about 100 000 members of the People's Party — as well as 142 election candidates. At the election, Communists frightened voters into voting for Communist candidates. To no-one's surprise, they won the election, winning 394 seats out of the 444. The 'free democratic' election was over: the government which Stalin wanted had been elected.

From "The Cold War and After" by J F Aylett, a British Historian

Source C: A cartoon called **'A Peep Under the Iron Curtain'** drawn in 1946.

Source D: George Marshall, US Secretary of State, speech at Harvard University (5th June, 1947).

It is logical that the United States should do whatever it is able to do to assist in the return of normal economic health in the world, without which there can be no political stability and no assured peace. Our policy is directed not against any country or doctrine but against hunger, poverty, desperation and chaos. Its purpose should be the revival of a working economy in the world so as to permit the emergence of political and social conditions in which free institutions can exist.

Worked Example 2

2 Study **Sources A to D** and then answer **all** parts of Question 2.

(a) Explain what you can learn from **Source A** about President Truman's attitude and intentions towards Communism.

(5 marks)

(b) Do **Sources A and B** agree about the methods by which Communist governments were established in Eastern Europe after the Second World War?

(6 marks)

(c) Is **Source C** an accurate interpretation of the division between east and west Europe by 1946? Use **Source C and your own knowledge** to answer the question.

(10 marks)

(d) How useful is **Source D** in explaining the reasons behind Marshall Plan aid? Explain your answer using **Source D and your own knowledge**.

(9 marks)

(e) **Use your own knowledge** to explain how a Cold War developed between the United States and the Soviet Union by 1949.

(15 marks)

Begin your answer by focusing on what the question asks you to do. Include your main point.

2 a) The first part of President Truman's speech is a strong criticism of Communism, and by implication, the Soviet Union. By 1947 the Soviet Union had control over most of Eastern Europe. Communist governments had been established *(Use background knowledge to place your answer in context.)* in countries occupied by the Red Army after the Second World War. Source A shows that Truman believed that the majority of people living in Eastern Europe had Communism forced upon them. He uses strong language, words like 'terror and oppression', to create an impression of people living in fear, fed propaganda from the Communist-controlled media.

The second part of Truman's speech suggests *(Make inferences from the sources. Using terms like 'suggests' signposts inferences.)* that he was prepared to go further than just criticising Communism. He states that the United States would 'support' resistance from 'free peoples'. By this he probably meant those prepared to rebel against Communist governments. However, it is not clear from Source A what this support would entail. This speech *(Recognise limitations in the source. 'However' is a useful word to help signal this.)* does suggest that Truman favoured an aggressive policy against Communism. Although the Soviet Union is not named in this extract, it was clearly Truman's intended target.

Quotes should be short phrases or words that are distinctive and will make an impact. Avoid long quotes. It's fine to paraphrase rather than copying the source directly.

2 b) Sources A and B do agree about some methods used to establish Communist governments by 1947. The main point of agreement concerns the way *(First identify the main point of agreement.)* in which Communists were elected. Source A suggests that Communist elections were 'fixed'. Source B reinforces this point when it states that the Communists won 'to no-one's surprise' and shows how this happened. Opponents of Communism were imprisoned

Worked Example 2

and intimidation was used to force people to vote for Communists. This also supports the view expressed in Source A that fear was used to impose Communism.

Sources A and B also agree about who controlled these elections. In Source A President Truman clearly implies that the Soviet Union was controlling events in Eastern Europe, including elections. Source B specifically refers to Stalin as the person who influenced the election in Poland in 1947. As Stalin was the leader of the Soviet Union, this shows that the sources are in agreement.

Now mention any points on which the sources disagree. 'Whereas' is a useful word for doing this.

The main difference between the two sources is that Source A is a list of criticisms directed against the nature of Communist government by a known opponent, <u>whereas</u> Source B reports the details of just one election in one country in 1947. Source B does not provide information about other aspects of Communist rule. Despite this, both Sources A and B agree that elections in Eastern Europe, by 1947, were being rigged, under the influence of Stalin.

The conclusion summarises the main points of agreement.

2 c) Source C is a British cartoon drawn in 1946, the same year that Winston Churchill gave a speech to an American audience warning of an 'iron curtain' that now divided Europe into east and west. Source C is an interpretation of this division.

Source C depicts the Iron Curtain as a physical barrier. This is partially accurate, as it gradually came to consist of fences, wire and guard towers, and from 1961, the Berlin Wall.

However, perhaps Churchill intended the Iron Curtain to be a metaphor for the difficult relationship between east and west Europe that developed into the Cold War. Source C accurately reflects the atmosphere of mistrust and hostility that characterised this period. Churchill is seen peeping under the 'curtain'. He looks suspicious. A man on the western side is trying to see through the 'curtain' with binoculars. This refers to the spying that became a feature of the Cold War. A clear warning of 'No Admittance' is painted on the curtain. 'By order, Joe' is a reference to Joseph Stalin, the Soviet leader. He sought to protect Communist Eastern Europe from the influence of the capitalist West by restricting access for Westerners. Source C also makes clear the Soviet domination of the East by showing a Soviet flag flying. By 1946, the Red Army occupied most of Eastern Europe and the process of establishing Communist governments had started — armed guards are shown along the 'curtain'.

Source C depicts heavy industry in the East. There are factories, cranes and smoking chimneys. This may be a reference to the insistence of Stalin at the Potsdam Conference in 1945 to take industrial equipment from Germany as reparations after the Second World War.

Worked Example 2

The western allies had wanted to rebuild Germany. Again, the cartoon accurately reflects the divisions, in the form of disagreements between East and West. *It is helpful to refer back to the question to give the response a focus.*

In conclusion, Source C shows several reasons why the metaphor of the iron curtain accurately reflects divisions between east and west by 1946. Despite the unrealistic depiction of the iron curtain, the cartoon does give a reasonable interpretation of Cold War developments at this time. The only concern would be that in 1946 the iron curtain was yet to solidify. It could be argued that it didn't become fixed until the crisis over Berlin in 1948-9. *— Try to find a limitation if at all possible.*

Begin your answer by focusing on the question. Include your main point.

2 d) Source D is useful in helping us to understand how the United States government wanted to present the Marshall Plan aid to the American people and to the rest of the world. Source D makes it clear that the economy of Europe was a major concern. In his speech Marshall talks about 'normal economic health' and the 'revival of a working economy'. The USA wanted Europe to recover quickly, partly so that Europe would then be able to afford American exports again. The US government also believed that strong economies were needed in Europe to stop the spread of Communism. Source D links 'economic health' with 'political stability'. What Marshall really means is that economic health would bolster capitalist governments against Communism. By June 1947 Communist governments controlled by Moscow had been imposed on most of Eastern Europe. US motives can be seen in the fact that Congress did not agree to give aid until Czechoslovakia turned Communist in 1948. With this in mind, Marshall's comment that the policy was not aimed at any 'country or doctrine' is probably a lie — It was clearly directed against the Soviet Union. **Use precisely selected knowledge to explain extracts from the source.**

In Source D Marshall refers to some of the problems facing Europe after the end of the Second World War. Marshall had toured Europe and had calculated that $13 000 million was needed to finance the Marshall Plan. The American people would have to pay the bill and so in his speech he uses words like 'hunger', 'desperation' and 'chaos' to gain a sympathetic response and to give the impression that help is needed urgently.

In conclusion, Source D is useful to help us see how Marshall Plan aid was promoted as a relief fund for struggling European countries. There were however other, more selfish reasons not mentioned in the speech that Marshall may not have wished to draw attention to.

2 e) In February 1945, the leaders of the USA, Britain and the Soviet Union met at Yalta. These three countries had fought together, but at the meeting differences arose between Stalin, and his democratic allies, the American President, Roosevelt and Winston Churchill, the

Worked Example 2

British Prime Minister. *The introduction should establish the key countries and individuals involved.*

A major cause of tension was disagreement over Eastern Europe's future. Stalin believed the Soviet Union had been left to fight Germany alone, losing over 20 million lives. Britain and America were hostile to Communism, and Stalin feared they might attack. To counter this, Stalin sought to create a Communist 'buffer zone' out of the countries liberated by the Red Army — Poland, Czechoslovakia, Hungary, Romania and Bulgaria became satellite states controlled by the Soviet Union. Stalin demanded Germany be kept weak. The Allies wanted a strong Germany to stop the spread of Communism, and a free Eastern Europe, but the area was occupied by the Red Army. In the end it was agreed that Germany be split into four zones — an American zone, a Soviet, a British and a French. Berlin would also be split into four.

Western hostility towards Communism also increased tension. In 1946 Churchill described the division between east and west Europe as an 'iron curtain'. Roosevelt was replaced by the more aggressive President Truman, who said he was 'going to get tough with the Russians'. Truman implied the Soviet Union controlled its satellite states through terror. In 1947 he launched the Truman Doctrine, promising help to any country threatened by Communism. Together with Marshall Aid, this was seen by Stalin as a direct attack on Soviet control of Eastern Europe. He refused to allow 'iron curtain' states to apply for aid, and instead set up COMECON — a rival funding programme to help Communist countries rebuild.

Nuclear weapons were also a major cause of increasing tension. The Americans did not inform their Russian allies of their development and use of an atomic bomb on Japan. When Stalin found out, he was furious, and believed the USA was intending to use nuclear weapons against the Soviet Union. He instructed his scientists to begin work on a Soviet A-bomb. When this was developed in 1949, it heralded the start of a nuclear arms race which became one of the characteristics of the Cold War. The arms race necessitated an increase in spying, and the threat of nuclear war caused deep mistrust between the USSR and the West.

It's a really good idea to identify which cause you think is the most important — it shows the Examiner that you have an opinion. The most serious cause of tension, however, was Berlin. Stalin was determined to push the Allies out of Berlin and in 1948 isolated the city by closing all the road and rail links. The Allies responded by airlifting supplies to their zones. In the end, Stalin did not dare attempt to shoot down the Allied planes as it would risk almost certain war and he had not yet developed nuclear weapons to match the Americans. The Berlin Blockade was lifted in 1949, but the damage to superpower relations was considerable. Both sides sought to consolidate their position by forming military alliances. NATO was set up in 1949, and the Warsaw Pact in 1953. The Cold War had started.

The Great Powers in Europe 1900

To really get to grips with <u>why the war started</u>, you'll need to know about the background to it.

There were **Five** main **Rival Nations** in **Europe**

1) BRITAIN ruled an empire of over <u>one quarter</u> of the world's people, and owned <u>rich industries</u>. Britain was an island, so it had a <u>strong navy</u> to protect itself and its colonies from invasion. During the 19th century, Britain had followed a policy of '<u>splendid isolation</u>' — it didn't get involved in European politics.

2) FRANCE also had an <u>overseas</u> empire. The French were <u>bitter</u> about losing Alsace and Lorraine to Germany in the Franco-Prussian War in 1871.

3) RUSSIA was poor, but the <u>biggest country</u> in Europe. It was ruled by Tsar Nicholas II. It had <u>no lands</u> overseas, but wanted land in Europe and Asia with <u>access</u> to the <u>sea</u>.

4) AUSTRIA-HUNGARY was a central European empire, made up of 10 different nationalities — many of whom wanted <u>independence</u>. It was ruled by the Emperor Franz Joseph I.

5) GERMANY had a <u>small empire</u> ruled by Kaiser Wilhelm II. The Kaiser was <u>jealous</u> of Britain's superior <u>sea power</u> and rich colonies. He wanted to increase German influence and wealth abroad. The Kaiser described Germany's small empire as its '<u>place in the sun</u>', and was keen to expand it.

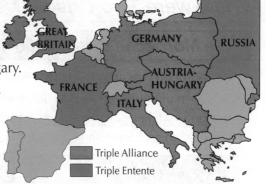

BRITAIN	185 warships
	700 000 men
FRANCE	62 warships
	1 000 000 men
RUSSIA	30 warships
	1 200 000 men
AUSTRIA-HUNGARY	28 warships
	800 000 men
GERMANY	100 warships
	2 000 000 men

Approx. sizes of European Armies and Navies in 1914

Alliances were formed for **Security**

Countries often made agreements to help each other out.

1) 1879: <u>Dual Alliance</u> between Germany and Austria-Hungary.

2) 1882: <u>Triple Alliance</u> when Italy joined the Dual Alliance.

   These alliances created a large group of allies in <u>Central Europe</u> — making both <u>France</u> and <u>Russia</u> nervous.

3) 1892: <u>Franco-Russian Alliance</u> against the Triple Alliance.

4) 1904: <u>Entente Cordiale</u> between Britain and France.

5) 1907: The <u>Anglo-Russian Entente</u> completes the <u>Triple Entente</u> between Russia, Britain and France.

Kaiser Wilhelm II

These ententes were <u>not military agreements</u> — but they ended up involving the military because of the tensions between the Triple Alliance and the Triple Entente.

These alliances and ententes created <u>more tension</u> between the major powers. Following the Franco-Russian Alliance, Germany had a <u>fear of encirclement</u> — it was worried about being attacked on two fronts at the same time. <u>Russia</u> was worried about <u>Austria's intentions</u> towards the Balkans. Meanwhile, <u>Britain</u> and <u>Germany</u> competed to build the <u>best navy</u> in the world...

International politics — a sneaky business...

Countries make <u>alliances</u> with nations who share their ideas. It's also a way of <u>ganging up</u> on enemies. <u>Scribble</u> a list of the <u>main strengths</u> of these countries and the <u>alliances</u> they formed.

Tension Builds — 1900-1914

Europe was drifting towards a major war — and Germany and Britain played a big part.

Germany and Britain began an Arms Race

1) The Kaiser wanted Germany to be a major world power, but he needed a bigger navy. Germany began to follow a policy known as 'Weltpolitik' — a more aggressive foreign policy aimed at increasing military strength and expanding Germany's empire.

2) Between 1900 and 1914 Germany attempted to double the size of its navy.

3) Britain had a policy called the Two Power Standard — the Royal Navy always had to be as big as the next two strongest navies in Europe put together. It meant Britain would never be outnumbered at sea.

4) Britain responded to Germany's improvements in 1906 by building the first Dreadnought — a new and superior kind of battleship.

5) Germany built its own version in 1907-8 — but, by 1912, Britain had a new, bigger kind.

6) By 1914 Britain had 29 Dreadnoughts and Germany had 17.

The Major Powers made Plans for War

1) Faced with enemies on both its eastern and western borders, Germany came up with the Schlieffen Plan in 1905. The plan was that in a war, Germany could defeat France before Russia mobilised, and then fight Russia afterwards.

2) France prepared Plan 17 to recapture Alsace and Lorraine from Germany.

3) Britain created an Expeditionary Force of 150,000 men, ready to travel immediately to Europe in case of war. The Territorial Army was also set up.

4) Russia started to build up its army in 1909 in case of war.

There were Two Crises over Morocco

The Moroccan Crisis 1905-6

1) Morocco was an uncolonised African country, but France wanted to add it to its empire.

2) Germany objected — and demanded an international conference on Morocco's future.

3) At the Algeciras Conference in 1906, Germany was forced to back down by British, Italian, Russian and Spanish support for France taking control of Morocco's police and banks.

The Agadir Crisis 1911

1) The French sent troops to Fez to fight Moroccan rebels.

2) Germany accused France of trying to take complete control over Morocco.

3) Germany sent a warship called the *Panther* to Agadir, hoping to force France to give them the French Congo.

4) Britain was worried that Germany might build a naval base at Agadir, which would threaten key British sea routes — so Britain also sent warships.

5) Germany backed down and recognised French influence in Morocco. The Germans felt increasingly anti-British.

Countdown to conflict — only a matter of time...

There you go then, three major factors in the start of the First World War. As soon as the arms race began, it was clear a war was possible — Germany was trying to overtake British power.

Trouble in the Balkans

The <u>Balkans</u> were known as 'the powder keg of Europe' — a spark of trouble could mean chaos.

The **Balkans** were **Controlled** by the **Turkish Empire**

1) The Balkans were a very <u>poor area</u> of south-eastern Europe.

2) The <u>Turkish Empire</u> (also known as the Ottoman Empire) was <u>very weak</u>. It suffered from increasing <u>corruption</u> and the <u>rise of nationalism</u> among many of the countries it controlled. People called it '<u>the Sick Man of Europe</u>'.

Other powers wanted **Influence**

The Balkans 1912 (before the First Balkan War)

1) GERMANY wanted to build a <u>railway</u> to the East through the Balkans.

2) AUSTRIA-HUNGARY wanted to <u>stop</u> Serbia from stirring up the <u>Slavic</u> people inside its own lands. The Slavs wanted <u>independence</u> and hoped Serbia (a Slavic country) would help them.

3) RUSSIA is also a Slavic country. It wanted <u>sea access</u> from the Black Sea to the Mediterranean, through straits controlled by the Turkish Empire.

4) ITALY wanted to control the other side of the Adriatic Sea. It took <u>Tripoli</u> in North Africa in 1911.

In 1908 **Austria-Hungary** annexed **Bosnia & Herzegovina**

1) Austria-Hungary had been given control of <u>Bosnia</u> by an 1878 treaty. They wanted to make it an <u>official part</u> of their empire. They cut a <u>deal</u> with Russia — who would support this '<u>annexation</u>' if Austria-Hungary backed Russian hopes of getting access for its warships through the <u>Turkish Straits</u>.

2) Russia <u>didn't get</u> what it wanted, as other powers stood against it — but Austria-Hungary <u>went ahead</u> with the annexation. Russia protested, but <u>Germany</u>, Austria-Hungary's ally, <u>backed</u> them. Russia wasn't strong enough to intervene against them both. This left Russia feeling <u>angry</u> and <u>humiliated</u>.

Two Wars created more tensions

The **First Balkan** War

Greece, Bulgaria, Serbia and Montenegro formed the <u>Balkan League</u> and <u>attacked</u> the Turkish Empire in 1912. The Turks were <u>beaten</u> easily and were driven out of the Balkan area and forced to <u>give up</u> their lands.

The **Second Balkan** War

In 1913 the Balkan League <u>quarrelled</u> — Bulgaria went to <u>war</u> with Greece and Serbia. Turkey and Romania <u>joined</u> the Greek and Serbian side and Bulgaria was soon <u>defeated</u> — losing land to the four victors.

The Balkans after the Second Balkan War (note increased size of Serbia)

In both of these wars, the British tried to <u>keep the peace</u>, instead of supporting Russia, who were on Serbia's side. Germany saw this as a sign that the <u>Triple Entente</u> was <u>weak</u>.

There'll be more trouble in the Balkans...

Tension in the Balkans was a main cause of World War One. The <u>Slav question</u> is key here — Serbia wanted to <u>unite</u> the Slavs in the region and was <u>angry</u> about the annexation of Bosnia.

The Outbreak of War

Tension suddenly exploded into the <u>First World War</u> — and it began in the <u>Balkans</u>.

The **Black Hand** was a **Serbian Nationalist Group**

1) The <u>Black Hand</u> was started in Serbia with the aim of <u>uniting</u> all the Serbian peoples.
2) Austria-Hungary had <u>many Serbian citizens</u> and feared a <u>rebellion</u> in its lands, especially in Bosnia.

Franz Ferdinand's Assassination spelled trouble

Archduke Franz Ferdinand was the heir to the Austro-Hungarian throne. He went to Bosnia to try to <u>strengthen</u> the <u>loyalty</u> of the Bosnian people to Austria-Hungary.

Princip - The Serbian student who shot the heir to the Austro-Hungarian throne

Dimitrijevic — Leader of the Black Hand

The Archduke was killed by a <u>Serb student</u> called Princip in Sarajevo in <u>June 1914</u>.
Princip was a <u>Black Hand member</u> — Austria was furious.

Events *Moved Quickly* towards *War*

The <u>sequence of events</u> is important. Also remember the <u>Triple Alliance</u> and the <u>Triple Entente</u> (see p.19) because they <u>determined</u> how the two sides shaped up for World War I.

23 JULY	Austria-Hungary blames the Serbian government for the assassination, demanding compensation and the right to send troops into Serbia.
28 JULY	Serbia refuses to let these troops in. Austria-Hungary declares war on Serbia and shells Belgrade.
29 JULY	Russia begins mobilising troops ready to help Serbia.
30 JULY	Germany demands that Russia stop mobilising.
1 AUGUST	Russia refuses. Germany declares war on Russia.
2 AUGUST	France begins mobilising to help Russia.
3 AUGUST	Germany declares war on France.
4 AUGUST	Germany sends troops through Belgium to attack France, following the Schlieffen Plan. Belgium is neutral, and Britain has agreed to protect Belgium. Britain orders Germany to withdraw. Germany refuses. Britain declares war on Germany.
6 AUGUST	Austria-Hungary declares war on Russia.

Now count the <u>number of days</u> in which all this happened — not much time for sensible thinking.

The First World War — everybody got sucked in...

I know, it's all a bit complicated. Make sure you know the <u>sequence of events</u> and how the alliance system meant Russia helped Serbia, so Germany helped Austria-Hungary, etc., etc...

Revision Summary

Time for the best part of every section — the page with those fab revision questions to see how much you remember. I know it's a bit boring, but it's something you've got to do. It'll help you learn everything in the section — which you'll be really grateful for when you're sat in the exam. When you've finished the questions, check the answers you weren't sure about. Then have another go...

1) Which of the Great Powers had the biggest empire in the world in 1900?

2) Which two bits of land had France lost to Germany in 1871?

3) Who ruled over Germany at the time?

4) Which of the major powers had (1) the largest navy? (2) the largest army?

5) List the key alliances between 1882 and 1907 which split the major powers into two opposing camps.

6) Name the type of battleship which figured strongly in the naval arms race.

7) What dispute was settled by the Algeciras Conference in 1906?

8) Write a paragraph on the Agadir Crisis of 1911.

9) What was the nickname given to the Turkish Empire to show its weakness?

10) Give reasons why Germany, Austria-Hungary, Russia and Italy all wanted influence in the Balkans at this time.

11) What did Austria-Hungary do in the Balkans in 1908? Why was it potentially so serious?

12) Which Balkan states started the Balkan League? When?

13) What was the First Balkan War about? When did it happen?

14) What happened in the Second Balkan War? How did this leave Serbia?

15) Who were the Black Hand? What did they want to achieve?

16) Who was the heir to the Austro-Hungarian throne at the time? Where was he visiting in June 1914? What happened to him there?

17) What did Austria demand from Serbia after the assassination?

18) What did Russia do when Austria-Hungary declared war on Serbia?

19) What was Germany's reaction to Russia's action?

20) What did France do after Germany's declaration of war on Russia?

21) What was the name of the German plan to invade France through Belgium?

22) Why did Britain decide to declare war on Germany?

23) How many days passed between Austria-Hungary's demand to Serbia and Britain's declaration of war on Germany?

24) Write down at least four reasons for the outbreak of World War I.
(Think about the whole section.)

Exam Practice

Study **Source A** and then answer the questions below.

Source A:
Sultan Mehmed V Reshad of Turkey (1844-1918), pictured with Kaiser Wilhelm II, and Franz Joseph of Austria-Hungary; the three emperors of the Central Powers in World War I, 1915. The caption reads, "United in War".

© Mary Evans Picture Library/
Grenville Collins Postcard Collection

The Causes of the First World War

1 (a) Between 1900 and 1914 there were many rivalries between the great powers of Europe. Alliances were made so each country could expect help in a conflict with a rival power.

Describe the main features of the alliances which existed in Europe by 1914.

(4 marks)

(b) Source A suggests something about the relationship between Germany, Austria-Hungary and Turkey in the early part of WWI.

Do you agree with this view of the countries' relationship at the start of WWI?

Explain your answer by referring to the purpose of the source, as well as using its content and your knowledge.

(6 marks)

(c) Which of these was the more important reason for the start of WWI:
  • The assassination of Archduke Franz Ferdinand on 28 June 1914;
  • The arms race between Britain and Germany between 1900 and 1914?

You must refer to both reasons when explaining your answer.

(10 marks + 3 marks for SPaG)

The Causes of the First World War

2 (a) What does Source A tell us about the relationship between Germany and its allies in the early part of WWI?

(4 marks)

(b) Explain why the Moroccan Crises of 1905 and 1911 increased tension between the great powers.

(6 marks)

(c) "The assassination of Archduke Franz Ferdinand was the main reason why WWI began." How far do you agree with this statement? Explain your answer.

(10 marks + 3 marks for SPaG)

The Peace Settlement

World War One lasted from <u>1914-1918</u>. Fighting ended with the armistice on November 11th 1918. The winners (Britain, France and the USA) then had to agree a <u>peace treaty</u> with the losers.

There were **Three Concerns** to think about

1) <u>Millions</u> of people were <u>dead</u> or <u>injured</u>. Countries like Belgium and France were <u>devastated</u> and the main powers had <u>spent too much</u> money on the war.

2) Many people wanted Germany to take all the <u>blame</u>, especially in Britain and France — so Germany and their allies <u>weren't allowed</u> to take part in the talks.

3) Everyone wanted to make sure a war like this <u>wouldn't happen again</u>, but they <u>couldn't agree</u> on how to do this — the system of alliances had obviously <u>failed</u>.

The **Big Three** were **France**, **Britain** and the **USA**

1) All three countries had ideas about the settlement, and they often <u>disagreed</u>.

2) So a <u>compromise</u> was reached — only some of their ideas became part of the settlement.

3) The key fact to remember is that the French had <u>suffered badly</u>, and the British had <u>also suffered</u> — this meant they both wanted to <u>punish</u> the Germans.

"Punish Germany hard to keep France safe."

"Punish Germany - but not too much."

"Let's be generous, to stop wars happening again."

George Clemenceau
French P.M.

David Lloyd George
British P.M.

Woodrow Wilson
US President

But people in the USA had <u>suffered less</u> — so they were less emotional and wanted to stay <u>impartial</u>.

Wilson suggested **14 Points**

1) President Wilson had come up with the <u>Fourteen Points</u> in January 1918 when the Germans were asking for a truce.

2) Germany <u>rejected</u> them then, but when the fighting ended they changed their minds and wanted to base the <u>peace settlement</u> on them.

3) The Allies <u>refused</u> Wilson's Points because the Germans had rejected them before.

4) But the Fourteen Points were an important part of the <u>peace process</u> — especially point 14 which called for a <u>League of Nations</u> to settle disputes. This was going to become very important between the two world wars.

● WILSON'S FOURTEEN POINTS ●
JANUARY 1918

1. No secret treaties
2. Free access to the sea for all
3. Free trade between countries
4. Disarmament by all countries
5. Colonies to have a say in their own future
6. Russia to be free of German troops
7. Belgium to be independent
8. Alsace-Lorraine to go to France
9. New frontier between Austria & Italy
10. Self-determination for people of Eastern Europe
11. Serbia to have access to sea
12. Self-determination for people in Turkish Empire
13. Poland to be independent with access to the sea
14. League of Nations to settle disputes

The Fourteen Points — giving peace a chance...

Once the war was over you'd have thought the squabbling would stop, but instead the winners argued about what should happen next. Don't forget the reasons why Britain and France had <u>different ideas</u> from the USA. Then scribble a list of the <u>Fourteen Points</u> and get it learnt.

The Versailles Treaty

Wilson's Fourteen Points would have been pretty good for the Germans — but things didn't work out that way. After a lot of negotiating, the reality was the Treaty of Versailles.

The **Treaty of Versailles** was signed in **June 1919**

1) This treaty (agreement) dealt with Germany, but the other defeated countries made separate treaties.

2) This map shows the key changes, so go around it carefully and make sure you know who got what.

3) Start by looking at the land Germany lost — especially Alsace and Lorraine (A), the large piece of land to the west of Germany.

4) The Rhineland (R) was demilitarised — Germany wasn't allowed to have troops there as it was close enough to invade France and Belgium from.

5) Look at the new countries set up, particularly the ones near Germany. Some contained many different nationalities within their borders. They were potentially unstable.

Key:
- Countries made from the Turkish Empire
- Countries made from Austria-Hungary
- Countries made from the Russian Empire
- Land taken from Germany
- Demilitarised Zone

THE SETTLEMENT AFTER THE FIRST WORLD WAR

The **Results** of the **Versailles Treaty** were **Severe**

1) It wasn't just land that Germany lost. Article 231 of the treaty said Germany had to take the blame for the war — the War-Guilt Clause.

2) Germany's armed forces were reduced to 100 000 men, only volunteers, without armoured vehicles, aircraft or submarines, and only 6 warships.

3) Germany was forced to pay £6600 million in reparations — payments for the damage caused. The amount was decided in 1921 but was changed later. It would have taken Germany until the 1980s to pay.

4) Germany lost its empire — areas around the world that used to belong to Germany were now called mandates, and they were going to be run by...

5) ...the League of Nations, which was set up to keep world peace — you're going to have to learn a lot more about this organisation.

Versailles — no treats for the Germans...

This treaty was the key document in Europe for the next 20 years — and it was a major cause of the Second World War. The Germans were very unhappy with the results of the treaty, and it would cause major problems later...

Reactions to the Treaty

A lot of people <u>didn't like</u> the Treaty of Versailles — Lloyd George and Wilson thought it wouldn't work, and Clemenceau was criticised by many French people who thought it wasn't harsh enough.

Some people said the Treaty was Fair

1) Some people thought the Treaty of Versailles was fair because the war had caused so much <u>death and damage</u>.
2) They thought <u>Germany</u> had to be <u>made weaker</u> so it couldn't go to war again.
3) People in France and Britain wanted <u>revenge</u> — politicians listened to them so that they could stay in power.

Others said the Treaty was too Harsh

1) The Germans were left <u>weak</u> and <u>resentful</u> — this could lead to <u>anger</u> and cause future trouble, like another war.
2) The treaty <u>wouldn't</u> help rebuild European <u>trade</u> and <u>wealth</u> — Germany <u>couldn't afford</u> the reparations, and many of the new countries were poor.
3) The peacemakers faced problems and <u>pressure</u> from the people at home.

Germany Hated the Treaty of Versailles

The Germans were very <u>bitter</u> about the treaty because they...

Problems were Building up for the Future

1) Europe <u>couldn't recover</u> properly while countries like Germany remained <u>poor</u>.
2) Self-determination would be <u>difficult</u> in new countries like Poland and Czechoslovakia where many people from <u>different nationalities</u> had been <u>thrown together</u> as an artificial country.
3) German <u>anger</u> would lead to <u>trouble</u> in the future. The Germans called the treaty a '<u>Diktat</u>' — they had <u>no choice</u> about accepting it.
4) Without Germany, Russia or USA in the <u>League of Nations</u>, it'd be <u>hard</u> to keep the peace.

After the Treaty — there may be trouble ahead...

I'm afraid we've got more treaties to come — but the key here is that you understand the <u>main points and effects</u> of the Treaty of Versailles. Scribble two lists — one for the reasons some people thought the treaty was <u>too harsh</u>, and the other with the reasons some people said it was <u>fair</u>. Remember — you need to be able to give <u>both sides</u> of the case.

The Other Treaties

<u>Versailles</u> was really only about <u>Germany</u> — other treaties dealt with the rest of the losers.

Four more treaties *Caused Trouble*

TREATY	DEALT WITH	MAIN POINTS
ST. GERMAIN 1919	AUSTRIA	Separated Austria from Hungary. Stopped Austria joining with Germany. Land taken away, e.g. Bosnia. Made Austria disarm. Created new countries (see p.26).
TRIANON 1920	HUNGARY	Land taken away, e.g. Croatia. Made Hungary disarm. Created new countries (see p.26).
NEUILLY 1919	BULGARIA	Lost some land. Lost access to the sea. Made Bulgaria disarm.
SÈVRES 1920	TURKEY	Lost land — part of Turkey became new mandates, e.g. Syria. Lost control of the Black Sea.

1) <u>New countries</u> like Czechoslovakia and Yugoslavia were formed out of Austria-Hungary.

2) Austria and Hungary's <u>separation</u> was important — and the fact that Austria <u>wasn't allowed</u> to <u>join</u> with Germany. Both Austria and Hungary <u>suffered</u> badly after the war.

3) The <u>Turks hated Sèvres</u>. Turkish nationalists like Mustafa Kemal <u>resisted</u> the treaty and forced some later changes — at the <u>Treaty of Lausanne</u> in 1923. This <u>reduced</u> the amount of territory to be lost by Turkey and <u>scrapped all reparations</u>.

4) The <u>Arabs</u> who fought alongside the Allies <u>didn't gain as much as they'd hoped</u>.

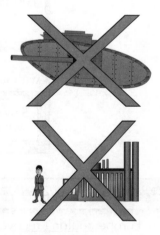

The Treaties had *Similar Results*

1) All the defeated countries <u>lost land</u>, and had to <u>disarm</u>.

2) They were all <u>punished</u>, following the pattern of Versailles.

3) Versailles, St. Germain and Trianon were the harshest treaties — Germany, Austria and Hungary lost <u>valuable industrial land</u>. Bulgaria wasn't so badly treated because it hadn't played such a big part in the war.

4) Countries which were <u>created</u> or <u>increased</u> because of the treaties — like Czechoslovakia, Yugoslavia and Poland — were now governing people of many <u>different nationalities</u>.

5) <u>Czechoslovakia</u>, for example, had <u>Germans</u>, <u>Slovaks</u>, <u>Hungarians</u>, <u>Poles</u>, <u>Ukrainians</u>, and over 6 million <u>Czechs</u>. Tricky one deciding what language to speak.

Czechoslovakia

The treaty was a charmer — so disarming...

You'd be smart to get the names of the treaties and the countries involved all learnt now. Learn the <u>five key results</u> of the treaties and the <u>patterns</u> that show how they all followed the example of Versailles. The new countries were <u>artificial</u> — and would cause big problems later.

Revision Summary

Time for some magnificent mind-bending questions yet again — just so you know how you're getting on. The important thing is to see what you know and to work out what you don't. Then go back over the section and have another go at these spiffing questions. Keep at it until you can get every single one of them right — I know it sounds much too hard, but you can do it... It's the only way to win yourself top marks when the exams come around.

1) On what date did the fighting end in the First World War?

2) Who were the 'big three' who led the talks at Versailles?

3) Which of the big three wanted Germany punished most?

4) Who came up with the Fourteen Points?

5) When was the Treaty of Versailles signed?

6) Which area of Germany was demilitarised?

7) What was Article 231 of the Versailles Treaty?

8) What size armed forces was Germany allowed?

9) How much was Germany expected to pay in damages? What were the payments called?

10) What were 'mandates'?

11) Give three reasons why the Treaty of Versailles could be seen as fair.

12) Give three reasons why the Treaty of Versailles could be seen as too harsh.

13) Explain why the Germans hated the Treaty of Versailles.

14) Name the other treaties which followed Versailles. Write briefly what each one did.

15) Name at least three nationalities living in the new Czechoslovakia.

Exam Practice

Study **Source A** and then answer the questions below.

Source A:
Photograph (circa 1919) showing the skeletons of German warplanes in a scrapyard in Munich as a result of the terms of the Treaty of Versailles which stripped Germany of her armaments.

© Mary Evans Picture Library /WEIMAR ARCHIVE

The Peace Settlement

1 (a) In January 1918 President Woodrow Wilson proposed a peace plan containing 14 points, which he hoped would be the basis of a treaty to end the fighting in World War One.

Describe the main features of Wilson's Fourteen Points.

(4 marks)

(b) Source A suggests that the Treaty of Versailles virtually destroyed Germany's armed forces.

Do you agree that Germany's armed forces were virtually destroyed?

Explain your answer by referring to the purpose of the source, as well as using its content and your knowledge.

(6 marks)

(c) Which of these was the more important reason for Germany's resentment of the Treaty of Versailles:
  • Reparations;
  • Territorial losses?

You must refer to both reasons when explaining your answer.

(10 marks + 3 marks for SPaG)

The Peace Settlement

2 (a) What does Source A tell us about the impact of the Treaty of Versailles on Germany's armed forces?

(4 marks)

(b) Explain how Germany was punished by the Treaty of Versailles.

(6 marks)

(c) "The Treaty of Versailles was unfair." How far do you agree with this statement? Explain your answer.

(10 marks + 3 marks for SPaG)

The League of Nations

There were high hopes for the League of Nations. Lots of people admired its moral principles.

The League came from the Fourteen Points

1) The flags show the four main aims of the League.
2) The rest of the diagram shows how the League was organised and which parts of the organisation were responsible for what.

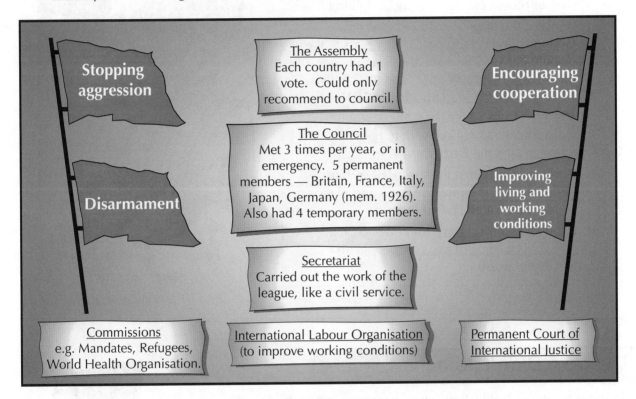

The League was intended to Police the World

1) It began work in January 1920.
2) There were 42 members to start with, and around 60 by the 1930s.
3) All the members followed a Covenant (agreement) of 26 rules.
4) Every member country had a vote in the Assembly.
   Only some member countries could vote in the Council.
5) The League could warn countries in disputes, apply economic sanctions (block international trade with misbehaving countries), then send troops in.
6) The League tried to improve social conditions, working on health, slavery and refugees.
7) The Permanent Court of International Justice decided on border disputes between countries. Everyone hoped this would avoid another major war.

Policing the nations — in a league of its own...

The main thing you need to know here is how the League was supposed to work, and its main aims and intentions. Scribble down lists of these to make sure you know everything you need to know about the purpose of the League of Nations.

Problems with the League of Nations

The League of Nations had good _intentions_, but not everyone was on board....

There were some early **Successes**

1) The League _resolved_ several difficult situations over territorial claims — _without_ fighting.

2) It solved the dispute in 1921 between Germany and Poland over _Upper Silesia_, the dispute between Sweden and Finland over the _Aaland Islands_ in 1921, and the conflict when _Greece invaded Bulgaria_ in 1925. These _successes_ gave it a _good reputation_.

3) It also did a lot of good work to _help refugees_ after the First World War.

4) It worked to combat the spread of serious _diseases_ such as leprosy, malaria and plague — and inoculated against them.

5) It fought against _slavery_, and tried to create _better working conditions_ for people all across the world.

The **USA Didn't Join** the League

Wilson was very ill by this time, and Congress _rejected_ the League. The USA never became a member. Learn these reasons why:

1) The people of America _hadn't liked_ the Versailles treaty, and _refused_ to accept it. They thought the League of Nations was _connected_ to it.

2) They believed it would be _too expensive_ — many people wanted to stay out of Europe, and wanted only to worry about American affairs. This attitude was called _isolationism_.

3) Many thought that all people should be _free under democracy_. They weren't willing to be dragged into wars to help countries like Britain and France keep _undemocratic colonies_.

4) Wilson's political _enemies_ wanted to make him _unpopular_, and get rid of him.

It started off so well — but hit a major snag...

The League did help to sort some things out at the start, but without the USA it all began to go _wrong_. Make sure you can name all of the _early successes_ of the League of Nations, as well as the reasons the USA _didn't join_ up.

Problems with the League of Nations

After a promising start, the League couldn't live up to expectations, especially when it had conflicts to deal with.

The League Wasn't Powerful Enough

1) Britain and France were in charge, but neither country was strong enough after the war to do the job properly.

2) Economic and military sanctions could only work if a powerful nation like the USA was applying them. Most countries were too busy rebuilding to be able to apply them.

3) Germany and communist Russia were not allowed to be members when the League was first formed.

4) The League had no army of its own, and most members didn't want to commit troops to war. Some countries like Italy were quite prepared to ignore the League.

5) The organisation was a disaster — in the Assembly and the Council everyone had to agree before anything could happen. The Court of Justice had no powers to make a country act.

Two Conflicts caused the League Problems in 1923

THE CORFU INCIDENT

1) The Italian leader Mussolini occupied the Greek island of Corfu in 1923 after the murder of an Italian diplomat.

2) Mussolini demanded financial compensation and an apology from Greece.

3) The League demanded that the money should be paid to them, not Italy.

4) But Mussolini got the decision overturned and received the money and the apology he wanted. The League looked weak.

FRENCH OCCUPATION OF THE RUHR

1) Germany failed to keep up with its reparation payments.

2) In retaliation, France invaded and occupied an industrial region of Germany called the Ruhr in 1923.

3) The League of Nations didn't intervene.

4) The United States helped resolve the situation with the Dawes Plan (see p.34).

5) France withdrew from the Ruhr in 1925.

Big problems — hardly the Premier League...

The League was doomed from the start, I'm afraid — but you need to be able to argue for the good and the bad sides of the League. The biggest problem it had was when the USA didn't join — even though the idea had come from the US President in the first place.

More International Agreements

Despite problems with the League of Nations, countries were learning to get on with each other.

Agreements were made in the 1920s

1) Between 1921 and 1929, the political situation seemed to be getting better as countries tried to cooperate.

2) There were loads of important agreements over arms reduction and economic aid.

3) Germany even accepted her new western borders.

WASHINGTON CONFERENCE 1921
USA, Britain, and France reduced size of navies

RAPALLO TREATY 1922
Russia and Germany resumed diplomatic relations

GENEVA PROTOCOL 1924
Tried to make countries use the League to sort out disputes

DAWES PLAN 1924
USA plan to lend money to Germany and extend payments

LOCARNO TREATIES 1925
Germany agreed to western borders set at Versailles

KELLOGG-BRIAND PACT 1928
65 nations agreed not to use force to settle arguments

YOUNG PLAN 1929
Reduced reparations by 75%, gave Germany 59 years to pay

There seemed to be a Chance of Lasting Peace

1) The Washington Conference showed that some countries were keen on disarmament.

2) The Geneva Protocol seemed to be strengthening the League of Nations.

3) The Dawes Plan and the Young Plan were helping Germany to recover — this would create increased trade and cooperation.

4) The Locarno Treaties suggested that Germany was at last prepared to accept the terms of the Versailles Treaty. The Germans joined the League of Nations in 1926.

5) The Kellogg-Briand Pact seemed to be a step towards lasting peace.

But all of these agreements had Problems

1) After the Washington Conference, nobody wanted to reduce arms further — the League had failed in its disarmament plans. Defeated countries were angry they had been forced to disarm.

2) The benefits of the Dawes and Young Plans were wiped out by the economic Depression (see p.35) which was soon to affect everybody.

3) Countries began to make agreements without the League of Nations because they didn't trust it to be effective — France made treaties with several countries because it didn't trust Germany. The Locarno Treaties had nothing to do with the League of Nations.

4) Germany agreed to its western borders at Locarno, but nothing was said about the East — which worried Czechoslovakia and Poland.

5) No one knew what'd happen if a country broke the Kellogg-Briand Pact.

Everybody agreed — to disagree...

The main point here is that everybody was willing to agree, but only up to a point. Sooner or later there was going to be a real crisis. Scribble a list of these agreements with their dates and what they tried to do, and what problems they had.

The Effects of the Great Depression

One of the things that really <u>undermined</u> the <u>League of Nations</u> was the <u>Great Depression</u>...

The American *Stock Market Crashed* in 1929

1) In the 1920s, the USA was the <u>most prosperous</u> country in the world, with <u>high wages</u> and <u>mass production</u> of goods. The 'Booming Twenties' saw billions of dollars <u>loaned</u> by the USA to help European countries <u>recover</u> from the effects of the First World War. American companies were <u>selling</u> lots of goods, so people <u>borrowed</u> money to <u>buy shares</u> in them.

2) But <u>problems</u> started to emerge. Many American producers <u>overproduced</u> — there was too much <u>supply</u> and not enough <u>demand</u>. There was <u>competition</u> from countries like Japan.

3) In <u>1929</u>, the American <u>stock market crashed</u> — people realised some companies were doing badly and rushed to <u>sell their shares</u>.

4) <u>Wall Street</u> is the trade centre for the USA — by October 1929 the selling was <u>frantic</u>, and <u>prices dropped</u> because people no longer wanted to buy shares at high prices.

5) Businesses <u>collapsed</u> and thousands of people were <u>ruined</u> — by the end of the month they were selling shares for whatever they could get for them. This was the start of the <u>Great Depression</u> — a global <u>economic downturn</u>.

The *Depression* caused big problems in *America*

1) In 1929 the USA <u>stopped</u> lending money abroad and <u>called in</u> its loans.

2) By 1930 nearly 2000 banks had <u>collapsed</u> as people <u>rushed</u> to <u>withdraw</u> savings.

3) Three years later there were over <u>12 million</u> people <u>unemployed</u> in the USA.

The Depression *Affected* other *Industrial Countries*

1) Most <u>industrial countries</u> were <u>affected</u> — banks failed, industries struggled, and trade ground to a halt. The <u>least affected</u> country was the USSR, which had a <u>communist</u> system.

2) Within three years there were over <u>2.5 million</u> people <u>unemployed</u> in Britain, and more than 30 million unemployed in the industrial countries of the West.

3) Germany, which had <u>relied</u> on American loans, was particularly <u>badly affected</u>, with banks failing, exports suffering and unemployment rising to over <u>6 million Germans</u> by 1932.

The Depression made the *League's* work more *Difficult*

1) The Depression caused widespread <u>poverty</u>. People were <u>more likely</u> to <u>support</u> extreme <u>right-wing leaders</u> — hoping they'd provide strong government.

2) In 1933, the <u>Nazis</u>, led by Adolf Hitler, were elected in <u>Germany</u>. The Nazis wanted to <u>defy</u> the <u>League of Nations</u> by overturning the Treaty of Versailles.

3) The Depression meant that countries like Britain and France were <u>less willing</u> to <u>help</u> the League by getting involved in resolving international conflicts. They wanted to concentrate on dealing with <u>domestic problems</u> like unemployment.

4) The Depression was also a factor in some <u>international conflicts</u>, e.g. the Manchurian Crisis (see p.36).

The Wall Street crash — a depressing subject...

The Depression didn't just affect the world economy — it affected world <u>politics</u> too. Countries that had nearly recovered from World War One found themselves in dire straits again.

The Manchurian Crisis

On the other side of the world, <u>Japan</u> had suffered badly during the <u>Depression</u>.

The USA saw **Japan** as a **Threat**

1) Japan had been at <u>war</u> with Russia in 1904.

2) Japanese industries had <u>grown</u> while Europe was busy fighting World War I.

3) The USA was <u>worried</u> about Japanese <u>competition</u>, and tried to <u>limit</u> its power and <u>reduce</u> the size of its navy.

4) When the Depression <u>wrecked</u> Japanese industries, the military leaders and business interests in Japan called for <u>military expansion</u> to strengthen the country.

Japanese Aggression led to the Manchurian Crisis

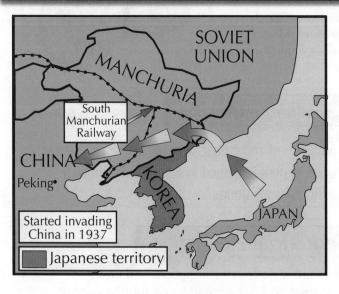

1) Japan had a <u>large</u> army and navy. Since 1905, it had <u>controlled</u> the territory of the South Manchurian Railway.

2) In September 1931, it used the excuse of a disturbance to <u>take</u> Mukden and send its troops to <u>overrun</u> the rest of Manchuria.

3) The Japanese <u>pretended</u> to give Manchuria independence. They put a weak leader called <u>Puyi</u> (who'd been the last emperor of China) on the throne so they could <u>control him</u>.

4) The League of Nations sent Lord Lytton to <u>assess</u> the situation. He produced a <u>report</u>, which said the Japanese had been <u>wrong</u>, but the League <u>didn't do</u> anything else — it failed to stop Japan and end the crisis.

> This was the <u>first major challenge</u> for the League of Nations, and the whole world saw it <u>fail</u> to confront the Japanese aggression.

The **League** was **Weakened**

1) Japan <u>refused</u> to accept Lord Lytton's report and <u>withdrew</u> from the League in 1933.

2) In 1933 the Japanese <u>invaded</u> China's Jehol Province, which bordered Manchuria.

3) Dictators like Hitler and Mussolini saw the obvious <u>weakness</u> of the League.

4) Japan signed a <u>treaty</u> with Germany in 1936 and in 1937 started to <u>invade</u> China — again the League did <u>nothing</u> to stop it.

The League of Nations — a Drama out of a Crisis...

This is where things started to go <u>seriously wrong</u> for the League of Nations. Japan's suffering in the Depression made them look for ways to get stronger — by <u>expanding</u> and <u>attacking</u> other countries. The League's weakness meant it'd only be a matter of time before <u>someone else</u> tried too.

The Invasion of Abyssinia

Next it was the <u>Italians</u> who tested the strength of the League of Nations.

*Italy was ruled by **Mussolini's Fascists***

1) Italy was under the control of <u>Benito Mussolini</u> and his <u>Fascist Party</u>.

2) Mussolini had been made Prime Minister in 1922 after threatening to take power by <u>marching on Rome</u>. He used his new position to change the <u>voting rules</u>, and in the 1924 election the <u>Fascists</u> swept to <u>power</u>.

3) From 1925, he began to change Italy into a <u>dictatorship</u>.

4) Opposition political parties were <u>banned</u>.
He used a harsh <u>secret police</u> against his opponents.

> In the early 1930s, Mussolini was more on the side of <u>France</u> and <u>Britain</u>. He joined them at the Stresa Conference in 1935 to stand <u>against</u> a possible <u>German invasion of Austria</u>.

*Mussolini **Invaded Abyssinia** for **Four Reasons***

1) Italy had been <u>defeated</u> by Abyssinia in 1896 and the Italians wanted <u>revenge</u>.

2) Abyssinia — now called Ethiopia — was <u>well positioned</u> for Italy to add to her lands in Africa.

3) Mussolini had seen Japan <u>get away</u> with the Manchurian invasion <u>despite</u> the League of Nations' threats.

4) He dreamed of making Italy a <u>great empire</u> again.

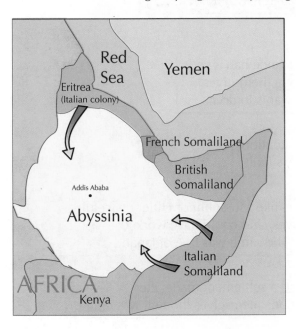

1) In October 1935, Mussolini sent <u>troops</u> with heavy artillery and tanks to <u>invade</u>.

2) The Abyssinian leader <u>appealed</u> directly to the League of Nations for help.

3) The League of Nations imposed <u>economic sanctions</u>, but delayed banning oil exports in case the USA didn't support them.

4) Britain and France <u>didn't close</u> the Suez Canal to Italian ships — so supplies got through despite the sanctions.

5) By May 1936 Italy had <u>conquered</u> all of Abyssinia.

Italy took advantage while the League was weak...

Mussolini was building up a <u>Fascist dictatorship</u> in Italy, and the weak League of Nations <u>could not prevent</u> his invasion of Abyssinia. Make sure you can give reasons <u>why</u> he did it, and <u>how</u> he got away with it.

The Failure of the League of Nations

It's important to see <u>why</u> the idea of the League of Nations <u>didn't work</u>.

The **League of Nations** appeared **Ineffective**

1) The League's <u>reputation</u> was in <u>tatters</u>. But Italy became more <u>confident</u> — and started making pacts with the fascist leader of Germany, Adolf Hitler.

2) Mussolini and Hitler agreed the <u>Rome-Berlin Axis</u> in 1936, and in 1937 Italy <u>joined</u> Japan and Germany in the <u>Anti-Comintern Pact</u>.

3) Italy also attacked Albania in 1938, and signed the <u>Pact of Steel</u> with Hitler in 1939.

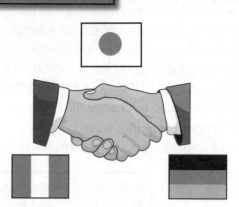

The League **Didn't Achieve** its original **Aims**

The League set out to prevent <u>aggression</u>, to encourage <u>cooperation</u>, to work towards <u>disarmament</u> and to prevent a major <u>war</u> breaking out again. In the end, it failed on all these.

The League did have some <u>success</u> in improving the lives of ordinary people around the world — combating slavery and poor working conditions — but this <u>wasn't</u> its main purpose.

There are **Arguments** in **Defence** of the League...

It was always going to be tough...

1 Once the USA <u>refused to join</u>, Britain and France had a very difficult task — when they <u>weren't</u> that <u>strong</u> themselves. You can't enforce sanctions if nobody else wants to do it.

2 The <u>Depression</u> made the political situation <u>tougher</u> worldwide — it was nobody's fault.

3 <u>No organisation</u> could have <u>stopped</u> leaders like Mussolini or Hitler peacefully. Italy and Germany were members themselves, and could have worked harder for the League instead of against it. The same was true of Japan.

4 The League of Nations had to <u>defend</u> a settlement made after World War I which many of the nations themselves thought was <u>unfair</u>.

Some world problems were out of its league...

Once again, the League was <u>too weak and ineffective</u>. Its failure to protect Abyssinia would have dire consequences. The new alliance between <u>Mussolini's Italy</u> and <u>Hitler's Germany</u> gave Germany the extra strength it needed to bounce back after the losses of Versailles.

The Failure of the League of Nations

...and there are **Arguments Against** the League

It made some big mistakes...

1 The <u>Manchurian</u> crisis was the turning point — the League should have <u>resisted</u> Japan.

2 Too many members <u>didn't</u> keep to the <u>rules</u>. When they were attacked for it, they simply <u>left</u> the League, e.g. Germany and Japan in 1933, Italy in 1937.

3 Britain and France <u>didn't lead strongly</u>, and were often very <u>slow</u> to do things.

4 Members of the League who could have <u>opposed</u> aggression <u>didn't</u> want to <u>risk</u> a war.

5 <u>Ambitious</u> members like Hitler and Mussolini <u>weren't dealt</u> with strongly enough.

6 Instead of cooperation, it let the old system of secret <u>alliances</u> creep back.

The League had **Successes** and **Failures**

PROS	CONS
• Early minor successes in preserving peace between minor powers	• Rise of dictators
• Helped European rebuilding and aided refugees of the war	• Manchurian crisis 1931
• Improved health & labour conditions around the world	• Failure of disarmament conference 1932
• USA supported it with loans	• Germany and Japan left 1933
• Kellogg-Briand Pact 1928 made a general statement against war	• Abyssinian crisis 1935
• Provided the groundwork for the United Nations	• Rome-Berlin Axis 1936
	• German aggression
	• Italy left 1937
	• USSR left 1939
	• Spanish civil war 1936-9
	• Powerless to prevent World War II

For and against — now you be the judge...

Make sure you know the League's <u>original aims</u> and can give your own verdict on whether the League can be <u>blamed</u> for its problems, or if they were <u>unavoidable</u>.

Revision Summary

Here are a few more cracking questions for you to have a go at. Don't skim past this page —
you need to make sure you've learnt everything in this section before you go any further...

1) List the four main aims of the League of Nations.

2) Which countries were permanent members of the Council?

3) Name three early successes which the League enjoyed.

4) Give four reasons why the USA would not accept membership of the League of Nations.

5) Why did Britain and France find it difficult to lead the League?

6) Which two important nations apart from USA were not members at the beginning?

7) Write brief notes to show the importance of the Corfu Incident in 1923.

8) Why did the French occupy the Ruhr in 1923?

9) Briefly explain the purpose of the following international agreements:
   a) the Dawes Plan
   b) the Kellogg-Briand Pact
   c) the Young Plan

10) Describe a weakness of the Locarno Treaties.

11) What event sparked off the global depression in 1929?

12) The Depression started in America. How did it affect other countries?

13) Why did the Depression make the work of the League of Nations more difficult?

14) Why did the USA see Japan as a threat?

15) Why did Japan invade Manchuria?

16) Why did the Manchurian crisis make the League of Nations look weak?

17) Who was the leader of the Fascist Party in Italy in the 1920s?

18) Give four reasons why Italy invaded Abyssinia in 1935.

19) Why did the Abyssinian crisis make the League of Nations appear weak?

20) Who signed the Pact of Steel?

21) Give four ways in which the League of Nations could be judged a success.

22) Give four ways in which the League of Nations could be judged a failure.

Exam Practice

Study **Source A** and then answer the questions below.

© Mary Evans Picture Library

Source A:
A German cartoon published in 1919 entitled "A Sound Basis for the League of Nations", showing the Big Three leaders (Lloyd George, Clemenceau and Wilson) as angels standing over prostrate Germany.

The League of Nations

1 (a) The League of Nations was set up to find peaceful solutions to international disputes.

Describe how the League of Nations intended to solve international disputes before they turned into wars.

(4 marks)

(b) Source A suggests a view about the aims of the League of Nations.

Do you agree that this was a main aim of the League?

Explain your answer by referring to the purpose of the source, as well as using its content and your knowledge.

(6 marks)

(c) Which of these was the more important reason for the failure of the League of Nations:
  • The USA did not join the League when it was set up in 1920;
  • The Manchurian Crisis of 1931?

You must refer to both reasons when explaining your answer.

(10 marks + 3 marks for SPaG)

The League of Nations

2 (a) What does Source A tell us about opposition to the League of Nations?

(4 marks)

(b) Explain how the Great Depression affected the work of the League of Nations.

(6 marks)

(c) "The weaknesses in the organisation of the League of Nations meant it was doomed to failure from the start." How far do you agree with this statement? Explain your answer.

(10 marks + 3 marks for SPaG)

The Rise of the Dictators

Poor conditions in 1930s Europe saw the rise of <u>dictators</u>, and increasing international <u>tension</u>.

Problems and Fears aided the rise of Dictators

Dictatorship might seem a scary idea, but for some people it solved a lot of <u>worrying issues</u>.

1) <u>LOCARNO</u> had only settled the <u>western</u> borders of Germany. The borders on the East were vulnerable if Germany wanted to expand — people wanted strong leaders to <u>protect</u> them.

2) <u>DEPRESSION</u> still affected most countries, causing widespread <u>unemployment</u> and <u>poverty</u>. People welcomed <u>strong governments</u> who could put things right.

3) <u>DEMOCRACY</u> was often <u>blamed</u> for the bad conditions — democratic governments seemed unable to prevent them happening or to improve the situation.

4) <u>COMMUNISM</u> was seen as a threat to all of Europe after the Russian Revolution in 1917 — people looked to strong leaders to fight the threat of <u>world revolution</u> by the workers.

5) <u>ISOLATIONISM</u> continued — the USA <u>stayed out</u> of world affairs, and Britain and France weren't strong enough to oppose the large numbers of foreign dictators.

6) <u>FRANCE</u> was still suspicious of Germany and was building <u>strong defences</u> along the Maginot Line — many Germans felt they needed a strong leader against this French threat.

7) <u>DISARMAMENT FAILED</u> — most countries <u>refused to disarm</u> to the same level as Germany in 1932. Germany saw this as <u>unfair</u> and became determined to rebuild their armed forces.

Dictatorships popped up All Over Europe

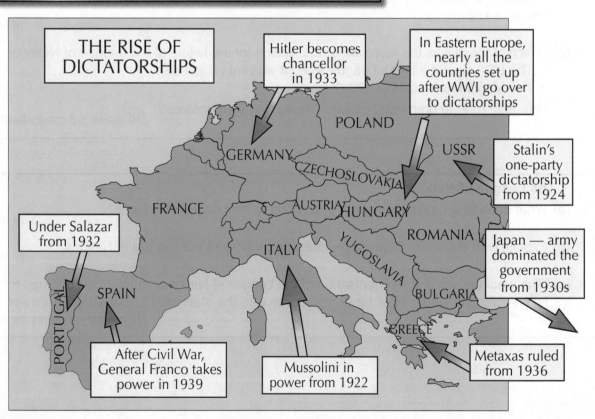

Dictatorship — simply irresistible...

This is really important stuff to learn. Europe was full of tension because of the <u>economic crisis</u> and the <u>threat of war</u> that still came from German anger over the Versailles Treaty. There was a power vacuum — people were afraid that no one was in control, so they turned to <u>dictators</u>.

Hitler's Foreign Policy

Hitler rose to power during a time of depression and international tensions in Europe — and his aggressive foreign policy just made things worse...

The atmosphere in Europe was Tense

1) All the League of Nations' attempts at disarmament had failed.
2) Democracy had collapsed in much of Europe. Several countries were led by aggressive leaders who wanted to take over new territories, and weren't worried about defying the League of Nations.
3) Italy and Japan both invaded other countries' territory (see p.36-37) — and the League of Nations did virtually nothing to stop them.
4) Germany still resented its treatment after the First World War.
5) France had never stopped distrusting Germany.
6) Britain didn't want to get dragged into a war, whatever the reason.

German discontent helped Hitler rise to Power

1) During the Depression, extremist parties flourished (see p.35). There was widespread poverty and unemployment — people wanted strong leadership.
2) Adolf Hitler, the leader of the Nazi Party, got to power in Germany in 1933.
3) The main aims of Hitler's foreign policy were:

> 1) He wanted the Versailles Treaty to be overturned. Hitler hated the treaty which he saw as unfairly weakening Germany (see p.27).
>
> 2) He wanted rearmament. Germany had been forced to reduce its armed forces under the Versailles Treaty. Hitler wanted Germany to be a strong military power.
>
> 3) He wanted all German-speaking peoples to be united in a German Reich (empire). This would mean annexing Austria, and taking territory from Poland and Czechoslovakia which had German minorities. This idea was known as Grossdeutschland — meaning "Great Germany".
>
> 4) He wanted to expand Germany's territory by taking land from peoples he saw as inferior, such as the Slavs. This expansion would provide more Lebensraum (which means "living space") for the German people.

Hitler Prepared for German Expansion

1) In 1933, Hitler withdrew Germany from the League of Nations' Disarmament Conference. He later withdrew Germany from the League of Nations itself.
2) In 1934, Hitler agreed a 10-year friendship pact with Poland — which had the effect of weakening Poland's alliance with France.
3) In March 1935, he brought in military conscription in Germany — breaking the terms of the Versailles Treaty. This was condemned by France, Britain and Italy.
4) In June 1935, Hitler reached a naval agreement with Britain. It allowed Germany to build up to 35% of British naval strength and up to 45% of their submarine strength. This agreement implied that Germany had a right to rearm — breaking the Treaty of Versailles.

Hitler didn't lack ambition...

Hitler was an ambitious and ruthless leader. He wanted to make Germany a strong military power which could dominate Europe — and didn't care if he broke the rules to do it.

The Rhineland and Austria

Hitler's foreign policy became increasingly aggressive...

Hitler's first Territorial Success was in the Saar

1) The Saar was an industrialised region of Germany about 30 miles wide, bordering France.

2) Under the Treaty of Versailles, the Saar was put under the control of the League of Nations for 15 years from 1920. The plan was for the territory's status to be decided by popular vote in 1935.

3) In the January 1935 plebiscite (referendum), 90% of voters chose reunion with Germany — showing Hitler's popularity. The Saar was returned to Germany in March.

In March 1936 Hitler sent Troops into the Rhineland

1) The Rhineland was demilitarised by the Treaty of Versailles. Germany accepted this by signing the Locarno Treaties in 1925 (see p.34).

2) But the League of Nations was busy with Italy's invasion of Abyssinia. Hitler saw his chance.

3) Russia and France had recently made a treaty against German attacks. Hitler claimed that this threatened Germany, and that he should be allowed to put troops on Germany's borders.

4) Hitler reckoned Britain wouldn't get involved. But he was unsure how France would react.

5) The German forces had orders to pull out immediately if the French army moved in. But France was in the middle of an election campaign — so no one was willing to start a war with Germany. The League of Nations and Britain were angry but refused to take action.

> Hitler was breaking part of the Treaty of Versailles — and no one tried to stop him.

Hitler then turned his attention to Austria

1) Hitler believed Germany and Austria belonged together. He wanted "Anschluss" (union).

2) In 1934, a Nazi revolt in Austria failed, after Mussolini moved Italian troops to the Austrian border, scaring Hitler off.

3) But by 1936, Hitler and Mussolini had become allies.

4) Hitler encouraged Austrian Nazis to stage demonstrations and protests. In February 1938, he demanded that an Austrian Nazi called Seyss-Inquart be made Minister of the Interior.

5) Instead, the Austrian Chancellor Schuschnigg called a plebiscite on whether Austria should remain independent. But Hitler couldn't be sure he'd get the result he wanted.

6) Hitler threatened to invade if Schuschnigg didn't resign. Schuschnigg couldn't take the risk — he and his cabinet resigned, except for Seyss-Inquart, who invited the German army into Austria to "restore order".

> On 15th March 1938, Hitler entered Vienna to proclaim the Greater German Reich. Austria and Germany were united.

The late 1930s — storm clouds gathering...

Hitler was rapidly gaining power — after the humiliations of Versailles, Germany was on the up. Write a list of the main reasons why Hitler got away with sending troops into the Rhineland.

Czechoslovakia and Munich 1938

Czechoslovakia was afraid that Hitler, after taking over Austria, would try the <u>same thing on them</u>.

*Hitler put **Pressure** on **Czechoslovakia** in 1938*

1) <u>Czechoslovakia's</u> borders had been set at Versailles. The <u>Sudetenland</u> was a part of western Czechoslovakia which had a <u>large population of Germans</u> — about 3 million.

2) Britain, France and the USSR agreed to <u>support the Czechs</u> if Hitler invaded.

3) Hitler promised the British PM, <u>Neville Chamberlain</u>, that he <u>wouldn't invade</u> Czechoslovakia.

4) But soon Hitler claimed that the Czech government was <u>discriminating</u> against the Germans in the Sudetenland. The Nazis organised <u>demonstrations</u> in the Sudetenland demanding that the area should become <u>part of Germany</u>.

5) In <u>May 1938</u>, Hitler threatened to <u>go to war</u>. The Czech leader, Benes, was ready to fight.

6) But Chamberlain and the French PM Daladier then <u>put pressure</u> on the Czechs to give <u>concessions</u> to Hitler to avoid a war.

*Chamberlain **Negotiated** with Hitler*

1) In September 1938, Chamberlain <u>flew twice</u> to Germany, where he met Hitler to <u>negotiate</u>.

2) But Hitler <u>changed his demands</u>, and set a date of <u>1st October</u> to "rescue" the Sudeten Germans. Chamberlain called this <u>unreasonable</u>, and the British Navy was mobilised for war.

3) Then on 29th September, Hitler invited Chamberlain, Daladier and Mussolini to a <u>conference</u> in Munich. Mussolini put forward a plan (really written by the German Foreign Office).

4) After discussions, the four leaders produced the <u>Munich Agreement</u>. This <u>gave</u> the Sudetenland to Germany but guaranteed the <u>rest</u> of Czechoslovakia would stay put. Chamberlain gave in to Hitler's demands because he <u>believed</u> Hitler would honour his promise.

> The Munich Agreement was all about <u>appeasement</u> — giving aggressive countries like Germany and Italy <u>what they wanted</u> in order to <u>avoid</u> a major war.

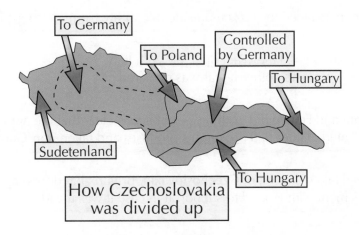

How Czechoslovakia was divided up

Appeasement — "Peace for our Time"...

Czechoslovakia was understandably <u>wary</u> of Hitler, but Chamberlain didn't want to cause a war by <u>refusing his demands</u> — meaning the Czechs lost part of their land. Make sure you know what <u>appeasement</u> was — and scribble a list of the <u>events</u> of the Czech crisis.

Czechoslovakia and Munich 1938

Most people were glad there wouldn't be a war — but in a poll soon after the Munich Agreement, over 90% of British people asked said they didn't trust Hitler.

Not Everyone was Happy with the Munich Agreement

1) It seemed like Chamberlain had prevented war. He claimed the agreement meant "peace for our time", and he flew back to Britain to a hero's welcome.
2) But Czechoslovakia and the USSR weren't invited to the Munich Conference. So the Czechs weren't even consulted on their own future.
3) And the USSR, who had big concerns about Hitler, were horrified at the agreement.

Many at the time Supported Appeasement

Appeasement may seem a bad idea now, but at the time, many people supported it.

1) No one in Britain wanted a war, and some people felt the Treaty of Versailles was unfair to Germany — so Hitler should be allowed to rebuild its power.
2) Many British politicians feared communism and the USSR much more than Hitler — they wanted Germany as a buffer between Britain and the USSR.
3) Britain's economy and armed forces were weak. Some historians say Chamberlain gave in to Hitler in order to buy time for rearming.

In March 1939 Hitler took over the Rest of Czechoslovakia

1) After losing the Sudetenland, Czechoslovakia began to descend into anarchy. Slovakia began to demand independence.
2) Hitler persuaded the Czech president to allow German troops in to "restore order".
3) In May 1939, Germany signed the "Pact of Steel" with Italy. They promised to support each other if war was declared.
4) Britain and France did nothing — but it was clear that the appeasement policy had failed. Hitler had broken his promises and taken non-German lands.
5) Once the Nazis had taken the rest of Czechoslovakia, Britain abandoned appeasement and made an agreement with Poland to support it in case it was invaded.

Appeasement seemed like a good idea at the time...

Although the Munich Agreement was all about avoiding a war, it caused major problems for Czechoslovakia, and upset the USSR. By the time it was clear that Hitler had broken his promises it seemed too late to prevent conflict...

Poland and the Outbreak of War

The situation in Europe was getting very <u>heated</u>. Countries were <u>angry</u> and <u>suspicious</u> of each other, and Hitler seemed to be getting <u>exactly what he wanted</u> while Britain and France did <u>nothing</u>.

The **USSR** made a **Pact** with **Hitler**

1) The USSR (Soviet Union) <u>joined</u> the League of Nations in 1934, and signed a <u>treaty</u> with France in 1935 <u>against</u> Hitler. The Soviet leader, Stalin, was <u>suspicious</u> of the Nazis.

2) But the USSR <u>never trusted</u> the French, and <u>couldn't</u> understand why nobody stood up to Hitler earlier. After Munich, Stalin decided to <u>negotiate</u> with Germany to <u>protect</u> the USSR.

3) The <u>Nazi-Soviet Pact</u> was signed in August 1939. The USSR and Germany agreed <u>not</u> to attack each other. They also <u>secretly planned</u> to carve up another country — <u>Poland</u>.

4) They agreed that if Germany invaded Poland, the USSR would get Latvia, Estonia, Finland and East Poland — but Hitler <u>never</u> really <u>intended</u> to let them keep those areas.

On <u>1st September 1939</u> Hitler <u>invaded Poland</u>. This was too much — Britain and France ordered him to leave. He ignored them and Britain <u>declared war</u> on Germany on <u>3rd September 1939</u>.

The **Road** to the **Second World War**

These are the <u>three key areas</u> you need to cover in your revision of this topic:

 Make sure you learn the final steps to war between 1936 and 1939 — the <u>sequence of events</u> is very important and you should practise the different names and spellings.

 Be clear on the <u>reasons</u> why nobody stopped Hitler sooner — e.g. the <u>weakness</u> of the League of Nations, the policy of <u>appeasement</u> and the <u>secret plotting</u> of the USSR etc.

 Remember the <u>long-term causes</u> of tension during the 1920s and 1930s — think about the <u>problems</u> caused by the Versailles Treaty and the League of Nations, and the <u>consequences</u> of the worldwide economic problems during the Depression (look back at Sections 2 and 3).

Twenty years on — Europe was at war again...

This is really important stuff. Remember — there were <u>long-term causes</u> as well as the <u>short-term ones</u>. Scribble a quick summary of the <u>Nazi-Soviet pact</u>. Then test your memory of Hitler's actions in the Rhineland, Austria, Sudetenland, Czechoslovakia and Poland.

Revision Summary

Yes, it's time for some more revision questions — just what you need to test your knowledge of this section. This is a really important section because it sits right in the thick of the action. All the problems after the First World War and then during the Depression suddenly came to a head. The key is to make sure you understand all of the different causes of the Second World War. Don't forget — it wasn't just one thing but a whole combination of long- and short-term causes. So start by working through these questions. Remember — you need to practise them till you know all the answers by heart.

1) List as many reasons as you can why several dictators came to power in Europe in the 1930s.

2) What was the name of the dictator who ruled in Italy?

3) Give four aims of Adolf Hitler's foreign policy in the 1930s.

4) Why did Hitler hate the Treaty of Versailles?

5) What conference did Hitler withdraw from in 1933?

6) When did Hitler bring in military conscription in Germany?

7) What was the result of the plebiscite (referendum) in the Saar in 1935?

8) Where did Germany send troops in 1936? Explain why nobody stopped them.

9) What was the name given to the joining of Germany and Austria? How did Hitler achieve it?

10) Name the area of Czechoslovakia that Hitler wanted in 1938.

11) What was agreed in the Munich Agreement in 1938?

12) What was appeasement? Give three reasons why it was a popular policy in Britain at the time.

13) What was the Pact of Steel?

14) Why did the Soviet Union make an agreement with Germany in 1939?

15) What happened after Hitler invaded Poland in September 1939?

16) Explain four causes of the Second World War.

Exam Practice

Study **Source A** and then answer the questions below.

Source A:
German postcard published 1 October 1938, thanking the Führer for taking the Sudetenland.

WIR DANKEN UNSERM FÜHRER

© Mary Evans Picture Library

Causes of the Second World War

1 **(a)** At the Munich Conference of September 1938 the British, French and Italians agreed that Germany could take over the Sudetenland in Czechoslovakia.

Describe the main features of the policy of appeasement.

(4 marks)

(b) Source A suggests Hitler's invasion of the Sudetenland was popular with the German people.

Do you agree that Hitler's policy of increasing German territory was a popular one?

Explain your answer by referring to the purpose of the source, as well as using its content and your knowledge.

(6 marks)

(c) Which of these was the more important reason for the start of WWII, in September 1939:
- Chamberlain's policy of appeasement;
- The Nazi-Soviet Pact of August 1939?

You must refer to both reasons when explaining your answer.

(10 marks + 3 marks for SPaG)

Causes of the Second World War

2 **(a)** What does Source A tell us about the popularity of Hitler's foreign policy in the 1930s?

(4 marks)

(b) Explain why Hitler challenged the Treaty of Versailles after 1933.

(6 marks)

(c) "The policy of appeasement was a mistake."

How far do you agree with this statement? Explain your answer.

(10 marks + 3 marks for SPaG)

Causes of the Second World War

3 This question is about the events leading to the start of WWII, in September 1939.

(a) Describe two ways in which Germany challenged the Treaty of Versailles between 1933 and 1938.

(4 marks)

(b) Briefly explain how Britain and France appeased Germany between 1936 and 1938.

(6 marks)

(c) Explain why war broke out in September 1939.

(10 marks + 3 marks for SPaG)

Planning the Post-War Future

The Second World War lasted from <u>1939-1945</u>. The <u>main winners</u> were Britain, the USSR and the USA. Two main <u>summits</u> were held between the Big Three allies during 1945 to decide on the future of Germany and Eastern Europe. These were the <u>Yalta</u> conference and the <u>Potsdam</u> conference.

There were **Three Major Decisions** at Yalta in 1945

The "big three" allied leaders — British Prime Minister <u>Winston Churchill</u>, US President <u>Roosevelt</u> and USSR leader <u>Stalin</u> — had already met at a conference in Tehran in 1943. They met again for the <u>Yalta Conference</u> in February 1945 — to plan what they wanted to happen <u>after</u> the war (although the conflict was still ongoing at this point).

1) Germany was to be <u>split</u> into four zones of occupation.
2) <u>Free elections</u> for new governments would be held in countries previously occupied in Eastern Europe.
3) The <u>United Nations</u> would <u>replace</u> the failed League of Nations.

Then the **Situation Changed**

1) Roosevelt died and was succeeded by <u>Harry Truman</u>, who was <u>suspicious</u> of the USSR.
2) In Britain, the Conservative PM Winston Churchill was replaced by Labour's <u>Clement Attlee</u>.
3) The USSR <u>expanded westwards</u> into Finland, Czechoslovakia, Romania and the Baltic states.

The allies were now <u>suspicious</u> of each other. Stalin wanted to <u>control</u> <u>Eastern Europe</u> so didn't want elections there — the USA and Britain suspected this. Truman and Attlee were new to their jobs — Stalin thought they'd be <u>weak leaders</u> so he could do <u>whatever he wanted</u>.

Agreements were Made at **Potsdam** in August 1945

<u>Germany surrendered</u> in <u>May 1945</u>. The allies made more decisions about <u>post-war Europe</u>:

1) The new <u>boundaries</u> of <u>Poland</u> were agreed.
2) The allies decided to <u>divide</u> Germany and Berlin between them.
3) They agreed to legal <u>trials</u> at Nuremberg of Nazi leaders for <u>war crimes</u>.

Yalta learn this page — it's important...

Plenty for you to learn here — things changed fast after the war. Make sure you can list the decisions made at both <u>Yalta</u> and <u>Potsdam</u>. Also, remember that two of the Big Three <u>changed leaders</u> — you need to know what <u>difference</u> this made.

Increasing Tensions

After World War Two, the USA and USSR were the major world superpowers.
Unfortunately, relations between them went rapidly downhill...

The USA and USSR had very **Different Ideologies**

Although the USA and USSR had been allies during the Second World War, they
had very different beliefs. The USSR was communist. The USA was capitalist.
After the end of the Second World War, the two countries became rivals.

1) Economically, communism meant state
   control of industry and agriculture. The USA,
   by contrast, valued private enterprise — the
   'American Dream' was that anyone could work
   their way to the top to be wealthy and successful.

2) Politically, communism meant a one-party state.
   The USA valued political freedom.

3) Communism aimed at world revolution, and so
   it was seen by Americans as a danger to their
   democracy. Likewise, the communists feared
   worldwide American influence.

The **USA** and the **USSR** began an **Arms Race**

The USA and USSR became very competitive — each wanting to be the strongest, and
feeling threatened by the other. There was an arms race to have the most powerful weapons.

1) Germany surrendered in May 1945, but
   the war against Japan continued. In August
   1945, the USA dropped two atom bombs on
   Japan — destroying the cities of Hiroshima
   and Nagasaki. These bombs were incredibly
   powerful and thousands of civilians were killed.
   Japan surrendered immediately after this.

2) The USA had kept the atom bomb (A-bomb)
   secret from the USSR until just before it
   was used in Japan. For four years, the USA
   was the world's only nuclear power.

3) But in 1949, the USSR exploded their own
   A-bomb. The USA developed the even more
   powerful hydrogen bomb (H-bomb) in 1952.
   The USSR had followed with their own by 1955.

When Superpowers fall out — they do it in a big way...

Although they had similar power, the USA and USSR were worlds apart in their ideologies.
They both felt under threat from the other, so they needed to prove just how strong they were
by building deadly nuclear weapons — making the world more dangerous in the process.

Increasing Tensions

The tension between the two countries got <u>worse</u> as they increased their nuclear power.

The USSR became *Influential* in *Eastern Europe*

1) At the end of the Second World War, the USSR's <u>Red Army</u> occupied Eastern Europe. Stalin had <u>no intention</u> of keeping the promise he made at Yalta to allow <u>free elections</u> in Poland.

2) Between 1945 and 1948, Stalin installed pro-Soviet <u>"puppet" governments</u> in Poland, Hungary, Romania, Bulgaria and Czechoslovakia. Free speech was suppressed.

3) Non-communist parties were <u>banned</u>, and even communist parties were controlled by the <u>Cominform</u> (Communist Information Bureau) to consist solely of <u>Russian-style</u> communists.

4) <u>Comecon</u> (the Council for Mutual Economic Assistance), set up in 1949, worked to <u>nationalise</u> the states' industries and <u>collectivise</u> agriculture.

5) For a while it seemed that <u>Czechoslovakia</u> might remain democratic. But when the Communist Party seemed likely to lose ground in the next election, it <u>seized power</u> in February 1948.

6) The <u>exception</u> to Soviet domination was <u>Yugoslavia</u>, which had freed itself from the Germans without the Red Army. Yugoslavia was communist but more <u>open</u> to the <u>West</u>. Its leader, <u>Tito</u>, argued with Stalin over political interference. Stalin cut off aid but <u>didn't invade</u>.

There was an *'Iron Curtain'* between East and West

1) Increasing tensions between the USA and the USSR became known as the '<u>Cold War</u>'.

2) It was called the <u>Cold War</u> because there <u>wasn't</u> any direct fighting — instead both sides tried to gain the upper hand with alliances and plans.

3) Both sides were <u>afraid</u> of another war because of the huge power of <u>atomic weapons</u>.

4) Countries in <u>Western Europe</u> tended to support the <u>USA</u>. Most countries in <u>Eastern Europe</u> were dominated by the <u>USSR</u>.

5) In a famous speech, Winston Churchill warned there was an <u>Iron Curtain</u> dividing Europe.

The Iron Curtain — it just wouldn't wash...

Nuclear weapons were capable of wiping out <u>entire cities</u> in one go — people thought it could be the end of humankind if a proper war broke out, which is why both sides were so <u>cautious</u>. The tensions between the USA and USSR affected the countries in between, on <u>both sides</u> of the Iron Curtain.

US Influence and the Berlin Blockade

If there was one thing the USA didn't want, it was for the whole world to go communist.

The USA was Worried about the Spread of Communism

President Truman was worried that other countries might also fall to communism.
Truman tried to stop the spread of communism in two main ways:

1) The Marshall Plan

This promised American aid to European countries to help rebuild their economies — West Germany benefited massively. The USA was worried that if Western Europe remained weak it might be vulnerable to communism.

2) The Truman Doctrine

The USA would support any nation threatened by a communist takeover. For example, the USA gave $400 million of aid to Turkey and Greece to try to stop communism spreading. A civil war had started in Greece in 1946 between the pro-Western government and communists — Truman wanted to give the government all the help he could.

In 1948 the USSR and the West Disagreed over Berlin

BERLIN

French Sector

British Sector

Soviet Sector

USA Sector

In East Germany (controlled by USSR)

1) There were four zones of occupied Berlin. The USA and Britain agreed to combine their zones into a zone called Bizonia in 1947.

2) The French agreed to combine their zone with them — the new western zone had a single government, and a new currency to help economic recovery.

3) The Soviet Union opposed these moves. Stalin wanted to keep Germany weak — so he decided to blockade Berlin.

4) Berlin was in Eastern Germany, which was controlled by the USSR — so Stalin ordered that all land communication between West Berlin and the outside world should be cut off.

West Berlin survived because of the Berlin Airlift. Between June 1948 and May 1949, the only way of obtaining supplies from the outside world was by air. By 1949, 8000 tons of supplies were being flown into West Berlin each day.

In 1949 Stalin Ended the Blockade

1) Two new states were formed — West Germany (German Federal Republic) and communist East Germany (German Democratic Republic).

2) In 1949 the Western Powers formed NATO (the North Atlantic Treaty Organisation) against the communist threat. The Eastern Bloc formed the Warsaw Pact in 1955 — a military treaty designed to counter NATO.

Two Germanies — and two German football teams...

Don't forget, the Cold War never led to any real fighting between the USA and USSR. Instead they seemed to be playing a giant game of chess. Make sure you know the two US policies intended to stop Europe turning communist, and the events that led to Germany being split up.

The Hungarian Rising

Soviet policy softened a little after Stalin's death — but the <u>problems</u> were still far from over.

Stalin died in 1953

Joseph Stalin

1) Stalin's death was a big <u>turning point</u>.
   He'd been the USSR's leader since the 1920s.

2) Soviet policy seemed to <u>change</u> under the new leader <u>Khrushchev</u>
   — he was critical of Stalin, and his policies seemed <u>less harsh</u>.
   This became known as "<u>de-Stalinisation</u>" and caused
   a "<u>thaw</u>" in the Cold War.

3) Khrushchev was in favour of <u>peaceful coexistence</u>
   between capitalist and communist states.

4) He made gestures of <u>friendship</u> to the USA — e.g. he <u>met</u> with US President Eisenhower at the
   <u>Geneva Summit</u> in 1955, and in 1959 he became the first leader of the USSR to <u>visit the USA</u>.
   He <u>freed</u> some prisoners and <u>reduced censorship</u> in the USSR. He also signed the <u>Austrian
   State Treaty</u> in <u>1955</u> along with the US, France and Britain (agreeing to withdraw occupying
   troops from Austria and allow it to become an independent state).

Hungary was treated Differently at first

1) After the war, the USSR helped put <u>Rákosi</u>, a brutal Stalinist, in charge of Hungary.
   His <u>authoritarian</u> regime became increasingly unpopular.

2) In October 1956, the people of Budapest <u>protested</u> against the government of Rákosi.

3) The <u>secret police</u>, who'd executed or imprisoned thousands of Hungarians, were <u>hunted down</u>.

4) Khrushchev <u>allowed</u> the liberal Nagy to become Hungarian <u>Prime Minister</u>.

5) <u>Austria</u> (which borders on Hungary) declared itself a <u>neutral state</u> in 1955.
   Nagy hoped that Hungary could also be a <u>neutral state</u>.

> In November 1956 Nagy announced that Hungary would <u>withdraw</u> from
> the Warsaw Pact and hold free elections — <u>ending communism</u> there.

Soviet Tanks Invaded Hungary

1) Over 20 000 Hungarians were <u>killed</u>.

2) Nagy was <u>arrested</u> and later <u>hanged</u>.

3) The Hungarian government asked the UN
   for <u>help</u>, but the USSR <u>vetoed</u> the draft resolution
   calling on them to <u>remove their tanks</u>.

4) Western countries <u>condemned</u> the USSR's actions, but the US <u>couldn't</u> come to Hungary's <u>aid</u>
   without risking a <u>nuclear war</u>. So they used the invasion as anti-USSR <u>propaganda</u>.

5) Kádár became Prime Minister and <u>ensured loyalty</u> towards the USSR.

6) The incident showed that despite the "<u>thaw</u>" in policy, Khrushchev could still be <u>harsh</u>.

Things got better — then worse again...

Even after Stalin's death, the USSR still wanted <u>tight control</u> of Eastern Europe.
New leader Khrushchev tried to warm up international relations, but used military force to regain
control over Hungary when their liberal leader turned against communism.

The Berlin Wall

The Cold War continued to get <u>worse</u>...

The **Berlin Wall** was built in 1961

1) Between 1949 and 1961, more than 2½ million people <u>left East Germany</u> for the West through East Berlin. The communist government of East Germany was <u>worried</u> by this trend.

2) In <u>1958</u> Khrushchev tried to solve the problem by issuing the <u>Berlin Ultimatum</u> — a demand that the US, France and Britain remove their troops from West Berlin <u>within six months</u>. It was <u>refused</u>.

3) In 1961 Khrushchev <u>tried again</u>. He gave another six-month ultimatum over West Berlin, but again this was <u>refused</u>.

4) So, on 13 August 1961, a 30-mile <u>barrier</u> was built across the city of Berlin overnight. The Berlin Wall was fortified with <u>barbed wire</u> and <u>machine gun</u> posts, and separated East Berlin from West Berlin.

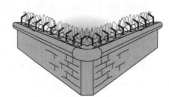

5) Anyone who tried to <u>escape</u> East Berlin was <u>shot</u>. West Berliners were suddenly <u>separated</u> from relatives in the East — for the next 30 years.

The **USA** supported **West Berlin**

John F Kennedy

In a famous speech in West Berlin on 26 June 1963, US President Kennedy declared his commitment to <u>protect</u> West Berlin, and his <u>solidarity</u> with its people. Kennedy said, "<u>Ich bin ein Berliner</u>" (I am a Berliner).

U-2 was an American **Spy Plane**

1) The U-2 spy plane was designed to fly so <u>high</u> it would usually be <u>undetected</u>.

2) It meant the USA could secretly get <u>information</u> about the USSR's weapons. It reassured President Eisenhower that the USSR didn't have as many missiles as they claimed.

3) The USSR <u>shot down</u> a U-2 in <u>1960</u>. Eisenhower <u>lied</u>, denying it was a spy plane. But the USSR then produced the <u>pilot</u> (alive) and the plane wreckage as evidence.

4) The USA and USSR were supposed to be attending <u>talks</u> together in <u>Paris</u> a few days later. This summit <u>fell apart</u> because of the U-2 crisis. Khrushchev demanded an <u>apology</u> from the USA, but Eisenhower <u>refused</u> — so Khrushchev <u>went home</u>.

Wall to Wall problems...

Overnight, the East was cut off from the West, with Berlin split into two halves. The Berlin Wall isolated the communist East even more, and support grew for West Berlin. The situation got even frostier when the USSR caught the USA spying on them red-handed.

The Prague Spring and the Arms Race

The problems <u>increased</u> as both sides developed bigger and better <u>technology</u>.

The **Arms Race** continued through the 50s and 60s

1) In 1957, the Soviets test-fired the first <u>Intercontinental Ballistic Missile</u> (ICBM), and also launched <u>Sputnik 1</u>, the world's first <u>artificial satellite</u>.

2) This new technology <u>frightened</u> the West as it was now clearly possible to launch a <u>nuclear missile attack</u> on the USA from the USSR.

3) But the USA soon made advances. The USA's <u>Atlas ICBM</u> was launched in 1957, and in 1960 the Polaris missile was the first <u>submarine-launched ICBM</u>.

4) The number of American ICBMs <u>increased</u> from 200 in 1961 to 1000 in 1967. Then the USSR began <u>catching up</u> again as American resources were diverted into the Vietnam War. Both sides now had enough bombs to <u>destroy</u> each other many times over.

5) As well as the arms race, there was a <u>space race</u>. The USSR got the <u>first man in space</u> — Yuri Gagarin in 1961. The US were the first to get men on the <u>Moon</u> in 1969.

Czechoslovakia Rebelled against Communism in 1968

1) Alexander <u>Dubcek</u> became Czechoslovakian leader in 1968 and made <u>changes</u> to the country:

- Workers were given a <u>greater say</u> in the running of their factories.
- <u>Travel</u> to the West was made available for all.
- Living standards were to be <u>raised</u>.
- <u>Free elections</u> were to be held.
- <u>Opposition</u> parties would be permitted.

This was called the '<u>Prague Spring</u>'.

2) Dubcek was still a <u>communist</u>. He was careful to reassure the USSR that Czechoslovakia <u>wouldn't</u> leave the <u>Warsaw Pact</u> — unlike Hungary in 1956.

3) But the USSR was worried — it didn't want the <u>Eastern Bloc</u> to be <u>weakened</u>.

4) On 21st August 1968, 500 000 Soviet troops <u>invaded</u> Czechoslovakia and Dubcek was <u>removed</u> from office. Soviet control was restored. Many countries <u>criticised</u> the Soviets, but no action was taken. A UN draft resolution condemning the invasion was <u>vetoed</u> by the USSR.

5) Soviet leader <u>Leonid Brezhnev</u> (who had replaced Khrushchev in 1964) announced that in future the USSR would <u>intervene</u> in any country where <u>socialism</u> was under <u>threat</u>. This became known as the <u>Brezhnev Doctrine</u>.

Communism — the Bloc Party...

The superpowers were <u>super-competitive</u>. They kept trying to get one up on each other — who could have the biggest guns, bombs, spaceships... And neither wanted to <u>lose face</u>. Make sure you know the facts about the <u>tensions</u> and <u>rebellions</u> in Eastern Europe because of the <u>Cold War</u>.

The Cold War in Asia

In 1949 the <u>Communist State of China</u> was set up by Mao Tse-tung — this meant that the USA was <u>also worried</u> by the communist threat in <u>Asia</u>.

In 1950 *War* broke out in *Korea*

Communist North Korea went to <u>war</u> with South Korea in order to <u>reunite</u> the country — this was seen as a <u>direct challenge</u> from communism to the West. The USA and the Western powers <u>intervened</u> on behalf of the United Nations to stop communism spreading.

The *UN Aim* was to *Resist* Communist North Korean *Aggression*

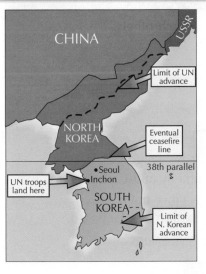

1) The UN ordered an immediate <u>attack</u> against the North Koreans. <u>UN forces</u> landed at Inchon and <u>drove</u> the North Koreans <u>back</u> over the 38th parallel by September 1950.

2) President Truman allowed General MacArthur (UN commander) to <u>invade</u> North Korea — most of the UN force were Americans.

3) This worried China, who <u>feared</u> a Western <u>invasion</u>.

4) In October 1950, China joined the North Koreans in an <u>attack</u> which drove the UN forces back, and <u>captured</u> Seoul (the capital of South Korea) by January 1951. A UN counteroffensive retook the city, and drove the North Koreans back to <u>near the original border</u>.

5) MacArthur wanted to attack China but Truman <u>disagreed</u> — after arguing with the President, MacArthur was <u>sacked</u>.

6) Truman looked for peace and a <u>ceasefire</u> was <u>agreed</u> in 1953.

A *Communist Government* came to power in *North Vietnam*

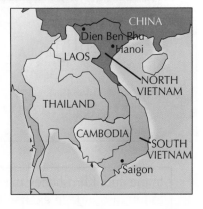

1) <u>Indochina</u> was a <u>French colony</u> that covered a large area of South-East Asia. In the 1940s and 1950s there was a <u>revolt</u> against the French — which turned into a long and bloody <u>war</u>. The resistance fighters were backed by <u>communist China</u>.

2) The <u>Geneva Conference</u> in 1954 was a meeting of international leaders to sort out problems in Asia — including this <u>conflict</u>.

3) Under the terms of the Geneva Accord, France <u>withdrew</u> from Indochina. Vietnam (formerly part of Indochina) was <u>partitioned</u> into <u>communist North Vietnam</u> and <u>democratic South Vietnam</u>. Laos and Cambodia were set up as <u>independent states</u>.

The Asian Cold War — pretty hot really...

There you are, the main events of the Korean War — but you just need to learn the <u>key points</u>. <u>The Korean War</u> was a dangerous moment that could easily have become a World War — make sure you know the <u>main reasons</u> why the <u>UN invaded</u> and why <u>China fought back</u>.

The Cuban Missile Crisis

The USA wanted to keep all countries close to its shores friendly.

Cuba was *Only 100 Miles* from the *USA*

Fidel Castro

1) Since 1952, Cuba had been <u>ruled</u> by Batista, a ruthless and corrupt military <u>dictator</u>. Batista allowed American businessmen and the Mafia to make <u>huge profits</u> in a country where <u>most people</u> lived in <u>poverty</u>.

2) In 1953 <u>Fidel Castro</u> attempted to <u>overthrow</u> the government, but he was <u>defeated</u> and <u>imprisoned</u>. After his release in 1955, he fled Cuba.

3) In 1956 Castro returned and began a <u>guerrilla war</u>. By 1959, he had enough support to take Cuba's capital, Havana, and <u>successfully</u> overthrow the government.

Castro wanted to *Get Rid* of *American Influence*

1) Castro made a big impact. He <u>shut down</u> the gambling casinos and the brothels. He also <u>nationalised</u> American-owned sugar mills.

2) The USA <u>cut off</u> diplomatic <u>relations</u> with Cuba.

3) Castro began to work with the USSR — he'd always been <u>influenced</u> by <u>communism</u>.

4) The USSR offered to buy Cuba's sugar <u>instead</u> of the USA.

Cuban *Rebels* in America plotted an *Invasion*

1) In 1961, President Kennedy authorised a CIA-trained <u>invasion</u> of Cuba by anti-Castro rebels.

2) In April 1961, the rebels landed in the <u>Bay of Pigs</u>, but the USA <u>didn't give</u> them air <u>support</u> as they had promised. The rebels were easily <u>defeated</u> — it was a bit of a fiasco.

3) This invasion meant Castro decided that Cuba needed <u>Soviet military assistance</u>.

Soviet *Nuclear Missiles* were shipped to Cuba

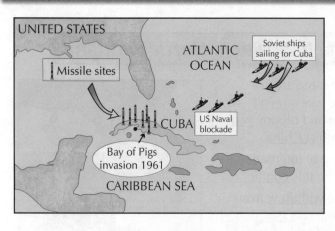

1) In 1962, the USA's U-2 spy planes <u>detected</u> Soviet missiles in Cuba. From Cuba these missiles could be used to <u>attack</u> US cities with very little warning.

2) President Kennedy ordered a <u>naval blockade</u> of Cuba. All Soviet ships were to be <u>stopped</u> and <u>searched</u> to prevent further missiles being transported to Cuba.

3) Kennedy <u>demanded</u> that Khrushchev <u>withdraw</u> his missiles and <u>prepared to invade</u> Cuba. The Soviet ships steamed on to Cuba.

4) The world was on the brink of <u>nuclear war</u>...

In the end, Khrushchev made a deal to <u>remove</u> the missiles from Cuba and ordered his <u>ships</u> to <u>turn around</u>. In exchange the US <u>lifted</u> the <u>blockade</u>, promised to <u>not invade</u> Cuba — and <u>secretly</u> agreed to <u>remove</u> their <u>missiles</u> from <u>Turkey</u>, which bordered the USSR.

U-2 were spy planes — I always thought they were a rock band...

The <u>13 days</u> of the Cuban missile crisis were the closest the world's been to nuclear war. There was a stalemate with nuclear weapons because if one side fired, so would the other and <u>everyone</u> would be destroyed. It was a <u>no-win situation</u>.

Vietnam and the USA

The USA was <u>scared</u> of countries turning communist — they didn't want to be <u>outnumbered</u>.

The **Domino Theory** of **Communism**

The <u>domino theory</u> says that when you knock over the first domino in a line the rest will fall down too.

The USA thought this would happen if <u>one country</u> was knocked over by the <u>communist threat</u> — soon all the <u>nearby countries</u> would turn communist as well.

So China, North Korea and North Vietnam could knock down the South Vietnamese domino.

The **USA** tried to **Protect South Vietnam** from **Communism**

Dwight D Eisenhower

1) The Truman Doctrine meant America was willing to provide <u>aid</u> to <u>South Vietnam</u> to stop it falling to communism. President Eisenhower supported the choice of <u>Diem</u> as <u>leader</u> of South Vietnam. He was a <u>corrupt</u> and <u>unpopular</u> ruler — but he was <u>anti-communist</u>.

2) Under <u>Eisenhower</u>, and later <u>Kennedy</u>, the USA gave loads of <u>money</u> to South Vietnam. They also sent military '<u>advisers</u>' — there were 12 000 American soldiers in Vietnam by 1962. The communist threat remained, and the US became <u>more involved</u> in countering it.

In 1963 **President Johnson** changed **US Policy**

The President was <u>determined</u> to keep South Vietnam <u>free</u> from <u>communism</u>:

1) He <u>increased troop numbers</u> from 23 000 in 1964 to 180 000 in 1965 and 500 000 in 1967.

2) He began a <u>bombing campaign</u> against communist North Vietnam.

Lyndon B Johnson

Domino Theory — not an easy game...

Protecting South Vietnam from communism was <u>crucial</u> for the USA so that it didn't spread throughout the whole of South Asia. They tried all sorts of <u>strategies</u> — giving them money, aid, soldiers, and eventually <u>bombing</u> North Vietnam.

Vietnam and the USA

The USA tried to stop the spread of communism in Vietnam by <u>military force</u>, but they <u>didn't expect</u> Vietnam to put up so much of a <u>challenge</u>...

The war became *Unpopular* in the *USA*

1) The <u>Tet Offensive</u> by the North Vietnamese in 1968 took the Americans by <u>surprise</u>.

2) The offensive was beaten but there were <u>heavy casualties</u> — about 14 000 US soldiers were killed in action in 1968.

3) The American public saw <u>brutal images</u> of the war on <u>TV</u>. They were also shocked by news of the 1968 <u>My Lai massacre</u> where civilians were murdered by US troops.

4) The war was very <u>expensive</u>, costing millions of taxpayers' dollars to support and finance.

Richard Nixon

President *Nixon* tried to *Finish* the war

1) American troops were gradually <u>withdrawn</u> from Vietnam — in 1972 only 47 000 were left.

Vietcong Supply Lines (Ho Chi Minh Trail)

2) Instead the US started <u>training</u> the South Vietnamese to fight the <u>Vietcong</u> — the communist guerrillas fighting in South Vietnam.

3) Heavy <u>bombing</u> of North Vietnam and Cambodia began, aimed at <u>destroying</u> North Vietnamese <u>supply lines</u> — the Ho Chi Minh trail. It was hoped this would <u>force</u> a <u>peace</u> settlement.

4) In 1973 a <u>ceasefire</u> was agreed and the US <u>pulled out</u> of Vietnam — but the fighting between the North and South <u>continued</u>. By 1975 the South Vietnamese capital <u>Saigon</u> had been <u>captured</u> by the North Vietnamese army.

The US had *Failed* to stop *Communism* from *Spreading*

The Americans were effectively <u>defeated</u> in Vietnam for six main reasons:

1) The Vietcong treated the South Vietnamese <u>well</u> and gained their <u>support</u>.

2) American bombing killed many <u>civilians</u> and made North Vietnam more <u>determined</u>.

3) Vietcong guerrillas were very <u>skilful</u> soldiers. They didn't fight in open warfare, but used tactics like <u>sudden raids</u> and <u>ambushes</u>. They didn't wear uniforms and often operated in small groups.

4) American troops <u>weren't used</u> to fighting in the jungle.

5) The North Vietnamese had the <u>support</u> of China and the USSR.

6) American <u>public opinion</u> had turned against the war.

Vietnam — apocalypse then...

Phew, loads for you to learn here. Remember — the <u>domino theory</u> explains why the USA thought Vietnam was so important in the first place, so learn it right now. And while you're at it, scribble down some details about the war in Vietnam so you can say <u>how</u> and <u>why</u> it didn't work.

Revision Summary

Yes, it's time for those awesome revision questions again — I know it's a pain, but there's no way round it. It's the best way to test yourself on this stuff. So if you want to get the grades, you've really got to put the work in now. An important thing to remember here is that the USA and USSR were the only countries who were strong enough to interfere in world affairs after the Second World War — everybody else was too busy rebuilding their economies and industry. Make sure you can answer all of these lovely questions — and if you have problems go back over the section until you've got the lot sorted. So get going.

1)   Name the two conferences held by the Big Three in 1945.
2)   Which political leader was present at both of these conferences?
3)   Was the USSR capitalist or communist?
4)   Describe the difference between capitalism and communism.
5)   Where and when did the USA use its atomic bombs?
6)   When did the USA develop a hydrogen bomb?
7)   Explain how the USSR developed a sphere of influence in Eastern Europe.
8)   Which Eastern European country was communist but not under the USSR's influence?
9)   What phrase did Winston Churchill use to describe the separation of Western Europe from Eastern Europe?
10) What was the Marshall Plan?
11) What was the Truman Doctrine?
12) Why did disagreements occur over the administration of Berlin in 1948?
13) What was the Berlin Blockade, and how did the Western powers deal with it?
14) Give the full official names of the two new states formed in Germany.
15) What does NATO stand for?
16) When did Stalin die?
17) Why was there a "thaw" in the Cold War when Khrushchev first came to power?
18) Why did Soviet tanks invade Hungary in 1956?
19) When was the Berlin Wall built?
20) What is a U-2?
21) Why did the U-2 crisis cause embarrassment for President Eisenhower?
22) Who got the first man in space — the USA or the USSR? What was his name?
23) What was the 'Prague Spring'?
24) Who set up the Communist State of China in 1949?
25) Who was the UN commander at the start of the Korean War?
26) What was decided about the future of Vietnam at the Geneva Conference in 1954?
27) Name the military dictator who was overthrown in Cuba in 1959.
28) How did Castro set about reducing American influence in Cuba?
29) Why did the world almost face a nuclear war in 1962?
30) Why did American public opinion turn against the war in Vietnam?
31) Give six reasons why the Americans failed to win the Vietnam War.

Exam Practice

Study **Source A** and then answer the questions below.

Source A:
Photograph showing Flight Lieutenant K.J. Ryall of the Royal Air Force handing over a sack, representing the millionth short ton of supplies to be flown into Berlin during the airlift, 18th February 1949.

© Illustrated London News Ltd/ Mary Evans Picture Library

The Origins of the Cold War

1 (a) By 1955 there was a 'Cold War' between the USA and the USSR.

Describe how the USA planned to stop the spread of communism after the end of WWII.

(4 marks)

(b) Source A suggests a reason why West Berlin did not become part of East Germany when the GDR was formed in 1950.

Do you agree that this was the main reason?

Explain your answer by referring to the purpose of the source, as well as using its content and your knowledge.

(6 marks)

(c) Which of these presented the biggest risk of starting a world war:
  • The Berlin Blockade;
  • The Korean War?

You must refer to both reasons when explaining your answer.

(10 marks + 3 marks for SPaG)

The Origins of the Cold War

2 (a) What does Source A tell us about the relationship between the 'West' and the USSR in 1949?

(4 marks)

(b) Explain why the USSR blockaded Berlin in 1948.

(6 marks)

(c) "The Berlin Blockade presented a bigger risk of a world war than the Korean War."

How far do you agree with this statement? Explain your answer.

(10 marks + 3 marks for SPaG)

The Origins of the Cold War

3 This question is about the development of a 'Cold War' between the USA and the USSR in the aftermath of WWII.

(a) Describe two ways in which the USA planned to stop the spread of communism after WWII.

(4 marks)

(b) Briefly explain why the Berlin Wall was built in 1961.

(6 marks)

(c) Explain why a 'Cold War' existed between the USA and the USSR by 1955.

(10 marks + 3 marks for SPaG)

Détente

After the <u>fear</u> and <u>panic</u> of the Cuban Missile Crisis, the USA and USSR made an effort to get on.

The **USA** and **USSR** wanted to **Avoid** a **Crisis**

The Cuban Missile Crisis of 1962 brought the world to the <u>brink of nuclear war</u>. Future <u>misunderstandings</u> between the Soviet Union and the USA <u>had to be avoided</u>.

1) A <u>telephone hotline</u> was set up between the Kremlin and the White House.

2) The Soviet Union and the USA <u>signed</u> a test ban treaty in 1963 to <u>stop</u> further nuclear weapons testing.

3) <u>Relations</u> between the superpowers still <u>weren't that friendly</u> though. In 1963 the American <u>president</u> John F Kennedy gave a speech in West Berlin <u>criticising communism</u>.

Détente — a period of increasing US–Soviet **Cooperation**

1) The USSR <u>couldn't afford</u> to continue building up its nuclear arsenal.

2) The US was trying to end the Vietnam War (see p.60) — an expensive and unpopular war against <u>communists</u>. The US hoped that <u>improving relations</u> with the <u>USSR</u> and <u>China</u> would <u>isolate North Vietnam</u> and force it to agree to a <u>peace settlement</u>.

3) From 1972, US President <u>Nixon</u> and the leader of the USSR, <u>Brezhnev</u>, began a series of <u>talks</u> aimed at improving relations. These were known as the <u>Brezhnev-Nixon summits</u>.

4) In 1972 the two superpowers <u>agreed</u> to <u>limit</u> their nuclear weapons when they signed the <u>Strategic Arms Limitation Talks Agreement</u> (SALT 1).

5) In <u>1975</u> the US, the USSR and other powers signed the <u>Helsinki Agreement</u>. This agreement officially recognised the European <u>borders</u> fixed at the end of the Second World War, including the <u>division of Germany</u>.

6) The Helsinki Agreement also included a commitment to <u>human rights</u> — for example, freedom of speech and travel. But since there was <u>no enforcement procedure</u>, these promises were not always kept by the communist countries.

7) China also wanted <u>détente</u>. Its relationship with the USSR had deteriorated, so China needed to gain the US as a powerful <u>ally</u>. It also <u>feared a war</u>, like the one in Vietnam, with the US.

8) In West Germany, the <u>Chancellor</u>, Willy Brandt, wanted better relations with the Eastern Bloc to <u>improve trade</u> and <u>reduce military tensions</u>.

SALT 2 wasn't **fully agreed** in time...

Talks continued throughout the 1970s with a view to <u>further limitation</u> of nuclear weapons. President Carter signed a <u>SALT 2</u> agreement in June 1979 at a US-USSR summit in Vienna — but the <u>Senate had not yet ratified</u> the treaty when the Soviet invasion of Afghanistan altered the political climate.

Détente — a chance for peace...

At last it seemed like the relationship between the USA and USSR was warming up, and <u>both sides</u> had good reasons to shake hands and make their <u>peace</u>. The superpowers were willing to sign <u>agreements</u> which would make the world a safer place for everybody.

The New Cold War

The Cold War had its <u>last gasp</u> in the 1980s as the tension mounted and the relationship between the USA and the USSR <u>got frostier</u>. This period is also known as the '<u>Second Cold War</u>'.

The **USSR** got bogged down in a war in **Afghanistan**

1) To prop up a pro-Soviet government besieged by rebels, the <u>USSR</u> invaded Afghanistan in <u>December 1979</u>. This decision turned out to be a <u>disaster</u>. The USSR got stuck with a seemingly <u>unwinnable</u> conflict in difficult <u>mountainous terrain</u>.

2) <u>American distrust</u> of the USSR increased. It worried the USSR had its sights on the <u>oil-rich Persian Gulf</u> (fairly close to Afghanistan). President <u>Carter warned</u> that the US would use <u>force</u> to <u>prevent</u> outside powers gaining control of the Gulf region. This warning became known as the <u>Carter Doctrine</u>.

3) The <u>SALT 2</u> agreement was being debated by the Senate. Carter <u>withdrew</u> it from consideration, and called for an <u>increase</u> in the <u>defence budget</u>.

4) During the 1980s the USA <u>aided the Afghan resistance</u> with military equipment.

5) Disagreement over Afghanistan led to a US <u>boycott</u> of the Moscow Olympics in 1980 — and in 1984 the Soviet team <u>boycotted</u> the LA Games.

6) The USSR finally <u>gave up</u> and began <u>withdrawing</u> their forces from Afghanistan in <u>1988</u>.

In 1980 the **New Cold War** began

The <u>war in Afghanistan</u> and the election of <u>Ronald Reagan</u> as US president in 1980 <u>ended détente</u>.

1) Ronald Reagan was a hardline <u>anti-communist</u>. He called the Soviet Union an "<u>evil empire</u>".

2) Reagan was keen to show off <u>American technology</u> and <u>power</u> through the development of <u>new weapons</u> — the start of another <u>arms race</u>.

3) The US developed and deployed medium-range <u>Cruise</u> and <u>Pershing nuclear missiles</u> which could be launched from almost anywhere.

4) The US also started to develop the <u>Strategic Defense Initiative</u> (SDI or Star Wars) for using laser weapons

Ronald Reagan

It wasn't peaceful for long...

The Afghanistan War was a bit like the <u>Vietnam War</u>. Like the USA in Vietnam (see p.59-60), the USSR was fighting there for years in difficult terrain, and ended up retreating. Make sure you can explain <u>why</u> détente ended with the election of Reagan and the Soviet war with Afghanistan.

The New Cold War

Whilst the tensions increased again between the USA and USSR,
things were getting heated in communist Poland...

Poland's People Rebelled in 1980

1) In the early 1970s Poland under its communist leader had achieved some rise in living
standards. But in the late 1970s the economy suffered from foreign debt and shortages.
In response the government raised prices.

2) In 1980 Lech Walesa led shipyard workers in the
port of Gdansk in protest against the increase in
food prices — with some success.

3) They set up their own independent trade union
called 'Solidarity' and demanded the right to
strike and to be consulted on all major decisions
affecting their living and working conditions.
Lech Walesa became the leader.

4) Solidarity became a broad-based anti-communist social movement which by the end of
1981 had 9 million members. Nothing like it had been seen before in the communist world.
The movement was especially strong because of the support of the Catholic Church.

5) The Polish communist government was in a fix. It was scared to ban Solidarity —
but neither could it meet demands for political reform, for fear of Soviet intervention.

The Military seized Control

In 1981 the Polish army leader General Jaruzelski, with Soviet support,
seized control of the country and declared martial law. As a result:

1) Solidarity was completely banned.
2) Lech Walesa was arrested and imprisoned.
3) The price of basic foodstuffs was increased by 40%.

Lech Walesa

Solidarity lived on as an underground organisation. Lech Walesa became
a symbol of resistance to Soviet oppression — he was awarded the Nobel
Peace Prize in 1983. In 1988 further nationwide strikes again forced the
government to negotiate with the union.

Solidarity — Rebels with a Cause...

There's plenty to learn here. The events in Poland are evidence of popular resistance to communism
in Eastern Europe — which would eventually lead to the fall of the USSR. Scribble a list of the reasons
behind the Solidarity movement in Poland, and how the communist government dealt with them.

The Soviet Withdrawal

Mikhail Gorbachev came to power in the USSR — and radically changed Soviet policies...

The Cold War created a Crisis in the USSR

1) The arms race with the USA was so expensive that Soviet living standards became worse as more money was spent on weapons.

2) Soviet farming was inefficient — there wasn't enough food and millions of tonnes of grain had to be imported from the USA.

3) The communist government was becoming more corrupt and was unable to give the Soviet people the same high living standards as people had in the West.

4) The war in Afghanistan was a disaster — it cost billions of dollars and 15 000 Soviet troops were killed.

Gorbachev introduced his 'New Thinking' Reforms

In 1985 Mikhail Gorbachev became General Secretary of the Communist Party. He was more open to the West than previous leaders. He introduced two major new policies — Glasnost and Perestroika.

Glasnost meant New Freedom and Openness	Perestroika meant Economic Restructuring
The Soviet people won new rights: 1) Thousands of political prisoners were released, including the leading dissident, Andrei Sakharov. 2) People were told about the atrocities committed by Stalin's government. 3) Free speech was allowed. 4) Military conscription was soon to be abolished.	1) Gorbachev wanted to make the Soviet system of central planning of production more efficient. 2) However, corruption in the Soviet economy was too great and he was unable to see through his plans.

These reforms were part of what is known as Gorbachev's 'New Thinking'. He didn't want to end communism, but he hoped that reform would help revive the USSR's struggling economy, which was falling further behind the US's and causing increasing discontent among the people.

Gorbachev changed Foreign Policy

Gorbachev's 'New Thinking' also covered foreign policy.

1) In 1987, a disarmament treaty was signed called the INF (Intermediate-Range Nuclear Forces Treaty). The USA and the USSR agreed to remove medium-range nuclear missiles from Europe within three years.

2) In 1988, Gorbachev announced the immediate reduction of the weapons stockpile and the number of troops in the Soviet armed forces.

Mikhail Gorbachev

3) Gorbachev tried to improve relations with the West. He met with the US President Reagan several times, for example at the Geneva Summit in 1985.

4) Gorbachev announced the complete withdrawal of Soviet troops from Afghanistan in 1988.

> In 1988, Gorbachev decided to abandon the Brezhnev Doctrine (see p.56). He told the United Nations that the countries of Eastern Europe now had a choice — the USSR wasn't going to control them any more.

It's feeling a bit less chilly in here...

By the late 1980s, the end of the Cold War was in sight. Don't forget — the attitude and leadership of Mikhail Gorbachev are the key to understanding why the situation changed.

The End of the Soviet Union

Communism toppled — and the Cold War was <u>finally over</u>...

Communism Fell all over Eastern Europe in 1989

1) Hungary <u>opened</u> its frontier with Austria in May.

2) <u>Free elections</u> were held in Poland in June. Solidarity won and a new non-communist government came to power.

3) Many <u>East</u> Germans <u>crossed</u> into Hungary, through Austria and into <u>West</u> Germany.

4) The <u>Berlin Wall</u> was <u>torn down</u> in November.

5) Anti-communist <u>demonstrations</u> took place in Czechoslovakia and the communist government <u>collapsed</u> in December.

6) In December a <u>revolution</u> began in Romania against the cruel and corrupt regime, and the dictator Nicolae Ceausescu was <u>executed</u> on Christmas Day.

7) The Warsaw Pact <u>ended</u> officially in <u>1991</u>.

In 1990 <u>Germany</u> was <u>reunified</u>. Communist East Germany and democratic West Germany were <u>one country</u> again after 45 years. For many people this was a powerful symbol that the communist experiment was over.

Communism was Rejected in the USSR

The main nationalities within the Soviet Union <u>demanded independence</u>, especially the Baltic republics — Latvia, Lithuania and Estonia. Gorbachev tried to <u>prevent</u> the rise of nationalism in the Baltic republics with military force, but gradually started to <u>lose control</u>.

An Anti-Communist Russian President was Elected in 1991

1) The newly elected President of Russia, <u>Boris Yeltsin</u>, was an <u>opponent</u> of Gorbachev, and became <u>popular</u> and <u>powerful</u>.

2) He demanded the <u>end</u> of communist domination and the <u>break-up</u> of the USSR. This led to a <u>crisis</u> in 1991.

The Attempted Coup of 1991 Failed

1) The old communist leaders <u>feared</u> the reforms, so they decided to <u>get rid</u> of Gorbachev.

2) A military group tried to <u>seize power</u> by capturing Gorbachev, but Yeltsin rallied the Russian people to <u>resist</u> and the army supported him, and the coup <u>failed</u>.

3) Soon the individual Soviet republics became <u>independent</u> — the USSR didn't exist any more.

4) Now Gorbachev had no power and had to <u>resign</u>. Communism in Russia was dead.

The end of communism — when the reds got the blues...

Phew, there's even more stuff to learn here — but you've got to do it. Scribble a paragraph on why <u>communism fell</u> in Russia, and why <u>1991</u> was so important.

The USA and the UN after the Cold War

After the Cold War ended, the USA had to find a new focus for its foreign policy.

The **USA** was now the **Sole Superpower**...

1) After the fall of the USSR, the USA was the only country with a military and economy strong enough to be able to take action across the globe — making it the world's only superpower.

2) The USA had the most powerful military in the world, even with post Cold War cuts in spending. Through the 1990s, the US's military expenditure made up more than a third of the world's military spending. No other country came close to spending as much as the US did.

3) The USA's economy was strong throughout most of the 1990s, remaining the biggest in the world while Russia struggled after the collapse of the USSR.

4) This gave the USA a lot of power to get involved in disputes around the world.

5) In the 1990s, the US saw itself as a champion of democracy and tried to be a force for freedom and democracy in the world.

...but it still wanted **Friends** in **Europe**

1) After the Cold War, Western Europe no longer needed protection from the USSR, so the USA reduced its military presence. US missiles were withdrawn from the UK in 1991.

2) The UK continued to be one of the USA's closest allies, supplying much of the support for the US-led interventions in Kuwait, Bosnia and Kosovo (see p.69-70).

3) Other European countries, such as France, the Netherlands, Czechoslovakia, Hungary and Poland, all contributed to the US-led UN coalition in the Gulf War (see p.69).

4) In 1999, three former Warsaw Pact members — the Czech Republic (which used to be part of Czechoslovakia), Poland and Hungary — joined NATO.

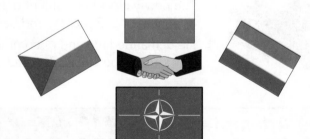

5) US involvement in Bosnia, Kosovo and Northern Ireland showed a US commitment to Europe.

There's no one left but US...

The important thing to remember here is that the end of the Cold War didn't mean the end of US foreign policy... They still thought it was important to get involved in conflicts all over the world.

The USA and the UN after the Cold War

The invasion of Kuwait was the <u>first</u> big post-Cold War crisis for the <u>US</u> and the <u>UN</u>.

The *Iraqi Invasion* of *Kuwait* was *Condemned Internationally*

1) In 1979, <u>Saddam Hussein</u> came to power in Iraq. He was a <u>ruthless</u> and <u>brutal</u> dictator, who had used <u>chemical weapons</u> against Iraq's Kurdish minority.

2) In 1990, Iraq invaded <u>Kuwait</u>, its southern neighbour. The UN <u>demanded</u> that Iraq withdraw, and introduced <u>sanctions</u> (a ban on people trading with Iraq).

3) When Iraq refused, the UN <u>authorised</u> the use of force to remove the Iraqi army from Kuwait. The USA supported UN demands for <u>Iraq</u> to withdraw from <u>Kuwait</u>.

4) In the <u>Gulf War</u> (1991), US President Bush (George W. Bush's father) was in charge of creating the coalition of international forces which <u>drove</u> Saddam Hussein's army out of Kuwait.

George Bush

The UN used *Tough Sanctions* against Iraq

1) The UN kept its <u>strict sanctions</u> against Iraq after the Gulf War. They hoped the sanctions would force Iraq to give up its <u>weapons of mass destruction</u> (biological and chemical weapons) and stop it from trying to get hold of or make more.

2) While these sanctions helped to cut the amount Iraq could spend on <u>weapons</u>, they <u>hurt</u> ordinary Iraqi people — shortages of <u>food</u> and <u>medicine</u> led to a big rise in the death rates of Iraqi children.

3) The UN tried to help the Iraqi people with the <u>Oil-for-Food Programme</u> — Iraq would be allowed to trade oil for food and medicines. This trade would be <u>carefully monitored</u> to make sure that oil exports weren't being used to buy weapons.

4) While it did <u>help</u> many Iraqis, the programme did face some accusations of <u>corruption</u> — it's believed that some <u>profit</u> was unlawfully made by UN and Iraqi officials.

The US continued to try to create *Peace* under *Clinton*

1) <u>Bill Clinton</u> defeated President Bush in the 1992 presidential election.

2) In 1992, just <u>before</u> President Bush <u>left office</u>, he authorised a US led UN <u>intervention</u> in <u>Somalia</u>. Somalia was suffering from a <u>chaotic civil war</u> and the US wanted to bring <u>peace</u> and <u>stability</u>.

3) In 1994, following the <u>death</u> of a number of <u>US troops</u>, President Bill Clinton pulled the US out.

4) Clinton also used <u>diplomacy</u> and US influence to try to secure <u>peace</u> between the <u>Israelis</u> and <u>Palestinians</u>, and he played an important part in the <u>Northern Ireland</u> peace process.

Bill Clinton

President Clinton was left to deal with the problems in Somalia...

Somalia was a big <u>turning point</u> for the US in the 1990s — after the deaths of US troops in Somalia, Clinton avoided using American ground troops in overseas conflicts.

The USA and the UN after the Cold War

Unfortunately, conflicts continued to spring up in the 1990s (and beyond)...

The USA continued to Promote Democracy

1) In 1991, Jean-Bertrand Aristide, the first democratically elected president of Haiti, was overthrown by the Haitian army.

2) The army ruled Haiti until 1994, when the US launched Operation Uphold Democracy.

3) As part of this operation, the US threatened to invade Haiti and forcibly remove the military leaders unless the Haitian army agreed to give up power peacefully.

4) Under the threat of invasion, the Haitian army agreed to restore Aristide as president. The operation was a success.

The USA were also Concerned with Human Rights

1) In 1994, after the break-up of Yugoslavia, there was a violent civil war and genocide in Bosnia.

2) The US did not want to send troops into Bosnia, so it led a NATO bombing campaign against the Bosnian Serbs in 1995.

3) The NATO bombing lifted the Bosnian Serbs' siege of Sarajevo and helped to end the conflict.

The crisis in Kosovo was a Big Test for the UN

1) In the late 1980s, the government of Serbia took away much of the independence that Kosovo, a mainly ethnic-Albanian area of Serbia, had previously had.

2) The ethnic Albanians formed a group called the Kosovo Liberation Army (KLA) to fight for independence. The Serbians fought back fiercely, killing hundreds.

3) To stop the violence, NATO began a bombing campaign against Serbia in 1999. This campaign was led by the USA.

4) After two months of bombing, Serbia agreed to remove its troops from Kosovo and allowed KFOR, a NATO-led multinational force, to take control of the region.

5) While the bombing campaign was successful in ending the conflict, civilian casualties, including the deaths of three Chinese citizens, made the US intervention controversial.

6) A UN task force called UNMIK was sent to help get Kosovo back on its feet, helping with policing and reconstruction. But the process was very slow, and ethnic tensions remained, sometimes turning into violence. Local Serbs felt that they were being forced into leaving.

7) There were also reports that KFOR and UNMIK personnel, who were immune from local prosecution, got involved in crime and violence in Kosovo.

The US and the UN have a mixed record, UN-surprisingly...

The UN was set up to promote peace and protect human rights. Although it has helped many people, it isn't perfect. Learn the UN's failures in Iraq (see p.69) and Kosovo, as well as its successes.

Revision Summary

There's just time for the best bit — some mega-magnificent revision questions for you. You've really got to test yourself here, because there were loads of facts in a very small section. See how many you can answer first go, then look back over the areas you weren't so sure about. Just keep coming back to those questions — by the time you sit the exam you should know them backwards... Well, forwards will do. So get busy and get this lot sorted.

1) Describe what 'détente' means in terms of USSR and USA relations.

2) What does 'SALT' stand for?

3) Why didn't the USA go through with the SALT 2 agreement?

4) Why did the USSR invade Afghanistan in 1979?

5) Which country gave military equipment to the Afghans fighting the USSR?

6) What was President Ronald Reagan's attitude towards the USSR?

7) What was the Strategic Defense Initiative?

8) Who was the leader of the Solidarity movement in Poland?

9) Give the name of the Polish army leader who seized power in 1981.

10) When was Mikhail Gorbachev appointed General Secretary of the Soviet Union's Communist Party?

11) Explain what is meant by the terms Glasnost and Perestroika.

12) Why was Perestroika unsuccessful?

13) What was agreed in the INF treaty?

14) What doctrine did Gorbachev abandon in 1988?

15) What year was the Berlin Wall torn down?

16) What year was Germany reunified?

17) What happened to Romanian dictator Nicolae Ceausescu in 1989?

18) What was the name of the President of Russia elected in 1991?

19) Briefly describe the events of the attempted coup against Gorbachev in 1991.

20) Which three countries joined NATO in 1999?

21) Why did the UN place sanctions on Iraq in 1990?

22) What was the Oil-for-Food Programme?

23) What was Operation Uphold Democracy?

24) What was the name of the UN force sent to help rebuild Kosovo?

Exam Practice

Study **Source A** and then answer the
questions below.

Source A:
*'Thank you Gorby', graffiti
on the Berlin Wall, 1990.*

The End of the Cold War & the Post Cold War World

1 **(a)** In December 1979 the USSR invaded Afghanistan. During the 1980s the USA aided
Afghan resistance to the Soviet invasion with military equipment.

Describe the main features of the new 'Cold War' of the 1980s.

(4 marks)

(b) Source A suggests a reason for the fall of the Berlin Wall.

Do you agree that this was the main reason for the fall of the Berlin Wall?

Explain your answer by referring to the purpose of the source, as well as using its content
and your knowledge.

(6 marks)

(c) What was the more important cause of the collapse of Soviet communism:
  • Economic problems;
  • Political change?

You must refer to both reasons when explaining your answer.

(10 marks + 3 marks for SPaG)

The End of the Cold War & the Post Cold War World

2 **(a)** What does Source A tell us about the role of Gorbachev in bringing about the fall of the
Berlin Wall?

(4 marks)

(b) Explain why the USSR struggled financially with the 'Cold War'.

(6 marks)

(c) "It was the Solidarity movement in Poland which did most to bring about the collapse of
communism in the Eastern Bloc."

How far do you agree with this statement? Explain your answer.

(10 marks + 3 marks for SPaG)

The End of the Cold War & the Post Cold War World

3 This question is about the events leading up to the end of the 'Cold War'.

(a) Describe two causes of the period of détente between the US and USSR from
1963 to 1979.

(4 marks)

(b) Briefly explain the key features of Gorbachev's reforms in the USSR in the 1980s.

(6 marks)

(c) Explain why communist leaders found it increasingly difficult to keep control of the USSR
and the Eastern Bloc in the period 1979-1991.

(10 marks + 3 marks for SPaG)

Terrorism

History didn't stop with the Cold War. This section is about current world issues that are rapidly finding their way into the history books — <u>terrorism</u> and the second <u>Iraq War</u>.

Terrorists use **Fear** to make a **Political Point**

1) Terrorism is the use of <u>fear</u> to achieve <u>political goals</u>. Terrorists use tactics such as <u>bombing</u> public places, taking <u>hostages</u> and <u>hijacking</u> aeroplanes.

2) It's usually <u>condemned</u> because it puts <u>innocent civilians</u> in danger.

3) Terrorists often claim that they use violence because they have <u>no choice</u>. They say it's the only way to get their <u>voice heard</u> — e.g. in a non-democratic state.

4) Sometimes a group is called "<u>terrorists</u>" by some people and "<u>freedom fighters</u>" by others. It all depends <u>how sympathetic</u> you are to what they're trying to achieve and on your views of their methods.

5) Terror networks are now <u>international</u>. Terrorist organisations trade with each other for <u>weapons</u> and <u>training</u>. Some terrorist groups receive money from <u>governments</u> who want to harm other countries without being held responsible.

The **PLO** used both **Terrorist Tactics** and **Diplomacy**

1) <u>Israel</u> was created in <u>1948</u> as a <u>homeland</u> for Jewish people after World War 2. The region had historical and cultural <u>significance</u> for Jews. However, there was <u>conflict</u> between the Jewish settlers and Palestinian Arabs who lived in the region. <u>750 000</u> Palestinians became <u>refugees</u>.

2) The <u>Palestine Liberation Organisation</u> (PLO) was created in <u>1964</u> by <u>Arab nationalists</u> who wanted to win Palestine back from Israel. <u>Yasser Arafat</u> became the <u>chairman</u> of the PLO in <u>1969</u>. He was a <u>strong leader</u>.

3) The PLO was made up of <u>different groups</u>. Arafat belonged to <u>Fatah</u> — the largest group, which was relatively <u>moderate</u>. Other groups were more <u>extreme</u>.

4) The PLO used <u>terrorist tactics</u>, e.g. the <u>1978 Coastal Road Massacre</u> killed 38 Israelis, including 13 Israeli children.

5) But it also wanted to be <u>accepted</u> as the <u>representative</u> of the Palestinian people.

6) The PLO eventually <u>reduced its demands</u>. In <u>1988</u> it agreed to a <u>two-state solution</u> which would <u>divide</u> Palestine into <u>separate</u> Jewish and Arab states.

Yasser Arafat

7) In the <u>Oslo Accords (1993)</u> the Israeli government recognised the PLO as the <u>legitimate representative</u> of the Palestinians. The PLO recognised that Israel had a right to exist in <u>peace</u>. Arafat became President of the new <u>Palestinian Authority</u>, which controlled some of the territory previously occupied by Israel.

Terrorism — a violent way to make yourself heard

All terrorists have an <u>agenda</u> which they want to be <u>acknowledged</u> by those in power. Sometimes, like the PLO, terrorist groups want to reclaim land they feel has been unfairly given away. Although some groups can be diplomatic and <u>negotiate</u> with the government, terrorism puts <u>civilians in danger</u> — which is why people want to put a stop to it.

Terrorism

Some terrorists are willing to <u>negotiate</u>, but extreme organisations tend to rely on <u>violence</u> alone.

Al-Qaeda is an International terrorist organisation

1) <u>Al-Qaeda</u> is a <u>global terrorist network</u> with <u>extreme</u> Islamic views. Its members want to create a unified Muslim nation with <u>strict religious laws</u> and <u>no Western influences</u>.

2) Its leader is <u>Osama bin Laden</u>, a <u>Saudi Arabian</u>. During the 1990s, the Taliban regime in Afghanistan supported al-Qaeda and allowed them to build <u>training camps</u> for terrorists.

3) "<u>Jihad</u>" is the Islamic idea of a "<u>spiritual struggle</u>", but some terrorists use it to mean "<u>holy war</u>". In <u>1996</u> al-Qaeda announced a jihad to remove foreign troops from Islamic lands.

4) In 1998 <u>bin Laden</u> announced that it was the duty of every Muslim to <u>kill Americans</u>.

Al-Qaeda have carried out a Number of Attacks

1) The <u>Khobar Towers bombing</u> in Saudi Arabia in 1996 was aimed at US servicemen (19 died). The East African <u>US Embassy bombings</u> in 1998 killed about 200 people, mostly locals.

2) Al-Qaeda attacked the <u>World Trade Center</u> in New York and the <u>Pentagon</u> in Washington on <u>11 September 2001</u>. The attack destroyed the twin towers and killed around 3000 people. It was the <u>worst terrorist attack in history</u>. In response, the <u>USA</u> declared a "<u>war on terror</u>" and <u>invaded Afghanistan</u>. They destroyed many terrorist <u>training camps</u>, but bin Laden wasn't captured.

3) Even with Osama bin Laden in hiding, the attacks continued, e.g. the <u>Bali nightclub bombings</u> in 2002 and many <u>suicide bombings in Iraq</u>.

4) <u>Bin Laden</u> was eventually <u>tracked down</u> and <u>killed</u> in Pakistan by a US military raid in <u>2011</u>.

Not all terrorist groups are willing to negotiate...

The PLO used violent tactics but eventually they were willing to <u>negotiate</u> in a peace process. Extreme terrorist groups like Al-Qaeda don't use <u>diplomacy</u> and won't <u>compromise</u>. They rely on <u>high profile attacks</u> to make headlines and promote their cause. You've probably heard a lot about them on the <u>news</u>, but make sure you know the facts for your <u>exam</u>.

Terrorism

Some terrorist conflicts can last for <u>decades</u>, such as the 'Troubles' in <u>Northern Ireland</u>...

The **IRA** wanted **Ireland** to be **United**

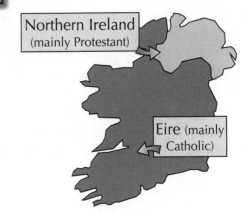

Northern Ireland
(mainly Protestant)

Eire (mainly
Catholic)

1) In 1921, Ireland was <u>divided</u> into <u>Eire</u> (the Catholic, southern part of the country) and <u>Northern Ireland</u> (the mainly Protestant northern area), which stayed part of the United Kingdom.

2) The <u>Protestant</u> majority living in the North <u>discriminated</u> against Catholics, for example in jobs and housing. In <u>1969</u> violence broke out in Northern Ireland over <u>civil rights</u> for <u>Catholics</u>.

3) The <u>Provisional IRA (Irish Republican Army)</u> wanted Northern Ireland to be united with Eire. They used <u>terrorist tactics</u>.

4) A long period of serious violence was known as the <u>Troubles (1969-1998)</u>. <u>Over 3000 people were killed</u> and many more were injured on both sides of the conflict.

5) There were <u>revenge killings</u> between the IRA and its opponents — the "loyalist" <u>UVF</u> (Ulster Volunteer Force) and <u>UDA</u> (Ulster Defence Association).

6) The IRA wanted to <u>wear down</u> the British government so they would eventually decide that defending Northern Ireland wasn't <u>worth the cost</u> in lives and resources.

The **'Troubles'** involved many **High Profile Attacks**

- From <u>1971</u> the IRA began <u>killing British soldiers</u>, including 100 British soldiers in <u>1972</u>.

- The IRA started bombing <u>commercial targets</u>, e.g. <u>Belfast city centre</u> in <u>1972</u>.

- In <u>1973</u> the bombing spread to <u>England</u>. In 1974, there were <u>pub bombings</u> in <u>Guildford</u> and <u>Birmingham</u>. The <u>Brighton hotel bombing</u> in <u>1984</u> was an attempt to kill Margaret Thatcher.

- In <u>1997</u> the IRA agreed to a <u>ceasefire</u>.

- In <u>1998</u>, the British and Irish governments, and most Northern Ireland political parties, including <u>Sinn Fein</u> (associated with the IRA), signed the <u>Good Friday Agreement</u>. It was a move towards <u>power-sharing</u> in Northern Ireland through new political bodies such as a <u>Northern Ireland Assembly</u>. It also included plans for the <u>decommissioning</u> of <u>weapons</u> by paramilitary groups, and a commitment to use only <u>democratic</u> and <u>peaceful</u> methods.

The Troubles were troubling times...

Terrorism and violence created a climate of fear in Northern Ireland during the 'Troubles' — for many the fighting was a way of life as it had been going on for so long. In the end it was <u>peaceful negotiation</u> and the 'Good Friday Agreement' that helped to bring progress.

The Iraq War

The decision to invade Iraq in 2003 was extremely <u>controversial</u>...

*The **First Gulf War** was in 1990-1991*

1) Iraq is made up of different ethnic groups. It's mainly <u>Arab</u>, but there's a strong <u>Kurdish minority</u> (17%) in the North. The main religion is Islam, which in Iraq is divided into a <u>Shia majority</u> and a <u>Sunni minority</u>.

2) <u>Saddam Hussein</u> came to power in 1979. His <u>Ba'ath Party</u> was socialist and secular (non-religious), but his rule <u>favoured the Sunni minority</u>.

3) The USA <u>supported</u> Iraq during its war with Iran in the <u>1980s</u>.

4) But after <u>Iraq invaded Kuwait in 1990</u> President Bush (George W. Bush's father) led international forces against Saddam Hussein in the <u>First Gulf War</u>.

*George W Bush wanted to **Remove Saddam** from **Power***

When <u>George W Bush</u> became US President in 2001, he wanted to invade Iraq.
He claimed that Saddam had links to <u>al-Qaeda</u> and was developing <u>weapons of mass destruction</u>.

In October 2002 Congress passed the <u>Iraq War Resolution</u>. This made the invasion of Iraq legal because it hadn't met the conditions of the 1991 <u>ceasefire</u>. Congress accused Iraq of developing <u>weapons of mass destruction</u> (WMD), <u>protecting terrorists</u> and acts of <u>brutality</u>.

In November 2002 the <u>UN Security Council</u> passed <u>Resolution 1441</u>, giving Iraq a <u>final chance</u> to give up its weapons, but Iraq didn't comply. Some people argue that the case should have gone back to the UN because Resolution 1441 <u>did not authorise</u> the invasion.

In March 2003, the US <u>invaded</u> Iraq. British Prime Minister <u>Tony Blair</u> supported US policy and <u>Britain</u> became America's main <u>ally</u> in the war.

*It turned out there weren't any **WMD***

After the invasion, it became clear that there was <u>no evidence</u> of <u>WMD</u> or links to <u>al-Qaeda</u>.
This was embarrassing for the USA so they put forward other arguments for the invasion:

1) Getting rid of a dictator and establishing <u>democracy</u> could be seen as <u>progress</u> for Iraq.

2) The war was justified by <u>Saddam's appalling human rights record</u>.

War — what was it for?

Whatever your views on the Iraq War, the reasons the USA gave for invading at the time were not backed up by the <u>evidence</u> they'd hoped for, despite a hunt for the suspected WMDs. The decision to invade was <u>controversial</u> here in the UK because so many people were <u>strongly against</u> going to war.

The Iraq War

Despite worldwide speculation, the initial invasion went ahead and had a speedy 'victory' —
but that wasn't quite the end of it...

Millions Demonstrated Against the War

There were anti-war protests involving millions of people in early 2003.

Some people didn't trust the USA's motives for war — they thought that the US wanted Iraq's oil supply and lied about the WMD.	Others felt uneasy about Western nations invading Iraq. Iraq had once been controlled by the British Empire — there were echoes of colonialism.	The idea of these Western, mainly Christian countries invading a Muslim country made some people feel uncomfortable.

Saddam's regime Crumbled in just over a Month...

1) In March 2003, coalition forces led by the US invaded Iraq.
2) They captured the capital Baghdad on 9 April. The coalition had about 200 000 ground troops who were far better equipped than the Iraqis, and had total air superiority.
3) On 1 May President Bush announced US victory in Iraq.

...but the Conflict went on

Saddam Hussein

1) After Saddam's defeat, there was widespread looting and civil disorder. The coalition forces lacked the manpower to deal with the problem.
2) Many members of the defeated Iraqi army became insurgents (resisting the invasion). They used weapons supplied by terrorists.
3) Saddam Hussein went into hiding but was captured in December 2003.
4) In 2004 resistance to the US coalition increased, helped by foreign fighters and al-Qaeda. Fighting included a 46-day battle for the city of Fallujah starting in November 2004. It was eventually won by US forces.
5) Over the next few years, 2 million Iraqis fled the country to escape the war. Some Iraqis were angry that the coalition couldn't protect civilians.
6) US soldiers were found guilty of abusing prisoners at Abu Ghraib prison in April 2004. This was a major blow to the moral justification for invading Iraq.

The invasion of Iraq divided public opinion...

...some people thought the war was justified, but others argued that it was illegal and wrong.

The coalition forces seemed to have won in just a short space of time, with Saddam Hussein captured and troops occupying Baghdad. The invasion caused massive disorder within Iraq though, so the army had to stay there for years to help sort out the mess, and try to protect the Iraqi civilians.

The Iraq War

The invasion was fairly <u>quick</u> and <u>easy</u>, but the conflict went on <u>longer</u> than anyone expected.

*Achieving **Democracy** and **Security** was a **Slow Process***

Coalition forces tried to <u>improve security</u>, but there was still some <u>resistance</u>.

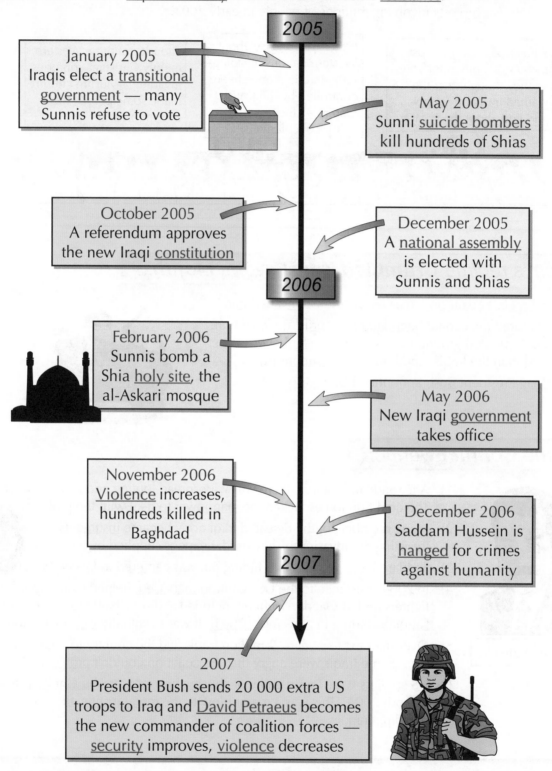

2005

January 2005
Iraqis elect a <u>transitional government</u> — many Sunnis refuse to vote

May 2005
Sunni <u>suicide bombers</u> kill hundreds of Shias

October 2005
A referendum approves the new Iraqi <u>constitution</u>

December 2005
A <u>national assembly</u> is elected with Sunnis and Shias

2006

February 2006
Sunnis bomb a Shia <u>holy site</u>, the al-Askari mosque

May 2006
New Iraqi <u>government</u> takes office

November 2006
<u>Violence</u> increases, hundreds killed in Baghdad

December 2006
Saddam Hussein is <u>hanged</u> for crimes against humanity

2007

2007
President Bush sends 20 000 extra US troops to Iraq and <u>David Petraeus</u> becomes the new commander of coalition forces — <u>security</u> improves, <u>violence</u> decreases

The Iraq war — the conflict and the debate continue...

Coalition forces couldn't just invade Iraq and then abandon the Iraqi people — they had a responsibility to leave the country in a stable condition. People who oppose the war criticise the US for its <u>lack of preparation</u> for the aftermath of the invasion and the chaos which followed.

Revision Summary

I know, I know, that was quite a lot of information in a deceptively small section. How sneaky.
Not to worry though, because here are some wonderful revision questions to test your knowledge
and make sure you understand it all. There are a few facts and figures to remember but it's all
really relevant to what's going on in the world today. It might even come in handy if you want to
impress strangers at parties with your thoughts on current world events.
Well, it's more interesting than talking about the weather and the price of onions anyway...

1)   What do terrorists use to achieve their political goals?

2)   Give three examples of terrorist tactics.

3)   What does PLO stand for?

4)   Who was made leader of the PLO in 1969?

5)   What was agreed at the Oslo Accords?

6)   What is the main aim of al-Qaeda?

7)   What is traditionally meant by 'jihad'? What do extremists sometimes use it to mean?

8)   Name three terrorist attacks carried out by al-Qaeda.

9)   Which area of Ireland is mainly Catholic and which is mainly Protestant?

10) Which terrorist group wanted Northern Ireland to be united with Eire?

11) What were the 'Troubles'?

12) What is the name of the Northern Ireland peace process agreement signed in 1998?

13) What are the two main branches of Islam in Iraq?

14) What did the Iraq War Resolution do?

15) What was Resolution 1441?

16) Give three reasons why some people opposed the war in Iraq.

17) When did US coalition forces invade Iraq and what date did President Bush claim victory?

18) When was Saddam Hussein captured?

19) What crime happened at Abu Ghraib prison?

20) When did the new Iraqi government come into office?

21) When was Saddam Hussein hanged? What crime was he found guilty of?

Exam Practice

Study **Source A** and then answer the question that follows.

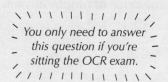
You only need to answer this question if you're sitting the OCR exam.

Source A:
A man walks past a UVF mural in the Shankill area of West Belfast

Rex Features

Current World Issues

1 (a) Describe the main features of the Troubles in Northern Ireland.

(4 marks)

(b) What does Source A tell us about relations between Catholics and Protestants in Northern Ireland during the 1970s and 1980s?

Use details of the source and your knowledge to explain your answer.

(6 marks)

(c) "The PLO and Al-Qaeda use similar methods to each other to achieve their aims."

How far do you agree with this statement? Explain your answer.

(10 marks + 3 marks for SPaG)

The Schlieffen Plan

This section covers the main events of the First World War. If you're revising this topic, you also need to learn about the causes and outbreak of the war — which are covered in Section 1.

The Germans had to **Fight France** and **Russia**

1) France had been defeated by Germany in 1870-71 and wanted revenge. The French had a secret plan — Plan 17 — to take back lands they had lost in 1871 — Alsace and Lorraine.

2) France had made a treaty with Russia in 1894, so Germany expected a Russian attack from the East to help France.

3) Germany would therefore have to fight on two fronts at once. The answer was the Schlieffen Plan, thought up in 1905 (see p.20).

> The SCHLIEFFEN PLAN aimed to attack and defeat France through Belgium before the Russians were ready, then turn back to fight the Russian Army.

The Schlieffen Plan 1905 - what the Germans wanted..........

⟹ German Forces
➡ French Forces

➡ British Forces
➡ German Forces
➡ French Forces

....and what they actually got in 1914.

The **Schlieffen Plan Didn't Work**...

1) Belgium refused to let the German army through to attack France. So Germany had to use force, which delayed their advance.

2) Britain had signed a treaty with Belgium in 1839 to protect it as a neutral country. When Germany refused to withdraw from Belgium, Britain declared war.

3) Russia was ready for war quicker than the Germans had expected. Many valuable German troops had to march East to face them instead of pushing on into France.

It didn't all go to plan for the Germans...

Germany thought that sending all the troops through Belgium into France would be easy, leaving them free to turn around to deal with the Russians — but they hadn't expected the Belgians to be so resistant, or the Russians to be so well-prepared.

Stalemate in the West

The First World War began a <u>new type of warfare</u> — and it was shockingly horrible.

A short period of **Open Warfare** followed

The early <u>battles</u> of the war in the West saw the two sides struggle for an advantage:

| MONS | — August 1914 — the <u>British Expeditionary Force</u> (BEF) — the first troops sent over from Britain — managed to slow down the German advance, but they didn't stop it. The German Kaiser called them a '<u>contemptible little army</u>'. |

| MARNE | — the Allied troops managed to <u>save Paris</u>, and forced the Germans to pull back to the river Aisne. The battle lasted five days. |

| YPRES | — where both sides '<u>dashed to the sea</u>' to stop the other side controlling the coastline. The Allied troops managed it, but with a terrible <u>loss of life</u>. |

Neither side could push the other back, so they dug <u>trenches</u> to stop the enemy advancing further. By the end of 1914, the trench lines stretched all the way from the Belgian coast down to Switzerland and the two armies had reached a <u>stalemate</u>.

Changes in Warfare meant **Stalemate in the Trenches**

1) <u>Nobody</u> was used to <u>trench warfare</u>.
   It took a long time to work out how to <u>break</u> the stalemate.

2) No one had commanded such <u>huge armies</u> before. They had to learn how.

3) It took <u>time</u> to train all the new soldiers. This was especially hard
   for the <u>British</u> who had had a small army before the war.

4) <u>New weapons</u> the armies had were generally better for <u>defence</u> than attack (see diagram).

5) Advancing troops <u>couldn't</u> hold on to the ground they won, and were pushed back.

6) Both sides were <u>well supplied</u>, and could always call up more arms and men.

7) <u>Conditions</u> were often appalling — <u>muddy</u> and <u>wet</u> — not suited for quick attacks.

8) <u>Artillery bombardments</u> were supposed to weaken enemy lines
   — but they just <u>warned</u> the enemy an attack was coming.

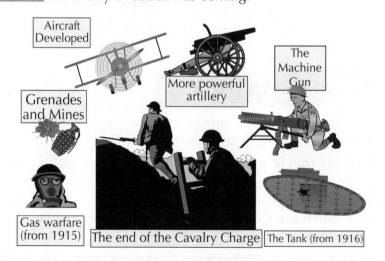

Aircraft Developed

Grenades and Mines

More powerful artillery

The Machine Gun

Gas warfare (from 1915)

The end of the Cavalry Charge

The Tank (from 1916)

Get all these facts en-trenched in your brain...

Once the armies were stuck in the trenches, there was no hope of it being <u>over by Christmas</u>.

Life in the Trenches

The Somme made it clear that <u>neither side</u> would win a breakthrough in this new kind of war.

The Generals Kept Sending Troops 'Over the Top'

<u>Both sides</u> often tried to break the deadlock by sending thousands of men across <u>No Man's Land</u>. The result was <u>huge slaughter</u> of infantry. But some battles did affect the whole war:

1) At the 2nd battle of <u>Ypres</u> in 1915, the Germans first used poison gas against the Allied troops.

2) At <u>Verdun</u> in 1916, the French, under General Petain, held the Germans back from the city.

3) This victory for France <u>boosted</u> French morale — Verdun became a symbol of French freedom and <u>demoralised</u> the Germans, who were sure it would fall.

4) In order to relieve the pressure on Verdun, the British began a <u>major attack</u> at the <u>Somme</u> (July-November 1916). At this battle the British army used a new invention — the <u>tank</u>.

The Somme was a **Major Battle** and a **Major Disaster**

<u>The Somme</u> was one of the <u>key</u> battles of the war. The British commander was <u>Sir Douglas Haig</u>.

After a massive artillery bombardment, the British soldiers were sent 'over the top' to charge the German trenches. They were under orders to advance slowly, not run. This gave the Germans time to get ready for the attack. The slow-moving British soldiers were an easy target. 57 000 Britons were <u>killed</u> or <u>wounded</u> on the first day alone. Later attacks were more successful, but the battle dragged on till November. Only about 12 km of land was gained in some places.

The Results of the Battle of the Somme

1) The <u>Germans</u> had found out about the offensive on the Somme <u>before</u> it happened, which meant that there was a <u>big</u> problem with keeping military secrets.

2) The <u>British artillery</u> had <u>failed</u> to break the enemy lines. It didn't even destroy their barbed wire, despite bombarding for several days.

3) The battle was <u>filmed</u> and shown back home. It gave people some idea of what the trenches were <u>really like</u> — but some footage was <u>faked</u> because the real battle was too horrific.

4) People at home started to openly <u>criticise</u> the generals and their tactics.

Trench Warfare — All quiet on the Western Front...

Phew, there's a lot for you to learn here. Have a go at covering the page and scribbling down everything you can remember about it. Then check what you missed, and <u>do it again</u>.

Life in the Trenches

Life in the Trenches was Hard and Dangerous

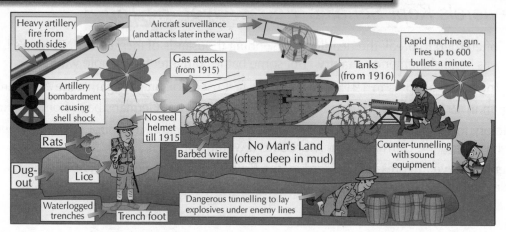

1) Life was almost <u>as dangerous</u> in the trenches as it was in No Man's Land.
2) Each man got paid <u>one shilling</u> (5p) a day, and their main rations were <u>bully beef</u>, <u>jam</u> and <u>tea</u>.

People *Still Can't Agree* whether the *Tactics* were Right

Many people <u>nowadays</u> still feel that the tactics used at the Somme and in other battles were <u>wrong</u>. Their picture of the First World War comes from <u>TV, books and films</u> — which often lay a lot of blame on Sir Douglas Haig, the "Butcher of the Somme". But in fact, it's much <u>more complicated</u> than that.

Here are some of the <u>main opinions</u> on both sides.

Arguments <u>supporting</u> Haig's tactics

- Haig's main <u>aim</u> was to <u>win</u> the war, <u>whatever the cost</u> — not to save lives.
- If the <u>British government</u> at the time had thought there was a better strategy, they could have replaced Haig — but they didn't.
- Some of <u>Germany's best troops</u> were <u>killed</u> at the Somme — and couldn't be replaced.
- Haig couldn't wait for more tanks before the Somme — he had to <u>relieve the pressure</u> on <u>Verdun</u>, or the whole war might be lost.
- By 1918, Haig had learnt to <u>adapt</u> these attacking tactics so that they became more <u>successful</u>. In 1918 the British pushed the Germans back at the Battle of Amiens.

Arguments <u>against</u> Haig's tactics

- <u>Hundreds of thousands</u> of men were <u>killed</u> under Haig's command. He is quoted as saying, "The attacks are to be pressed, regardless of loss."
- Haig could have <u>waited</u> for <u>more tanks</u> at the Somme, which might have saved many lives.
- Once he saw the first day's slaughter at the Somme, he could have <u>changed tactics</u>.
- Haig could have learnt from his mistakes sooner. Instead he stuck to <u>old-fashioned ideas</u> about war that had already been shown to be disastrous — costing many lives.
- Some junior officers claimed that Haig didn't take account of <u>bad weather conditions</u>.

Trying to win the war — at a huge cost...

Opinions on the <u>British tactics</u> are a tricky business. You've really got to watch out for people just repeating <u>modern ideas</u> about Haig. Make sure you learn the main opinions on <u>both sides</u>.

The Eastern Front

There wasn't just a Western Front... This was a <u>world war</u>, and you've got to know about the <u>Eastern Front</u> as well.

The **Russian Army** was Supposed to be **a Steamroller**

1) The <u>Allied plan</u> was for Britain and France to hold the German army up in the West, while the Russian army advanced from the East. This would <u>trap</u> the Germans between their enemies.

2) At the start of the war, British newspapers talked confidently about the <u>Russian steamroller</u> crushing opposition as it advanced into Germany. It <u>didn't</u> happen.

3) On the other hand, the Russians <u>did</u> catch the Germans out — they were ready in just <u>10 days</u> with <u>6 million men</u>. The Germans had to <u>send troops</u> East <u>before</u> they'd defeated France — so the Schlieffen Plan had <u>failed</u>.

But the **Russian Advance** was a **Failure**

1) The Russian Army <u>advanced</u> into Germany, but they <u>didn't</u> have enough <u>weapons</u>. Many soldiers had to wait for someone to be killed so that they could get hold of a rifle.

2) The Russian plans were <u>rushed</u> because of the need to advance quickly. They <u>weren't prepared</u> for a long campaign.

3) The army was <u>poorly organised</u>. Many officers were inexperienced and discipline was poor.

4) 150 000 Russians were <u>slaughtered</u> in 1914 at the battles of <u>Tannenberg</u> and the <u>Masurian Lakes</u> by German troops under von Hindenberg and Ludendorff.

5) After this the Russians were <u>driven back</u>, and the Germans and Austro-Hungarians advanced.

6) A <u>stalemate</u> soon developed on the Eastern Front. The war was now like a chess match. The war effort put a <u>great strain</u> on Russia, as civilians went hungry so the troops could be supplied.

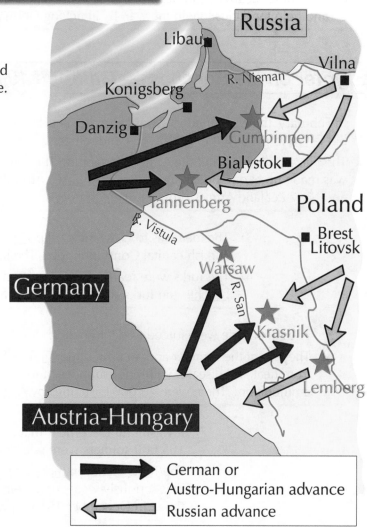

German or Austro-Hungarian advance

Russian advance

The Russian steamroller — it soon ran out of steam...

There you are then, just two key facts to learn here — what the Russians were <u>supposed</u> to do and what <u>really happened</u>. Remember — because the Russians were <u>ready</u> for war quickly the Schlieffen Plan <u>failed</u>. Scribble a list of reasons why the Russian advance was such a <u>disaster</u>.

The Gallipoli Campaign

The Ottoman Empire — which was centred on Turkey — was another enemy of the Allies.

The British Planned to Weaken Germany by Attacking Turkey

1) The Ottoman Empire had joined the war on the German side in November 1914. It attacked Russia in the hope of regaining a hold in the Balkans (see p.21).

2) Some leaders in Britain like Winston Churchill, the First Lord of the Admiralty, thought that Germany and Austria-Hungary could be weakened by attacking Turkey in the East.

The Plan was to Gain Control of the Dardanelles

1) Turkey controlled the Dardanelles — the narrow entrance to the Black Sea — and this was stopping Britain getting supplies through to Russia.

2) If Britain could land troops on the Gallipoli Peninsula they could take the Dardanelles, and then go on to take Constantinople, the capital of the Turkish empire.

3) Then other nearby countries like Greece and Romania might join in on Britain's side, and help the Allies to win the war, by attacking Germany from the East.

Slaughter on the Beaches — Gallipoli 1915

1) In February, the Navy tried to advance up the Dardanelles but failed to get past the Turkish forts and mines.

2) The Navy pulled out and the Army was sent in. The force was made up of one British division and ANZAC (Australian and New Zealand Army Corps) and French troops.

3) The idea was to cross the Gallipoli peninsula and capture the Turkish capital Constantinople. The land assault began in April.

4) The Turks were ready. By firing down from hills above the beaches the Turks stopped the Allies from advancing at all.

5) The Allied side were forced to dig trenches.

6) They spent the summer and autumn under fire, suffering from heat and disease, with poor supplies of food and ammunition. There were 40 000 casualties by August.

7) It wasn't till December that the evacuation began. 105 000 soldiers were withdrawn.

8) The Turks lost even more men than the Allies: 65 000 died. This seriously weakened their army, but it wasn't obvious at the time. In December 1915 it just looked like a complete mess.

Gallipoli — not exactly a nice trip to the seaside...

Turkey was important for the British — not only did it control a vital supply route to Russia, but it could also provide a way in to weaken Germany and Austria-Hungary. The Turks put up a massive resistance at Gallipoli which caused carnage for both sides.

The Gallipoli Campaign

The Gallipoli Campaign went horribly wrong for the British, and although they stopped the Allies advancing, the Turkish army suffered terribly too.

The **Disaster** was partly caused by **Bad Planning**

1) The Allied commanders didn't know the area, and didn't have proper maps.

2) They hadn't realised how strong and well-positioned the Turkish forces would be.

3) The chosen landing place was in difficult terrain — a narrow beach backed by steep hills.

Over a third of the ANZACs sent to Gallipoli died. Churchill was removed from his post as First Lord of the Admiralty, and the Dardanelles remained under Turkish control.

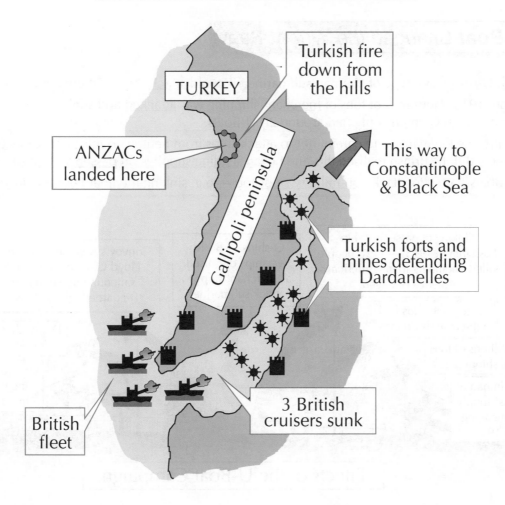

TURKEY

Turkish fire down from the hills

ANZACs landed here

Gallipoli peninsula

This way to Constantinople & Black Sea

Turkish forts and mines defending Dardanelles

3 British cruisers sunk

British fleet

It wasn't just the Western Front that had trench warfare...

Complicated stuff here and there's no way round it — you've got to learn what the Gallipoli campaign tried to achieve and why it went so horribly wrong. At the time there was so much confusion that it was months before the soldiers were evacuated from the beaches — by which time both sides had suffered tens of thousands of casualties, and appalling conditions.

The War at Sea

Blockades were more important than sea battles — stopping supplies getting to Germany.

The British Navy had **Four Important Jobs**

(1) To protect trade ships so that the Allies could remain supplied.

(2) To blockade ports, preventing the enemy being supplied.

(3) To carry troops to wherever they were needed.

(4) To protect British colonies overseas.

The **U-Boat** Changed the War at Sea

1) The U-Boat was a type of German submarine. It could attack ships without being detected.

2) From 1915, thousands of tons of merchant shipping was attacked and sunk, even though Germany only had around 20 U-Boats.

3) At first the Germans were careful not to attack ships from neutral countries or passenger liners. But the British realised this and began sending supplies on passenger liners too.

4) U-Boats started to attack non-military ships too — e.g. sinking the liner Lusitania in 1915.

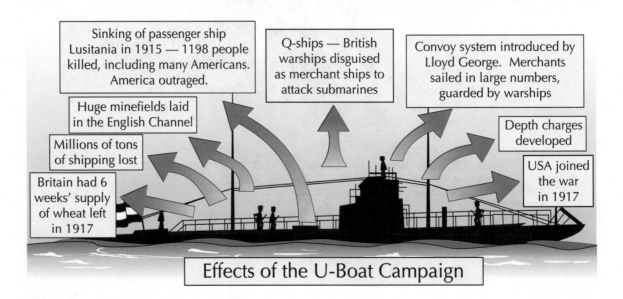

Sinking of passenger ship Lusitania in 1915 — 1198 people killed, including many Americans. America outraged.

Q-ships — British warships disguised as merchant ships to attack submarines

Convoy system introduced by Lloyd George. Merchants sailed in large numbers, guarded by warships

Huge minefields laid in the English Channel

Millions of tons of shipping lost

Depth charges developed

Britain had 6 weeks' supply of wheat left in 1917

USA joined the war in 1917

Effects of the U-Boat Campaign

Germany rocked the boat to control the seas...

The Navy was an important force in the war — but fighting battles at sea was not supposed to be on their agenda. Everything changed when the Germans started to use U-Boats to attack supply ships undetected, especially when they started attacking passenger ships too.

The War at Sea

With the threat of the German Navy at large, the British started to fight back to regain control at sea.

Major Battles were Too Risky

Both sides had raced to build Dreadnoughts — (see p.20). But neither side wanted to risk these expensive ships in too many big battles. The only large-scale battle between the Dreadnought fleets was the Battle of Jutland in May 1916. Around 250 ships clashed. The German Admiral von Scheer wanted to lure part of the British fleet out of their base to attack them. But more British ships came than he expected...

Both Sides said they won at the Battle of Jutland...

1) The British lost 14 ships, and the Germans 11.

2) They fought in the evening, when it was misty, so neither side could fire accurately.

3) The British ships generally suffered more damage than the Germans.

4) The German ships and firepower seemed stronger.

5) But the German fleet left the battle first, and never put to sea in any strength after that.

Meanwhile the U-Boat Seemed to be an Unstoppable Force

1) Over 0.5 million tons of shipping was sunk in April 1917 alone.
2) The U-Boat campaign was trying to starve Britain into submission.
3) To tackle this problem, Lloyd George introduced the Convoy System — where merchant ships travelled together in groups protected by warships — to keep Britain's supplies coming in.

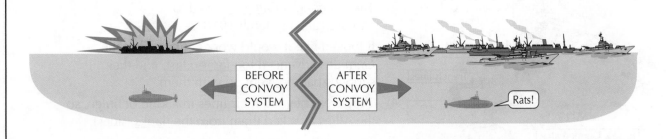

The war at sea — sailing to victory...

After rushing to build sophisticated battleships, neither side wanted to risk losing them. The only big sea battle was at Jutland, and even then the result was more or less a draw. There are loads of facts here — make sure you learn the reasons for avoiding major battles and the effects of the U-Boat threat.

The End of the Fighting

The Russians withdrew from the fighting — but the USA joined.

Russia **Pulled Out** of the War in **1917**

1) Tsar Nicholas II of Russia was a poor military commander.

2) To the south, the Brusilov Offensive advanced successfully into Austria-Hungary in June 1916, but was soon pushed back.

3) There was widespread starvation in the winter of 1916, and Nicholas II was forced out of power in 1917. The new Provisional Government continued the war, but was no more successful.

4) The Bolshevik Revolution in 1917 brought new leaders to power who decided to end the fighting. Russia signed the Treaty of Brest-Litovsk with Germany in 1918, giving Germany control of a large amount of Eastern territory in return for peace.

5) Two important results of Russia leaving the war were:

   i) The Allies were left to fight on without Russian help on an Eastern Front.

   ii) Germany was now able to pull back 1 million men to the Western Front.

In April 1917 the **USA** joined the **Allies**

1) In April 1917 the USA joined the war for two main reasons — the effects of the U-Boat campaign (100 American citizens were killed when the Lusitania was sunk in 1915), and a German attempt to encourage Mexico to attack the USA. This was a direct threat.

2) By now the fighting in Europe had become even fiercer. The French under General Nivelle had failed to push the Germans back.

3) The Allies fought the battles of Passchendaele and Cambrai in 1917. (The Battle of Passchendaele was also known as the Third Battle of Ypres — over 300 000 Allied troops were killed or wounded to win a few hundred metres of mud.)

Germany had to Attack Before all the Americans Arrived

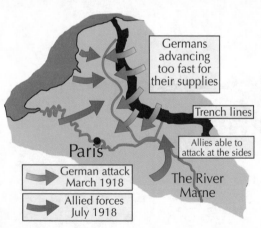

Germans advancing too fast for their supplies

Trench lines

Allies able to attack at the sides

Paris

German attack March 1918

Allied forces July 1918

The River Marne

1) The USA wasn't ready to send all its troops, so Germany made a last effort to break through.

2) The Ludendorff Offensive tried to capture Paris in March 1918.

3) It looked like it would work at first — but the Germans advanced too far too fast, and their supplies had not kept up with them.

4) They were beyond their lines in a kind of bulge, so the Allies attacked them from the flanks (sides).

5) Thousands of American troops were soon joining the Allies, and the Germans were pushed back.

6) Kaiser Wilhelm II abdicated and the new government agreed a ceasefire or armistice on November 11th 1918.

US and them — America made all the difference...

Here you go, three key events in the last two years of the war — Russia's withdrawal, the USA joining the struggle and Germany trying a final big offensive. It's important to learn them NOW.

Revision Summary

Don't just turn the page now — you really do need to have a go at these questions. It's the only way you can make sure you know this stuff well — and that's the only way you can guarantee doing well in your exams. See how many you can get right — and revise the stuff you get wrong.

1)   List three reasons why the Schlieffen Plan didn't work.

2)   How far did the trenches stretch by the end of 1914?

3)   Write down four new types of military equipment used during World War 1.

4)   When did the Germans first use poison gas against Allied troops?

5)   Give a summary of the events of the Battle of the Somme.

6)   Write a short paragraph for and against the tactics used by the Allies at the Somme.

7)   Give three reasons why the Russian Army did badly when they advanced on Germany in 1914.

8)   What was the original aim of the Gallipoli campaign?

9)   Give two reasons why the Gallipoli campaign failed.

10)   How did the ANZACs get their name?

11)   Give four important roles of the British Navy during the war.

12)   Name the new type of battleship built by Britain and Germany before the war.

13)   Give two reasons why the U-Boats caused Britain so many problems.

14)   Why isn't it clear who won the Battle of Jutland?

15)   Who was the Russian Tsar who was forced out of power in 1917?

16)   What was the name of the treaty made between Germany and Russia in 1918?

17)   Give two reasons why the USA joined the war in 1917.

18)   Why did the Ludendorff Offensive fail in 1918?

19)   Here's a list of important battles — put them into the order in which they happened, and note what was important about each one:
PASSCHENDAELE, MARNE, THE SOMME, 2ND BATTLE OF YPRES

Exam Sources

Study **Sources A to C** and then answer the questions that follow.

Source A

You only need to answer these questions if you're sitting the OCR exam.

© Mary Evans Picture Library

"The Gas Fiend" published in "Raemaeker's Cartoons", 1916. The book, devised by the UK War Department, contains work by Dutch Cartoonist Louis Raemaeker.

Source B

© Mary Evans Picture Library

A photograph published in 1915 showing a British Officer in 'anti-gas helmet' (gas mask) in a trench on the Western Front.

Source C

> Very successful attack this morning. All went like clockwork. The battle is going very well for us. Already the Germans are surrendering freely. The enemy is so short of men that he is collecting them from all parts of the line. Our troops are in wonderful spirits and full of confidence. All objectives achieved so far.

From a report by Sir Douglas Haig, the British Commander-in-Chief, on the first day of the Battle of the Somme, 1 July 1916.

Exam Practice

The First World War

1 (a) Study Source A.

What is the message of this cartoon?

Use the source and your knowledge to explain your answer.

(6 marks)

(b) Study Source B.

How far does this source prove that the British were well prepared to fight the Germans in 1915?

Use the source and your knowledge to explain your answer.

(7 marks)

(c) Study Source C.

To what extent does this give a true indication of the progress of the battle?

Use the source and your knowledge to explain your answer.

(7 marks)

2 (a) Describe the main features of the Schlieffen Plan.

(4 marks)

(b) Explain why the Schlieffen Plan failed.

(6 marks)

(c) "Sir Douglas Haig deserves the title 'Butcher of the Somme'."

How far do you agree with this statement? Explain your answer.

(10 marks + 3 marks for SPaG)

The Weimar Republic

Germany lost the First World War (1914-1918). The peace settlement was harsh on Germany — it said Germany should accept blame for the war and pay £6.6 billion in reparations.

A New Government Took Over When the Kaiser Abdicated

1) Kaiser Wilhelm II had ruled the German Empire as a monarch. At the end of the First World War there was a period of violent unrest in Germany — and the Kaiser was forced to abdicate in November 1918.

2) In early 1919, a new government took power led by Friedrich Ebert — it changed Germany into a republic. It was set up in Weimar, because there was violence in Berlin. Ebert became the first President, with Scheidemann as Chancellor.

Friedrich Ebert

3) Ebert was leader of the Social Democratic Party, a moderate party of socialists. The new government was democratic — they believed the people should say how the country was run.

4) The new German government wasn't invited to the peace conference in 1919 — and had no say in the Versailles Treaty. At first, Ebert refused to sign the treaty, but in the end he had little choice — Germany was too weak to risk restarting the conflict.

Reasons for Discontent

1) Thousands of people were poor and starving. An influenza epidemic had killed thousands.

2) Many Germans denied they had lost the war and blamed the 'November Criminals' who had agreed to the Armistice and the Treaty of Versailles.

3) Others blamed for losing the war included the communists, the government and the Jews.

4) The government was seen as weak and ineffective — the Treaty of Versailles had made living conditions worse in Germany.

The Weimar Constitution made Germany a Republic

THE WEIMAR GOVERNMENT

REICHSRAT
Upper house (could delay measures passed by Reichstag)

REICHSTAG
The new German parliament (elected by proportional representation)

PRESIDENT
Elected every 7 years. Head of army. Chooses the Chancellor.

Proportional representation is where the number of seats a party wins in parliament is worked out as a proportion of the number of votes they win. This was the system in Germany and it often led to lots of political parties in the Reichstag (German parliament) — making it harder to get laws passed.

The Weimar Republic

The *Weimar Republic* had Many *Problems*

1) It was <u>difficult</u> to make decisions because there were so <u>many parties</u> in the Reichstag.

2) It was hard to pick a Chancellor who had the <u>support</u> of most of the Reichstag.

3) The new government had to <u>accept</u> the Versailles Treaty, so they were <u>hated</u> by many Germans because of the loss of territory, the 'war guilt' clause, the reparations etc. (see p.27).

4) Some Germans joined paramilitary groups, such as the <u>Freikorps</u> (Free Corps) — <u>right-wing</u> groups made up of <u>ex-soldiers</u> who saw <u>communists</u> as a threat to <u>peace</u>.

5) Even though the <u>Freikorps</u> were <u>problematic</u> — they were <u>private organisations</u> not under government <u>control</u> — Ebert was happy to use them to <u>suppress</u> communist uprisings.

The Weimar Republic had many *Cultural Achievements*

1) Germany's capital <u>Berlin</u> became a <u>centre for culture</u> under the Weimar Republic.

2) There were advances in <u>art</u>, <u>architecture</u>, <u>music</u> and <u>literature</u>. German films were successful — e.g. 'Metropolis', directed by <u>Fritz Lang</u>.

3) Some developments were <u>bold</u> and <u>new</u>, like the drama of <u>Bertolt Brecht</u>. The <u>Bauhaus School</u> of <u>design</u> was highly influential.

4) The Weimar Republic encouraged new ways of <u>critical thinking</u> at places like <u>Frankfurt University</u>.

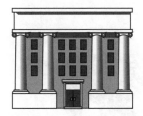

5) Not everyone approved of these cultural changes — the <u>cabaret culture</u> in Berlin was seen as <u>immoral</u> by some. The culture of the Weimar Republic <u>didn't survive</u> under the <u>Nazis</u>...

Weimar — not a kind of sausage...

The <u>Weimar Republic</u> was set up in a time of <u>defeat</u> — which made it unpopular right from the start. Don't forget — many German people <u>didn't accept</u> the peace settlements at the end of the First World War. Scribble a quick paragraph on the Weimar Republic and how it was set up.

Years of Unrest 1919-1923

Germany faced all sorts of <u>problems</u> in the years following the First World War.

Soon there were Riots and Rebellions

1) In 1919 the <u>Spartacists</u>, a communist group led by Karl Liebknecht and Rosa Luxemburg, tried to <u>take over</u> Berlin in the <u>Spartacist Revolt</u> — but they were defeated by the Freikorps.

Wolfgang Kapp

2) In 1920, some of the right-wing Freikorps themselves took part in the Kapp Putsch (Putsch means revolt) — led by Wolfgang Kapp, they <u>took over</u> Berlin to form another government. The workers staged a General Strike — Kapp <u>gave up</u>. The government <u>didn't</u> punish the rebels, because many judges <u>sympathised</u> with people like Kapp.

3) In 1922 Walter Rathenau was <u>killed</u> — he'd been the Foreign Minister who <u>signed</u> the Rapallo Treaty with Russia and was <u>Jewish</u>. Many Germans were now anti-Jewish (<u>anti-Semitic</u>).

In 1923 Germany Couldn't Pay the Reparations

France and Belgium occupied the Ruhr — the <u>richest</u> industrial part of Germany — to <u>take resources</u> instead. This led to fury in Germany, while workers in the Ruhr <u>refused</u> to work. German industry was devastated again, plunging the economy into <u>hyperinflation</u>.

	1918	Aug 1923	Nov 1923
Egg	1/4 Mark	5000 Marks	80 million Marks

HYPERINFLATION - THE PRICE OF AN EGG IN GERMANY

<u>Hyperinflation</u> happens when production can't keep up with the amount of money there is, so the <u>money</u> keeps <u>losing its value</u>.

Hyperinflation had Three Major Results

1) <u>Wages</u> were paid <u>twice a day</u> before prices went up again.
2) The middle classes lost out as <u>bank savings</u> became <u>worthless</u>.
3) The German <u>Mark</u> became <u>worthless</u>.

Hyperinflation — sounds good for blowing up balloons...

Remember that discontent in Germany got <u>worse</u> when the economy <u>went wrong</u> — but there were lots of other factors too. Now cover up the page and scribble down everything you can <u>remember</u>.

Stresemann and Recovery

In August 1923 Gustav Stresemann became Chancellor — he gradually led Germany back to recovery.

Stresemann wanted International Cooperation

Stresemann was Chancellor for a few months, then Foreign Minister. He believed Germany's best chance for recovery came from working with other countries, particularly the US.

1) In September 1923 he told the workers in the Ruhr to return to work, and in November 1923 he introduced a new German Mark called the Rentenmark to make the currency more stable.

2) In 1924 he accepted the Dawes Plan from the US, which reorganised reparation payments.

3) In 1925 the French and Belgian troops left the Ruhr.

4) In October 1925 he agreed to the Locarno Treaty where the western borders of Germany were agreed, but not the eastern. He won the Nobel Peace Prize for his efforts in this field.

5) In 1926, Germany joined the League of Nations, and became one of the permanent members of the Council.

6) In 1928, Germany was one of 65 countries to sign the Kellogg-Briand Pact. They promised not to use violence to settle disputes.

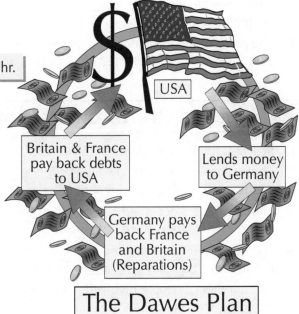

USA

Britain & France pay back debts to USA

Lends money to Germany

Germany pays back France and Britain (Reparations)

The Dawes Plan

7) In 1929, the US agreed to replace the Dawes Plan with the Young Plan — reparations would be reduced by three-quarters of the amount, and Germany was given 59 years to pay them.

Germany had Begun to Recover — but Depended on US Money

Gustav Stresemann

Life was beginning to look better for Germany thanks to the work of Stresemann. But he died in October 1929, just before the disaster of the Wall Street Crash (see p.35).

The plans he had agreed would only work if the USA had enough money to keep lending to Germany — but now it didn't. Things were suddenly going to get worse again.

Stresemann tied Germany's future to the US...

Because it was such a huge economic power, Stresemann believed that by making deals with the US he could make Germany strong again — both the Young and Dawes plans were US-led.

The Roots of the Nazi Party

The <u>Nazi Party</u> was a small organisation in the 1920s — but it had big ambitions...

Adolf Hitler was the Nazi Leader

1) Born in Austria in <u>1889</u>, Hitler had lived in Germany from 1912 onwards.
2) He'd been a brave <u>soldier</u> on the Western Front in World War I, winning the Iron Cross twice. He <u>couldn't accept</u> that Germany had <u>lost</u> the war.
3) In 1919, he joined the German Workers' Party, led by <u>Anton Drexler</u>. It was a tiny party — Hitler was the 55th member. In 1920 the name was changed to the <u>National Socialist German Workers' Party</u> (Nazis).
4) Hitler was a <u>charismatic speaker</u> and attracted new members. He took over the <u>leadership</u> of the party.
5) The party set up its own <u>armed group</u> called the <u>SA</u> — brown-shirted stormtroopers who protected Nazi leaders and <u>harassed</u> their opponents.

Hitler tried to Overthrow the Government in the Munich Putsch

1) In 1923, things were going badly for the Weimar Republic — it seemed <u>weak</u>.
2) Hitler planned to <u>overthrow</u> the <u>Weimar government</u> — starting by taking control of the government in a region called Bavaria.
3) Hitler's soldiers occupied a <u>beer hall</u> in the Bavarian city of <u>Munich</u> where local government leaders were meeting. He announced that the <u>revolution</u> had begun.
4) The next day Hitler marched into Munich supported by <u>several thousand armed men</u>. But the revolt quickly <u>collapsed</u> when <u>police</u> fired on the rebels.
5) The number of people involved, including the famous general Ludendorff, made it seem like a big <u>threat</u> to Weimar, but the Nazis had <u>little popular support</u> and it was all over <u>very quickly</u>.

Hitler wrote the book 'Mein Kampf' in Prison

1) Hitler was <u>imprisoned</u> for his role in the Munich Putsch.
2) He wrote a book in prison describing his <u>beliefs</u> and <u>ambitions</u>. The title 'Mein Kampf' means 'My Struggle'.

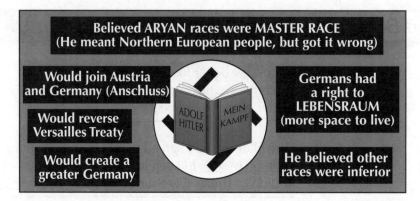

Believed ARYAN races were MASTER RACE
(He meant Northern European people, but got it wrong)

Would join Austria and Germany (Anschluss)

Would reverse Versailles Treaty

Would create a greater Germany

Germans had a right to LEBENSRAUM (more space to live)

He believed other races were inferior

The Nazis — ready to sweep to power...

Very few people supported the Nazis at this stage. There were <u>fewer than 30 000</u> members by 1925, and in the 1928 elections the Nazis had 12 Reichstag members, compared with 54 communists and 153 Social Democrats. All that was about to <u>change</u> though...

The Rise of the Nazis

The Depression hit Germany hard. The popularity of the Nazi Party soared as a result — people thought the Weimar government couldn't sort out Germany's problems.

After the Munich Putsch Hitler **Changed Tactics**

1) The Nazi party was banned after the Munich Putsch. After Hitler was released from prison, he re-established the party with himself as supreme leader.

2) By the mid-1920s, the German economy was starting to recover under Stresemann. As a result, general support for the Nazis declined and overturning the government through a coup no longer seemed realistic.

3) Hitler changed tactics — he now tried to gain control through the democratic system. The Nazi party network was extended nationally, instead of it being a regional party. Propaganda was used to promote the party's beliefs.

The **Great Depression** caused **Poverty** and **Suffering**

1) The Depression caused massive unemployment in Germany — over 6 million were unemployed by 1933.

2) In 1931, Germany's biggest bank collapsed. This made paying reparations (see p.26) more difficult.

3) Weimar governments kept changing during this time, but none managed to solve the economic problems.

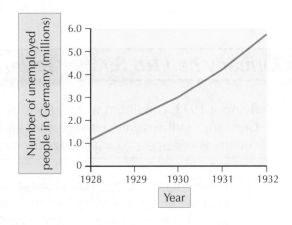

4) The Depression contributed to the collapse of the Weimar Republic. People hoped a new government could sort out the problems.

5) Extremist groups like the Nazis became more popular — they promised strong leadership.

The **Nazis** increased in **Popularity** during the **Depression**

1) The Nazis promised prosperity and to make Germany great again. This appealed to many of the unemployed, as well as to businessmen and young people.

2) Some people supported the Nazis' anti-communist and anti-Jewish views.

3) By 1930 Nazi membership grew to over 300 000.

Another depressing page...

In normal circumstances, the Nazis would have stayed a small, extremist group on the fringes of politics. Unfortunately the Depression gave them an opportunity to gain mainstream popularity.

The Rise of the Nazis

The results of the 1930 election were <u>encouraging</u> for the Nazi party...

The *Elections* of *1930* showed *Nazi Gains*

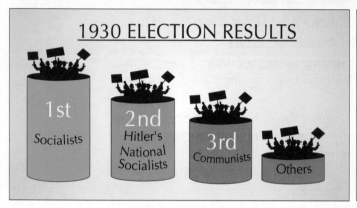

1930 ELECTION RESULTS

1st Socialists

2nd Hitler's National Socialists

3rd Communists

Others

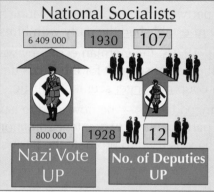

National Socialists

6 409 000	1930	107
800 000	1928	12

Nazi Vote UP

No. of Deputies UP

SHARE PRICES

DOWN

20%

Chancellor Heinrich Brüning <u>couldn't control</u> the <u>Reichstag</u> properly — there was a <u>big increase</u> in seats for both the <u>Nazis</u> (who won 107) and the communists (who won 77). Brüning had to rule by <u>emergency decree</u> as no single party had enough seats to control the Reichstag.

Germany had *No* Strong *Government*

1) By April 1932, conditions were <u>serious</u> in Germany. Millions were unemployed, and the country was <u>desperate</u> for a <u>strong</u> government.

2) President <u>Hindenburg</u> had to stand for <u>re-election</u>, because his term of office had run out. Hitler stood against him, and there was also a communist candidate.

3) Hindenburg, a national hero, said he'd win easily but <u>didn't</u> win a <u>majority</u> in the first election — in the second ballot he won 53%, beating Hitler's 36.8% of the vote.

Paul von Hindenburg

Hindenburg *Refused* to give the Nazis *Power*

1) Hindenburg <u>couldn't find</u> a Chancellor who had <u>support</u> in the Reichstag.

2) He appointed the <u>inexperienced</u> Franz von Papen.

3) In the July 1932 Reichstag elections, the Nazis won 230 seats — they were now the <u>biggest</u> party, but didn't have a majority in the Reichstag. Hitler <u>demanded</u> to be made Chancellor.

4) Hindenburg <u>refused</u> because he <u>didn't trust</u> Hitler and kept von Papen.

The Rise of the Nazis

The Nazis gained a lot of votes — but they used some <u>underhand tactics</u> to get them...

The Nazis *lost seats* in the *Elections*

1) The Nazis <u>lost</u> 34 seats in the November 1932 election — they seemed to be losing popularity.

2) Hindenburg replaced Papen as <u>Chancellor</u> with <u>Kurt von Schleicher</u>. Schleicher tried to <u>cause divisions</u> in the Nazi Party by asking another leading Nazi to be Vice-Chancellor — Gregor Strasser. But Hitler <u>stopped</u> Strasser accepting.

3) Papen knew that Hindenburg would get rid of Schleicher if he <u>failed</u> to get a <u>majority</u> in parliament, so he made a <u>deal</u> with Hitler. They agreed that if Papen persuaded Hindenburg to make Hitler Chancellor, Hitler would make Papen Vice-Chancellor.

4) In January 1933, Papen persuaded Hindenburg to replace Schleicher as <u>Chancellor</u> with Hitler — Papen argued that they would be able to <u>control Hitler</u> and use him as a puppet. He was <u>wrong</u>.

5) In March 1933, Hitler decided to call for <u>another election</u>, hoping to make the Nazis <u>stronger</u> in the Reichstag.

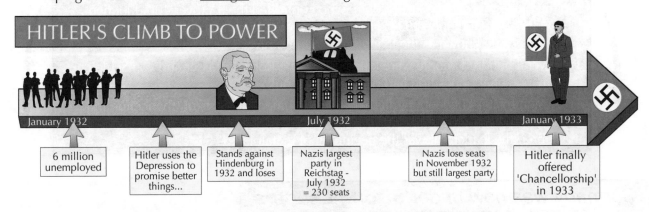

HITLER'S CLIMB TO POWER

January 1932   July 1932   January 1933

| 6 million unemployed | Hitler uses the Depression to promise better things... | Stands against Hindenburg in 1932 and loses | Nazis largest party in Reichstag - July 1932 = 230 seats | Nazis lose seats in November 1932 but still largest party | Hitler finally offered 'Chancellorship' in 1933 |

The Nazis used *Dirty Tricks* to *Win* in 1933

The Nazis did well in the elections because:

1) They <u>controlled</u> the news media.

2) Opposition meetings were <u>banned</u>.

3) They used the SA to <u>terrorise</u> opponents.

4) A <u>fire</u> broke out in the Reichstag building, and Hitler whipped up <u>opposition</u> against the communists, who he said started it. Mass arrests of communists followed.

5) Hitler was allowed <u>emergency decrees</u> to deal with the situation — and used these powers to <u>intimidate</u> communist voters.

HITLER BECOMES DICTATOR OF GERMANY

Reichstag fire enables him to increase control of Reichstag

Chancellor Hitler calls another election

Enabling Act

March 1933 Hitler forces through his Enabling Act

June 1934 Night of the Long Knives. Hitler removes opposition of Röhm

August 1934 Hitler takes over from Hindenburg. Now called 'Der Führer'.

Germany 1930-33 — a state of confusion...

Loads of facts here — but you <u>don't</u> need to learn them all by heart. The <u>key point</u> is the sequence of events. Hitler didn't come to power overnight — his support increased as the economy <u>got worse</u> and as the other political parties <u>failed to solve</u> Germany's problems.

Hitler Comes to Power

Once Hitler was Chancellor he set about strengthening his <u>power</u>...

Hitler **Changed** the **Law** to **Keep Control**

1) The Nazis won 288 seats but <u>no</u> majority — the communists still won 81.

2) So Hitler <u>declared</u> the Communist Party <u>illegal</u>.

3) This gave him enough <u>support</u> in parliament to bring in an <u>Enabling Bill</u> which was passed with threats and bargaining in March 1933.

4) This bill let him <u>govern</u> for four years <u>without</u> parliament and made all other parties illegal. Hitler was almost in full control.

The **Night** of the **Long Knives**

1) Hitler still had opposition — and was worried about <u>rivals</u> within the Nazi party.

2) The biggest <u>threat</u> was <u>Ernst Röhm</u>, who controlled the <u>SA</u> (over 400 000 men). On the 29th-30th June 1934, Hitler sent his own men to <u>arrest</u> Röhm and others. This became known as the 'Night of the Long Knives'.

3) Several hundred people were <u>killed</u>, including Röhm, Strasser and von Schleicher. Any potential <u>opposition</u> had been <u>stamped out</u>.

4) A month later <u>Hindenburg died</u>. Hitler combined the posts of Chancellor and President, made himself Commander-in-Chief of the army, and was called <u>Der Führer</u> (the leader). It was the beginning of <u>dictatorship</u>.

Germany was now under **Strong Leaders**

1) Germany was <u>reorganised</u> into a number of provinces. Each province was called a Gau (plural: Gaue), with a Gauleiter — a loyal Nazi — in charge of each.

2) Above them were the <u>Reichsleiters</u> who <u>advised</u> Hitler, e.g. <u>Goebbels</u> who was in charge of propaganda, and <u>Himmler</u> who was chief of the German police.

3) At the top was the <u>Führer</u> — Hitler himself — who was in absolute <u>control</u>.

4) Every aspect of life was carefully <u>controlled</u>, and only <u>loyal</u> Nazis could be <u>successful</u>.

Joseph Goebbels

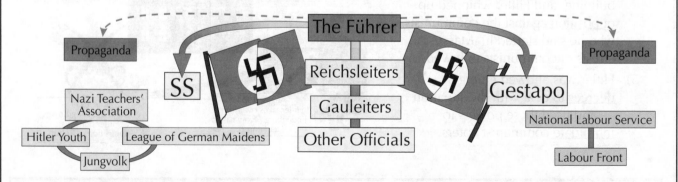

Hitler was obsessed with power...

Once elected the Nazis pretty quickly turned Germany from a democracy into a <u>dictatorship</u>. Hitler set himself up as a <u>supreme ruler</u> — Chancellor, President and army chief combined.

Nazi Methods of Control

The Nazis used many methods to control the German people — from persuasion to <u>violence</u>...

The Nazis used **Propaganda**

<u>Propaganda</u> means spreading particular ideas and <u>points of view</u> to try to control how people think. Nazi propaganda blamed the <u>Jews</u> and <u>communists</u> for most of Germany's problems.

1) The Nazis took over the <u>media</u>. They controlled <u>radio broadcasts</u>, and also used <u>films</u> and <u>posters</u> to spread their messages.

2) The <u>Ministry of Public Enlightenment and Propaganda</u> (founded in <u>1933</u>) was led by <u>Dr Joseph Goebbels</u>. All artists, writers, journalists and musicians had to <u>register</u> to get their <u>work approved</u>.

3) The Nazis organised huge <u>rallies</u> of party members to present an <u>image</u> of power and popularity. They also used the <u>1936 Berlin Olympics</u> as an opportunity for <u>international publicity</u>.

The Nazis used **Censorship**

1) The Nazis <u>censored</u> books, newspapers and other material.

2) Those who published anti-Nazi material risked <u>execution</u>.

3) The Nazis used censorship to encourage <u>nationalism</u> and <u>anti-Semitism (hatred of Jews)</u>. They praised patriotic German composers such as <u>Wagner</u> but banned the work of Jewish composers such as <u>Mendelssohn</u>.

Germany became a **Police State**

1) The <u>SS</u> (<u>Schutzstaffel</u>) began as a bodyguard for Hitler. It expanded massively under the leadership of Himmler during the 1930s. Its members were totally loyal to Hitler, and were feared for their <u>cruelty</u>. Himmler was also in charge of the <u>secret police</u> — the <u>Gestapo</u>.

2) After 1933 <u>concentration camps</u> spread across Germany and its territories to hold political prisoners and anybody else considered dangerous to the Nazis. Some of these were later turned into <u>death camps</u> (see p.110).

3) Local <u>wardens</u> were employed to make sure Germans were loyal to the Nazis. People were encouraged to <u>report disloyalty</u>. Many were arrested by the Gestapo as a result.

The Nazis saw the Church as a **Threat**

1) Many Nazis were against Christianity — its teaching of <u>peace</u> was seen as incompatible with Nazi ideas. However, the Nazis didn't want to <u>risk</u> an immediate attack on it.

2) Hitler signed the <u>Concordat</u> (an agreement) with the <u>Catholic Church</u> in 1933. Each side promised not to interfere with the other. However the Nazis did try to <u>curb</u> the influence of the church — and there were some Catholic <u>protests</u> against Nazi policies.

3) Hitler tried to unite the different Protestant churches into one Reich Church. He placed the Nazi Bishop Ludwig Müller at its head. Some church members split off in protest at this state interference. They formed the <u>Confessing Church</u> (see p.107).

4) Many clergy who stood up to the Nazi regime were sent to <u>concentration camps</u>.

This book wouldn't be available in Nazi Germany...

Imagine if the radio and newspapers all covered the <u>same news</u> in the same way, and featured all the <u>same opinions</u>. You might start to think that way after a while.

German Growth Under the Nazis

The Nazis took strict <u>control</u> of the economy.

Hitler gave **Work** to **6 Million Unemployed**

1) Hitler started a huge <u>programme</u> of <u>public works</u>, which gave <u>jobs</u> to thousands of people.

2) From 1933, huge motorways — <u>Autobahns</u> — were started. <u>Unemployment fell</u> dramatically.

3) But — the Nazis also <u>fiddled with the statistics</u> to make unemployment look <u>lower</u> than it really was. E.g. they didn't count women or Jewish people in the unemployment statistics — this is called "<u>invisible unemployment</u>".

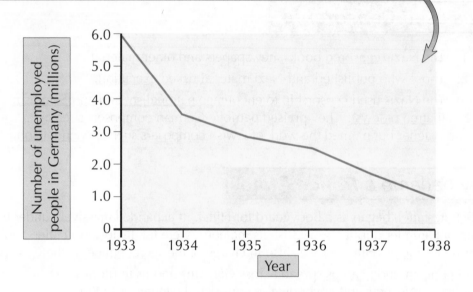

Number of unemployed people in Germany (millions)

Year

People were **Encouraged** to **Work** by **Rewards**

1) <u>All</u> men between 18 and 25 could be <u>recruited</u> into the <u>National Labour Service</u> and given jobs.

2) The Nazis got rid of trade unions. Instead workers had to join the Nazi's <u>Labour Front</u>.

3) The Nazis introduced '<u>Strength through Joy</u>' — a scheme which provided workers with <u>cheap holidays</u> and leisure activities. Another scheme, '<u>Beauty of Labour</u>', encouraged factory owners to <u>improve conditions</u> for their workers.

4) Output increased in Germany, and <u>unemployment</u> was almost <u>ended</u> completely. The Nazis introduced the <u>Volkswagen</u> (the people's car) as an <u>ambition</u> for people to aim for.

5) <u>Wages</u> were still relatively <u>low</u> though — and workers <u>weren't allowed</u> to go on <u>strike</u> or campaign for better conditions.

German Growth Under the Nazis

Hitler Re-armed the German Military

1) Another way to create work was to <u>build up</u> the armed forces.
The Nazis did this <u>secretly</u> at first, because the <u>Treaty of Versailles</u> had <u>banned</u> it.

2) Hitler <u>sacked</u> some of the generals, and <u>replaced</u> them with Nazi supporters. <u>Goering</u> was put in charge of the newly-formed <u>Luftwaffe</u> (airforce), which had been banned at Versailles.

3) In 1935, <u>military conscription</u> was reintroduced (drafting men into the army).

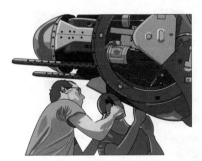

4) In 1936, the Nazis introduced a <u>Four-Year Plan</u> to <u>prepare</u> the country for <u>war</u>. <u>Industrial production</u> increased — many workers had to <u>retrain</u> in jobs that would help the war effort. The plan was to make Germany <u>self-sufficient</u>, so it wasn't reliant on foreign goods.

The outbreak of War changed the Economy

1) More men were drafted into the <u>army</u> — which meant more <u>women</u> had to work, especially after <u>1941</u> when German forces were doing badly in <u>Russia</u>.

2) <u>Albert Speer</u> was appointed Minister of Armaments in 1942. From 1942 to 1944 weapons production tripled.

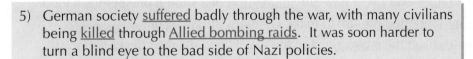

3) Later in the war, Germany used <u>slave labour</u> from conquered countries to help its war effort.

4) <u>Industries</u> which weren't related to the war effort were <u>neglected</u>.

5) German society <u>suffered</u> badly through the war, with many civilians being <u>killed</u> through <u>Allied bombing raids</u>. It was soon harder to turn a blind eye to the bad side of Nazi policies.

Hitler reduced unemployment — and gained popularity...

Hitler provided new jobs and helped Germany recover from the <u>Depression</u> (see p.99).

Young People and Women

The Nazis believed that to control the future they had to <u>influence</u> children and their mothers.

The Nazis created powerful **Youth Groups**

1) Hitler knew that <u>loyalty</u> from <u>young people</u> was essential if the Nazis were to remain <u>strong</u>.

2) Boys aged fourteen upwards were recruited to the <u>Hitler Youth</u>, which was <u>compulsory</u> from <u>1939</u>. Girls aged from fourteen joined the <u>League of German Maidens</u>.

3) Boys wore <u>military-style uniforms</u>, and took part in lots of <u>physical exercise</u>.
Girls were mainly trained in <u>domestic skills</u> like <u>sewing</u>.

4) The boys were being prepared to be <u>soldiers</u>, the girls to be <u>wives</u> and <u>mothers</u>.

The Nazis took over **Education**

1) Schools started teaching <u>Nazi propaganda</u>. Jews were banned from <u>teaching</u> in <u>schools</u> and <u>universities</u>. Most teachers joined the <u>Nazi Teachers' Association</u> and were trained in Nazi methods. Children had to <u>report</u> teachers who did not use them.

2) Subjects like history and biology were <u>rewritten</u> to fit in with Nazi ideas. Children were taught to be <u>anti-Semitic</u> and that <u>World War I</u> was lost because of Jews and communists.

3) <u>Physical education</u> became more important for boys, who sometimes played <u>war games</u> with live ammunition.

4) In universities students <u>burned</u> anti-Nazi and Jewish books, and <u>Jewish lecturers</u> were sacked.

Women were expected to raise **Large Families**

1) Nazis didn't want <u>women</u> to have too much freedom. They believed the role of women was to support their families at home. Women existed to provide children.

2) The <u>League of German Maidens</u> spread the Nazi idea that it was an honour to produce <u>large families</u> for Germany. Nazis gave <u>awards</u> to women for doing this.

3) At school, girls studied subjects like <u>cookery</u>.
It was stressed that they should choose '<u>Aryan</u>' husbands.

4) Women were <u>banned</u> from being <u>lawyers</u> in 1936 and the Nazis did their best to stop them following other professions. The <u>shortage of workers</u> after 1937 meant more women had to <u>go back to work</u>. Many Nazi men did not like this.

Eight Main **Reasons** for Hitler's **Popularity**

It's hard to imagine now, but the Nazis were <u>genuinely popular</u> with many Germans at the time.

1) He gave the Germans <u>jobs</u> after the struggles and unemployment of the 1920s.

2) The people were <u>taught</u> the Nazi way from an <u>early</u> age.

3) He made them <u>proud</u> internationally — Germans had felt humiliated for a long time.

4) People felt much <u>better off</u> as industry expanded.

5) Massive <u>rallies</u> every year gave the <u>impression</u> of a strong, prosperous nation.

6) The <u>army supported</u> his aim to make Germany strong again.

7) Businesses liked the <u>prosperity</u> and the way Hitler attacked the communists.

8) People were <u>frightened</u> to protest against Nazi methods — they knew they'd be arrested.

Hitler Youth — not like your local youth club, then...

Although the Nazis were <u>destroyed</u> in 1945, they expected to be in power a lot, lot longer. That's why they spent so much time and effort on the <u>young</u> — creating Nazis for the <u>future</u>.

Opposition to the Nazis

The Nazis had a tight grip on Germany, but some opposition remained.

Opposition was *Weak* under the Nazis

1) Most people who disagreed with the Nazis were afraid of the <u>SS</u> and the <u>Gestapo</u>. They were also afraid their friends and neighbours would <u>inform</u> on them if they criticised the regime.

2) Thousands of those who did voice opposition to the Nazis were sent to <u>concentration camps</u>.

3) Opposition <u>within</u> the party was <u>crushed</u> on the <u>Night of the Long Knives</u> (p.102).

4) Anti-Nazi activity had to be carried out in <u>secret</u> — which made it difficult for different groups to work together.

5) Nazi <u>propaganda</u> persuaded most people that they were better off under Hitler.

The Nazis *Overcame* most *Resistance*

1) Once in power, the Nazis banned <u>communist groups</u> and sent many communists to <u>concentration camps</u>.

2) Some opposition came from <u>religious groups</u>, especially after church land was confiscated.

3) <u>Jehovah's Witnesses</u> were persecuted for not supporting the regime, with many members sent to the concentration camps.

4) Some opponents of the <u>Reich Church</u> joined together as the <u>Confessing Church</u>. Hundreds of clergymen were arrested, including <u>Martin Niemöller</u>, one of the Confessing Church's founders.

5) Catholic dissent was more widespread after 1937, when <u>Pope Pius XI</u> sent out a letter protesting at German <u>nationalism</u> and <u>racism</u>, which was read out in Catholic churches.

6) Catholic <u>protesters</u> had some success in reducing Nazi interference with the Church.

Some young people joined the *White Rose* group

1) The <u>White Rose</u> group was an opposition movement led by students and lecturers from <u>Munich University</u> between 1942 and 1943. Among the leaders were brother and sister <u>Hans</u> and <u>Sophie Scholl</u>.

2) The group protested against the Nazi <u>discrimination</u> of <u>minorities</u> (see p.109-110).

3) Some male members of the group had served in the army and had been horrified by the <u>atrocities</u> carried out by the German army, including the <u>mass killing</u> of Jews.

4) They used <u>non-violent</u> methods and distributed <u>anti-Nazi leaflets</u> to encourage opposition.

5) In <u>1943</u> the group organised the first public anti-Nazi demonstration.

6) Many of the group were <u>arrested</u> by the Gestapo. Several of them were tortured and <u>executed</u>, including Hans and Sophie Scholl.

It wasn't easy to stand against the Nazis...

Some very brave people were prepared to make a stand against Hitler and the Nazis, but <u>fear</u> of the Gestapo and the SS meant that the opposition was <u>never</u> that strong.

Opposition to the Nazis

Opposing the Nazis was a <u>dangerous</u> business — these groups were literally risking their <u>lives</u>.

The *Edelweiss Pirates* were *Difficult* to control

1) The <u>Edelweiss Pirates</u> was the name given to groups of rebellious young people which had sprung up across Germany during the 1930s. Groups in different towns each had their own names, including the <u>Navajos</u> and the <u>Roving Dudes</u>.

2) They rejected <u>Nazi values</u> and didn't like being told what to do. They avoided joining the <u>Hitler Youth</u> and some members deliberately got into <u>fights</u> with the Hitler Youth.

3) They were <u>difficult to control</u> because they weren't a single organisation with clear leaders.

4) At first the Nazis mostly ignored them as they had no real <u>political agenda</u>.

5) However, during the <u>1940s</u>, they started distributing <u>anti-Nazi leaflets</u>. They also helped <u>army deserters</u>, <u>forced labourers</u> and escaped concentration camp <u>prisoners</u>.

6) The Nazis eventually cracked down on the groups. Many were arrested. In <u>1944</u>, several members of the Edelweiss Pirates in Cologne were publicly <u>hanged</u>.

Members of the *Kreisau Circle* were *Against Violence*

1) The <u>Kreisau Circle</u> was an anti-Nazi movement led by Helmuth von Moltke and Yorck von Wartenburg. It was made up of <u>churchmen</u>, <u>scholars</u> and <u>politicians</u>.

2) The group was <u>against</u> violence, so they didn't <u>actively resist</u> the Nazis. Instead they discussed how to make Germany a <u>better country</u> after the Nazis had fallen.

3) Some members of the Circle tried to <u>inform</u> Allied governments about the <u>dangers</u> and <u>weaknesses</u> of Nazi control.

4) In <u>1944</u>, members of the Kreisau Circle, including <u>Moltke</u>, were <u>arrested</u> and <u>executed</u>.

Resistance in the *Army* grew during the War

1) By 1944, some German military officers were <u>unhappy</u> with Hitler's <u>leadership</u> — they believed he was going to lead Germany to <u>defeat</u>.

2) There had been <u>plots against Hitler</u> from army officers before the war, but these became <u>more serious</u> after the German defeats at <u>El Alamein</u> and <u>Stalingrad</u> in <u>1942</u>.

3) One of the most famous was a plot by <u>Claus von Stauffenberg</u> (and other German officers). They planned to kill Hitler and wanted to install a moderate government, including members of the Kreisau Circle.

4) On <u>20 July 1944</u>, Stauffenberg put a <u>bomb</u> in a <u>briefcase</u> and left it in a meeting room by Hitler's chair. However, someone <u>moved the briefcase</u>. Although the bomb exploded, Hitler was unhurt.

5) Most of the plotters, including Stauffenberg, were quickly <u>captured</u> and <u>executed</u>.

Anyone would think Hitler wasn't very popular...

Some of those that opposed Hitler <u>protested peacefully</u>, but others were more <u>violent</u> and even tried to kill Hitler. Learn all these major <u>movements against Hitler</u> and the names of their leaders.

Persecution

The Nazis targeted <u>anyone</u> who they thought didn't fit into their idea of a '<u>pure Germany</u>'.

Hitler believed *Aryans* were a *Super-Race*

1) The Nazis believed <u>Aryans</u> (whites) were the '<u>master race</u>' and people of other ethnicities, like Jewish, Romani ('gypsies') or Slavic people (Russians and Poles), were <u>inferior</u>.

2) The Nazis <u>blamed</u> Jewish people for <u>problems</u> in <u>German society</u>.

3) The Nazis wanted a German population of only '<u>pure</u>' Aryan people who fitted their ideal. They wanted to <u>eliminate</u> people who were disabled, homosexual, held different beliefs, or weren't 'Aryan'.

4) Hitler was <u>angry</u> when an <u>African-American</u> called <u>Jesse Owens</u> took <u>four gold medals</u> at the <u>1936 Berlin Olympics</u>, and when the German World Heavyweight Boxing Champion Max Schmeling was beaten by another African-American, <u>Joe Louis</u>.

5) In the early 1930s the Nazis began to <u>sterilise</u> disabled people (preventing them from having children). By the late 1930s they had also begun a '<u>Euthanasia Programme</u>' — killing people suffering from <u>mental</u> or <u>physical disabilities</u>.

Persecution of the Jews *Increased* through the *1930s*

In 1935 Hitler passed the <u>Nuremberg Laws</u>

1) These laws <u>stopped</u> Jews being <u>German citizens</u>.
2) They <u>banned marriage</u> between Jews and non-Jews in Germany.
3) They <u>banned sexual relationships</u> between Jews and non-Jews.
4) These laws were later extended to cover both <u>Romani</u> and <u>black people</u>.

Kristallnacht 1938 — the <u>Night of Broken Glass</u>

1) A <u>Jew murdered</u> a German <u>diplomat</u> in Paris in November 1938.

2) There was <u>rioting</u> throughout Germany — thousands of Jewish shops were <u>smashed</u>, and thousands of Jews were <u>arrested</u>.

3) Nazi <u>propaganda</u> made people believe that the <u>Jews</u> were bad for Germany, so they should be sent to special <u>Concentration Camps</u>, or humiliated and maltreated in public.

4) Many people <u>believed</u> the camps were <u>work-camps</u>, where the Jews would work for Germany. Later, Nazi policy became more terrible as they tried to <u>exterminate</u> the Jewish race.

There was little *German Opposition* to the persecution

1) Everybody was <u>scared</u> of the SS and the Gestapo.

2) People were <u>better off</u> after years of hardship, and chose to <u>ignore</u> what they didn't like.

3) Goebbels' <u>propaganda</u> was so <u>effective</u> that people didn't get the whole story about what was really going on — but believed the Nazi government knew best.

4) <u>Opponents</u>, like the communists, had been <u>eliminated</u>.

Nazi Germany — a climate of cruelty and fear...

The Jewish people <u>suffered terribly</u> at the hands of the Nazis — and you need to know how.
This is horrific, and it's hard for us to understand how such cruelty could have been carried out.
Remember — other groups were also persecuted, including Roma (gypsies) and the disabled.

Persecution

The <u>Holocaust</u> was the persecution and <u>mass murder</u> of Jewish people by the Nazis.

Jewish people were **Moved** to **Ghettos**

1) Once the war was under way these <u>policies of persecution</u> began to get more and more <u>extreme</u>. The invasions of Poland and Russia meant <u>more</u> Jews came under Nazi control.

2) In 1940 the idea of deporting all the Jews from Europe to a Jewish reservation was <u>dropped</u>. Instead they were forced to move into <u>ghettos</u> — separate districts of cities which were usually <u>walled in</u> and policed by <u>armed guards</u>. The largest was in <u>Warsaw</u>.

3) Conditions in the ghettos were terrible. <u>Starvation</u> and <u>disease</u> killed thousands. A rebellion in the Warsaw ghetto in 1943 was ruthlessly put down.

4) When Russia was invaded in 1941, <u>Special Action Corps</u> followed the army with orders to <u>kill</u> every Jew they came across in the occupied towns and villages.

The Nazis began the **Final Solution** in 1942

1) The <u>Final Solution</u> was the Nazis' plan to <u>destroy</u> the Jewish people.

2) <u>Death camps</u> were built in Eastern Europe. <u>Gas chambers</u> were built for mass murder.

3) Mainly Jewish people were killed, but <u>other</u> groups were targeted as well, for example Slavs (Russians and Poles), Roma, black people, homosexuals, disabled people and communists.

4) <u>Heinrich Himmler</u>, head of the SS, was in overall charge of this 'final solution'.

5) Some death camps were: <u>Auschwitz</u>, <u>Treblinka</u>, <u>Sobibor</u>, <u>Chelmno</u>, <u>Belzec</u>.

6) By the end of the war, approximately <u>6 million Jewish people</u> had been killed by the Nazis.

7) The Nazis were also responsible for the deaths of over <u>200 000</u> Romani people and around <u>200 000</u> mentally and physically disabled people.

The Reaction of the **Jewish People**

1) They faced <u>death</u> for any resistance. Some <u>fled</u> into the forests, and formed <u>resistance groups</u> to blow up railway lines and attack German soldiers.

2) In some ghettos Jewish authorities thought the best way to save lives was to <u>cooperate</u> with the Nazis and to <u>produce goods</u> for them.

3) There was some <u>resistance</u> in the camps, and <u>escapes</u> from Sobibor and Auschwitz.

4) Reports of what was happening in the camps were <u>smuggled out</u>. Before the war ended, Nazi orders went out to <u>destroy</u> the camps and the evidence — but there <u>wasn't</u> time.

Holocaust means "Sacrifice" — Shoah means "Catastrophe"...

Holocaust is a term disliked by some Jewish people, who prefer to use the word <u>Shoah</u>. The Nazis organised and carried out murder on an industrial scale — deliberately killing millions of people.

Impacts of the Second World War

The Second World War had a big impact on German society.

The War forced Changes in the German Economy

1) In 1936, Goering introduced a Four-Year Plan to prepare the German economy for war.
2) The Nazis built up industries like weapons and chemicals at the expense of domestic goods.
3) By the outbreak of war, a quarter of the work force was working in war industries, especially weapons. Two years later, this had become three-quarters. Unemployment fell.
4) During the war, working hours increased to over 50 hours a week, and wages were lower than they had been under the Weimar Republic. Despite this, the German industry was not producing enough, and there were not enough workers.
5) Industry suffered as a result of the bombings. Industrial plants were bombed, particularly in the Ruhr, meaning factories had to be rebuilt.
6) In 1943, Albert Speer was appointed Minister for Armaments and Production. He reorganised industry and rapidly increased production, but the German industry still couldn't produce enough.
7) A lot of working-age Germans were conscripted into the army, so the Nazis used foreign workers to help keep the economy going. By 1944, around 20% of the workforce were foreigners — either civilians from occupied territories or prisoners of war.
8) At the start of the war, the Nazis had encouraged women not to work. However, by 1944 about 50% of the workforce were women.

The War Affected German Civilians

Bombings killed many civilians

1) From 1942, the Allies began to bomb German cities more heavily. Around half a million German civilians were killed, and many more were made homeless.
2) The bombing was often relentless — the US bombed by day and Britain bombed by night.
3) The German cities of Dresden, Berlin and Hamburg were all badly affected by bombing.

Rationing affected quality of life

1) Food and clothes rationing began in 1939, but while Germany was winning the war, most goods could still be acquired easily.
2) By 1942, German civilians were living off much less than British civilians. Civilians lived off rations of bread, vegetables and potatoes — these rations decreased as the war progressed.
3) It became nearly impossible to buy new clothes or shoes.

Propaganda encouraged loyalty to the Nazis

1) Nazi news media only reported wartime successes. This made the Nazis appear strong, but the public were misinformed.
2) Nazi propaganda warned Germans against non-Nazi groups, such as the Bolsheviks. Some people supported the Nazis because they were made to fear the alternatives.
3) In the last days of the war, Nazi propaganda encouraged members of the Nazi party, boys and old men to defend Berlin from the Russians to the last man.

The Second World War was tough on everyone...
There were very few people who were left unaffected by the War. War dominated daily life.

Revision Summary

Phew — it's question time again. Now's your chance to show off what you've learnt — and to find out what you still need to practise. Germany between the wars is a tricky subject — make sure you know about the long-term consequences of the Versailles Treaty, and the reasons for the weakness of the Weimar government. Most difficult of all, you've got to be able to give clear arguments for why Hitler was able to come to power. Remember — it doesn't matter if you can't answer all the questions first time. Go over the section again and keep trying, until you can answer every one. And there's no point in cheating by looking back — that won't help you in the exams. So let's get going.

1) What was the name of the first President of the Weimar Republic? Which party did he belong to?

2) Why was the government based at Weimar?

3) What was the name of the parliament in the Weimar Republic?

4) Name the force which was started to keep the peace in Germany.

5) Give three reasons for discontent in Germany after World War I.

6) Where did the Spartacist Revolt and the Kapp Putsch take place?

7) Give the main results of the French occupation of the Ruhr in 1923.

8) Write a paragraph outlining the work of Gustav Stresemann.

9) Which party was responsible for the Munich Putsch? Who was its leader?

10) Name the paramilitary force which was set up to support the Nazis.

11) What was the title of the book Hitler wrote in prison?

12) Who beat Hitler in the Presidential elections of April 1932?

13) How did Hitler use the Reichstag Fire?

14) What did Hitler's Enabling Bill allow him to do in March 1933?

15) What was the Night of the Long Knives?

16) What title did Hitler give himself on the death of Hindenburg in 1934?

17) What were Gaue?

18) Which Nazi was put in charge of propaganda? Write about some of the methods he used.

19) What was the SS? What was the Gestapo?

20) Give an achievement of the Nazi programme of public works.

21) What was the 'Strength through Joy' programme? What organisation did workers have to join instead of trade unions?

22) Name the leading Nazi who was put in charge of the Luftwaffe.

23) In what ways did the Nazis make sure that young people followed their cause?

24) Which organisation did teachers in Nazi Germany have to join?

25) Give eight reasons why the German people followed the Nazis.

26) Give two reasons why opposition was weak under the Nazis.

27) What was the name of the church set up by Protestants who opposed the Reich Church?

28) Name the black athlete who won four gold medals at the Berlin Olympics in 1936.

29) What were the Nuremberg Laws? What did they do?

30) Describe what happened on the 'Night of Broken Glass'.

31) What did the Four-Year Plan aim to do?

32) When was rationing introduced in Germany?

Exam Sources

Study **Sources A to D** below and then answer the questions that follow.

Source A

A German woman burns money to fuel her stove during the post World War I hyperinflation in 1923.

Source B

Many Germans denied they had lost the war and blamed the 'November Criminals' who had agreed to the Armistice and the Treaty of Versailles. Others blamed for losing the war included the communists, the government and the Jews.

Discontent in Germany after World War One.

Source C

A German propaganda poster from the 1930s. "Kraft durch Freude" was a Nazi motto meaning "Strength through Joy".

Source D

The government has ordered that the Hitler Greeting is to be used in conversation between teachers and pupils. Every day at the beginning of the first lesson, the pupils will get up from their places as soon as the teacher enters the class, stand to attention and each raise their outstretched arm level with their eyes. The teacher will go to the front of the class and offer the same greeting accompanied by the words 'Heil Hitler!' The pupils will reply 'Heil Hitler!'

A translated extract from a German newspaper published in the mid-1930s.

Exam Practice

Germany Between the Wars

1 **(a)** What does Source B suggest about the attitude of the German people towards the Weimar Republic and its government?

(4 marks)

(b) Explain why the Weimar Republic faced many problems between 1919 and 1923.

(6 marks)

(c) How useful is Source A for studying the effects of hyperinflation?

Use Source A and your knowledge to explain your answer.

(10 marks + 3 marks for SPaG)

Germany Between the Wars

2 **Study Source D and then answer both parts of the following question.**

(a) Using Source D and your knowledge, describe the ways in which the Nazis tried to influence German children between 1933 and 1939.

(8 marks)

(b) "The main reason why Hitler was appointed Chancellor in 1933 was because of the Depression."

Do you agree? Explain your answer.

(12 marks + 3 marks for SPaG)

Germany Between the Wars

3 **(a)** Explain how the Nazis controlled the German people between 1933 and 1939.

(8 marks)

(b) How successful were the Nazis in solving the unemployment caused by the Depression? Explain your answer.

(12 marks + 3 marks for SPaG)

Exam Practice

Germany Between the Wars

4 (a) Study Source A.

Why do you think that this photograph was published in Germany in 1923?

Use the source and your knowledge to explain your answer.

(7 marks)

(b) Study Source C.

What is the message of this poster?

Use the source and your knowledge to explain your answer.

(6 marks)

(c) Study Source D.

How far does this source prove that the Nazis were successful in winning the support of German people?

Use the source and your knowledge to explain your answer.

(7 marks)

5 (a) Describe the main features of the Weimar Constitution.

(4 marks)

(b) Explain how Stresemann brought stability to Germany between 1924 and 1929.

(6 marks)

(c) Explain the effects of the Munich Putsch on the methods used by the Nazi Party in their attempts to gain power between 1923 and 1933.

(10 marks + 3 marks for SPaG)

The USA's Reaction to World War One

After the First World War (1914-1918), the USA chose not to get involved in international affairs. This policy was known as isolationism.

The League was the idea of the American President

1) The League of Nations was largely the idea of the American president Woodrow Wilson. It was one of his Fourteen Points (see p.25) — fourteen principles on which he thought a peace settlement could be based.

2) He thought a League of Nations could act like a world parliament where the representatives of all the major powers would meet to discuss matters of international importance.

3) He was sure that such an organisation could prevent another world war.

Woodrow Wilson

But America Never Joined the League of Nations

1) A League of Nations was set up following the end of the First World War, as part of the Treaty of Versailles.

2) Wilson wanted the USA to join the League of Nations, but he needed the approval of the US Congress.

3) The problem was that most Americans didn't want to join.

4) The majority of the American people favoured 'isolationism' — they wanted the USA to remain isolated from foreign entanglements.

Americans Didn't Trust the League of Nations

1) Many Americans had been against the USA getting involved in the First World War and were upset by the loss of American lives.

2) They were worried that if America joined the League of Nations they would be obliged to interfere in conflicts that most Americans thought were none of their business.

3) The USA had a lot of citizens who were German or Austrian immigrants.

These people saw the League as linked to the hated Treaty of Versailles (see p.26). They were opposed to the USA joining an organisation that was forcing Germany to pay vast amounts in reparations (damages for the war).

4) Some Americans were suspicious of the French and the British. They were sure that the League would come under British and French control and that America would be called upon to help these countries defend their colonies. Many Americans felt that colonies didn't fit in with their ideas about freedom and democracy and should not be supported.

5) Other Americans were concerned that joining the League of Nations could cost them money. They were worried that the League would drag America into lots of expensive wars. Many businessmen contended that the US had grown prosperous by staying out of European affairs and that it should remain isolated from Europe.

The USA thought it was better off alone...

Perhaps it was a bit selfish of the USA to reject the League of Nations, but they probably did save themselves a lot of trouble and expense, at least in the short term. Make sure you learn all the reasons for their decision not to join.

Growth of Isolationism

America just wanted to be <u>alone</u>.

The USA *Entered Late* and *Gained From* World War One

1) The American economy <u>boomed</u> as a result of the First World War.
2) The USA exported <u>weapons</u> and <u>food</u> to Europe during the war.
3) The USA <u>joined</u> the Allied side in <u>1917</u> — but no fighting happened on American soil.
4) After the war, European countries whose industries had been damaged <u>bought American goods</u> with the help of <u>American loans</u>.

Cheap European Imports were seen as a Threat

1) American <u>businesses</u> were afraid that the USA would be flooded with <u>cheap European imports</u>.
2) <u>Unemployment</u> was higher in <u>Europe</u> so European workers were willing to work for <u>lower wages</u>. Businessmen were worried American consumers would start <u>buying European products</u> rather than the <u>more expensive</u> American ones.
   This would mean:
   - The <u>loss</u> of American <u>jobs</u>.
   - <u>Lower profits</u> for US companies.
   - Less money in <u>taxes</u> for the US government.

Warren G Harding raised tariffs to protect US Industry

Warren G Harding

1) Harding was elected President in 1921. He brought in the <u>Emergency Tariff Act</u> of <u>May 1921</u>. A tariff is a <u>tax</u> on imported and exported goods. The act <u>increased</u> the tariff rates on <u>imported farm products</u>.
2) In 1922, the <u>Fordney-McCumber Tariff</u> gave the President the power to raise and lower the tariff rates.
3) Harding used the Fordney-McCumber Tariff to <u>raise duties</u> on both <u>factory</u> and <u>farm</u> goods.
4) He hoped to <u>protect</u> America from "<u>unfair</u>" European competition.

Immigration Control was increased

Before the First World War, America had followed an 'Open Doors' policy that allowed almost <u>anybody</u> to move to the USA. But some Americans started <u>demanding</u> that this '<u>door</u>' be <u>closed</u>. The most <u>powerful</u> and <u>wealthy</u> cultural group in America at this time were people with mainly British ancestors — later known as the <u>White Anglo-Saxon Protestants</u> (WASPs).

1) Many WASPs believed that people such as <u>anarchists</u> and <u>communists</u> were coming into the USA and <u>undermining</u> the American way of life.
2) They were also alarmed at the number of <u>Asian</u>, <u>Catholic</u> and <u>Jewish</u> people who were entering the USA.

The WASPs had great influence in <u>Congress</u> (the American parliament). As a consequence President Harding decided to place <u>strict limitations on immigration</u>, especially from <u>Eastern</u> and <u>Southern Europe</u>. In <u>1921</u>, Congress passed an act which introduced a <u>quota system</u>. Annual immigration was reduced from over one million to about 150 000 in 1929.

Isolationism — it's tariffic...

After the First World War, Europe had lots of <u>problems</u>, while America had <u>relatively few</u>. By <u>limiting imports</u> and <u>reducing immigration</u>, the US sought to secure its peace and prosperity.

Prosperity in the 1920s

The 1920s were a time of <u>huge economic growth</u> in the US.

The *1920s were a Time of Plenty*

This decade was a '<u>boom time</u>' for many — incomes rose and standards of living improved.

1) There was <u>low inflation</u>, <u>low unemployment</u> and <u>low interest rates</u>.

2) Cities were rebuilt with tall <u>skyscrapers</u>, and major <u>road building</u> programmes were undertaken.

3) There was a <u>consumer boom</u>. More people could now afford items such as radios, refrigerators, washing machines, vacuum cleaners and telephones.

4) <u>Advertising</u> encouraged <u>more spending</u> and became a big business in itself, expanding into radio and film commercials.

5) <u>Hire purchase</u> (buying in instalments) was introduced to make <u>cars</u> affordable to average earners who could only buy them on credit. It encouraged more spending on <u>luxury goods</u>.

6) Republican government policy contributed to prosperity. The <u>reduction</u> of <u>income tax</u> left people with more money to spend. The government also promoted <u>cheap credit</u> through the <u>Federal Reserve Board</u> (central banking system). They encouraged banks to <u>lend money</u> on easier terms, which (in the short term) contributed to the boom.

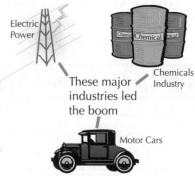

Electric Power

Chemicals Industry

These major industries led the boom

Motor Cars

The *Stock Market* boomed

1.5 million Americans <u>bought shares</u> in the 1920s. Before the price of shares began to rocket unrealistically in 1928, there were <u>sensible reasons</u> for buying them — people were investing in a real boom in production and consumption. It only started to go bad when people took to buying shares <u>on credit</u> in the hope of <u>selling them</u> at a profit (see p.125).

The *Motor Industry* led the way

1) The jobs of 1 in 12 workers were <u>linked to motor car production</u>.

2) Car production <u>boosted other industries</u> — steel, petrol, chemicals, glass and rubber.

3) Cars became more <u>affordable</u> — the Model T Ford cost less than $300.

4) Production of cars became dominated by <u>the big three companies</u> — Ford, Chrysler and General Motors.

5) Ford's factory used an <u>assembly line</u> system. It divided manufacturing tasks among a group of workers spaced alongside a <u>moving belt</u>. It made production far more <u>efficient</u>, which allowed for a huge reduction in price. By 1929, there was <u>one car</u> for every <u>five Americans</u>.

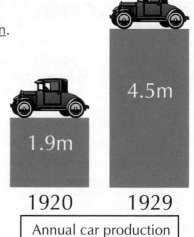

4.5m

1.9m

1920   1929

Annual car production

Boom in the US — revise this and prosper...

This page is really important. It shows you how the American economy really <u>took off</u> in the 1920s. Make sure you learn some of these <u>statistics</u> — they'll impress the examiners.

Poverty in the 1920s

While there was a boom for many Americans, for others life remained a struggle.

There was still Poverty

Wealth wasn't distributed evenly — there was a big gap between rich and poor in the USA.

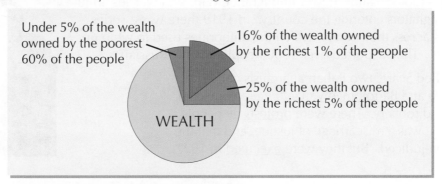

Under 5% of the wealth owned by the poorest 60% of the people

16% of the wealth owned by the richest 1% of the people

25% of the wealth owned by the richest 5% of the people

WEALTH

Some poverty was in Urban Areas

1) Monopolies (where a whole industry is owned or controlled by one company or alliance) kept prices high and wages low, by stopping competition for customers and workers.

2) Many African Americans had moved from the South to the northern states to work in war industries. They were often restricted by prejudice and poverty to living in poor districts.

3) Some urban poverty was produced by the pressure of numbers — many people moved to cities because of rural hardship.

"Old" industries Suffered

1) The coal industry did badly. Coal mining suffered from competition with oil. Cars and trucks began to take over from the railways, which were a major user of coal.

2) About 10% less coal was mined in 1929 than in 1919. More efficient mining technology also caused workers to be laid off, and those that remained saw their wages decrease. The mining towns suffered acute hardship.

3) In 1920 the wartime cotton boom collapsed. In 1921 the boll weevil — a beetle that feeds off cotton plants — destroyed 30% of the crop. In the mid-1920s the opposite problem, overproduction, caused prices to plunge.

Problems in Agriculture led to Rural Poverty

1) Farmers had prospered during the war. But during the 1920s, they grew more food than was needed. Overproduction led to falling prices and so to falling profits.

2) Taxes, mortgages and wages were rising, further reducing farmers' profits.

3) Foreign competition increased during the 1920s. European agriculture recovered from the war, while Canada, Russia, Argentina and Australia also competed on the world market.

4) The Republican government didn't believe in direct help to farmers. When Congress passed the McNary-Haugen bill, to allow the government to buy up farmers' crops, President Coolidge vetoed it twice — he thought it would encourage more overproduction.

5) For the first time ever, the American farm population began to shrink.

The Jazz Age wasn't all Bentleys and champagne...

There are always winners and losers — the 1920s were no different. It's important to remember that some people struggled through what are often thought of as the 'good times'.

Intolerance in the 1920s

Some groups in 1920s America suffered <u>discrimination</u> and <u>persecution</u>.

Prejudice against Immigrants led to the Red Scare

1) There was prejudice against <u>newer</u> immigrant groups and worries about <u>communist</u> agitators entering the country. In 1919 there was a series of <u>bombings</u> across the country, which the authorities used to whip up a '<u>Red Scare</u>'. They deported over 4000 people, mainly Russians.

2) During the Red Scare, two Italian anarchists called <u>Nicola Sacco</u> and <u>Bartolomeo Vanzetti</u> were convicted of murder and robbery. There were <u>protests</u> by people who argued it was a miscarriage of justice, and that the judge was prejudiced. But they were <u>executed</u> in 1927.

Systems were Introduced to Limit Immigration

- From 1917 immigrants had to pass a '<u>literacy test</u>' to enter.
- A <u>quota system</u> was introduced in 1921. This was replaced in 1924 by the <u>National Origins Act</u> which strictly <u>limited</u> immigration. This act <u>discriminated</u> against immigrants from Southern and Eastern Europe, and Asia.

The racist Ku Klux Klan (KKK) Expanded

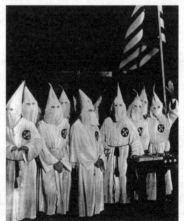

1) First formed in the 1860s, the Ku Klux Klan gained new <u>popularity</u> in the <u>early 1920s</u>.

2) The KKK was a <u>white supremacist</u> organisation based in the Southern states of the USA.

3) They <u>opposed</u> African Americans being given more <u>rights</u>. They were also prejudiced against immigrants, Jewish people and Catholics. They used <u>intimidation</u> and <u>violence</u>.

KKK members wore distinctive hoods and robes

4) KKK membership had grown to around <u>4 million</u> by <u>1925</u>.

5) In 1925, there was a scandal involving Indiana KKK leader <u>D.C. Stephenson</u> (he was convicted of kidnapping and second-degree murder). The organisation <u>lost much support</u>, and never regained such significant cultural and political power.

There was an ugly, violent side to American society...

Remember — there were <u>many groups</u> who were discriminated against in 1920s USA.

Intolerance in the 1920s

The persecution wasn't just carried out by <u>racist groups</u> such as the KKK — it was backed up by the <u>law</u>.

Some **Laws** were **Racist**

1) The '<u>Jim Crow Laws</u>' was a collective name for laws that <u>discriminated</u> against African Americans. These were more common in the <u>Southern States</u> of the USA.

> **DRINKING FOUNTAIN**
> **WHITE ONLY**

2) Some laws made it <u>difficult</u> for African Americans to <u>vote</u>. For example, it was law in some states that voters had to show that their <u>grandfathers</u> had <u>voted</u> — this <u>excluded</u> many African Americans whose <u>ancestors</u> were <u>slaves</u> with no voting rights (slavery was only abolished in America in 1865).

3) Some laws forced <u>white</u> and <u>African-American</u> people to use <u>separate</u> facilities, e.g. different schools, transport, parks, cafes and theatres. This was called <u>segregation</u>. Although the facilities were supposed to be "separate but equal", the ones provided for African Americans were usually <u>much worse</u>.

There was **Prejudice** against some **Scientific Ideas**

1) In 1925, a teacher called John <u>Scopes</u> was arrested for <u>teaching</u> Darwin's theory of <u>evolution</u> — which was against Tennessee state law.

2) He'd deliberately chosen to <u>take a stand</u> against the law.

3) The '<u>Monkey Trial</u>' became headline news. On appeal, Scopes's defence argued the law broke US Constitutional Amendments on <u>free speech</u> and separation of <u>church and state</u>.

4) Scopes was found <u>guilty</u> — but his lawyers had succeeded in making the <u>law</u> look very <u>foolish</u>.

They fought the law — and the law won...

If you were being persecuted in the USA today, you'd expect the law to be on your side, but in the 1920s it was a different story.

Prohibition and Organised Crime

In <u>January 1920</u> it became illegal to manufacture, distribute or sell alcohol. This was <u>Prohibition</u>.

In 1920 America tried to turn **Teetotal**

1) <u>Pressure</u> for Prohibition had built up over a <u>long time</u>. Some states were "<u>dry</u>" by 1917.

2) <u>Temperance movements</u> had been <u>campaigning</u> for Prohibition since the 19th century — they were popular in <u>rural areas</u>, and were often <u>Christian</u>. They claimed alcohol led to <u>violence</u>, <u>immoral behaviour</u>, and the <u>breakdown</u> of family life.

3) The <u>middle class</u> often blamed alcohol for <u>disorder</u> among immigrants and the working class. <u>Businessmen</u> blamed alcohol for making workers <u>unreliable</u>.

4) The First World War (which the USA joined in 1917) resulted in more support for Prohibition. Many breweries were owned by <u>German immigrants</u> — and the USA was fighting Germany.

5) <u>Opposition</u> to <u>Prohibition</u> was mainly in <u>urban</u> areas — especially cities in the northern states.

> <u>Saloons</u> were closed down. Buying alcohol illegally was <u>expensive</u>, which caused <u>consumption to decrease</u> — especially among the poor. The US authorities recruited over 1500 <u>agents</u> (later increased to 2800+) to enforce the law.

Organised Crime 'took over' the distribution of alcohol

Prohibition Crime and Gangsterism

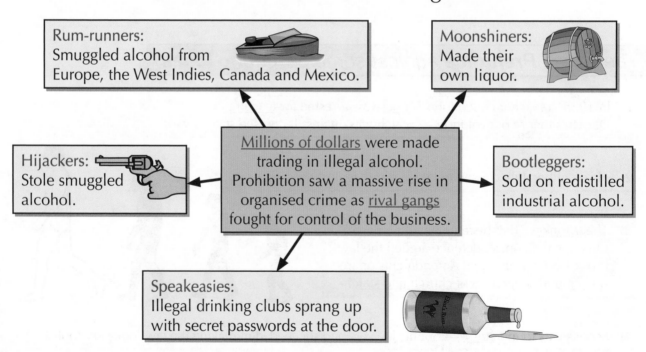

Rum-runners: Smuggled alcohol from Europe, the West Indies, Canada and Mexico.

Moonshiners: Made their own liquor.

Hijackers: Stole smuggled alcohol.

<u>Millions of dollars</u> were made trading in illegal alcohol. Prohibition saw a massive rise in organised crime as <u>rival gangs</u> fought for control of the business.

Bootleggers: Sold on redistilled industrial alcohol.

Speakeasies: Illegal drinking clubs sprang up with secret passwords at the door.

Alcohol was banned in America...

Despite Prohibition, people still wanted alcohol. This meant there was a lot of <u>money</u> to be made <u>supplying illegal alcohol</u>, so many criminals took this as an opportunity to make some <u>fast bucks</u>.

Prohibition and Organised Crime

Prohibition didn't bring peace to the US in the way many had hoped. If anything, things got more <u>violent</u>...

Al Capone was a Famous Gangster

In Chicago 1926-29, <u>gang warfare</u> led to almost <u>1300 murders</u>. <u>Al Capone</u> was a gang leader:

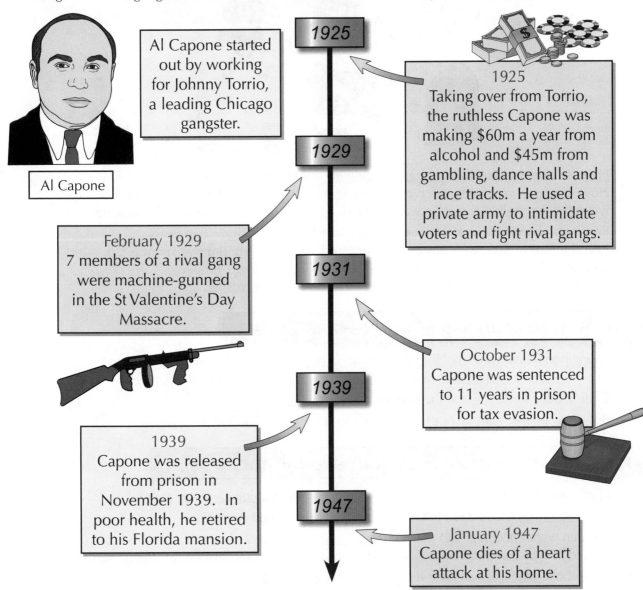

Al Capone

1925

Al Capone started out by working for Johnny Torrio, a leading Chicago gangster.

1925
Taking over from Torrio, the ruthless Capone was making $60m a year from alcohol and $45m from gambling, dance halls and race tracks. He used a private army to intimidate voters and fight rival gangs.

1929

February 1929
7 members of a rival gang were machine-gunned in the St Valentine's Day Massacre.

1931

October 1931
Capone was sentenced to 11 years in prison for tax evasion.

1939

1939
Capone was released from prison in November 1939. In poor health, he retired to his Florida mansion.

1947

January 1947
Capone dies of a heart attack at his home.

Prohibition finally ended in 1933

1) Enforcing Prohibition proved impossible because there was still a <u>public demand</u> for alcohol.

2) Prohibition led to <u>corruption</u> — judges and policemen took <u>bribes</u> from gangsters. Some policemen even got involved in bootlegging themselves. In 1930, <u>George Cassiday</u>, a bootlegger, revealed that he'd sold alcohol to most of Congress (the US parliament).

3) In his 1932 presidential campaign, <u>Roosevelt</u> (see p.129) promised to <u>repeal</u> Prohibition. Congress repealed Prohibition in December <u>1933</u>.

Prohibition — a tee-total disaster...

Prohibition failed because <u>demand</u> for alcohol continued. Criminals quickly moved in to supply people with <u>illegal liquor</u>, making huge profits and developing sophisticated <u>criminal networks</u>.

Social Developments

American society underwent <u>big changes</u> in the 1920s.

Many people had **More Money** to spend on **Leisure**

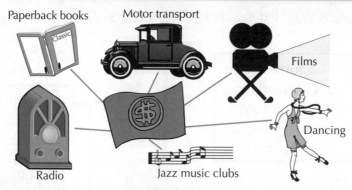

1) <u>Film</u> became the essential <u>mass entertainment</u> — and a multi-million dollar industry. Huge <u>cinemas</u> were built which could seat up to 4000 people. Films were silent until <u>1927</u>, when the first <u>"talking" picture</u> was released. <u>Hollywood</u> was the major film-making centre.

2) <u>Radio</u> also boomed. In 1921 there was just one <u>licensed station</u>. Two years later there were <u>508</u>. Millions of <u>sets</u> were sold. By 1929, $850m was spent on sets and parts every year. The <u>NBC</u> (National Broadcasting Company) was set up in 1926. By 1929 it had made $150m from <u>advertising</u>.

There were changing **Manners** and **Morals**

1) Young people enjoyed <u>smoking</u>, <u>dancing</u> and <u>cocktail parties</u>. Some women started to wear <u>lipstick</u>, <u>shorter skirts</u> and <u>high heels</u> (these women were called <u>flappers</u>).

2) Church attendance <u>fell</u> and the divorce rate <u>increased</u>.

3) But many people felt that permissiveness and <u>sexual freedom</u> had gone <u>too far</u>.

Women gained more **Freedom** and **Independence**

1) Films, popular songs and paperbacks encouraged <u>new fashions and freedom</u>.

2) Some <u>feminists</u> encouraged liberation, but had only limited success.

3) Women were encouraged to gain <u>economic independence</u> — some learnt a trade or trained as typists or secretaries. New <u>office jobs</u> provided employment for many women.

4) Household <u>gadgets</u> gave some relief from <u>domestic drudgery</u>.

5) Rising high school and college attendance meant women were <u>better educated</u> than before.

But **Traditional Views** continued

1) Some books and magazines tried to set '<u>decent</u>' standards.

2) Women were still expected to be <u>homemakers</u>.

3) In employment there was continuing <u>discrimination against women</u>.

4) The vast majority of working class women continued in <u>low-skilled, low-paid jobs</u>.

5) Traditional male values continued to emphasise the <u>superiority of men</u> in the 'public sphere'.

Sport also became a huge part of US life in the 1920s...

The 1920s were when sports became a big part of American life — millions watched baseball every year, making stars of players such as <u>Babe Ruth</u>. Another big-hitter was boxer <u>Jack Dempsey</u>, whose fights drew a live audience of tens of thousands, with millions tuning in on the radio.

The Wall Street Crash

Wall Street is the <u>major financial centre</u> in New York. Stocks and shares are bought and sold there.

Share Prices depend on the *Success* of a *Company*

You'll need to understand about <u>buying and selling shares</u>. Basically, here's how it works:

You buy shares in a company and the company uses your money.

If the company is successful then more people want to buy the shares. This pushes the price up.

A shareholder can sell shares and make a profit if the value has risen.

But if the company is not successful then people lose confidence and want to sell their shares. The price goes down and shareholders make a loss.

On *Black Thursday* share prices *Plummeted*

On Thursday 24th October 1929 around 13 million shares were sold. <u>Confidence</u> in the value of <u>shares</u> began to be <u>lost</u>. On 28th and 29th October, a series of sharp falls began in the value of shares.

- Some major stocks lost <u>three quarters</u> of their value.
- Prices continued to <u>fall for years</u>.
- At the lowest point in 1933, 83% of the stock market's value had been lost.

The *Fall* in *Share Prices* led to *High Unemployment*

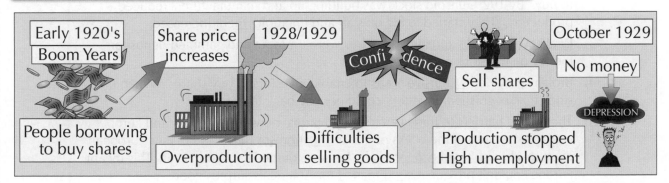

Too much share-ing can be a bad thing...

Speculating on the stock market means trying to make money by <u>buying and selling shares</u>. When it all went wrong, <u>everybody suffered</u> because of the awful effect on the economy...

The Wall Street Crash

The wealth of the 'boom years' of the early 1920s was like a <u>time bomb</u> — people spent money they <u>never really had</u>, so when the crash came it blew the economy to bits...

Efforts to Shore Up prices Failed

Most early losers were <u>large-scale speculators</u>. Leading financiers met to pool <u>$240m</u>. They used this to <u>buy shares</u> in an attempt to <u>restore confidence</u> and <u>stop panic</u>.

They failed — <u>panic selling</u> led to further falls.

- Investment trusts were unable to meet their obligations.
- <u>Defaulting</u> on debts led to other investors going bankrupt.
- People rushed to withdraw their savings from <u>banks</u>, causing many banks to go bust.

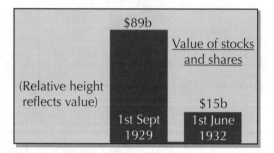

$89b

<u>Value of stocks and shares</u>

(Relative height reflects value)

1st Sept 1929

$15b

1st June 1932

Underlying Economic Problems contributed to the Crash

Though the 1920s had been a 'boom time' for many, there were <u>serious problems</u> with the economy. Prosperity depended on <u>people continuing to spend</u>. But many people had run up <u>large debts</u>, or had already bought the consumer goods they needed. After 1927 there was a <u>downturn</u> in demand.

This situation was <u>made even worse</u> for a number of reasons.

1) <u>Wealth was distributed unequally</u> — rising profits were not passed on to workers, so most people were too poor to spend more. This meant demand did not rise as fast as production.

2) There was <u>overproduction</u> — industry was producing more than people wanted to buy. By 1929, unsold stock was building up and manufacturers reduced production. They started to lay off staff and <u>unemployment</u> increased.

3) <u>Banks were largely unregulated</u>. They were unstable and gambled depositors' money on the stock exchange.

4) Brokers provided <u>expensive loans</u> to enable investors to <u>buy shares</u>. When the stock market crashed, investors could not pay back their loans.

5) There were <u>barriers to trade</u> (such as high tariffs) between the USA and Europe — partly because of the USA's policy of <u>isolationism</u> (see p.117). Plus European countries had <u>suffered economically</u> because of the First World War. This meant Europe <u>couldn't</u> provide a <u>good market</u> for America's surplus goods.

Wall Street '29 — a crash course in things going wrong...

When things started to look really bad for investors they started to <u>panic</u> — which only made things much <u>worse</u>. Make sure you can list <u>all of the reasons</u> why the situation got so bad.

Consequences of the Wall Street Crash

The crash <u>destroyed confidence</u>. People lost money and savings and there was no recovery in sight. A second long decline from mid-1931 to early 1933 resulted in <u>even more bankruptcies</u>.

The **Depression** hit all walks of life

1) The effects of the Wall Street Crash were immediate — from late 1929 to 1930, around <u>700 banks</u> closed. By mid-1932 around <u>5000</u> banks had folded — losing over $3 billion of deposits.

2) The <u>national income fell</u> from over $80b to just under $70b in the first year. By 1933 it had fallen as low as $40b.

3) The price of goods continued to fall. From 1929 to 1931 industrial production dropped by a third — <u>wages fell</u> and workers were laid off. 9% of workers (about 4.7 million) were unemployed by 1930. By 1933 a <u>quarter of the workforce</u> (about 13 million) were <u>unemployed</u>. Around 20 000 US <u>businesses folded</u> in 1932 alone.

4) The <u>price</u> of agricultural products <u>fell 60%</u> because of over-production and declining demand. It cost farmers <u>more</u> to harvest and transport their produce than they could make by <u>selling it</u> — fruit <u>rotted</u>, sheep were <u>killed and burnt</u>, wheat was not harvested and <u>debts increased</u>. Many bankrupt farmers were <u>evicted</u> or became tenants, <u>losing their independence</u>.

The Depression caused **Terrible Poverty**

1) Poverty led to <u>undernourishment</u>.

2) Thousands were made <u>homeless</u>. Some of the homeless built <u>shanty towns</u> to live in. These were nicknamed <u>Hoovervilles</u> after <u>President Hoover</u>.

3) Many people <u>moved</u> to seek work. Some fathers <u>abandoned</u> their families in the search for work.

TYPICAL DIET DURING THE DEPRESSION

Breakfast
Bread and coffee

Dinner
Bread, carrots and soup

4) <u>Migrant farm workers</u> roamed the countryside looking for work. Their situation was made worse by a period of <u>drought</u> in the Midwest, partly caused by <u>overuse of the land</u>.

5) Marriages were delayed and the <u>birth rate fell</u>.

The Depression Diet — not very appetising...

The Depression affected <u>everyone</u>, from businessmen to farm workers. It would have been difficult to see any light at the end of the tunnel if you had no <u>job</u>, no <u>home</u>, no <u>food</u> and no <u>independence</u>.

Consequences of the Wall Street Crash

The Depression was made <u>harder</u> for a lot of people because they had been used to <u>prosperity</u> and independence just a <u>few years earlier</u>.

Attempts were made to **Help People**

The Depression was a <u>shattering</u> and <u>demoralising</u> experience. Some people fought hard for survival and to keep their <u>pride</u>. State and charitable agencies tried to help people keep going.

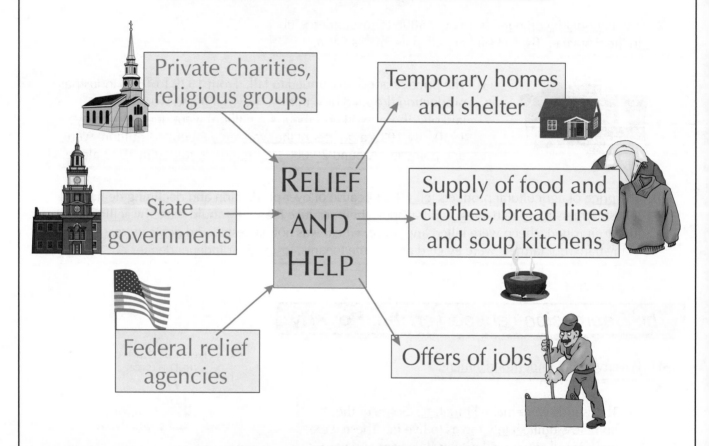

Private charities, religious groups

State governments

Federal relief agencies

RELIEF AND HELP

Temporary homes and shelter

Supply of food and clothes, bread lines and soup kitchens

Offers of jobs

Hoover passed some **Measures** which **Helped**

<u>President Hoover helped</u> by introducing some important economic policies:

- The <u>Emergency Relief and Construction Act</u> — this established the <u>Reconstruction Finance Corporation</u>, which provided <u>loans</u> to help <u>businesses</u>. The Reconstruction Finance Corporation was so <u>successful</u> that it continued under Roosevelt.

- The <u>Federal Home Loan Bank Act</u> — this gave banks access to low cost funds to encourage them to offer more mortgages. This meant that fewer people lost their homes, because they were able to <u>remortgage</u> when they got into <u>financial difficulty</u>. More mortgages also helped increase the demand for houses, which meant <u>more jobs</u> in construction.

John Steinbeck wrote about how hard it was...

His great novel <u>The Grapes of Wrath</u> tells the story of farmers forced to try their luck in California during the Depression. If you haven't got time to read it, try to find a copy of the film to watch...

Election of Roosevelt (FDR)

The Republican President Hoover tried to deal with the Depression — but he <u>failed</u>.

Not all of **Hoover's Measures** were **Successful**

1) He set up the <u>Federal Farm Board</u>, which was meant to help farmers work together to <u>stabilise crop prices</u>, but it failed to stop farmers from <u>over-producing</u>, so crop <u>prices</u> stayed <u>low</u>.

2) Hoover <u>agreed</u> to the <u>Smoot-Hawley Tariff</u> — a tariff that <u>increased</u> the <u>cost</u> of <u>importing goods</u> into the US, to make goods manufactured within America more <u>popular</u>. This tariff actually <u>harmed</u> US recovery because other countries raised their own tariffs in response, to <u>protect</u> their <u>own industries</u>. US exports to Europe more than halved between 1929 and 1932.

3) Hoover oversaw the creation of the <u>National Credit Corporation</u>. All the major banks were meant to pay into a <u>fund</u> that would make <u>loans</u> to <u>struggling banks</u> to stop them going bust. However, the scheme was <u>unsuccessful</u> because most banks didn't want to <u>help their rivals</u>.

For many people this was "<u>too little, too late</u>". Hoover persisted in his belief in '<u>rugged individualism</u>' — he believed that if the right conditions could be created, people would be able to <u>work themselves out of poverty</u> without direct assistance from the government. He therefore <u>refused</u> to offer any financial <u>relief</u> to individuals. This was very <u>unpopular</u>.

FDR was **Elected** in **1932**

1) FDR (Franklin Delano Roosevelt) had been a popular <u>governor of New York</u>. He ran a well-organised and <u>energetic election campaign</u> supported by wealthy backers. Influential supporters helped him with ideas and well-written speeches. So FDR looked like a winner.

2) Hoover wasn't helped by the '<u>Bonus Army</u>' protests in June 1932. 15 000 First World War army veterans gathered in Washington to demand extra bonus payments not due until 1945. Two protesters were killed by police, and many more were injured in army action to clear their encampments.

3) The <u>Democrats</u> swept to <u>power</u>, with FDR gaining 22 million votes and Hoover 15 million.

ELECTION PROMISES

Immediate action after the election

Relief and help for small banks and homeowners

A flexible approach for practical results

FDR thought that Federal government should act and lead on the economy

Prohibition to be ended

Happy times are here again...

The Great Depression was a terrible time. Hoover tried to help <u>big business</u> and the <u>economy as a whole</u>, but he did little to help <u>ordinary people</u>. That's why he lost to FDR in 1932.

The New Deal

Roosevelt now had to <u>deliver</u> his 'New Deal' to the American people.

FDR had 3 Main Aims

This was to be a '<u>New Deal</u>' for the American people.

> 1) <u>Relief</u> — to help to improve the lives of people.
>
> 2) <u>Recovery</u> — to begin to rebuild US industry and trade.
>
> 3) <u>Reform</u> — to change conditions to ensure future progress.

Franklin Delano Roosevelt

© Mary Evans Picture Library

Confidence had to be restored in **Banking** and **Finance**

1) There was a four-day '<u>bank holiday</u>' closure.

2) Healthy, sound banks <u>reopened</u>. <u>Weak banks</u> were reorganised under Federal supervision.

3) Laws were introduced to <u>insure deposits</u> and <u>limit speculation</u>.

4) The <u>stock market</u> was to be monitored more closely.

5) The USA was taken off the '<u>gold standard</u>'.

6) Bank failures fell — deposits rose — and <u>confidence</u> began to return.

Learn this and you can have an ice cream — a new deal...

Roosevelt gave speeches on the radio known as '<u>fireside chats</u>'. These urged listeners to have faith in the New Deal. Overall, he gave the American public a big old charm offensive.

The New Deal

FDR had to show that he was more than just a smooth talker, and put <u>measures</u> into place to <u>deliver his promises</u> right from the <u>start</u> of his term in office.

The 'Hundred Days' Launched Many New Measures

The "<u>Hundred Days</u>" was the first period of Roosevelt's term in office, during which he introduced many new acts. Much work was carried out by special <u>Federal agencies</u> (often called '<u>alphabet agencies</u>' because they were known by their initials). The most important were:

FERA	The <u>Federal Emergency Relief Administration</u> made $500m available to state and local government for emergency relief. This was used to give direct assistance to the poor, for example for dole payments and soup kitchens.
CCC	The <u>Civilian Conservation Corps</u> provided work for thousands of unemployed men in forestry, water and soil conservation projects. This was followed by the <u>Public Works Administration (PWA)</u> which provided work building roads, bridges, hospitals, schools and housing.
AAA	The <u>Agricultural Adjustment Administration</u> paid farmers to limit food production. This raised prices and increased incomes. The AAA also helped farmers modernise and rebuild their businesses.
NRA	The <u>National Recovery Act</u> drew up codes of fair competition, set minimum wages and a maximum eight-hour day. Trade unions were encouraged. This was a cooperative effort and relied on the voluntary agreement of business.
TVA	The <u>Tennessee Valley Authority</u>. See page 132 for details.
HOLC	The <u>Home Owners' Loan Corporation</u> helped people who were in danger of having their homes repossessed. It provided new long-term loans.

The Economy Strengthened a bit but Problems remained

1) Some agencies gave out money too <u>slowly</u>.

2) Stricter regulations on hours, wages and child labour <u>hurt small businesses and farmers</u>.

3) <u>Tenant farmers</u> continued to suffer — 3 million were displaced from the land (1932-5).

4) There was some <u>opposition to Federal control</u> — for example by the 'Liberty League' (1934-6). The Supreme Court raised <u>constitutional objections</u>, which delayed several of FDR's measures.

5) After an initial increase in industrial production the NRA encountered much opposition from business and was <u>unable to secure continued recovery</u>. Some argue that FDR didn't put enough money into reviving industry.

6) The <u>severe drought</u> and heat, on top of overfarming, led to the erosion of topsoil in large areas of the Midwest. Parts of Kansas and Oklahoma became '<u>dust bowls</u>'.

> But the fall in wages and prices was halted. <u>Employment</u> rose and, despite criticisms that Roosevelt was not being radical enough, the measures were very <u>popular</u>.

FDR and the FERA — feeding and confusing the masses...

President Roosevelt was obviously keen on his TLAs (three-letter abbreviations) — make sure you know what each of the <u>agencies</u> did, and what happened to the <u>economy</u>.

The TVA

There were still problems left that needed <u>action</u>...

The **Tennessee Valley Authority (TVA)**

1) The Tennessee Valley was one of the <u>poorest</u> <u>regions</u> in the country. <u>Overcultivation</u> had led to soil erosion and this had turned the land into a near desert.

2) Agriculture was in a dreadful condition and <u>industry</u> almost <u>non-existent</u>. Many local people were leaving the area to find work further west.

3) In 1933 the TVA was set up to <u>help</u> the area.

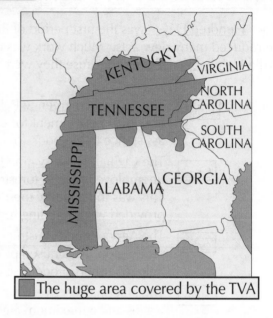

The huge area covered by the TVA

TVA brought **Construction Projects**

1) The TVA built a large number of <u>dams</u> to prevent the <u>flooding</u> that had been causing so much damage and to provide <u>irrigation</u> in times of drought.

2) <u>Trees</u> were planted to <u>prevent</u> more <u>soil erosion</u>.

3) The TVA constructed <u>power stations</u> which brought electricity to the area.

There was a huge <u>improvement</u> in the region's <u>economy</u>. The massive building projects provided thousands of <u>jobs</u> for local people. <u>Agriculture</u> began to prosper.

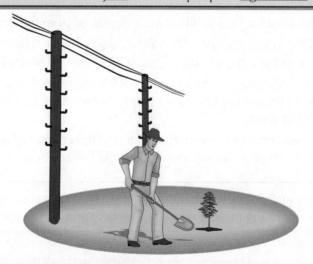

The TVA — rooting out the problems with the economy...

The Tennessee Valley relied on <u>agriculture</u> for its economy, and times had been hard for the farming industry. By providing water, trees and electricity, the TVA not only helped <u>save the land</u> from further ruin, but also gave people <u>new jobs</u> in construction.

The Second New Deal

After the popularity of the New Deal, a <u>newer deal</u> a few years later promised to take FDR's three aims <u>even further</u>.

The **Second New Deal** focused on **Social Welfare**

The Second New Deal began in 1935 and took the new ideas about <u>social welfare</u> and the <u>responsibilities of the state</u> even further. Roosevelt introduced new measures that would benefit the <u>elderly</u>, the <u>sick</u> and the <u>unemployed</u>.

> The Social Security Act was passed in 1935

1) This began America's state system of <u>old-age pensions</u>. Americans <u>over 65</u> received a government pension.

2) It also set up a plan for <u>unemployment benefit</u>. Both <u>employers</u> and <u>employees</u> paid into a fund so that the worker received a small amount of unemployment benefit if they lost their job.

3) It also set up schemes to help the <u>sick</u> and the <u>disabled</u>.

Unemployment in the USA

WE WANT JOB SECURITY

> The Wagner Act, 1935

This act gave workers the <u>right to join a trade union</u>. Companies were now forced by law to allow their employees to become members of a trade union.

> The Works Progress Administration (WPA), 1935

This was very like the Public Works Administration (see p.131), but it also <u>created jobs</u> for actors, artists, photographers and musicians. However, the USA still <u>lagged behind</u> countries like Britain and Germany in <u>social welfare provision</u>.

A new New Deal for y'all to remember...

A big change brought about by the New Deal was the acceptance that <u>the state</u> had a role in relieving the hardship of <u>individual citizens</u>. This was what the Second New Deal was all about.

Opposition to the New Deal

Although many Americans supported the New Deal, some people <u>opposed</u> Roosevelt's policies.

Some thought the New Deal had *Not Gone Far Enough*

Even though Roosevelt's economic policies had gone <u>further</u> than any other President before him, not everyone was <u>happy</u>.

> Senator Huey Long

1) The politician <u>Senator Huey Long</u> of Louisiana had a plan that he called '<u>Share Our Wealth</u>'.

2) Long wanted to <u>tax the rich</u> and give the money to the poor. He claimed that it would give every family an income of $5000 a year. The families would <u>spend</u> the money and this would create a bigger demand for goods and services and therefore <u>more jobs</u>.

Huey Long

3) Huey Long planned to stand against FDR in the 1936 <u>presidential elections</u> — but he was <u>assassinated</u> in 1935.

> Dr Francis Townsend

1) <u>Dr Francis Townsend</u> also criticised FDR. Dr Townsend recommended a plan by which every American over <u>60</u> was given a <u>pension</u> of $200 per month (a huge amount in the 1930s) on condition that they spent the lot within one month.

2) Dr Townsend said that this would give a <u>big boost</u> to the economy and get <u>unemployment down</u>.

> Father Charles Coughlin

1) Another critic was <u>Father Charles Coughlin</u>. Father Coughlin hosted a <u>popular radio show</u> in the 1930s. At the peak of his fame it's estimated that he had a regular audience of <u>tens of millions</u> of people every Sunday, making him very <u>influential</u>.

2) Coughlin <u>originally supported</u> Roosevelt's New Deal, but he turned <u>against</u> it because he thought it hadn't gone far enough and it didn't focus enough on helping the <u>working classes</u>.

Money, money, money...

America was (and to a great extent still is) attached to ideas of <u>free enterprise</u> and <u>minimal state</u> intervention in the affairs of individuals. This largely explains the opposition to FDR.

Opposition to the New Deal

While some people thought Roosevelt's New Deal hadn't gone <u>far enough</u>, others thought it had gone <u>too far</u>. It was <u>impossible</u> to make everyone <u>happy</u>...

Some thought the New Deal had **Gone Too Far**

Some <u>businessmen</u> and the <u>Republican party</u> took the view that the New Deal had gone too far.

1) Roosevelt's critics said that the New Deal made Americans <u>too dependent on government help</u>. These people believed that it was <u>wrong</u> for the government to <u>create work</u> and give Americans pensions and sickness benefits. Individuals should provide these things for themselves through their <u>own efforts</u>.

2) Some business people were angry that the New Deal allowed <u>trade unions</u> into the <u>workplace</u>. They said this was <u>unnecessary</u> government <u>interference</u> in the way that they ran their business affairs.

3) Some people condemned the New Deal measures as '<u>socialist</u>' and therefore <u>un-American</u>.

4) It was claimed that it was <u>wrong to tax the rich</u> to pay for the New Deal. The rich had earned their wealth through their <u>own efforts</u> and <u>enterprise</u>. By taxing the rich you discouraged them from wishing to <u>create more wealth</u>. This was a strongly <u>capitalist</u> viewpoint.

There was also **Opposition** from the **Supreme Court**

1) Most of the Supreme Court judges were <u>Republicans</u> and therefore <u>opposed</u> Roosevelt.

2) They used the <u>Schechter Poultry</u> '<u>sick chicken</u>' case in 1935 to <u>undermine</u> Roosevelt:

- Schechter Poultry had broken some of the <u>business codes</u> in Roosevelt's <u>New Deal</u>.

- These codes were supposed to ensure <u>fair wages</u> and <u>fair competition</u>.

- The Supreme Court felt that the President didn't have the power to tell people how to run their businesses — they declared that parts of the New Deal were <u>unconstitutional</u>.

3) Roosevelt asked the Congress to allow him to put six <u>Democrats</u> on the Supreme Court so that this would not happen again. However, many Americans felt that this would be a violation of the constitution and Roosevelt was <u>forced to back down</u>.

4) The Supreme Court began to take a more lenient view of the New Deal and the argument died down. However the objections did succeed in <u>delaying</u> some of FDR's policies.

The 'sick chicken' case made Roosevelt as sick as a parrot...

That's enough bird-based banter for now. The point is that Roosevelt really <u>struggled</u> to get <u>support</u> for his New Deal, but most of the opposition was politically led. Make a note of the key opponents.

How Successful Was the New Deal?

You need to know how <u>successful</u> the <u>New Deal</u> was, so make sure you learn this page.

The **New Deal** really was **New**

1) The New Deal was a <u>new idea</u> — it was the <u>first time</u> the US government had seriously <u>intervened</u> in the US <u>economy</u> to help the poorest Americans.

2) President Hoover had favoured a more <u>traditional approach</u> — he didn't think the government should tell people how to run their businesses. He promoted the ideas of <u>self-reliance</u> and <u>cooperation</u>. He wanted people to work their <u>own way</u> out of <u>debt</u> and <u>help others</u> do the same — without relying on direct help from the government.

3) FDR was more <u>radical</u> — he thought the government should be <u>actively responsible</u> for <u>helping struggling</u> US citizens caught up in the Depression. That's why he introduced the <u>New Deal</u>.

The New Deal had considerable success in its **Main Aims**

Give aid to the needy

1) The <u>FERA</u> did a <u>good job</u> in providing the needy with much-needed <u>emergency aid</u>.

2) From 1935 onwards, the elements of a basic <u>welfare state</u> were established — <u>unemployment benefit</u> and <u>pensions</u> were introduced, and the government intervened to ensure better working conditions and a <u>minimum wage</u>.

Restore stability to America's banking and financial system

1) Roosevelt successfully resolved the <u>banking crisis</u> with the <u>Emergency Banking Act (EBA)</u>.

2) This <u>restored</u> people's <u>confidence</u> in the <u>banks</u> and people began to deposit their money in them once again.

Reduce unemployment and restore prosperity

1) The New Deal created <u>millions of jobs</u> through the various agencies such as the CCC and the PWA. When Roosevelt became president in 1933, unemployment stood at <u>13 million</u>. In 1940, the figure was <u>8 million</u>.

2) However, though the 1940 figure is an improvement on the one for 1933, it is important to remember that there were <u>only 1.5 million people out of work in 1929</u>. So the New Deal did not actually bring back the low unemployment levels of 1920s America.

3) In 1937, another depression hit the American economy and unemployment rose in 1938 to over 10 million. The New Deal therefore <u>failed</u> to solve America's <u>unemployment problem</u>.

World War Two solved the **Unemployment Problem**

It was the outbreak of the <u>Second World War</u> in Europe that brought the jobless total down.

1) In March 1941 the <u>Lend-Lease Act</u> authorised the President to lease or sell military equipment and supplies to the British and other countries on the Allied side for their fight against Germany. From then on, the US geared production to <u>war needs</u>, eventually supplying her allies with <u>$50 billion</u> worth of food, armaments and equipment.

2) America's entry into the <u>war</u> in December 1941 <u>increased the demand</u> for military equipment. This, together with <u>recruitment</u> into the armed forces, put an end to high unemployment.

The end of the Depression — I feel better already...

Roosevelt achieved a lot, but he could only <u>relieve</u> the worst of the <u>hardship</u>. It took major changes in economic conditions, caused by the <u>Second World War</u>, to finally fix the unemployment problem.

Revision Summary

You've read the section, now try these revision questions, just to check that you've got the whole thing stored safely in your brain. Don't forget — if you get any wrong, look back through the section, learn it properly and then try again...

1) Which American President came up with the Fourteen Points?

2) Name the policy followed by the USA in their dealings with other countries after the First World War.

3) Write a short paragraph explaining why many people in America didn't want to join the League of Nations.

4) Who became President in 1921?

5) What did the Fordney-McCumber Tariff allow the US President to do?

6) How did the Republican government's policies encourage the economic boom in the 1920s?

7) Explain how the motor industry contributed to American prosperity in the 1920s.

8) Why did agriculture not share in the boom?

9) Why were there protests about the trial of Sacco and Vanzetti?

10) What did the Ku Klux Klan believe in? Who did they persecute?

11) Why was John Scopes prosecuted in the so-called 'Monkey Trial'?

12) When was Prohibition introduced?

13) Explain the following terms: speakeasy, rum-running, moonshine.

14) What crime was Al Capone convicted of in 1931?

15) Name three forms of entertainment which first became popular in the 1920s.

16) Explain how the social position of women changed in the 1920s.

17) What year did the Wall Street Crash happen?

18) Explain four economic problems that contributed to the Wall Street Crash.

19) How many Americans were unemployed by 1933?

20) What were Hoovervilles?

21) Explain why Hoover lost the 1932 election.

22) Who won the 1932 election? What were his three main aims?

23) Name three 'alphabet agencies' and explain how they helped America through the Depression.

24) What does TVA stand for? What did it do?

25) Name two acts passed in 1935 as part of the 'Second New Deal'.

26) Why did Huey Long oppose the New Deal?

27) Explain why some businessmen and members of the Republican party opposed the New Deal.

28) How successful was the New Deal in achieving its three main aims?

29) What finally solved America's unemployment problem?

Exam Sources

Study **Sources A to C** below and then answer the questions that follow.

Source A

© Mary Evans Picture Library

A photograph showing workers on the Ford assembly line, 1929

Source B

THE ILLEGAL ACT.

President Roosevelt. "I'M SORRY, BUT THE SUPREME COURT SAYS I MUST CHUCK YOU BACK AGAIN."

A cartoon from 1935 illustrating the attempt by Roosevelt to end the depression. The caption reads "I'm sorry, but the Supreme Court says I must chuck you back again".

Source C

The slogan of progress is changing from the full dinner plate to the full garage. Our people have more to eat, better things to wear and better homes. Wages have increased, the cost of living has decreased. The job of every man and woman has been made more secure. We have in this short period decreased the fear of poverty, the fear of unemployment, the fear of old age.

From a speech made by Herbert Hoover on 22 October 1928, during his campaign for the presidency.

Exam Practice

The USA 1919-1941

1 (a) What does Source A suggest about the reasons why the USA experienced an economic boom in the 1920s?

(4 marks)

(b) Describe the measures taken by the American government to reduce immigration after WWI.

(6 marks)

(c) How useful is Source C for studying the effects of the economic boom on the lives of the American people?

Use Source C and your knowledge to explain your answer. *(10 marks + 3 marks for SPaG)*

The USA 1919-1941

2 Study Source B and then answer both parts of the following question.

(a) Using Source B and your knowledge, describe the opposition to the New Deal.

(8 marks)

(b) "The First and Second New Deals successfully solved the problems of the depression."
Do you agree? Explain your answer.

(12 marks + 3 marks for SPaG)

The USA 1919-1941

3 (a) Describe the changes in American society that occurred in the 1920s.

(4 marks)

(b) Explain why Prohibition was introduced in the 1920s.

(6 marks)

(c) Was Prohibition impossible to enforce? Explain your answer.

(10 marks + 3 marks for SPaG)

140

Exam Practice

The USA 1919-1941

4 (a) Study Source A.

What does this photo tell us about life in the USA during the 1920s?

Use the source and your knowledge to explain your answer.

(6 marks)

(b) Study Source B.

Why do you think this cartoon was published in the USA in 1935?

Use the source and your knowledge to explain your answer.

(7 marks)

(c) Study Source C.

How far does this source prove that all Americans benefited from the economic boom of the 1920s?

Use the source and your knowledge to explain your answer.

(7 marks)

5 (a) Describe the opposition to the New Deal.

(4 marks)

(b) Explain why the Wall Street Crash happened in October 1929.

(6 marks)

(c) Explain how the depression affected the lives of ordinary Americans.

(10 marks + 3 marks for SPaG)

The USA 1919-1941

6 (a) Explain how the Republican government of Herbert Hoover attempted to deal with the problems of the depression.

(8 marks)

(b) Was the Wall Street Crash the main cause of the depression?

Explain your answer.

(12 marks + 3 marks for SPaG)

Russia Under the Tsars

Before the First World War, the <u>Tsar</u> held supreme power in Russia.

The **Government** of the Russian Empire was **Unpopular**

Tsar Nicholas II

<u>Absolute ruler</u>: His dynasty had ruled Russia for 300 years. Increasingly unpopular.

<u>Peasants</u>: 85% of people. Poor people using old, inefficient farming methods.

<u>Industrial workers</u>: Had low wages and poor working conditions. Industry was growing.

1) The Tsar was all-powerful — he ruled <u>without a parliament</u>, and most of the country's wealth and land was owned by a small noble class. The Church taught that the Tsar must be <u>obeyed</u>.

2) Peasant villages were controlled by the <u>mir</u> — a local council who interfered in everyone's business and had the power to <u>decide</u> whether a peasant was <u>allowed</u> to own or rent <u>land</u>.

3) The growth of <u>industry</u> meant there was a large working population in the towns — but conditions in the towns were <u>cramped</u> and the workers were <u>badly paid</u>.

4) In 1905 Russia was <u>defeated</u> in a war with Japan.

5) Poor conditions led to <u>strikes</u> and <u>demonstrations</u> — on 'Bloody Sunday' troops fired into a crowd of peaceful demonstrators in St Petersburg. There was <u>nearly</u> a popular <u>revolution</u>.

The Tsar allowed some **Change** and set up a **Parliament**

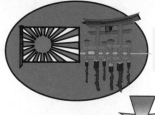

In <u>1905</u> Russia lost a war with Japan.

There were <u>food shortages</u>, <u>demonstrations</u> and <u>strikes</u>.

The <u>Duma</u> was set up. This was an elected assembly or <u>parliament</u>.

1) In the first <u>Duma</u> of 1906, the liberal <u>Constitutional Democratic Party</u> (known as the Cadets) won a majority. They demanded <u>control</u> of <u>taxes</u>, as the Tsar had promised them.

2) Instead he <u>dismissed</u> the Duma and many Liberals <u>fled</u> to Finland. New elections were held.

3) This time the Duma was even more radical — members of the <u>Marxist SDLP</u> (Social Democratic Labour Party — see p.145) <u>won</u> some seats from the Cadets. When the Tsar wanted to <u>arrest</u> several SDLP members as terrorists the Duma <u>refused</u> — so the Tsar <u>dismissed</u> it too.

4) The next two Dumas <u>obeyed</u> the Tsar (1907-1914). The SDLP were not allowed to run as candidates and any known '<u>troublemakers</u>' were arrested and <u>imprisoned</u>.

5) The press was <u>censored</u> and a secret police was used to <u>spy</u> on people the Tsar feared.

6) The situation of the people hadn't improved and there was still a lot of <u>discontent</u> among the <u>poor</u> working classes.

Tsarist Russia — dumb and Duma...

Make sure you know <u>how</u> the situation in Russia <u>changed</u> after 1905. Popular pressure for change forced the Tsar to make concessions — but he managed to keep hold of power. In some ways 1905 can be seen as a sign of the bigger changes to come.

Countdown to Revolution

Stolypin introduced new economic reforms. Unfortunately, they didn't have the effect he wanted...

Attempted *Reform* hit *Problems* — *1906 to 1911*

1) Prime Minister Stolypin wanted economic reforms — he was afraid that badly run industry could get out of control.

2) He ended the control of the mir over how land was distributed. Hard-working peasants could now rent or buy land to farm themselves — helped by special Peasant Banks. These better-off peasants were known as kulaks.

3) The mir system continued but became less efficient when the kulaks left — causing problems for the country's food supply.

4) Peasants in the mir farms resented the wealth of some kulaks.

5) Reform needed peace, but Europe was heading for war (see section 1).

6) Stolypin was murdered in 1911 by a revolutionary.

Russia Entered *World War One*

It wasn't long before Russia got involved in the War...

1) When Austria-Hungary declared war on Russia's ally Serbia, Russia entered the war.

2) At first, the war actually increased patriotism and loyalty to the Tsar — the Russian people unified, hoping for a short and victorious war.

3) However military leadership was bad and early casualties were high:

At the Battle of Tannenberg, August 1914, a grudge between Russian generals led to a split in the Russian forces. The Germans took advantage, and out of 150 000 Russian soldiers only 10 000 escaped being killed or captured.

At the Battle of the Masurian Lakes, September 1914, Germany attacked the rest of the Russian force that had split at Tannenberg. The Russians were outnumbered — by the end of the battle they had lost more than 100 000 men.

4) Shocked by these defeats, the Tsar made himself commander in chief in 1915. This meant he was often away at the Eastern Front — leaving his unpopular wife in charge in the capital.

Russia got involved with World War One...

Things just went from bad to worse in Russia. The failure of Stolypin's reforms caused big problems amongst the peasants and kulaks. Then, when Russia decided to get involved in World War One, they lost thousands of soldiers at the Battle of Tannenberg and the Battle of the Masurian Lakes.

Countdown to Revolution

Attempts were made to fix Russia's problems, but <u>World War I</u> made everything more difficult.

The *First World War* caused more *Problems*

Patriotism and <u>loyalty</u> to the Tsar were <u>revived</u>. People wanted a short and victorious war, but:

1) There were <u>high casualties</u> — 1 800 000 Russian soldiers dead by the end of 1917.

2) There was a <u>shortage</u> of rifles and equipment. By 1916, the overloaded <u>railway system</u> had virtually <u>collapsed</u>, which meant that although armament factories were producing plenty of supplies, they <u>couldn't</u> be <u>delivered</u> to the front line.

3) Military <u>leadership</u> was <u>bad</u> — the Tsar took <u>personal command</u> in 1915.

4) The Russian army was <u>pushed back</u> by the <u>Germans</u> and there was a stalemate (see p.85).

5) In 1914, the government <u>abandoned</u> the <u>gold standard</u>, which linked the value of the rouble to Russia's gold reserves. This allowed the government to <u>print</u> as many <u>bank notes</u> as it wanted, but this led to <u>inflation</u>, and wages could not keep up with <u>rapidly rising prices</u>.

6) There was widespread hunger and <u>food and fuel shortages</u> at home.

Rasputin undermined the *Tsar's Authority*

Tsar Nicholas's wife was influenced by a 'Holy Man' called <u>Rasputin</u> who claimed supernatural powers to treat the Tsar's son for haemophilia — a disease where the blood won't clot. She relied heavily on his advice and was <u>accused</u> of having an <u>affair</u> with him.

Rasputin

Rasputin became <u>powerful</u> and even sacked and appointed government ministers. The aristocracy felt <u>threatened</u> by his <u>influence</u> over the royal family and he was <u>killed</u> by angry nobles in 1916 — but the Tsar's <u>authority</u> had been <u>undermined</u>.

A revolution was brewing...

The <u>impact</u> of the <u>First World War</u> led to dissatisfaction within Russia. The Tsar also made big mistakes — allowing <u>Rasputin</u> so much power, and taking <u>personal command</u> of the army, which meant he could be <u>blamed</u> for the disastrous war effort. It was only a <u>matter of time</u> before a <u>revolution</u>...

The Provisional Government

By 1917 the people of Russia had had enough, and <u>revolted</u> against the Tsar.

The 'February' Revolution of 1917

1) Demonstrations and food <u>riots</u> suddenly broke out in the capital city of Petrograd.

2) The Tsar had <u>lost support</u> and control — when his <u>soldiers</u> were ordered to fire on the mobs many refused or <u>deserted</u> to join the rioting workers.

3) The Tsar <u>gave up</u> the throne. A Provisional Government was formed under the leadership of Prince Lvov until July, and then Kerensky. Russia was now a <u>republic</u>.

4) The main revolutionary parties were taken by surprise — this was a real <u>people's revolution</u> caused by sudden risings of <u>workers</u> and <u>soldiers</u> sick of the war, <u>shortages</u> and high <u>prices</u>.

5) This meant that the new government could face <u>opposition</u> from the revolutionaries, who wanted power for themselves — among them, a group from the SDLP called the <u>Bolsheviks</u>.

The Provisional Government had Problems

1) It <u>wasn't</u> supposed to <u>stay</u> in power — but the economic crisis made <u>elections impossible</u>.
2) <u>Inflation</u> grew even <u>worse</u>. Prices were ten times higher than 1914 by November 1917.
3) Food shortages became worse and peasants began to <u>seize land</u> from noble estates.
4) The new government <u>didn't end</u> the war — soldiers and sailors began to <u>mutiny</u>.
5) A <u>network</u> of <u>Soviets</u> (see p.146) was established — the <u>Petrograd Soviet</u> became an alternative government. Key workers were told to strike to <u>undermine</u> the Provisional Government.
6) The Petrograd Soviet issued '<u>Order No. 1</u>', which said that soldiers shouldn't obey orders from the Provisional Government if they were opposed by the Soviet.

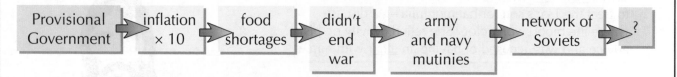

The Soviets demanded an <u>end</u> to the war, but the army <u>attacked</u> the German forces in June 1917. After early Russian success the Germans <u>counter-attacked</u>, forcing a <u>retreat</u> and the <u>collapse</u> of morale and discipline in the Russian army.

Disasters on the battlefield weakened the Provisional Government...

In 1905, <u>defeat</u> in the war against Japan weakened the Tsar. The First World War did the same, but worse. Defeat was a major factor in the fall of the Tsar, and had a <u>similar effect</u> on the Provisional Government, who continued to fight the Germans <u>unsuccessfully</u>.

The Bolsheviks

The Bolshevik Party wanted power in Russia — it held <u>Marxist</u> beliefs.

Marxism said Capitalism was Wrong

1) Capitalism is the economic system based on <u>business</u> — selling things to make a <u>profit</u>.

2) <u>Marx</u>, a 19th-century political thinker, said this was <u>unjust</u> because thousands of workers were receiving low wages for labour that made a tiny elite class very rich.

3) According to Marx, history is a process of <u>development</u> towards an ideal society — change comes because of <u>class struggle</u> between the middle class and working class.

4) He said this would in time lead to a <u>violent revolution</u> by the workers. After the revolution, the means of <u>production</u> would be used for everyone's benefit and <u>shared</u> — this is called <u>communism</u>.

The SDLP were the Marxist Party in Russia

In the late 1890s and early 1900s, the SDLP (Social Democratic Labour Party) <u>encouraged</u> the industrial workers in the towns to <u>protest</u> against their terrible living conditions. They hoped to <u>create</u> a situation where a <u>Marxist revolution</u> could take place. Many of them were <u>exiled</u> by the Tsarist government — this was one reason they weren't involved in the February Revolution.

The Bolsheviks came out of the SDLP

Lenin

1) At the Social Democrat Conference of 1903, the SDLP <u>quarrelled</u> over whether to become a <u>mass party</u> (open to anyone) or to remain a <u>small party</u> of dedicated members working towards revolution.

2) The party <u>split</u> into <u>Bolsheviks</u> who wanted a small party and were led by <u>Lenin</u>, and <u>Mensheviks</u> led by <u>Martov</u> who wanted a mass party.

Vladimir Ilyich Lenin was the Bolshevik leader. He was a <u>clever thinker</u> and a <u>practical</u> man — he knew how to take advantage of events.

Learn your theory — it's easy Marx...

Make sure you know <u>how</u> the Bolsheviks were formed and <u>what</u> they stood for. Remember, the Bolsheviks wanted to bring about a revolution, and in Lenin they had just the man to make that happen.

The Bolsheviks

Lenin was crucial to the Bolsheviks.

The Bolsheviks were a Small Party

1) At first, the Bolsheviks were too small a party to make much impact on the workers.

2) During the war, Lenin was in exile in Switzerland. The Bolsheviks just wanted a defensive war until he came back. When the February Revolution came, he returned to Russia to rally the Bolshevik cause.

3) The Germans helped him to return in a sealed train in April 1917, because they hoped he would cause another revolution and that Russia would end the war.

Lenin's 'April Theses' Urged Revolution

1) Lenin issued a document called the April Theses, promising 'peace, bread, land and freedom'.

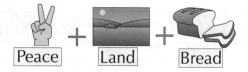

Peace + Land + Bread

2) He called for an end to the 'capitalist' war, and demanded that power should be given to the Soviets — elected committees of workers, peasants and soldiers which had started up in 1905 and had given leadership to the people during the February Revolution.

3) He demanded a revolution against the Provisional Government as soon as possible.

4) The Bolsheviks gained increasing support among workers and soldiers with their slogan:

All power to the Soviets

Lenin called for "peace, bread, land and freedom"...

Lenin's April Theses, which promised 'peace, bread, land and freedom', made more and more people (particularly workers and soldiers) decide to support the Bolsheviks. As a result, it looked like a Russian revolution was on the horizon... maybe even on the next page...

The Bolsheviks Seize Power

The Bolsheviks <u>took advantage</u> of the people's unrest to gain more support and stir up further revolts.

The *Bolsheviks* Prepared for Further *Revolution*

1) In July 1917 the Bolsheviks tried to <u>take control</u> of the government but were <u>defeated</u> and <u>Lenin</u> was forced to leave the country and <u>flee</u> to Finland. Kerensky had turned public opinion against him by accusing him of being a German agent.

2) <u>Leon Trotsky</u> led the <u>Red Guards</u> — a Bolshevik military force. At the same time, the Bolsheviks won control of the Soviets, and Trotsky became <u>Chairman</u> of the Petrograd Soviet.

3) Peasants <u>attacked</u> kulaks (see p.142) and <u>took land</u> from the Church and nobles.

4) Many <u>soldiers</u> started to <u>desert</u> from the army and returned home.

General Kornilov Attempted a *Military Coup*

1) In September 1917, the Russian Commander in Chief, General <u>Kornilov</u>, turned his army back from the Front and <u>marched against</u> the Provisional Government, determined to seize power.

2) Kerensky had to <u>give weapons</u> to the Bolsheviks and the Petrograd Soviet to <u>save</u> his government from a military takeover.

3) <u>Bolshevik</u> railway workers and <u>Red Guards</u> were waiting to stop Kornilov's advance — but all his soldiers <u>deserted</u> him and he fled.

4) The Bolsheviks were now the <u>real power</u> in Russia, and Lenin <u>encouraged</u> Trotsky to prepare plans for seizing power.

The *October Revolution* of 1917

The <u>Bolshevik Central Committee</u> under Lenin <u>voted</u> for <u>revolution</u>. Detailed plans were made by Trotsky to seize important buildings in Petrograd and arrest Ministers.
The revolution started on <u>24th October</u> and the Bolsheviks were in control by the next day.

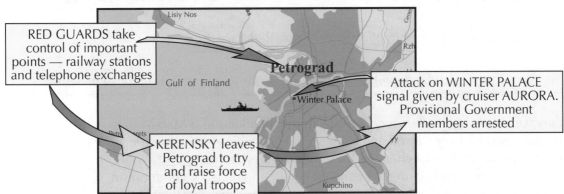

There were only 250 000 Bolsheviks in Russia, controlling a small part of the country — <u>civil war</u> was inevitable as there were <u>many</u> people who were <u>opposed</u> to Bolshevik rule.

> Lenin was <u>ruthless</u> and <u>determined</u> to keep power. He knew a strong government was needed — so the ideals of communism had to wait.

The Bolshevik Press — it was red all over...

The Russian calendar was behind the Western one at this time — by about <u>two weeks</u>. This means that the 'October' Revolution took place in our <u>November</u>, and the 'February' Revolution in our <u>March</u>. The Bolsheviks changed their calendar to the same system as ours in <u>1918</u>.

The Bolsheviks Seize Power

The October Revolution was just what Lenin and the Bolsheviks needed to take over the government.

The Bolsheviks Established Control

1) The All-Russian Congress of Soviets gave power to the Soviet Council of People's Commissars under Lenin, on 26th October 1917.

2) Soldiers were sent into the countryside to seize grain to feed the towns.

3) The Bolsheviks controlled the main centres of power and used telegraph communications to spread their revolutionary message to local groups.

4) Elections were held for a new constituent assembly. Bolsheviks won 168 seats out of 703, with most seats going to the Socialist Revolutionary Party (SRP), who had peasant support.

5) After one day the Red Guards closed down the Assembly — January 1918.

6) The Bolsheviks became the Communist Party, the only legal party in Russia.

7) Lenin made two decrees (orders) — the Decree on Land nationalised all land in Russia and the Decree on Peace called for peace with Germany.

The Reasons for the Bolshevik Success

1) They were strong in key political and administrative centres — especially Petrograd.

2) They had their own trained military force — the Red Guards.

3) They were ruthless and planned clear strategies — they were prepared for swift action.

4) They were practical — they recognised that the time for a true Marxist revolution was a long way off and so they changed their policies in order to seize power at the first chance. They claimed they ran a socialist government which was trying to create the right conditions for communism in the long term — so in the short term they could do whatever they liked.

5) The continuing problems of war and famine, and the breakdown of law and order, weren't dealt with by the Provisional Government, who had become a weak target.

6) The vision and ability of Lenin — he was a quick-thinking leader who inspired his party.

"Learn it all well" — Lenin's Decree on Revision...

The October Revolution was one of those big moments in history when a relatively small group of people had a huge impact. Make sure you learn the reasons why the Bolsheviks were successful.

1918 — Ending the German War

The Bolsheviks took Russia out of one war, and <u>prepared</u> for another one.

The Germans were Advancing

1) The Bolsheviks signed an <u>armistice</u> with the Germans, hoping to <u>delay</u> the peace treaties because they thought there might be a communist <u>revolution</u> in Germany too.

2) This didn't happen, and the German armies <u>advanced</u> — so the Bolsheviks quickly <u>agreed</u> to the harsh terms of the <u>Treaty of Brest-Litovsk</u> in March 1918.

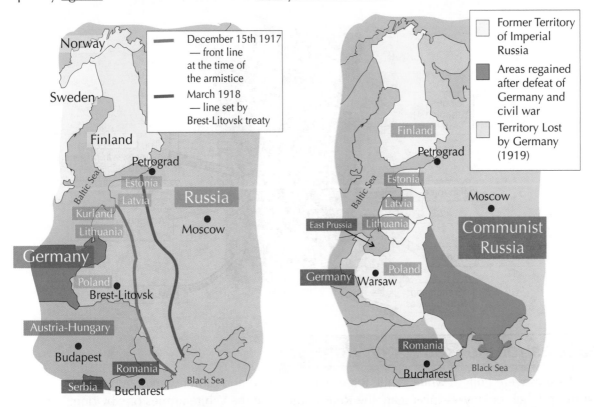

Germany was <u>defeated</u> by the Western Allies later in 1918 and some lands were regained.

A Civil War was Inevitable

Lenin and Trotsky were prepared for this. The reasons the civil war broke out were:

1) The communists had seized power suddenly and <u>repressed</u> the elected <u>Constituent Assembly</u> — they had also <u>outlawed</u> political opposition, so many people saw them as a danger.

2) Anti-communist army officers were no longer fighting Germany — many were <u>royalists</u> and wanted the return of the Tsar — and now they could <u>attack</u> the communists.

3) Communism wanted a <u>world revolution</u> — the <u>Comintern</u> (the Communist International) was formed under <u>Zinoviev</u> to promote revolution abroad and to encourage friendly governments in nearby European countries.

> The government moved from Petrograd to <u>Moscow</u> in <u>1918</u> — Leon Trotsky began to build an <u>efficient</u> Red Army to fight the civil war.

The civil war — not a very polite affair...

Remember — a civil war was the last thing Russia needed after the disasters of the First World War, but the communists knew it was coming, which was why they made peace with Germany at <u>any cost</u>. Scribble down the names of the <u>lands lost</u> by Russia.

The Civil War 1918-1921

The first big challenge for the new Bolshevik government was the brutal <u>civil war</u>.

Anti-Communist forces surrounded Red Russia

1) These armies were called the '<u>Whites</u>' — the colour of the Tsarist state.

2) There were many White groups who often had <u>different aims</u> and purposes — a key problem.

3) Britain, France and the USA sent troops to help the Whites — trying to <u>restart</u> the <u>Eastern Front</u> against Germany, and worried by communist ideas of world revolution.

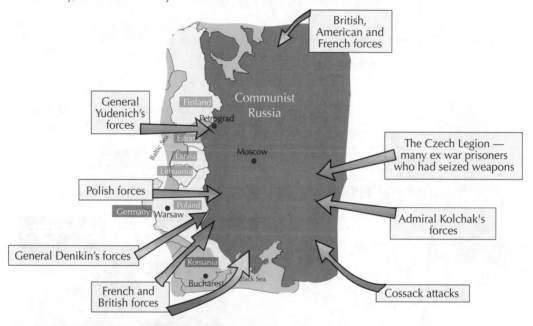

Reasons for the Red Army Victory

1) Red forces were <u>united</u>, while White forces were <u>divided</u> and didn't work together to surround their enemy — this meant the Reds could fight the White armies one by one, instead of fighting on several fronts at the same time. Trotsky was also a <u>brilliant leader</u>.

2) White forces were a long way apart and <u>couldn't</u> stay in touch to <u>coordinate</u> attacks. Some had <u>different</u> political <u>opinions</u> — which meant they didn't want to work together.

3) <u>Patriotic</u> Russians <u>supported</u> the Reds — the Whites were led by nobles and foreign armies.

4) <u>Foreign</u> military support was soon <u>withdrawn</u> as it became clear the Reds would win.

5) The communists <u>controlled</u> the main cities and <u>communications</u> systems — and the railways.

6) The strict and ruthless laws of <u>War Communism</u> helped obtain supplies for the Reds.

7) When the Red Army had defeated its enemies in Russia it <u>carried on</u> and pushed into Poland, hoping to <u>link up</u> with communists in Germany to <u>spread</u> revolution throughout Europe — but it was <u>defeated</u> by the Poles outside Warsaw in late 1920. The war ended with a treaty in 1921.

The Bolsheviks Killed their Enemies in the 'Red Terror'

1) Using the <u>secret police</u> (Cheka), the Bolsheviks executed '<u>enemies</u>' of the state, including members of the <u>aristocracy</u> and the <u>Church</u>, and anyone they feared might be <u>against</u> them.

2) This included the <u>Tsar</u> and his entire <u>family</u> who were <u>executed</u> by the Bolsheviks in 1918 because Lenin feared that they could become a <u>symbol</u> for the <u>opposition</u>.

3) The 'Red Terror' lasted until 1922. It's estimated that up to 500 000 Russians <u>died</u>.

Success in Europe — the Reds go marching on...

Plenty for you to learn here — focus on the <u>strengths</u> of the Reds and the Whites' <u>lack of coordination</u>.

War Communism and Mutiny

The Red Army won the civil war by being <u>united</u> and strictly <u>organised</u> — and <u>War Communism</u> was a big contributor to the victory.

War Communism — a **Strict System** to **Win** the War

1) Farms and factories were put under <u>state</u> control — private trade was banned.

2) <u>Food was taken</u> for soldiers and industrial workers — peasants who <u>refused</u> to hand it over to the Red Army were shot or sent to forced <u>labour camps</u>.

3) Industrial workers <u>weren't allowed</u> to <u>strike</u> or be absent from work. They could be sent to any region. Experts were brought in to improve efficiency.

4) <u>All adults</u> had to <u>work</u> except for pregnant women and the sick.

5) The results were <u>famine</u> and <u>decline</u>.

Food shortages from 1920 — and famine from 1921 — over 7 million people died of hunger

Worthless currency abandoned — wages paid in fuel and food

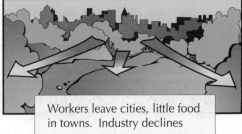

Workers leave cities, little food in towns. Industry declines

The **Kronstadt** Naval Base **Mutinied**

The sailors were <u>unhappy</u> with the lack of progress, the famine and the terror. They <u>mutinied</u> and seized the base near Petrograd, in February 1921.

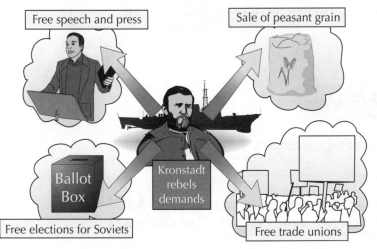

Free speech and press

Sale of peasant grain

Ballot Box

Kronstadt rebels demands

Free elections for Soviets

Free trade unions

1) The Kronstadt sailors had <u>supported</u> the communists in 1917 — especially <u>Trotsky's leadership</u> in Petrograd.

2) Despite this, Lenin and Trotsky were <u>worried</u> that dissent might <u>spread</u> when the ice around the island base <u>thawed</u> and let the sailors leave.

3) Trotsky <u>ordered</u> the Red Army to <u>put down</u> the mutiny.

4) The Red Army <u>attacked</u>, losing many men, but <u>captured</u> it in a brutal battle.

5) Many rebels were <u>killed</u> in the fighting — those who were left were either <u>executed</u> or <u>imprisoned</u> as traitors.

There were other revolts — peasants in Tambov Province <u>robbed</u> food convoys and many factories suffered <u>strikes</u> and <u>unrest</u>.

War Communism — not an overwhelming success then...

Whilst it helped the Red Army win the civil war, War Communism had a <u>negative effect</u> on the state — causing famine, a decline in industry, and several revolts.

The New Economic Policy

The Bolsheviks survived in part due to Lenin's willingness to change a <u>failing policy</u>.

Lenin Decided to Change Communist Policy

1) Communism was pushing ahead '<u>too fast</u>' — Trotsky had recognised the economic crisis in 1920 and suggested a <u>change of policy</u> to encourage businesses. Lenin <u>rejected</u> this at first.

2) Now the civil war was won, the communists needed to <u>keep control</u> of public opinion.

3) This meant a policy of <u>complete party unity</u> — no dissent or splits allowed.

4) In 1921 Lenin introduced the <u>New Economic Policy (NEP)</u> to restore <u>order</u> and increase <u>prosperity</u> after the chaos of revolution, civil war and War Communism.

The New Economic Policy Reversed War Communism

1) Peasants could <u>sell</u> surplus food produce and pay <u>tax</u> on profits.

2) <u>Small businesses</u>, like shops and small factories, no longer <u>had</u> to be state-owned — they could therefore make a profit.

3) Vital <u>industries</u> such as coal, iron, steel, railways, shipping and finance stayed in state hands. But here experts were brought in on <u>higher salaries</u>, and extra wages were paid for <u>efficiency</u>.

The <u>NEP</u> allowed <u>economic recovery</u> — by 1928 industrial and food production levels were about the same as in 1914, and some people grew rich.

Communist political Control Grew

1) A 'purge' in 1921 <u>expelled</u> about a third of Party members — those who <u>didn't agree</u> with Lenin.

2) Communist governments were <u>imposed</u> in areas <u>recaptured</u> in the civil war, against the will of independent nationalists such as in the <u>Ukraine</u>.

3) A <u>new constitution</u> established the <u>USSR</u> — Union of Soviet Socialist Republics.

4) Each Republic had a government with some policy freedom, but they all <u>had</u> to be communist, and the system was run centrally by the <u>Politburo</u> — the senior council.

The New Economic Policy — so new it wasn't even communist...

The NEP <u>reversed</u> War Communism. The easiest way to get them learnt is to <u>compare</u> the two. Scribble a list of the <u>main details</u> of each policy — especially the differences between them.

The New Economic Policy

A lot had happened in Russia while Lenin was around — he made a huge impact.

Lenin Died on Jan 21, 1924

1870	Lenin born.
1898	First Congress of the SDLP.
1903	Bolsheviks (majority) split from Mensheviks (minority).
1917	February — First Revolution — Provisional Government (Kerensky).
	April — Lenin outlines plans to overthrow government.
	July — Bolshevik rising defeated.
	October — Bolshevik communist revolution and takeover.
1918	March — Peace treaty with Germany (Brest-Litovsk)
1918-21	Civil war. Reds vs Whites.
1921	Famine. Kronstadt rebellion. New Economic Policy.
1922	Lenin ill after a stroke. Policy led by Stalin, Zinoviev and Kamenev.

Lenin died in 1924. Stalin organised his funeral, and against Lenin's own wishes, his body was embalmed and placed on public display in Moscow. Petrograd was renamed Leningrad in his honour.

Lenin's Key Strengths as a Leader

1) His organisation and leadership of the Bolshevik party transformed it.

2) He had a pragmatic and realistic approach to problems.

3) He was able to 'seize the moment', which was vital in the Bolsheviks gaining power.

4) He could be ruthless — he set up the Cheka (secret police) and the labour camps. He also wasn't afraid to use force to put down the Kronstadt mutiny.

5) He was able to change his policies — e.g. he was able to adopt War Communism to win the civil war, and then to introduce the NEP afterwards to help the economy recover.

Bolshevik Success also relied on Trotsky

Trotsky too played a huge part in the revolution. He was a great theorist and speaker — much of the tactical planning for the Bolshevik seizure of power was his. He also put together the Red Army that won the Civil War. And he was prepared to be brutal, as in the crushing of the Kronstadt mutiny (see p.151).

Never underestimate Lenin's importance...

Lenin was a real driving force behind the Bolshevik Party. Make sure you know specific examples of how he personally contributed to their success. And don't forget to learn Lenin's five key strengths.

The Struggle for Power

Lenin's death meant that there was a <u>vacancy</u> at the top of the Party.

Several **Leaders Struggled** to **Succeed Lenin**

1) <u>TROTSKY</u> was the most able, and <u>popular</u> with the <u>army</u> and <u>Party members</u>. He led the Red Army brilliantly during the civil war, but some people thought he was too <u>arrogant</u>, and he lacked support in the Politburo. He had been a <u>Menshevik</u> and he often made enemies.

2) <u>ZINOVIEV</u> and <u>KAMENEV</u> were left-wingers who agreed with Trotsky's ideas about <u>state control</u> of land and continuing the <u>revolution</u>. But they were determined to <u>stop Trotsky</u> becoming Party leader. Zinoviev was a popular man and had been a friend of Lenin.

3) <u>STALIN</u> didn't seem likely to lead the party. He had accumulated power through <u>good organisation</u> 'behind the scenes' in his work as <u>General Secretary</u> of the Party.

<u>Lenin's testament</u> talked about who might succeed him — he said <u>Trotsky</u> was <u>arrogant</u> but <u>able</u> and said <u>Stalin</u> should be <u>removed from office</u> because he was <u>too rude</u> and <u>ambitious</u>.

Trotsky and *Stalin* Had a *War of Ideas*

Leon Trotsky

...wanted <u>revolution</u> to <u>spread</u> to other countries — he called for the USSR to work for a world revolution.

Joseph Stalin

...and most of the Party wanted a period of <u>peace</u> and <u>rebuilding</u> in the USSR — 'Communism in one country'.

How *Stalin* Made Himself *All-Powerful*

1) Stalin controlled the Communist Party — he <u>appointed</u> people <u>loyal</u> to him to senior positions.

2) This meant Stalin's <u>rivals</u> had <u>no support</u> in the Party, and he <u>suppressed</u> Lenin's testament.

3) Only <u>Party members</u> could hold <u>government positions</u> and they were <u>chosen</u> by Party <u>voting</u>. It was a <u>one-party state</u>.

4) By the late 1920s Stalin had enough Party support to have his <u>rivals voted out</u> of power.

Stalin was a spin doctor — he changed the revolution...

The key factor in Stalin's rise was <u>Party control</u>. Remember, the Party <u>wasn't</u> the same as the government. But the USSR's constitution could be <u>abused</u> by anyone controlling the Party.

The Struggle for Power

Stalin was <u>single-minded</u> on his way to the top — and <u>terrifying</u> when he got there.

Stalin was *Ruthless* in *Destroying Rivals*

1) Born in 1879 in the Republic of Georgia, his real name was <u>Joseph Jughashvili</u>. He had studied to become a priest, but became a Bolshevik. He changed his name to <u>Stalin</u> ('man of steel') when he was imprisoned as a revolutionary.

2) He was an <u>organiser</u> who began by making speeches, organising strikes, and organising bank raids to aid Bolshevik funds. He was <u>efficient</u> at routine organisation which many thought was dull.

3) His power base came from being <u>General Secretary</u> of the Party after 1922 — by controlling Party appointments he could <u>control</u> who was given government roles, and chose people <u>loyal</u> to him.

4) By 1930 he was undisputed leader of Russia, but he became <u>terrified</u> that others wanted to <u>overthrow</u> him — this made him <u>determined</u> to <u>get rid</u> of rivals.

Stalin *Destroyed* the *Leftists* and the *Rightists*

1) Stalin <u>joined</u> Zinoviev and Kamenev <u>against</u> Trotsky — who was dismissed as Commissar for War in 1925. '<u>Socialism in one country</u>' became Party policy in 1925.

2) Trotsky was isolated — and <u>thrown out</u> of the Communist Party in 1927.

3) <u>New</u> members were elected to the Politburo, <u>loyal</u> to Stalin. At this time Stalin <u>supported the NEP</u> and gradual reform of the economy. The '<u>leftist</u>' Zinoviev and Kamenev were <u>dismissed</u> from the Politburo because they believed in <u>fast economic modernisation</u> (one of Trotsky's main ideas). They joined Trotsky to protest against Stalin and were expelled from the Party.

4) Trotsky was <u>exiled</u> to Kazakhstan in 1928, and forced to <u>leave</u> the USSR in 1929.

5) But in 1928 Stalin adopted <u>fast modernisation</u> instead of the NEP. This swing to the left meant he could now <u>remove</u> the leading figures on the <u>right</u> of the party, such as Bukharin and Rykov who supported the NEP, and could have been a threat to his position.

6) By 1929 he was in <u>complete control</u> as leader of the Communist Party and the USSR.

A man of steely determination...

Stalin was <u>highly organised and efficient</u>, which helped him to overcome rivals in his quest for power. He gained control by <u>removing</u> all his opponents from the party, and appointing people who <u>supported</u> him instead.

The Terror and the Purges

Stalin tightened his brutal grip on the USSR.

The **Kirov Murder** Began a **Purge**

1) Kirov was the popular head of the Party in Leningrad — he was murdered in 1934.

2) Some historians think Stalin was responsible for his death — in 1956 Stalin's successor, Khrushchev, blamed Stalin for the murder, but there is no clear proof.

3) Immediately Stalin ordered a purge of people he believed were involved in a conspiracy against Kirov and against himself — but Kirov's murderer was never put on trial.

4) In 1935-6, many 'old' communists like Zinoviev and Kamenev were arrested and charged in 'show trials'. They were forced by torture or threats to confess to betraying Stalin.

5) No one knows exactly what was true and what was invented by Stalin's torturers.

6) One claim was that the exiled Trotsky was plotting with senior leaders to take power.

Soon the Purges Reached **Ordinary People**

1) Anyone suspected of disloyalty to Stalin was taken away by the NKVD (the new secret police).

2) Most were shot or sent to labour camps.

3) People who wanted to avoid arrest did so by providing information about others — even if it was false.

4) Stalin's wife killed herself (or was murdered) after a purge at the university where she was a teacher.

5) The exiled Trotsky condemned Stalin's purges from his home in Mexico, calling for a new revolution. In 1940 he was murdered by one of Stalin's agents.

6) The total number of people killed by Stalin's regime is uncertain — but some estimates are as high as ten million.

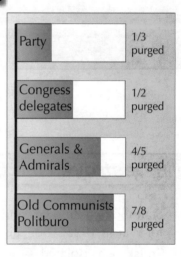

Party	1/3 purged
Congress delegates	1/2 purged
Generals & Admirals	4/5 purged
Old Communists Politburo	7/8 purged

The Purges **Weakened** the USSR

The terror slowed down by the end of the 1930s, but it had serious consequences:

1) Many of the most gifted and able citizens had disappeared — killed or sent to camps.

2) The army and navy were seriously weakened by the loss of most of the senior officers.

3) Industrial and technical progress was hampered by the loss of top scientists and engineers.

4) In 1936 a new constitution was brought in — every four years there were elections and only official Party candidates were allowed to stand. Power was kept in the Politburo.

The purges — a vicious circle...

Confusing stuff — but you need to get it straight. Under torture people invented all sorts of things to try to save themselves. Stalin started to believe there really was a plot against him.

Stalin the Dictator

Before long, Stalin had <u>complete control</u>.

Stalin **Controlled** all **Information**

1) Artists and writers had to <u>follow</u> the <u>Party line</u>, creating 'useful' art for the workers.
2) Newspapers, cinema and radio spread <u>propaganda</u> about the <u>heroic workers'</u> <u>struggle</u> and Stalin's great <u>leadership</u> and <u>personality</u>. Criticism was <u>banned</u>.
3) <u>History</u> was <u>rewritten</u> so that Stalin became more <u>important</u> in the story of the October Revolution than he really had been at the time.
4) <u>Trotsky</u> became a '<u>non-person</u>' — his name was removed from history books and articles, and his picture was rubbed out of old photos as though he had never existed.
5) <u>Photographs</u> were <u>altered</u> to show Stalin as a close friend and ally of Lenin.

> <u>Top Tip</u>: source material in the exams could be <u>propaganda</u> — opinion and not just fact. To get top marks you've got to say which points are true and which aren't, and explain what <u>opinion</u> the source expresses.

The Communists **Attacked** the **Church**

1) The Russian Orthodox Church had been a powerful <u>supporter</u> of the <u>Tsar</u>.
2) The communist <u>government</u> began to <u>take</u> Church property and land — these were valuable assets for the Party. Christians were persecuted as a political threat to communism, and priests were <u>murdered</u> or <u>exiled</u>.
3) In 1929 the Church was <u>banned</u> from any activity except leading worship.
4) By 1939 a <u>few hundred</u> churches <u>remained active</u> — the state claimed the promise of free conscience in the 1936 constitution was being honoured.
5) <u>Many</u> people were <u>still believers</u> — nearly half the population in 1940.

Stalin's Russia was a **Dictatorship**

1) Stalin <u>ran everything</u> — his policies were often completely different from communist ideas.

2) Party '<u>apparatchiks</u>' — members loyal to Stalin — received <u>privileges</u> like holidays, flats etc.

3) Most people lived in <u>fear</u> but were <u>unable</u> to speak out.

Stalin got stronger — the USSR suffered...

Sources often mix facts with opinions. Your job is to <u>separate</u> the two, and work out why a source gives a particular <u>opinion</u>, and why it may <u>ignore</u> some of the facts. Think about <u>who</u> wrote it, <u>why</u> they wrote it, and <u>when</u> they wrote it — how much they <u>really</u> knew.

The Five-Year Plans

The Party used targets to <u>increase the pace</u> of industrialisation.

The USSR still had a **Poor Economy**

1) The NEP had made some progress, but more rapid <u>growth</u> was <u>needed</u> for the USSR to <u>catch up</u> with the industrialised West and their economies.

2) Stalin adopted Trotsky's ideas for a programme of <u>fast state-controlled modernisation</u> to speed up production. Lenin's policy of the NEP was dropped.

3) The state took over planning for industry and agriculture with a commission called <u>Gosplan</u> to set targets for achievement.

The **First Five-Year Plan** was started in **1928**

1) A <u>Five-Year Plan</u> set <u>targets</u> for all basic industrial factories and workers.

2) The plan concentrated on basic <u>heavy industry</u> — coal, steel, railways, electricity, machinery.

3) Actual <u>production</u> figures were <u>lower</u> than the targets, but remarkable <u>growth</u> in <u>output</u> was achieved.

In 1933 a **Second** Five-Year Plan was **Started**

1) Some parts of the second plan were achieved, but <u>fear</u> at the rise of Adolf Hitler in Nazi Germany meant more <u>development</u> took place in the <u>armaments</u> industry than any other.

2) A <u>third</u> Five-Year Plan started in 1938, but was even more <u>disrupted</u> by war preparation and the German invasion of 1941.

> In under 10 years, the USSR had almost <u>doubled</u> its industrial output — the price was <u>misery</u> and <u>low living standards</u> for Soviet workers.

There were **Serious Problems** with the **Plans**

1) <u>New towns</u>, <u>cities</u> and <u>industrial zones</u> were set up — often with <u>poor-quality</u> housing.

2) <u>Long hours</u> were worked for <u>low pay</u>, and higher wages were offered to foreign workers with special skills required to work on new schemes.

3) <u>Bonuses</u> were given for workers who could improve upon production targets as an inspiration to others — e.g. Alexei <u>Stakhanov</u>, whose coal-mining team dramatically increased its output — but these were often <u>unrealistic targets</u> for most workers.

4) Much of the work was done by forced <u>labour camps</u> of criminals and political prisoners.

5) The targets were <u>propaganda</u> tools — the government said they'd been broken but often it's hard to tell how much was really achieved and how much was just propaganda.

Five years — I've got a cunning plan...

Communist Party propaganda used Stakhanov as an image of a <u>heroic worker</u> in the press and news reels. A <u>'Stakhanovite' movement</u> began which encouraged workers to match this ideal.

Collectivisation

Communism was <u>forced</u> on the countryside.

Food Production had to be *Increased*

1) It was vital to <u>increase</u> the <u>food supplies</u> to workers in the towns and cities or the five-year plans <u>wouldn't</u> succeed.

2) Millions of peasants <u>hid</u> food away and <u>didn't support</u> the communists.

3) They were often <u>poor</u> and had no time-saving equipment.

4) Many richer peasants, or <u>kulaks</u> (see p.142), were <u>influential</u> in the villages, which annoyed the local Communist Party secretaries.

In 1929 Stalin began Collectivising All Farms

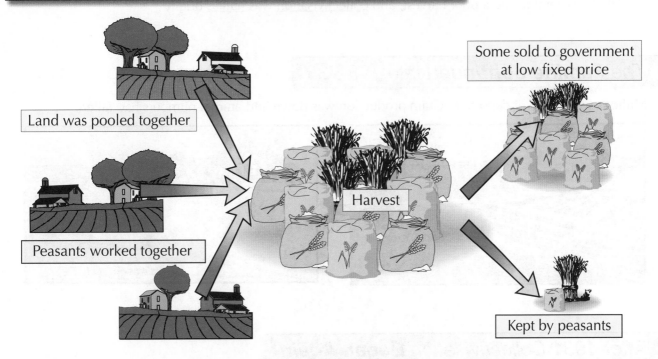

Land was pooled together

Peasants worked together

Harvest

Some sold to government at low fixed price

Kept by peasants

Peasants were forced to <u>collectivise</u> — although they could keep small plots of land of their own for fruit, vegetables and animals. There would now be <u>extra machinery</u> for use on the larger farms.

Share and share alike...

The misery didn't stop with the workers in towns and cities — before long the peasants in the countryside were <u>forced to cooperate</u> with the Five-Year Plans too. They had to <u>share their farmland</u> and <u>sell</u> most of what they grew cheaply to the government.

The Results of Collectivisation

Collectivisation led to <u>appalling conditions</u> in the countryside...

There were **Problems** with Collectivisation

1) The <u>speed</u> of change required would <u>destroy</u> the <u>traditional</u> peasant way of life.
2) The peasants <u>resisted</u> this change and didn't want to give up land — especially the kulaks.
3) The collectives were forced to grow <u>particular crops</u> needed for industry, export or food for workers, and they had to supply a <u>specific amount</u> to the state, whether the harvest was good or bad. <u>Party officials</u> were brought in to run collectives — this was <u>resented</u>.

Stalin **Declared War** on the **Kulaks**

1) Some of the peasants <u>refused</u> to collectivise, and Stalin <u>blamed</u> the <u>kulaks</u>.
2) Stalin sent troops to <u>attack</u> what he called these 'enemies of the people'.
3) An estimated 3 million kulaks were killed. Some were <u>shot</u>. Others died from <u>starvation</u> or cold either on the way to <u>labour camps</u> or during their time working there.
4) Some villages were <u>surrounded</u> and <u>destroyed</u> — many kulaks <u>burnt</u> their own crops and <u>killed</u> livestock in protest. This contributed to a <u>famine</u> in the Ukraine — around 5 million people died.
5) 1930 saw famine and a poor harvest, and <u>collectivisation</u> was <u>halted</u> briefly.

The **Famine Continued** into 1932-33

Millions were dead or deported. Grain production was down and animal numbers had fallen.

After 1931 Collectivisation **Began Again**

1) By 1939 it was almost complete — <u>99%</u> of farming land had been <u>collectivised</u>.
2) The <u>kulaks</u> had been <u>eliminated</u> and the peasants left were afraid of communist power.
3) The <u>Communist Party</u> held absolute <u>authority</u> throughout rural Russia as it did in the cities.

Putting the farms together — a collective disaster...

This is all pretty vicious I'm afraid — and it's going to get worse. <u>Collectivisation</u> is a really important topic — it was intended to <u>help</u> the five-year plans but the effects were horrific. Don't forget to learn the <u>main problems</u> with collectivisation. And remember that when things went wrong Stalin looked for someone to blame — the <u>kulaks</u> were scapegoats here.

The Results of Collectivisation

Collectivisation brought agriculture under <u>communist control</u> — but at a cost.

There were **Pros** and **Cons** to Collectivisation

In exam questions you may be presented with different interpretations of this issue.
Remember often these are opinions, mixing facts and ideas, and not always telling the truth:

The Positive View

1) It ended the forced <u>exploitation</u> of peasants by greedy landlords and got rid of the <u>greedy</u> and <u>troublesome</u> kulaks.
2) It helped peasants <u>work together</u>.
3) It provided <u>large-scale organisation</u> of food production for the farms.
4) This was <u>communism in practice</u>.
5) Soviet propaganda showed collective farms as a <u>triumph</u> for the state, and created a <u>myth</u> of the <u>happy worker</u>.

The Negative View

1) The changes were enforced by the <u>army</u> and by <u>law</u> — there was <u>no choice</u>.
2) The kulaks were <u>scapegoats</u> for inefficient food production in the past.
3) The policy led to the <u>murder</u> and <u>imprisonment</u> of millions of people.
4) The new system <u>didn't work</u> at first and a <u>bad harvest</u> combined with kulaks destroying crops and animals caused a <u>serious famine</u> — killing more people.

State Farms were an Extension of Collective Farms

1) Land was <u>owned</u> completely by the <u>state</u>, and peasants worked as labourers — so they <u>received wages</u> even if the farm did badly.
2) Food was <u>delivered</u> to the state, and farm workers <u>bought</u> food with their wages.
3) This was <u>closer</u> to the communist <u>ideal</u> than the collective, but they were very <u>expensive</u> to establish and run. Few farms of this type existed by 1940.

Propaganda and scapegoats — Stalin's key tactics...

Another important page for you to learn here — two views of collectivisation. Remember that neither side is giving pure facts — they're mixing them with opinions. It'll be up to you to tell <u>opinions</u> and <u>facts</u> apart in the exam, and use them to give a <u>balanced answer</u> to the question.

Life in the Soviet Union

Everyday life was <u>difficult</u> for many citizens of the USSR, but some did <u>better</u> than others.

Conditions were *Harsh* for millions of people

1) <u>Life was hard</u>, but it was <u>dangerous</u> to grumble — people feared being taken away by the secret police. Millions were shot or taken to labour camps during the purges (p.156).

2) Life in the <u>cities</u> was tough. <u>Discipline</u> was strict in the factories, and wages were low.

3) However, as a result of the rapid <u>industrialisation</u> there was almost <u>no unemployment</u>.

4) Life was probably worse for those in the countryside as a result of the <u>forced collectivisation</u>. Most people lived in <u>rural areas</u>, and in general they were far poorer than those in the cities. Only about a <u>quarter of Party members</u> were of <u>peasant origin</u>.

Some groups were "More Equal" than others

<u>Communism</u> was supposed to be about <u>equality</u>, but some people were better off than others.

1) <u>What people could buy</u> depended on a <u>system</u> based on <u>social grouping</u> — farmers, factory workers, engineers and Party managers had different places in the hierarchy. Those high up in the Party got the best goods and services. This also decided the standard of <u>medical treatment</u> people received.

2) <u>Social mobility</u> did increase as a result of the <u>technical colleges</u> which were opened during the first <u>Five-Year Plan</u>. Thousands of workers achieved <u>promotion</u> through <u>education</u>.

There were mixed fortunes for the **Ethnic Minorities**

1) Early Bolshevik ideology <u>supported</u> the rights of ethnic minorities, but the USSR <u>didn't grant</u> any real political <u>independence</u> to its non-Russian republics.

2) Some minorities suffered forcible <u>population transfers</u>. Stalin ordered <u>mass deportations</u> of ethnic Poles during the <u>1930s</u> and of people from the Baltic states after 1940. Many were sent north-east to Siberia.

3) The USSR followed a policy of '<u>decossackisation</u>'. The Cossacks — a <u>military people</u> who had mostly fought against the Bolsheviks during the civil war (see p.150) — were forced from their traditional homeland.

4) Although communism was against <u>anti-Semitism</u>, <u>Stalin distrusted Jews</u> — partly because his enemy <u>Trotsky</u> was Jewish. Many <u>victims of the purges</u> were Jewish.

Women were supposed to be **Equal**

1) The revolution gave women <u>legal equality</u>. <u>Divorce</u> was simplified. The state provided many <u>communal creches</u>, <u>kitchens</u> and <u>laundries</u>, to help women to work outside the home on an equal basis with men.

2) During <u>1919-30</u> the Women's Department of the Communist Party — the <u>Zhenotdel</u> — organised political <u>training conferences</u> attended by <u>millions</u> of women. But there were always far fewer women than men in the Party.

3) In the 1930s Stalin introduced legislation to <u>restrict divorce</u> and reduce women's independence. The emphasis was increasingly on <u>stability and discipline</u>, rather than on equality. Women were expected to go out and work, while still fulfilling traditional roles when they got home.

Not an easy time to be Russian — or Ukrainian, Georgian...

Communist rule didn't affect everybody in the same way. Although it was terrible for many millions of people, for others there were <u>opportunities</u> they'd never have had under the Tsar.

Revision Summary

And now it's time for your favourite part of every section — those sublime revision questions.
I bet you can't wait — but remember that this is a really big topic. Make sure you know the order of
events and be careful about mixing facts and opinions — especially with source questions.
Give all sides of the story.

1) What was the name of the last Tsar?

2) What was the Duma?

3) Explain the impact that the First World War had on Russia.

4) Who was Rasputin?

5) Why was Kerensky's government 'Provisional' — and what does this mean?

6) Give three problems the Provisional Government faced.

7) What were the main beliefs of Marxism?

8) Why were communists split into Bolsheviks and Mensheviks?

9) What did the 'April Theses' promise?

10) Which General marched against the Provisional Government in September 1917?

11) How did the Bolsheviks seize power in 1917?

12) Give four reasons for the Bolsheviks' success.

13) Why were the Bolsheviks prepared to agree to the Brest-Litovsk Treaty?

14) Consider the events of the civil war — why did the 'Reds' win and the 'Whites' lose?

15) What were the results of the civil war on the economy, farming and industry?

16) What was the Kronstadt rebellion and how was it dealt with?

17) Write down the main features of the New Economic Policy, and its results.

18) When did Lenin die?

19) Write a short summary of Lenin's achievements.

20) What was the main difference in ideas between Stalin and Trotsky?

21) Why was Joseph Stalin able to win the struggle for power?

22) What were the purges?

23) What was the NKVD?

24) How were religion and the Church changed by Stalin's rule?

25) Explain or make a diagram to show the aims of the first Five-Year Plan.

26) Make summary notes/diagrams to explain how a collective farm worked.

27) Why were many peasants opposed to a collective farm system?

28) Why was the early 1930s a time of famine?

29) Why did Stalin want to get rid of the 'kulaks' in the countryside?

30) Why were people afraid of complaining about working conditions in Stalin's Russia?

31) Which element of the first Five-Year Plan helped increase social mobility?

32) What was the name for the policy the USSR brought against the Cossacks?

Exam Sources

Study **Sources A to C** below and then answer the questions that follow.

Source A

Тов. Ленин ОЧИЩАЕТ землю от нечисти.

© Mary Evans Picture Library/Rue des Archives/PVDE

"The sweep of Lenin's brush" — a propaganda poster by Victor Deni in 1920. It shows Lenin sweeping the world of royalty and capitalists at the time of the Russian revolution.

Source B

A painting showing Stalin at the hydroelectric complex at Ryon in the Caucasus Mountains, 1935.

Source C

There was no law and order. Every day there were hundreds of reports about the destruction of shops and homes, beatings up and attacks on officers. In the countryside, the burnings and destruction of country houses became more frequent. Military discipline collapsed. There were masses of deserters. The soldiers, without leave, went off home in great floods. They filled all the trains, kicked out the passengers and threatened to bring the whole transport system to a standstill.

From N. Sukhanov, describing the situation in Russia in September 1917. Sukhanov was a journalist who wrote his eyewitness account of the revolution in 1922.

Exam Practice

Russia 1905-1941

1 **(a)** What does Source A suggest about the events of 1917?

(4 marks)

(b) Explain why the Bolsheviks won the civil war of 1918-21.

(6 marks)

(c) How useful is Source C for studying the reasons why the Bolsheviks were successful in taking power from the provisional government in October/November 1917?

Use Source C and your knowledge to explain your answer.

(10 marks + 3 marks for SPaG)

Russia 1905-1941

2 **Study Source B and then answer both parts of the following question.**

(a) Using Source B and your own knowledge, describe the ways in which Soviet industry changed during the 1930s.

(8 marks)

(b) "The main reason why Stalin was able to become a dictator was his use of propaganda in the 1930s."

Do you agree? Explain your answer.

(12 marks + 3 marks for SPaG)

Russia 1905-1941

3 **(a)** Explain how Soviet industry changed during the 1930s.

(8 marks)

(b) How successful was the policy of collectivisation?
Explain your answer.

(12 marks + 3 marks for SPaG)

Exam Practice

Russia 1905-1941

4 (a) Study Source A.

What is this poster trying to tell us about the events of 1917?

Use the source and your knowledge to explain your answer.

(6 marks)

(b) Study Source B.

Why do you think this painting was produced in the Soviet Union in 1935?

Use the source and your knowledge to explain your answer.

(7 marks)

(c) Study Source C.

How far does this source prove that the Bolsheviks were successful in taking power in October/November 1917 because the Provisional Government had already collapsed?

Use the source and your knowledge to explain your answer.

(7 marks)

5 (a) Describe what happened at Kronstadt in 1921.

(4 marks)

(b) Describe the key features of the New Economic Policy.

(6 marks)

(c) Explain the effects of War Communism on the Russian people.

(10 marks + 3 marks for SPaG)

The Impact of the Cold War

The Cold War was a long period of hostility between the USA and USSR post-1945.
No direct fighting took place between the two sides — but the situation was very tense.

The USA and USSR became Rivals after World War 2

1) The USA and USSR were allies during the Second World War. After the war, they were the two biggest powers in the world — often called superpowers. They soon became rivals.

2) Ideologically, they were very different. The USA was capitalist. The USSR was communist.

Early events in the Cold War

1) In the aftermath of the war, the USSR developed a sphere of influence in Eastern Europe. Most Eastern European countries had communist governments installed by the USSR.

2) In 1947, US President Truman promised support to countries threatened by communist takeover — this became known as the 'Truman Doctrine'.

3) Truman also gave economic aid to Western European countries — hoping that this would help protect them from communist influence. This was called the Marshall Plan.

4) There was a crisis in Berlin in 1948-1949. The USSR, USA, France and Britain each had a zone they controlled in post-war Berlin. The USSR was angry when the other three decided to combine their zones. The USSR stopped supplies getting by land to West Berlin — so supplies had to be airlifted in (see p.53).

5) In 1949, the North Atlantic Treaty Organization (NATO) was formed — a defensive alliance between America and Western European countries.

Events in the Far East made the Cold War worse

1) Communists came to power in China in 1949. They were led by Mao Tse-tung.

2) In 1950, communist North Korea invaded non-communist South Korea. The United Nations intervened to stop the communists taking over South Korea.

See p.57 for more on the Korean War.

3) Once the UN forces had pushed them back past the original border, the communist Chinese sent an army to help the North.

4) The US General MacArthur, in charge of the UN forces, wanted to hit back at China itself. President Truman, afraid of starting World War 3, refused and insisted on a limited war.

5) In 1953 the Korean War ended with the pre-war border restored.

General MacArthur

I spy — communists everywhere...

In the 1950s, there was huge fear and suspicion of communists in the USA. To understand why, you need to learn this stuff about the Cold War and what was going on in the world.

The Red Scare

There was a 'Red Scare' in the 1950s — people were panicked by the communist threat.

Americans' *Fear* of *Communism* increased

1) American suspicions of the USSR grew — they thought it wanted world domination.

2) Under the 1947 Federal Employee Loyalty Program government employees were subjected to security checks. Their loyalty was questioned if they belonged to organisations with liberal ideas on race, disarmament or workers' rights.

3) Alger Hiss, a former senior member of the US State Department, was accused of spying and imprisoned for lying in court in 1950. This was an embarrassment to the US government.

4) By the 1950s, concerns about communism had started to cause a climate of fear and panic in the USA — this was called the Red Scare.

The HUAC hunted for *American Communists*

1) The House Un-American Activities Committee (HUAC) was set up to investigate subversive activities. During the 1940s and 1950s it became focused on finding communists in the USA.

2) In 1947 HUAC began investigating the film industry, asking suspects at its hearings, "Are you now or have you ever been a member of the Communist Party?"

3) A group of directors and writers who refused to answer were blacklisted (meaning they would not be offered work in the industry again) and jailed. They became known as the Hollywood Ten. Hundreds more people were blacklisted in the following years.

4) Some famous actors like Humphrey Bogart supported the Hollywood Ten — but it didn't make any difference in the end. Some of those blacklisted went to Europe to find work.

5) Blacklisting also happened in broadcasting, schools and universities.

> **The FBI also investigated communists in America**
>
> J Edgar Hoover, director of the Federal Bureau of Investigation (FBI), was obsessed with "subversives". He kept thousands of secret dossiers on left-wing activists and thinkers, including six Nobel Prize-winning authors. The FBI conducted loyalty probes of millions of government employees.

Red Scare — BOO!

The playwright Arthur Miller was blacklisted for refusing to give information to HUAC. He wrote a play called 'The Crucible' about a 17th century witch-hunt — a symbol for the investigation of suspected communists in 1950s America.

McCarthyism

People were so afraid of communism that they often believed accusations in the press without needing proof. McCarthy took advantage of this and the witch-hunt became known as McCarthyism.

McCarthy made Accusations with little evidence

1) In 1950, Senator McCarthy gave a speech during which he waved what he claimed was a list of 205 communists in the State Department (the US Foreign Office). He claimed some were giving information to the USSR — putting America at risk.

2) No one ever got a look at the list and many of the accusations were never proved. But newspapers published his allegations, and many people believed him.

3) McCarthy investigated possible communists. During Senate hearings he intimidated witnesses and pressured people to accuse others. He destroyed the careers of thousands of people.

> McCarthy's activities were made possible by an already existing climate of fear. China had gone communist. The Russians had the bomb. And in 1951 two members of the US Communist Party, Julius and Ethel Rosenberg, were convicted of passing atomic secrets to the Russians. They were executed in 1953.

Ethel and Julius Rosenberg

McCarthy Lost Popularity because of his Bullying Tactics

1) In 1953 McCarthy turned on the Army, accusing it of covering up communist infiltration. In the televised Army-McCarthy hearings in 1954, his bullying of witnesses turned public opinion against him. His Senate colleagues finally voted 67-22 to censure him in December 1954.

2) However, anti-communist feeling remained strong. The Communist Control Act in 1954 allowed dismissal from the civil service for political beliefs.

Senator McCarthy

McCarthyism — fear and loathing in the USA...

McCarthy ruined people's lives with his investigations — they often couldn't defend themselves because people were so willing to believe the allegations in the media. His bullying was eventually stopped but it was too late for many of those he accused.

Introduction to the Vietnam War

There's a <u>lot to learn</u> about Vietnam, so here's a page giving you the <u>rundown</u> on the whole thing.

The *First Vietnam War* was fought against the *French*

1) In the <u>19th century</u>, Vietnam was ruled by the <u>French</u>. During <u>World War Two</u>, a communist group called the <u>Viet Minh</u> were formed — they wanted Vietnam to become <u>independent</u>.

2) Between <u>1946</u> and <u>1954</u>, the Viet Minh fought the French for <u>independence</u>. The <u>USA</u> supported France because they feared that if Vietnam became independent, <u>communism</u> would spread in the Far East. This was known as the '<u>domino theory</u>' (see p.59).

3) By 1954, many French forces were based in a military stronghold at <u>Dien Bien Phu</u>. They hoped to draw the Viet Minh into a <u>battle</u> and <u>defeat</u> them once and for all.

4) The Viet Minh <u>attacked</u> but the French had <u>underestimated</u> their strength. After weeks of fighting, the French were <u>defeated</u> and they left Vietnam. The country was <u>split</u> into two — North Vietnam became <u>communist</u>, while South Vietnam had a pro-western, anti-communist government.

Kennedy Increased US Involvement in Vietnam

1) The US had given <u>military help</u> and <u>advice</u> to the French to help prevent the spread of communism.

2) After the split, the US supported the president of South Vietnam, <u>Ngo Dinh Diem</u>, despite the fact that he was very corrupt. The US provided his regime with <u>financial help</u> and <u>political</u> and <u>military advice</u>.

3) In 1960, the communist <u>National Liberation Front</u> was formed in opposition to Diem's government. The military arm of this group became known as the <u>Vietcong</u>.

4) US <u>President Kennedy</u> was determined to stop the spread of communism in Asia. He sent financial aid, military equipment and over <u>12 000</u> military advisers to South Vietnam.

The *US* sent *More Troops* to *Vietnam*

1) After Kennedy was assassinated, <u>Lyndon B. Johnson</u> became the new president of the USA.

2) In <u>1964</u>, US ships were attacked by the North Vietnamese. This became known as the <u>Gulf of Tonkin Incident</u> (see p.174), and it led to <u>full-scale war</u> in Vietnam. President Johnson sent aircraft to attack North Vietnam and ground troops to South Vietnam.

3) By 1965, Johnson increased the number of ground troops to <u>125 000</u> men. By 1968 there were over <u>500 000</u> US troops in Vietnam.

4) The US troops found it <u>hard</u> fighting the Vietcong in the jungle — so they used tactics such as <u>heavy bombing</u> and <u>chemical weapons</u> instead (see p.173).

5) In <u>1968</u>, the Vietcong and the <u>North Vietnamese Army</u> (NVA) launched an <u>all-out attack</u> on the South — the <u>Tet Offensive</u>. Although the US recovered most of their losses after three days, fighting continued for <u>several weeks</u>. Eventually, the US <u>defeated</u> the Vietcong and NVA forces.

6) The Tet Offensive was a <u>victory</u> for the US, but it had taken them <u>by surprise</u>, and had led many Americans to <u>oppose</u> the war. After Tet, the new president, Richard Nixon, promised to <u>withdraw</u> US troops from Vietnam and negotiate '<u>peace with honour</u>'.

The US and Vietnam — in for a penny, in for a pound...

During the <u>1960s</u> and <u>1970s</u>, the USA feared the <u>spread of communism</u>. That's what drove the US to support South Vietnam, but the <u>more support</u> it gave, the <u>harder</u> it was to <u>pull out</u>.

Fighting the Vietcong

The <u>Vietcong</u> were <u>supported</u> by the <u>NVA</u> — but they weren't a trained army. They weren't as <u>well armed</u> as the US troops, but they turned out to be a <u>tough enemy</u> to fight.

The *Vietcong* were experienced *Guerrilla Fighters*

1) <u>Guerrilla warfare</u> is used when <u>small military units</u> want to <u>avoid open battle</u> with a <u>larger</u>, <u>better armed</u> opponent. It involves tactics such as <u>raids</u> and <u>ambushes</u>.

2) The Vietcong were <u>very experienced</u> in guerrilla warfare — the Viet Minh had used guerrilla tactics against <u>Japan</u> and <u>France</u> during World War Two and the First Vietnam War.

3) The Vietcong hoped that guerrilla warfare would <u>exhaust</u> the US troops, lower morale, encourage <u>desertion</u> and encourage South Vietnamese soldiers to <u>defect</u>. The Vietcong wanted the Americans to leave so that they could unify Vietnam as an <u>independent country</u>.

The Vietcong were *Hard* to *Pin Down*

The Vietcong used a number of <u>guerrilla tactics</u> that made fighting them very <u>difficult</u>.

1) They worked in <u>small groups</u> and launched <u>surprise attacks</u> on US troops. They knew the land well, so they could choose <u>when</u> and <u>where</u> to attack.

2) In the jungle, they used <u>hidden traps</u> to kill or injure US soldiers. For example, explosives triggered by tripwires and covered pits filled with bamboo spikes.

3) They hid in <u>underground tunnels</u>. These tunnel systems were very <u>complex</u>, and some even had <u>army barracks</u> and <u>hospitals</u>.

4) They blended in easily with Vietnamese <u>villagers</u>. This made it <u>difficult</u> for the US troops to <u>identify</u> Vietcong soldiers.

5) The Vietcong often <u>returned</u> to areas where the US had <u>driven them out</u>. The US army seemed to be making <u>little progress</u>.

The Vietcong's tactics made them <u>strong</u>, but the US army had <u>weaknesses</u>. Most US troops in Vietnam were <u>very young</u> — in their early twenties. Many had been drafted (conscripted) and <u>didn't want to be there</u>. Most only served <u>one year</u>. This gave them <u>little time</u> to gain <u>experience</u> of fighting in the jungle.

The US couldn't fight them if they couldn't find them...

The US had a massive amount of <u>military power</u>, but in the jungle they weren't able to use it to its <u>full potential</u>. Make sure you learn the <u>tactics</u> the Vietcong used and why they were so <u>effective</u>.

Fighting the Vietcong

The US troops needed ways to overcome the Vietcong's guerrilla tactics.

The Ho Chi Minh Trail was Crucial for the Vietcong

1) The Ho Chi Minh Trail was a North Vietnamese supply route. It passed through Laos and Cambodia.

2) The trail allowed soldiers, supplies and weapons to be sent from North Vietnam to support the Vietcong in South Vietnam.

3) The trail was used throughout the war and it allowed the Vietcong to keep on fighting.

4) The US tried to bomb the trail but never managed to break it. It was difficult to bomb paths in the jungle as new routes could easily be created. Also, the trail was actually a system of trails which were often added to. Some trails were just decoy routes to confuse the Americans.

The US launched Major Military Operations

The US used a variety of methods to try to combat the guerrilla tactics of the Vietcong.

Operation Rolling Thunder

1) Operation Rolling Thunder was a huge bombing campaign against North Vietnam which ran from March 1965 until 1968. It was meant to destroy North Vietnam's industry and stop supplies arriving from China.

2) The US hoped that if North Vietnam was weakened, it wouldn't be able to supply the Vietcong.

3) The operation wasn't successful. Vietnam's economy relied on farming, not factories, so it wasn't badly affected. Supplies from China continued to arrive.

'Hearts and Minds'

1) The US wanted to win South Vietnamese 'hearts and minds', so they wouldn't help the Vietcong.

2) They did this by providing free health care and training programmes for Vietnamese villagers.

3) It wasn't very successful because South Vietnamese civilians had been badly affected by the USA's 'search and destroy' tactics and chemical weapons (see next page).

4) The US was also unpopular because it supported the corrupt South Vietnamese government.

The Ho Chi Minh Trail was vital for the Vietcong...

The catchily named Ho Chi Minh Trail provided important supplies for the Vietcong, helping them to successfully fight the Americans. It was one of the key reasons why the US failed to defeat the Vietcong.

Fighting the Vietcong

Some of the tactics used by the US were quite controversial...

The US adopted *Extreme Tactics* to try to *Win* the *War*

The US used harsh measures to try to eliminate the Vietcong, including chemical warfare.

'Search and Destroy'

1) 'Search and destroy' was a tactic which focused on killing enemy troops. Instead of securing territory, US forces would simply hunt the Vietcong and clear them out of villages. Villages suspected of supporting the Vietcong were often destroyed. Afterwards, the US troops would move on to another village or return to base.

2) It was difficult to spot Vietcong soldiers from ordinary villagers, so innocent people were sometimes interrogated or even killed. This made the US unpopular.

3) US troops sometimes made brutal attacks to get revenge for their losses. This also made the US unpopular around the world.

Chemical Weapons

1) Napalm was a burning chemical jelly which stuck to people and objects. It was used to destroy hidden targets and burn areas of jungle. It caused many civilian casualties, and its use was widely criticised.

2) Agent Orange was a chemical which destroyed trees and plant life. The US used it to try to remove big parts of the jungle where the Vietcong hid. It was also used to destroy food supplies. It was used on trees and crops, but it was very harmful, and caused cancer and birth defects.

'Search and Destroy' led to the *My Lai Massacre*

1) In March 1968, a 'search and destroy' mission in the village of My Lai led to the murder of over 300 unarmed civilians, including women and children.

2) At first, the US Army tried to cover up the incident — early reports claimed that around 20 civilians had been accidentally killed.

3) But the massacre was revealed by the media in autumn 1969. The news horrified the public and led to a high profile investigation (see p.174).

Vietnam was an especially awful war...

Both the Vietcong and the US troops used increasingly brutal tactics as the war raged on. But it was the sheer scale of the damage caused by US tactics that caused the most outrage.

TV and Media Coverage

Hundreds of journalists covered the war in Vietnam. Their reporting was very influential.

Media Coverage led many people to Oppose the War

1) The presence of the media in Vietnam meant that the
   US public could see what the war was really like.

2) During the 1960s, more and more people owned televisions. A lot of Americans
   watched news about the war every night, so they knew that the death toll was rising.

3) Reporting was mostly upbeat until the Tet Offensive in 1968 (see p.176). Footage
   of the Tet Offensive, including scenes showing the Vietcong inside the walls of
   the US embassy, made many people think that the US was losing the war.

4) A famous photograph from the Tet Offensive shows a South Vietnamese police
   chief shooting a handcuffed Vietcong soldier in the street. This made many people
   think that the US and the South Vietnamese were just as brutal as the enemy.

5) Walter Cronkite was a respected news reporter. After the Tet Offensive,
   Cronkite said that the situation in Vietnam was at a 'stalemate'.
   His opinions made some US citizens pessimistic about the war.

The Tonkin Incident was Exaggerated

1) On the 2nd August 1964, a US ship, the USS Maddox,
   was attacked in the Gulf of Tonkin by North Vietnam.

2) Two days later, more attacks on the USS Maddox and the USS Turner Joy
   were reported. However, there was no proof that these attacks took place.

3) President Johnson announced these suspected attacks, and the
   story was printed in US newspapers. Johnson made the attacks
   seem very serious, and he wanted to take action to appear tough.

4) The attacks gave Johnson public and political support for taking further action in
   Vietnam. Congress (the US parliament) passed the Gulf of Tonkin Resolution, which
   gave Johnson permission to use 'all necessary steps' to 'prevent further aggression'.

5) In the late 1960s, it was revealed that the second attacks may not have happened.
   This made many Americans feel that they'd been tricked into the war.

Evidence from My Lai was released in the press

1) In 1968, over 300 Vietnamese civilians were killed in the My Lai Massacre
   (see p.173). Photographs of the incident were printed in the media in 1969.

2) Public opinion about My Lai was divided — many Americans were horrified by the massacre,
   and the news increased anti-war feeling. Others believed that the massacre was an unfortunate
   consequence of the war, and that the My Lai villagers were probably helping the Vietcong.

3) In the early 1970s, several of the soldiers who had taken part in the massacre
   were brought to trial. Only one officer, Lieutenant William Calley, was
   convicted. He was sentenced to life in prison, but he was released in 1974.

4) Opinion polls showed that most Americans believed that Calley had just been following orders.
   Despite this, other polls showed that a majority of Americans opposed the war in Vietnam.

Vietnam — the first TV war...

The media played a crucial role in encouraging people to support the war, and then to oppose it.

Anti-War Protests

During the 1960s, a <u>strong culture</u> of <u>protest movements</u> developed in the US.

Many *Anti-War Demonstrations* were held

Chicago Anti-War Protests

1) In 1968, the <u>Democratic Party</u> held its convention in Chicago.
2) The Democrats chose Hubert Humphrey (Johnson's Vice President) as their presidential candidate. <u>Anti-war protestors</u> believed that Humphrey would continue Johnson's Vietnam policies.
3) <u>Violent demonstrations</u> took place and were broadcast on <u>television</u>. 12 000 police and over 5000 National Guardsmen dealt with the protests — over <u>500 arrests</u> were made.
4) The Republican candidate, <u>Richard Nixon</u>, promised to secure '<u>peace with honour</u>' in Vietnam, and <u>end</u> the <u>violent protests</u> at home. <u>Nixon won</u> the 1968 election, but it was very close.

Vietnam Veterans' Protest

1) The <u>Vietnam Veterans Against the War</u> (VVAW) was an organisation of soldiers who had fought in Vietnam and wanted the war <u>to end</u>.
2) In <u>April 1971</u>, the VVAW held a <u>week</u> of <u>protests</u> in Washington DC. Over 1000 veterans threw their medals onto the steps of the <u>Capitol</u> — the building where US Congress (parliament) meets.
3) The VVAW protests <u>divided public opinion</u>. Some people felt that Vietnam veterans were <u>worth listening to</u>. Others felt that the demonstrations were <u>unpatriotic</u>.

The *Kent State University* protest ended in *Tragedy*

1) Nixon's decision to <u>invade Cambodia</u> (see p.176) sparked off several <u>student protests</u>, including one at <u>Kent State University</u>, Ohio, in May 1970.
2) The <u>Governor of Ohio</u> used the <u>National Guard</u> to deal with the protestors. The students were <u>angry</u> that soldiers had been used and violence broke out.
3) The National Guard used <u>tear gas</u>, and when this didn't disperse the students, they <u>opened fire</u>. Four students were <u>killed</u>. The incident <u>outraged</u> many people and caused <u>riots</u> at other universities across America. Some believed that the <u>protestors</u> were <u>to blame</u> for the outbreak of violence, but some believed that they had a <u>right</u> to protest.

The *Fulbright Hearings* were a media sensation

1) Senator <u>Fulbright</u> was chairman of the Senate Foreign Relations Committee. Among other things, the committee discussed ways to <u>end the war</u> in Vietnam.
2) In 1971, Fulbright organised a series of <u>hearings</u> from people who both supported and opposed the war. One of the most important testimonies came from <u>John Kerry</u> (a member of the VVAW).
3) In his <u>testimony</u>, Kerry spoke about the <u>Winter Soldier Investigation</u>. In this investigation, several veterans had admitted to <u>committing offences</u> in Vietnam such as rape, torture, and the destruction of entire villages and the people who lived there.
4) The hearings were <u>widely covered</u> in the news. Kerry was the first veteran to speak so publicly about the war and his testimony was a <u>media sensation</u>. Many saw him as a <u>hero</u> for revealing the truth, but others believed he had <u>betrayed</u> the army and the US.

The Vietnam War divided public opinion in America...

It's difficult to know how most US citizens felt about Vietnam. Despite the large number of protests, President Nixon believed that the '<u>silent majority</u>' of US citizens <u>supported the war</u>.

Trying to End the War

As the war in Vietnam progressed, it became more and more <u>unpopular</u> in the US.

The *Tet Offensive* worried the *US Public*

1) The <u>Tet Offensive</u> (January 1968), was the <u>biggest attack</u> of the war by the <u>Vietcong</u> and the <u>North Vietnamese Army</u> (NVA). Around 80 000 Vietcong troops <u>attacked US bases</u> throughout South Vietnam, including the capital <u>Saigon</u>.

2) The NVA and the Vietcong hoped that the <u>South Vietnamese</u> citizens would join them when they saw the attack and they could <u>force the US out</u> of Vietnam.

3) However, the South Vietnamese <u>did not</u> support the attack. The Vietcong and the NVA were <u>pushed back</u> after three days of fighting. The Vietcong was <u>almost completely destroyed</u>.

4) This was a <u>clear victory</u> for the US. The US Commander, <u>General Westmoreland</u>, believed that the US could soon '<u>finish the job</u>'.

5) However, the attack had taken the US <u>by surprise</u>. The US public saw images of mass <u>destruction</u> and death. The Tet Offensive made the Vietcong <u>seem strong</u>.

6) Many Americans wanted to <u>end</u> the war. When General Westmoreland requested <u>200 000</u> extra soldiers it was very <u>unpopular</u> with the public.

7) President Johnson <u>didn't run</u> for re-election. The new president, <u>Richard Nixon</u>, promised to <u>end the war</u>. He wanted peace without it looking like the US was <u>admitting defeat</u>.

Vietnamisation was Nixon's *New Strategy*

1) Nixon had promised to <u>withdraw US troops</u> from Vietnam. This meant that the <u>South Vietnamese Army</u> (the ARVN) would have to fight the North Vietnamese <u>alone</u>.

2) The US <u>invested</u> money in the ARVN to <u>recruit</u> more troops and provide <u>training</u> and <u>weapons</u>. This was called <u>Vietnamisation</u>.

3) Vietnamisation was largely <u>unsuccessful</u> because ARVN troops <u>lacked discipline</u>. The remaining US troops were also demoralised — they felt that the US wasn't <u>committed</u> to Vietnam, and they were simply <u>waiting</u> to be <u>sent home</u>.

Richard Nixon

Nixon tried to *Pressure North Vietnam* to make *Peace*

Along with Vietnamisation, Nixon used <u>aggressive tactics</u> to force <u>peace talks</u>.

Cambodian Campaign	Laos Campaign
1) In <u>1969</u>, Nixon began a <u>bombing campaign</u> in <u>Cambodia</u> to try to destroy the <u>Ho Chi Minh Trail</u> and pressure North Vietnam to make peace.	1) In <u>1971</u> the <u>South Vietnamese Army</u> attacked the Ho Chi Minh Trail in <u>Laos</u>.
2) He also sent in <u>30 000</u> US <u>ground troops</u> to destroy communist bases and supplies.	2) US troops couldn't enter Laos, but they provided <u>air support</u>.
3) However, crossing into Cambodia led to more <u>anti-war demonstrations</u> (see p.175).	3) Although many communist supplies were <u>destroyed</u>, the South Vietnamese army was quickly <u>driven out</u> of Laos.
4) Anti-war feeling led Congress to <u>cut</u> military spending and <u>cancel</u> the <u>Gulf of Tonkin Resolution</u> (see p.174). This made it <u>difficult</u> for Nixon to carry on the war.	

President Nixon — bombing his way to peace...

Nixon hoped that <u>heavy bombing</u> would <u>pressure</u> North Vietnam into signing a <u>peace agreement</u>.

Peace and Defeat

A peace deal for Vietnam took a <u>long time to negotiate</u>, and the peace <u>didn't last</u> very long...

Initial **Peace Talks** were **Unsuccessful**

1) <u>Peace talks</u> with North Vietnam were first held in <u>Paris</u> in <u>1968</u>, under President Johnson. In <u>1969</u>, Nixon also held <u>secret</u> peace talks — but both were <u>unsuccessful</u>.

2) North Vietnam was in <u>no hurry</u> to make peace, and it <u>refused</u> to <u>withdraw its troops</u> from South Vietnam. The North Vietnamese government believed that <u>anti-war protests</u> in the US and military <u>spending cuts</u> would soon <u>force Nixon</u> to make <u>peace</u>.

Peace was agreed at the **Paris Peace Conference**

On <u>27th January 1973</u> both sides signed the <u>Paris Peace Accords</u>. The key agreements were:

- The president of South Vietnam, <u>General Thieu</u>, could stay in power.
- The <u>NVA</u> could <u>stay</u> in areas of South Vietnam which it already <u>controlled</u>.
- All <u>US prisoners of war</u> would be <u>released</u>.
- All <u>US troops</u> would <u>leave Vietnam</u> within <u>two months</u>.

Both sides wanted to **Reach a Deal**

North Vietnam	USA
1) The US had <u>improved</u> its <u>relations</u> with <u>China</u> and the <u>USSR</u>. These countries were North Vietnam's <u>allies</u>. They <u>encouraged</u> North Vietnam to make <u>peace</u>.	1) The war was becoming <u>increasingly unpopular</u> in the US.
2) In December 1972, the US launched its '<u>Christmas bombing</u>' of North Vietnam. The renewed bombing made North Vietnam eager for the US to leave.	2) It was <u>difficult to finance</u> the war after Congress cut military spending.
3) The North Vietnamese government wanted a chance to <u>recover</u> and <u>rebuild</u>, and then mount a <u>final assault</u> on South Vietnam.	3) It seemed the war would <u>drag on</u> for a long time.

The **Fall of Saigon** showed that **Peace** had **Failed**

1) US troops were <u>gradually</u> being withdrawn from 1969, but once the <u>peace treaty</u> was signed, <u>all remaining troops</u> left Vietnam.

2) By <u>1974</u> the US had withdrawn all its <u>troops</u>, and Congress had stopped all <u>financial help</u> to the country as well — South Vietnam was left to <u>defend itself</u>.

3) North Vietnam <u>invaded</u> South Vietnam in <u>late 1974</u>. They advanced rapidly against the <u>weak</u> and disorganised South Vietnamese forces. In <u>April 1975</u>, they took control of the South Vietnamese capital, Saigon.

4) Helicopters landed on the roof of the <u>US embassy</u> to pick up the last remaining diplomats. This <u>evacuation</u> was broadcast <u>on television</u>. Many Americans who watched it felt that the chaotic scenes were an <u>embarrassment</u> for their country.

Saigon, 1975 — a not quite honourable exit...

Some argued that the US evacuation was a <u>success</u>, with thousands of people lifted to safety. Others believed it was <u>chaotic</u> and <u>disorganised</u> and that evacuation should have begun <u>earlier</u>.

The Civil Rights Struggle in the 1950s

In the 1940s and 1950s, African Americans were still denied the rights promised by the <u>American constitution</u>. Many states were still <u>segregated</u> (see p.121) and <u>racist attitudes</u> were common.

African Americans fought in **World War 2**

1) World War 2 started in 1939, but the <u>USA</u> didn't join the fighting until <u>December 1941</u>.

2) About a <u>million</u> African Americans fought in the American <u>armed forces</u> during the war.

3) The army was <u>segregated</u> — African Americans served in <u>separate military units</u> to whites.

4) African Americans saw action on <u>all fronts</u> and often distinguished themselves in the fighting, for example in the <u>Battle of the Bulge</u> in 1944 and at <u>Iwo Jima</u> in 1945.

5) However, because of racism, <u>no</u> African Americans were awarded the <u>Medal of Honor</u>.

6) Some <u>concessions</u> were made for the sake of <u>military efficiency</u>. African Americans were admitted to the <u>Marine Corps</u> for the first time. The first <u>African-American fighter pilots</u> flew combat missions.

7) African-American soldiers fought for <u>freedom</u> abroad — but returned home to a society in which they were <u>oppressed</u> and <u>discriminated against</u>.

8) After the war, in <u>1948</u>, President Truman ended segregation in the <u>armed forces</u>.

African Americans remained **Second-Class Citizens**

In 1941, President Roosevelt had signed an executive order <u>banning racial discrimination</u> in <u>defence industries</u>. This caused <u>resentment</u> from some white workers. <u>Race riots</u> broke out in the industrial city of <u>Detroit</u> in 1943 — during which 25 African Americans and 9 white Americans were killed.

In the <u>South</u> of the USA, <u>segregation</u> was enforced by <u>law</u> in most aspects of <u>daily life</u> — schools, restaurants, theatres, workplaces, public transport and public toilets. Most white people thought this was <u>normal</u> and unremarkable. In the <u>North</u>, there was some <u>informal segregation</u> — reflecting and reinforcing African Americans' <u>lower social status</u>. Average wealth and living standards remained comparatively low for African Americans across the whole country.

The <u>Ku Klux Klan</u> (see p.120) was a <u>secret</u> organisation that believed in <u>white supremacy</u> — and used <u>violence</u> to intimidate African Americans. It had declined in popularity by the 1940s but was <u>still active</u> — and many people still shared its beliefs.

Civil Rights — in the land of the not-yet free...

Despite gaining freedom from slavery after the civil war, African Americans were still <u>heavily oppressed</u> in the South. See pages 120-121 for more on how prejudice was rife in pre-war America. Make sure you learn about the impact of World War 2, and how bad things remained at home.

The Civil Rights Struggle in the 1950s

With the help of the <u>Supreme Court</u>, the African Americans began to gain civil rights.

Justice lay in **Enforcing** *the* **Constitution**

The USA's <u>Declaration of Independence</u> and <u>Constitution</u> promise <u>all citizens</u> certain <u>rights</u>, including equal protection by the law. One strategy for gaining civil rights for African Americans was to appeal back to these <u>iconic American documents</u>. This approach, combined with <u>non-violent protest</u>, was pursued by <u>organisations</u> such as:

- The <u>NAACP</u> — National Association for the Advancement of Colored People, founded in 1909 — funded court cases challenging discrimination.

- <u>CORE</u> — the Congress of Racial Equality, founded in 1942 — dedicated to non-violent protest.

- The <u>SCLC</u> — Southern Christian Leadership Conference, founded in 1957 by Martin Luther King and Ralph Abernathy — used the churches' strength for protests.

- The <u>SNCC</u> — Student Nonviolent Coordinating Committee, formed in 1960.

The Supreme Court ruled against **Segregated Education**

1) Following campaigns by the NAACP, the <u>US Supreme Court</u> — which interprets the Constitution — ruled in the case <u>Brown v Board of Education of Topeka (1954)</u> that <u>racial segregation</u> in <u>state schools</u> was <u>unconstitutional</u>.

2) Since the <u>Constitution</u> is the <u>highest law</u> of the land, the federal (central) government was obliged to intervene when it was contradicted by <u>local state law</u>.

3) In 1957 President Eisenhower ordered 1000 paratroopers to the <u>Central High School</u> campus at <u>Little Rock</u>, Arkansas, to enforce the admission of <u>nine African-American pupils</u> in the face of local <u>mob violence</u>.

4) In 1962, <u>James Meredith</u>, an African American, had to have the protection of federal troops as he registered as a student at the <u>University of Mississippi</u>.

5) In both the above cases the <u>state governor</u>, backed by passionate <u>public support</u> from white people for segregation, did all he could to <u>defy</u> the federal authorities.

All men are created equal...

... or so says the <u>Declaration of Independence</u>, which, along with the <u>Constitution</u>, has a lot to say about <u>freedom</u> and <u>equality</u> — but African Americans still had to struggle to achieve theirs.

Civil Rights Movement in the 1960s

Small defiances by ordinary people often had a big impact for the civil rights movement.

The *Montgomery Bus Boycott* — a victory for *Integration*

Rosa Parks

1) In 1955 in Montgomery, Alabama, Rosa Parks refused to give up her seat on the bus for a white man. She was arrested.
2) Black ministers, led by 26-year-old Martin Luther King, organised a bus boycott in protest. African Americans supported the boycott by walking to work or sharing cars for a year, until the Supreme Court finally ruled that Alabama's bus segregation laws were unconstitutional.
3) The success of this peaceful protest was inspirational to all who opposed segregation in the South.

The *Civil Rights Acts* of 1957 and 1960 were ineffective

1) The 1957 act created a Civil Rights Commission to investigate obstruction of voting rights.
2) The 1960 act increased record-keeping and supervision of voting procedures.
3) Neither act achieved much in practice, but a small beginning had been made by Congress.

Non-Violent Protest won support

1) Martin Luther King and other activists used peaceful protests like marches, sit-ins and freedom rides (see box below) — gaining publicity and sympathy for the cause.
2) Many peaceful protests were undertaken by civil rights activists:

- In 1960, four African-American students started a series of sit-ins at segregated lunch counters at the Woolworths in Greensboro, North Carolina. These protests spread and some succeeded in forcing the desegregation of facilities.
- The Freedom Rides of 1961, organised by CORE and the SNCC, saw groups of African Americans and white Americans sitting together on bus trips into the South. Segregation on bus services had been ruled unconstitutional by the Supreme Court. There was a violent reaction to the Freedom Rides by some white people in the South — such as the burning of a bus at Anniston, Alabama.

The *Birmingham* victory convinced the *President*

1) President Kennedy (who came to power in 1961) at first gave limited support for African-American civil rights. He didn't want to alienate Southern white voters.
2) King and the SCLC organised protests in Birmingham, Alabama in April 1963. Protesters were met by police with fire hoses, truncheons and police dogs. Images of the harsh treatment of the protesters in the media gained support for their cause. King and hundreds of others were jailed. But in the end the Birmingham authorities gave way and agreed some concessions.
3) President Kennedy decided it was time to send a major Civil Rights Bill to Congress.

Civil Rights — a victory for non-violence...
King was influenced by Gandhi, who used non-violent civil disobedience against the British in India.

Civil Rights Movement in the 1960s

Martin Luther King, the first president of the SCLC, was committed to <u>non-violent struggle</u>.

Next came **Pressure** on **Congress**

Martin Luther King

1) In August 1963, 250 000 demonstrators marched on Washington, where King spoke of his <u>dream</u> of a non-racist America.

2) But when Kennedy was <u>assassinated</u> in November 1963, his Civil Rights Bill had still not passed. He was replaced by President Johnson.

3) Despite the fact that Kennedy was from <u>liberal Massachusetts</u> in the North, and Johnson from <u>segregated Texas</u> in the South, it was Johnson who was more effective in achieving civil rights.

Important Acts were passed in **1964** and **1965**

1) The <u>Civil Rights Act</u> of <u>1964</u> empowered the federal government to <u>enforce desegregation</u> in all public places. This was a big victory for the civil rights movement.

2) <u>Voting rights</u> were still a problem. In theory, African Americans could vote, but in the South all kinds of <u>local rules</u> were invented to stop them.

3) In the "<u>Freedom Summer</u>" of 1964 thousands of student volunteers spent vacations in Mississippi in a drive for <u>voter registration</u>. Three of these students were <u>murdered</u>.

4) In March 1965 the police in Selma, Alabama, used <u>clubs</u> and <u>tear gas</u> on civil rights marchers and again the brutality was televised. In response, King — who had been awarded the <u>Nobel Peace Prize</u> in 1964 — led a march through Alabama from Selma to Montgomery.

5) In <u>August 1965</u> Johnson signed the <u>Voting Rights Act</u>. Federal registrars would now enforce voting rights. This was another <u>major success</u> for the civil rights movement.

There was still **Discrimination** and **Unrest**

1) Formal civil rights <u>weren't enough</u> to help African Americans trapped in <u>poverty</u>.

2) The <u>Vietnam War</u> began to absorb funds which might otherwise have been available for more spending on <u>social programmes</u>.

3) Some African Americans became <u>impatient</u> with King's leadership and <u>non-violent</u> methods.

4) There were many inner-city <u>riots</u> by African Americans in the mid-1960s. 34 people were killed in a 6-day riot in the <u>Watts</u> district of Los Angeles in <u>August 1965</u>. The <u>8-day Detroit riot</u> of <u>July 1967</u> left 43 dead.

Martin Luther King was **Assassinated** in **1968**

1) In <u>1966</u> Martin Luther King went north to <u>Chicago</u> to organise marches against discrimination in <u>housing</u> — a problem not dealt with by the 1964 Civil Rights Act.

2) The government gave no support because President Johnson was angered at the "<u>ingratitude</u>" of black leaders who had <u>criticised</u> his <u>Vietnam War policy</u>.

3) Congress did pass an effective Civil Rights Act for <u>housing</u> after King's <u>assassination</u> in April 1968 had triggered more riots in more than 100 <u>cities</u>.

Martin Luther King — he had a dream...

Throughout the 60s, the peaceful protests led to some <u>serious changes</u> in law, such as the Civil Rights Act, and the Voting Rights Act — although the progress was <u>limited</u> by poverty, war, and the assassinations of both Kennedy and King.

Civil Rights Movement in the 1960s

The late 1960s and early 1970s saw the rise of a more <u>confrontational approach</u> to civil rights.

Some groups favoured *Violent Protest*

Malcolm X, an African-American Muslim, <u>rejected</u> integration and non-violence. He called the peaceful march on Washington the "<u>farce on Washington</u>". His preaching drew converts to the African-American separatist organisation, the <u>Nation of Islam</u>. Malcolm X developed more 'inclusive' views and left the Nation of Islam in 1964. He was <u>killed</u> by Nation of Islam members in February <u>1965</u>.

In 1966 SNCC chairman Stokely Carmichael popularised the "<u>Black Power</u>" slogan. Under his leadership, the SNCC <u>expelled</u> its white members. In Newark in 1967, after a riot in which over 20 African Americans had been killed by police, a <u>Black Power</u> conference passed resolutions calling for a <u>separate African-American nation</u> and <u>militia</u>.

The <u>Black Panther Party</u> was founded in 1966 by <u>Huey P. Newton</u> and <u>Bobby Seale</u>. Its members wore uniforms and went on armed patrol, claiming to defend African Americans from police violence. They also carried out programmes of <u>education</u> and <u>healthcare</u> for <u>African Americans</u>.

Affirmative Action gave African Americans opportunities

1) President Johnson sought to combat the under-representation of African Americans in many areas of <u>employment</u> with a <u>preferential hiring policy</u>.

2) Under President Nixon, people began to criticise this policy as "<u>reverse discrimination</u>".

3) However, from 1969 Nixon encouraged the growth of African American-owned businesses with the Small Business Administration's <u>set-aside programme</u>. This guaranteed that a proportion of government contracts would be awarded to ethnic minority owned firms.

4) During the 1970s attempts were made to integrate <u>schools</u> by "<u>busing</u>" children from different areas to make sure <u>schools</u> were ethnically mixed. It caused much <u>resistance</u> — many white Americans moved out to the suburbs or put their children in private schools to avoid it.

African-American Athletes protested at the *Olympics*

1) At the 1968 Mexico Olympics two African-American athletes, <u>Tommie Smith</u> and <u>John Carlos</u>, won medals in the men's 200m sprint.

2) During the playing of the national anthem, they bowed their heads and gave the <u>Black Power salute</u> — a <u>raised fist</u> — in protest at the <u>racism</u> and <u>hardship</u> suffered by African Americans back home.

3) The two athletes were <u>thrown out</u> of the Olympic team and <u>sent home</u>. Reaction in the US was largely <u>negative</u>, and the two athletes found later life hard with the <u>notoriety</u> they had gained.

4) The image of the two athletes with raised fists became an important <u>symbol</u> of the <u>Civil Rights struggle</u>.

The Black Panthers — a cat-aclysmic shift in the struggle...

Black Power and African-American separatism were <u>frightening</u> developments to many Americans — including those in positions of power. But groups like the Black Panthers also did a lot of good in helping their communities.

Civil Rights of Hispanic Americans

African Americans weren't the only group in the USA who <u>struggled</u> against <u>discrimination</u>.

People emigrated from **Latin America** to the USA

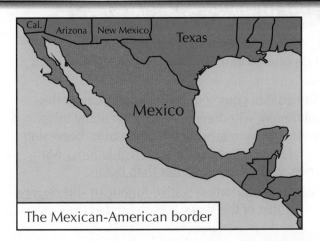

The Mexican-American border

1) The states <u>bordering Mexico</u> — Texas, New Mexico, Arizona and California — attracted much immigration from Mexico and other countries in Latin America.

2) To help the wartime <u>labour shortage</u>, from 1942 the <u>Bracero Program</u> allowed Mexican labourers to <u>work temporarily</u> in the US. The scheme lasted till 1964.

3) Millions more came as <u>illegal immigrants</u> — the <u>2000-mile border</u> was difficult to police.

4) Mexican Americans faced <u>segregation</u> in schools, housing and employment.

The war sparked an era of **Progress**

1) Hundreds of thousands of Hispanic Americans served in the <u>US armed forces</u> in World War 2.

2) There was some <u>racism</u> against Hispanic Americans. In 1943 Los Angeles erupted in the <u>Zoot Suit Riots</u> — American sailors spent 10 days seeking out and beating up Latino teenagers.

3) After the war, the <u>League of United Latin American Citizens</u> and the <u>American GI Forum</u> mounted legal challenges to overturn school segregation in California and the exclusion of Mexican Americans from Texas juries.

4) In <u>1954</u> the Supreme Court in the case <u>Hernandez v Texas</u> declared that the 14th Amendment outlawing racial discrimination applied not just to African Americans but to <u>all races</u>.

5) Founded in 1968, the <u>Mexican American Legal Defense and Educational Fund</u> (MALDEF) became the most prominent Mexican-American civil rights organisation.

Cesar Chavez led the farm workers

1) Cesar Chavez, the grandson of Mexican immigrants, formed the <u>United Farm Workers</u> union in <u>1962</u>. From 1965 he organised a <u>10-year campaign</u> to improve the pay and working conditions of migrant workers, including a nationwide <u>grape boycott</u> in 1967.

2) In <u>1975</u> the <u>Agricultural Labor Relations Act</u> protected the right of farm workers to unionise. Chavez's success played a part in raising awareness of the wider struggle for <u>Hispanic-American rights</u>.

United Farm Workers' flag

The **1965 Immigration Act** loosened restrictions

1) US immigration rules were based on a system of national <u>quotas</u> designed to reflect the <u>existing ethnic structure</u> of the USA. In the 1960s liberals denounced this as <u>race bias</u>.

2) The <u>1965 Immigration Act</u> set preference categories based less on <u>country of origin</u> and more on <u>kinship relations</u> and <u>occupation</u>. Immigration from Latin America and Asia increased.

The Zoot Suit Riots — a fashion crime...

<u>Zoot suits</u> were over-sized suits popular with Latin American teenagers in the 1940s. Some people said they <u>wasted material</u> — bad in wartime. But hardly justification for a riot...

Civil Rights of Native Americans

Native Americans suffered discrimination. Traditionally many tribes had led a nomadic lifestyle on the plains — but white settlers in the 19th century had forced them off much of the land.

Native American *Land* and *Independence* was under *Threat*

1) The 1934 Indian Reorganization Act had halted previous attempts to break up tribes and enforce assimilation. Now substantial self-government was offered to tribes who wanted it, in an effort to restore their sovereignty and cultural autonomy.

2) After World War 2, Congress reverted to the earlier goal of complete assimilation. Under this 'termination' policy, started in the 1950s, the government withdrew benefits from many tribes. Many reservations (areas set aside for Native Americans) were absorbed by the states, becoming new counties. 'Terminated' tribes now had to pay state taxes and obey state regulations. Many had to sell land or mineral rights to outside interests, and were left poorer than before.

3) In the 1960s the Supreme Court began issuing decisions supporting Native American sovereignty and recognising the tribes' legal status as higher than that of the states, which limited the power of the states over the reservations.

AIM struggled for *Native American Rights*

1) The American Indian Movement (AIM) was formed in 1968 in response to police harassment in Minneapolis. It became a national organisation concerned also with issues such as living standards and treaty rights.

2) In 1972 AIM members joined with seven other organisations in the Trail of Broken Treaties, a march on Washington. The protesters vandalised the headquarters of the Bureau of Indian Affairs (BIA) — the federal agency which manages the reservation system.

3) Civil disobedience 'fish-ins' brought success in the 1974 Boldt Decision in favour of Native American fishing and hunting rights.

4) By 1980 Native Americans had succeeded in forcing the government to return some important tribal lands and to provide compensation for some confiscated lands.

5) The 1978 Indian Religious Freedom Act guaranteed protection for forms of religious worship and access to sacred sites.

There was conflict at *Wounded Knee* in *1973*

1) A faction at the Oglala Sioux reservation, opposed to corruption in the way the reservation was managed, invited AIM to join a protest.

2) The protesters seized the village of Wounded Knee at gunpoint. Soon they were surrounded by a military cordon. The siege lasted for 71 days. Shots were exchanged and two people were killed.

3) The symbolism of the site — scene of an 1890 massacre of Sioux by the Army — ensured national media attention.

4) Eventually, after a negotiated settlement of the local issues, the siege ended in a triumph for AIM.

Russell Means — one of AIM's leaders in the '70s

Native American Rights — AIM to learn the whole page...

Wounded Knee is a place with very heavy significance in Native American history. The 1890 massacre of Sioux is generally regarded as the final event in the Native American struggle against the expanding USA. So the siege there in 1973 made people sit up and take notice.

Women's Rights

The feminist movement gained momentum in the <u>1960s</u> — and won <u>better rights</u> for women.

Women began to challenge **Discrimination at Work**

1) In 1960 women usually worked in <u>low-paid jobs</u> such as <u>nursing</u>, <u>teaching</u>, and <u>clerical</u> and <u>domestic</u> work. During the 1960s, women made up around <u>33-43 per cent</u> of the total workforce, but their average earnings remained around <u>60 per cent</u> that of men.

2) <u>Eleanor Roosevelt</u> pressured President Kennedy into creating a <u>Presidential Commission on the Status of Women</u> (1961) with herself as its head.

3) The <u>1963 Equal Pay Act</u> made it <u>illegal</u> to pay women less than men for the <u>same job</u>. But the Equal Employment Opportunity Commission was <u>understaffed</u> and there was little to stop employers giving <u>different job titles</u> to men and women doing the <u>same activities</u>.

4) <u>Title VII</u> of the <u>1964 Civil Rights Act</u> prohibited discrimination in <u>employment</u> on the basis of <u>sex</u>. But enforcement was <u>slow</u> to follow.

5) Available from 1960, the <u>contraceptive pill</u> ('the Pill') made it easier for women to postpone having children while they started a <u>career</u>.

Eleanor Roosevelt

The campaign group **NOW** was formed in 1966

1) <u>Betty Friedan</u> in '<u>The Feminine Mystique</u>' (<u>1963</u>) criticised the isolation of women in the household — saying many <u>felt trapped</u> in the homemaker role.

2) Friedan was one of the founders of the <u>National Organization for Women</u> (<u>NOW</u>) — founded in 1966 to campaign for women's <u>legal</u>, <u>educational</u> and <u>professional equality</u>.

3) NOW pressured Congressmen into passing the <u>Equal Rights Amendment</u> (ERA) in 1972 — but the Amendment failed to achieve ratification by the necessary three-quarters of states.

4) Opposition to the ratification of the ERA included women who wanted a return to "<u>traditional</u>" femininity. Conservative activist <u>Phyllis Schlafly</u> organised a group called "<u>Stop ERA</u>".

5) However, the objectives of ERA were largely achieved by other means — especially a more vigorous enforcement of <u>Title VII</u> of the <u>1964 Civil Rights Act</u>.

6) <u>Title IX of the Educational Amendments Act</u> (<u>1972</u>) forced government-funded <u>educational establishments</u> to provide equal facilities and opportunities for both sexes.

> Feminists began to campaign against the <u>objectification of women</u>. Feminists protested at the 1968 <u>Miss America beauty pageant</u> — they crowned a sheep their own 'Miss America'.

The right to **Abortion** was a **Controversial Issue**

> Feminists argued that women had the <u>right</u> to choose <u>abortion</u>. The Supreme Court ruled in the case <u>Roe v Wade</u> (<u>1973</u>) that state laws <u>banning abortion</u> were <u>unconstitutional</u>. But in response to pressure from religious groups, Congress passed the <u>Hyde Amendment</u> in 1976. This stopped <u>Medicaid</u> (the medical assistance programme for the poor) from funding abortions.

Women's liberation — get learning NOW...

The women's movement <u>achieved</u> a lot for women — including basic rights we take for granted nowadays like equal pay and equal educational opportunities.

Student Protest and Youth Culture

The 1960s were a decade of <u>student protest</u> and youthful discontent.

There were some **Big Political Issues** *in the* **1960s**

1) The <u>civil rights movement</u> was at a peak in the 1960s (see p.180-182). Students and young people were often involved in the <u>protests</u> and <u>campaigns</u>.

2) The American government was also stuck in a <u>long war</u> in <u>Vietnam</u> (see p.170-177). Many young people were opposed to the US's <u>motives</u> and the <u>tactics</u> it used in the war.

3) Young people were the group most affected by the war because of the <u>draft</u> (conscription).

4) In <u>October 1967</u>, over 50 000 students and others opposed to the war took part in a march on the Pentagon during <u>Stop the Draft Week</u>.

Student Groups *organised major* **Protests**

| The SDS |

1) The <u>Students for a Democratic Society</u> (<u>SDS</u>) was formed in <u>1959</u>. In the early 1960s many of its members worked for <u>civil rights</u> — which taught them <u>protest tactics</u>.

2) As the <u>Vietnam War</u> continued, the SDS became a leading group for <u>anti-war protests</u>.

3) In April 1968 they led a student <u>takeover</u> of <u>Columbia University</u> to protest against the <u>Vietnam War</u> and against <u>segregation</u>. The takeover lasted for 8 days and resulted in around <u>700 arrests</u>.

| The SNCC |

1) The <u>Student Nonviolent Coordinating Committee</u> (<u>SNCC</u> or 'snick') was formed in <u>1960</u> by students who wanted to campaign for civil rights.

2) The SNCC helped organise the <u>Freedom Rides</u> (see p.180) as well as the <u>Albany Movement</u> — a series of <u>sit-ins</u> in Albany, Georgia between <u>1961</u> and <u>1962</u>.

3) From 1966 the SNCC strongly opposed the war in Vietnam and organised increasingly <u>militant protests</u>, particularly against <u>the draft</u>.

The **'Swinging Sixties'** *challenged traditional values*

1) Many young people <u>experimented</u> with <u>new lifestyles</u> involving rock music, psychedelic drugs, sexual freedom and religious experimentation.

2) Events included the San Francisco "<u>Summer of love</u>" (1967) and the <u>Woodstock Music Festival</u> (<u>1969</u>).

3) <u>Protest singers</u>, such as Bob Dylan, wrote songs about <u>political issues</u> like the Vietnam War and the civil rights movement.

4) By 1967 there were <u>hippy</u> areas in most American cities — populated by "drop-outs" from mainstream life. Not all young people took part though — some still had <u>traditional values</u>.

Stop the draft — it's getting chilly in here...

The 1960s were a time of fervent student protest and activism. There were <u>big cultural changes</u> too — the 'swinging sixties' were a break with what had gone before...

Revision Summary

It's another glorious revision summary. It's the usual drill — answer all the questions, then see what you got wrong and revise any weak spots. You'll be an old hand at it by now.

1) What was the Marshall Plan?

2) What was the name of the American general in charge of UN forces in the Korean War?

3) What was the 'Red Scare' in the 1950s?

4) What was the 'Hollywood Ten'?

5) Who was the director of the FBI during the Red Scare?

6) Why did Senator McCarthy lose popularity?

7) What was the name of the military arm of the National Liberation Front?

8) Name two tactics used by the Vietcong.

9) What were the two main aims of 'Operation Rolling Thunder'?

10) What was the Gulf of Tonkin incident?

11) What was the name of the massacre that journalists revealed in 1969?

12) At which US university were four students killed in anti-war protests in May 1970?

13) What was the name of the offensive the Vietcong and the North Vietnamese army launched in January 1968?

14) Give two reasons why the North Vietnamese government were willing to make a ceasefire deal in 1973.

15) What was segregation?

16) What does NAACP stand for?

17) What was the ruling in the case Brown v Board of Education of Topeka (1954)?

18) What act of resistance did Rosa Parks make to segregation in 1955?

19) What major civil rights march happened in 1963?

20) Who was murdered during the 'Freedom Summer'?

21) When was Martin Luther King assassinated?

22) How did Malcolm X's approach differ from Martin Luther King's?

23) Why was President Johnson's preferential hiring policy criticised?

24) What were the Zoot Suit Riots?

25) Who founded the United Farm Workers union in 1962?

26) What does AIM stand for?

27) Describe the events at Wounded Knee in 1973.

28) What Act made it illegal to pay women less than men for the same job?

29) What was the name of Betty Friedan's famous 1963 book?

30) What was the ruling about abortion in the case Roe v Wade (1973)?

31) What was the SDS?

Exam Sources

Study **Sources A to D** below and then answer the questions that follow.

Source A

"The March on Washington" — a photograph showing Freedom Walkers, 28th August 1963.

Source B

A photograph showing a civil rights sit-in by John Salter, Joan Trumpauer and Anne Moody at Woolworths' lunch counter in Jackson, Mississippi, America, 28 May 1963.

Source C

A photograph showing a billboard in Selma, Alabama, on US Route 80 highway, 22 March 1965. Over 300 civil rights marchers, led by Martin Luther King Jr., used US Route 80 en route to Montgomery.

Source D

It ought to be possible, therefore, for American students of any color to attend any public institution they select without having to be backed up by troops. It ought to be possible for American consumers of any color to receive equal service in places of public accommodation, such as hotels and restaurants and theaters and retail stores, without being forced to resort to demonstrations in the street, and it ought to be possible for American citizens of any color to register and to vote in a free election without interference or fear of reprisal. It ought to be possible, in short, for every American to enjoy the privileges of being American without regard to his race or his color. In short, every American ought to have the right to be treated as he would wish to be treated, as one would wish his children to be treated. But this is not the case.

Part of a radio and television report to the American people on civil rights by President John F. Kennedy, June 11 1963.

Exam Practice

The USA 1945-1975

1 Study Source A and then answer both parts of the following question.

   (a) Using Source A and your knowledge, describe how pressure was exerted in order
      to secure civil rights for African Americans.

                                                   (8 marks)

   (b) Non-violent protest was the most effective tactic used in the struggle for greater
      civil rights for African Americans in the USA.
      Do you agree? Explain your answer.

                       (12 marks + 3 marks for SPaG)

The USA 1945-1975

2 (a) Study Source C.

     Why was this poster put up in the USA in 1965?
     Use the source and your knowledge to explain your answer.

                                               (7 marks)

   (b) Study Source D.

     To what extent does this show President Kennedy to be the most important politician in the
     era of the civil rights struggle?
     Use the source and your knowledge to explain your answer.

                                               (7 marks)

   (c) Study Source B.

     What message would this photograph have sent when published?
     Use the source and your knowledge to explain your answer.

                                               (6 marks)

3 (a) Describe the provisions and effects of the Immigration Act of 1965.

                                                   (4 marks)

   (b) Explain the significance of the events that took place at Wounded Knee in 1973.

                                                   (6 marks)

   (c) The following people were all equally significant in the struggle for civil rights in the USA.
     (i)   President Johnson
     (ii) Rosa Parks
     (iii) President Nixon

How far do you agree with this statement?
Explain your answer referring only to (i), (ii) and (iii).

                                         (10 marks + 3 marks for SPaG)

Exam Practice

The USA 1945-1975

4 Study Source B.

What can you learn from Source B about the civil rights movement in the USA in 1963?

(5 marks)

5 Study Source C and use your own knowledge.

Does the message on this poster surprise you?

Use details of the source and your own knowledge to explain your answer.

(7 marks)

6 Study Sources A, B and D and use your own knowledge.

Do these sources support the view that the African-American civil rights campaign achieved its aims without violence?

Explain your answer, using the sources and your own knowledge.

(8 marks)

7 Study Sources A and C.

How useful are Sources A and C as evidence of the beliefs and actions of Martin Luther King?

Explain your answer.

(8 marks)

8 Study all the sources and use your own knowledge.

"Martin Luther King was the most influential figure in the struggle for civil rights for African Americans in the USA."

How far do the sources in this paper support this statement?

Use details from the sources and your own knowledge to explain your answer.

(12 marks + 3 marks for SPaG)

The Need for Reform

In the 1890s many people in Britain weren't just poor, they were desperate.
There was no government help for the old, ill or unemployed.

Poor People faced serious hardship in the 1890s

1) The only help available for very poor people was workhouses run by local councils.
They provided basic food and lodging in exchange for long hours in brutal conditions.
Many people saw going to the workhouse as shameful.

2) There was serious unemployment in some industries, and no 'dole' or unemployment benefit.

3) Old people who had no savings or family suffered very badly — there were no
government pensions. The only option for many old people was the workhouse.

4) Housing in poor areas was damp, cold and didn't have proper sewage systems. It was easy
to get ill in these conditions, which meant missing work, and maybe losing your job.

5) Many people couldn't afford doctors or medicine.

6) Many children had to go to work from an early age, and so missed getting an education.

7) Large numbers of people couldn't even afford to eat properly. Out of all the men
recruited to fight in the Boer War (1899-1902), half were malnourished.

Two reports said a Third of British people were Poor

Not everybody believed that poverty was all that bad — especially rich people.
Two reports said that poverty was serious, and that it affected large numbers of people.

Charles Booth published the first edition
of *Life and Labour of the People* in 1889.
This showed that 30% of people in
London were living in severe poverty,
and that it was sometimes impossible
for people to find work, however hard
they tried. He also showed that wages
for some jobs were so low that they
weren't enough to support a family.

Life and Labour
of the People

Charles Booth
1889

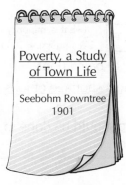

Poverty, a Study
of Town Life

Seebohm Rowntree
1901

Seebohm Rowntree had a factory in York.
He didn't believe the problem was as
bad there as in London — so he did a
survey of living conditions. The report
of his findings, *Poverty, a Study of Town
Life* (published 1901) showed that 28%
of people in York were so poor that they
couldn't afford basic food and housing.

Rowntree — social reformer AND inventor of Fruit Gums...

Life was hard for a lot of people in 1890s Britain. Learn the examples of the problems facing poor
people, and about the two reports. Scribble them down, and check you've got them right.

The Need for Reform

At the start of the new century, the issues with poverty in Britain could no longer be <u>ignored</u>. Both politicians and the general public began to admit that <u>something</u> needed to be done.

Public Opinion on helping poor people began to Change

There was <u>no way</u> you could put <u>a third of the population</u> into the workhouse. Britain needed a new <u>approach</u> to deal with poverty. Many people had an <u>opinion</u> on how it should be done.

1) Popular and well-respected writers like <u>George Bernard Shaw</u>, <u>J. Galsworthy</u>, <u>Charles Dickens</u> and <u>H. G. Wells</u> wrote about how poor people lived. They said the poor needed help, and the government should <u>pass laws</u> to make sure it happened.

2) People involved in <u>public health</u> and <u>medicine</u> said the government should get <u>more involved</u> in health issues.

3) <u>Socialists</u> argued that wealth should be more <u>equally spread</u> between working people and people like factory owners and land owners, who were traditionally the richest.

4) The <u>Labour Party</u> was the only mainstream socialist political party. They argued that the government should give <u>financial help</u> to the poorest members of society. Labour was attracting more and more <u>working-class supporters</u>.

A Royal Commission investigated Poverty

In <u>1905</u> the <u>Conservative</u> government set up a <u>Royal Commission</u> to look at the <u>Poor Law</u>. This was the 19th-century law which <u>set up</u> the workhouses and other help for the poor. The Commission was supposed to decide whether the <u>help</u> given by the Poor Law was <u>good enough</u>. But the members of the Commission <u>couldn't agree</u> about what <u>caused</u> poverty, so they published <u>two reports</u>:

THE MAJORITY REPORT (what the majority of the commission thought)

- If people were poor it was their <u>own fault</u>.
- They made themselves poor by <u>gambling</u> and <u>drinking</u> — so they didn't deserve help.
- Enough was being done for the poor <u>already</u>.

THE MINORITY REPORT (what a minority of the commission thought)

- People <u>couldn't help</u> being poor.
- <u>Illness</u>, <u>old age</u> and a <u>shortage of jobs</u> made people poor.
- They thought <u>more should be done</u> to prevent people being poor.

What the Dickens could be done about the poor?

By 1905, most people realised that there <u>was</u> a problem with poverty in Britain, but it was less clear what should be done about it. The political parties and the medical professions had their own ideas, but the majority of the commission felt that the poor should <u>help themselves</u> as it was their own fault.

Conservatives, Liberals and Labour

Pressure was growing for the government to deal with poverty. The main parties — the Liberals and Conservatives — traditionally felt it wasn't the government's role. But things were changing.

The political parties had **Different Attitudes** to **Poverty**

The oldest, most powerful political parties — the Liberals and the Conservatives — didn't really agree with giving government help to people. They believed that:

1) the government should interfere as little as possible in people's lives
2) it was wrong to raise taxes as people should decide how to spend their own money
3) giving poor people money was morally wrong as it undermined their independence.

The Labour Party didn't have many MPs before 1906, but they did have growing support from working people. They believed that:

1) the poorest people in society should get government help
2) the government should get the cash to pay for this from taxes
3) the government should also take over (nationalise) the major industries and make use of the profits.

Some Liberals and some Conservatives were more open to the idea of the government helping the poor — especially if it helped their party win votes from Labour.

After **1906** the **Liberals** brought in **Social Reforms**

1) In 1906 the Liberal Party won a landslide general election victory over the Conservatives.

2) 29 Labour Party MPs were elected — giving them a good position to push for help for the poor.

3) The Minority Report, the success of the Labour Party, and pressure from the general public all encouraged the Liberals to bring in laws to deal with poverty.

4) The Liberals had to compete with Labour for the support of working-class voters — this led to the emergence of "New Liberalism" which favoured government intervention to help the poor.

5) The poor physical condition of volunteers for the Boer War had been a shock. If Britain was involved in a major war, it would need a healthy working class to fight as soldiers.

6) David Lloyd George and Winston Churchill* were the MPs who worked hardest to drive the bills through. They wanted to help the poor, but were also keen to make a name for themselves.

David Lloyd George — so good they named him thrice...

We're used to the idea of benefits and pensions being paid by the government, but at the time this was a new idea. Scribble down the reasons why the Liberals brought in social reforms after 1906.

Laws to Help Children and Old People

The Liberals <u>didn't plan</u> to help <u>everyone</u> — just the people with the <u>worst problems</u> — children from poor families, old people, ill people, and people who were out of work or badly paid. Unfortunately they've left you <u>reams of laws</u> to learn...

Children needed **Special Protection**

In <u>1906</u> the <u>School Meals Act</u> allowed <u>LEAs</u> to supply <u>free</u> school meals paid for out of <u>rates</u>.

> <u>LEAs</u> = Local Education Authorities.
> They were in charge of running state schools.
> <u>rates</u> = local council tax

In <u>1907</u> LEAs started giving children at their schools <u>free medical inspections</u>. Many of them built clinics where they could hold the inspections.

In <u>1908</u> Parliament passed the <u>Children and Young Persons' Act</u> (also known as the <u>Children's Charter</u>) to give children some legal protection. The Charter made it illegal for children younger than <u>16</u> to <u>buy cigarettes</u>, <u>go into a pub</u> or <u>beg</u>. It also set up special <u>juvenile courts</u> — so <u>young offenders</u> wouldn't be <u>tried</u> in an <u>adult court</u>.

<u>Herbert Samuel</u> from the Home Office tried to help <u>young offenders</u>:

> 1) He set up special prisons, known as <u>borstals</u>, for young offenders — so they wouldn't have to go to adult prisons.
> 2) He set up the <u>probation service</u> to try to keep young people from reoffending.

Elderly people got **State Pensions**

In <u>1908</u> <u>David Lloyd George</u> was Chancellor of the Exchequer. He introduced the <u>Old Age Pensions Act</u>. These are the most important bits of the Act:

> 1) The pension was for people <u>over 70</u> on low incomes.
> 2) The scheme was <u>non-contributory</u> — you didn't have to pay money in to get a pension when you retired. The pensions were paid for by money raised through <u>ordinary taxes</u>.
> 3) In the <u>1908</u> budget <u>£1 200 000</u> of tax money was set aside to pay for pensions.
> 4) Single people with an income of <u>less than £21 per year</u> got 5 shillings per week. <u>Married couples</u> with an income of <u>less than £21 per year</u> got 7s 6d (7 shillings & 6 pence) per week.
> 5) Anyone whose income was <u>between £21 and £31 per year</u> got a smaller pension.
> 6) People with an income of <u>over</u> £31 per year didn't get a pension at all.
> 7) The first pensions were paid on <u>1 January 1909</u>.

Although Labour said 5 shillings was <u>too little</u>, the pension was <u>immensely popular</u>. Lloyd George took the <u>credit</u>.

Remember the aim <u>wasn't</u> to help everyone, just the <u>poorest people</u>.

> "We are lifting the shadow of the workhouse from the homes of the poor."

David Lloyd George

The Old Age Pensions Act — an over-70s free-for-all...

Children got <u>legal protection</u>, <u>school dinners</u>, <u>medical check-ups</u> and <u>borstal</u>. Old people got pensions. Make sure you know the dates and names of the acts.

Laws Protecting Working People

The Liberals also passed laws to help <u>working people</u>. Get all of these <u>clear</u> in your mind now — you need to know the <u>name</u> and <u>date</u> of each act, and <u>what it did</u> to help people.

The **National Insurance Act** of **1911**

In <u>1911</u> Lloyd George introduced the <u>National Insurance Act</u>.
Lloyd George got a lot of the ideas for this Act from a <u>similar scheme</u> running in <u>Germany</u>.

> The Act came in two parts. Part One's covered here. Part Two's covered on the next page.

Part One helped with **Health Insurance**

Part One was to help workers pay for <u>health insurance</u>. The insurance was to pay for <u>treatment</u> and provide <u>sick pay</u> when people were too ill to work. The National Insurance Act said the government would <u>top up</u> the money that workers paid into insurance schemes.

1) The Act covered workers earning <u>less than £160 per year</u>.

2) <u>Each week</u> workers paid <u>4 old pence</u> out of their wages into a <u>central fund</u>.
   Employers added <u>3 old pence</u> per week and the government added another <u>2 old pence</u> per week.

3) Sick pay of up to <u>10 shillings per week</u> was paid to <u>male</u> workers if they were off work ill for more than <u>four days</u>. This sick pay would be paid for several months. The worker was also entitled to <u>medical attention</u>.

> 4) Women <u>didn't pay as much</u> in or <u>get as much</u> out, because they <u>didn't earn as much</u> in the first place
>
> 5) Women were paid <u>7s 6d</u> a week <u>sick pay</u>.
> They also got a one-off <u>maternity grant</u> of <u>30 shillings</u>.

6) <u>Names</u> of workers on the National Insurance scheme were put on a special list known as a <u>doctors' 'panel'</u>. Doctors were <u>paid</u> a sum by the government for every patient on the panel.

7) The scheme was organised through organisations approved by the government — <u>friendly societies</u>, <u>trade unions</u> and <u>private insurance companies</u>.

8) The scheme caused <u>controversy</u> — Conservatives said the government had <u>no right</u> to force people to contribute from their wages, and many socialists said there should be <u>higher taxes on rich people</u> to pay for it instead of workers having to contribute. But it was still <u>passed</u>.

> <u>friendly society</u> = a kind of voluntary society in which members paid a subscription in exchange for financial and medical help if they became sick.

> "Workers are getting nine pence for four pence."

> <u>Ten million workers</u> now had health insurance.

David Lloyd George

I can't wait to find out what happens in part two...

These laws were to help some of the <u>poorest</u> people in the country. Remember that Britain was a lot more <u>industrial</u> at the time, so there were more <u>accidents</u> and <u>industrial illnesses</u>.

Laws Protecting Working People

Here's <u>Part Two of the National Insurance Act</u>, and a couple of other Liberal laws to help <u>workers</u>.

Part Two set up Unemployment Benefit for a few trades

<u>Part Two</u> of the National Insurance Act provided <u>unemployment benefit</u> for workers in <u>shipbuilding</u>, <u>iron founding</u> and <u>construction</u>. These were industries where workers were quite <u>regularly</u> out of work for <u>several weeks</u> at a time.

It was a <u>contributory scheme</u>. <u>Employers</u> and <u>employees</u> each paid <u>2½d</u> per week into an <u>unemployment fund</u> and the <u>government</u> paid 1¾d.

In return workers were paid <u>7 shillings</u> per week for up to <u>15 weeks</u> in any one year if they were <u>unemployed</u>. Payment started from the <u>second week</u> of unemployment.

The Trade Boards Act of 1909 set a Minimum Wage

<u>Winston Churchill</u> and <u>William Beveridge</u> put together the <u>Trade Boards Act</u> in <u>1909</u> to help <u>sweated industry</u> workers.

<u>Sweated industries</u> included tailoring, lace-making and cardboard-box making. The workers were often women or foreign immigrants who worked from home doing long hours for low wages.

1) The Act set up <u>trade boards</u> for each of the 'sweated industries'.
2) Every board was made up of <u>equal numbers</u> of workers and employers, and a <u>neutral chairman</u>.
3) The board's job was to decide a <u>minimum wage</u> for the <u>industry</u>.
4) Employers paying <u>less</u> than their trade board laid down could be <u>fined</u>.
5) <u>Factory inspectors</u> made sure the Act was put into practice.

By <u>1914</u> <u>half a million workers</u> were covered by the trade boards and so had the security of a <u>minimum wage</u>.

The Labour Exchanges Act set up Job Centres

Churchill and Beveridge also worked together on the <u>Labour Exchanges Act</u>. This was passed in <u>1909</u> too.

1) <u>Labour exchanges</u> were like job centres. Unemployed workers could go there to find out about <u>job vacancies</u>.
2) Within five years there was a network right <u>across Britain</u>.
3) <u>One million jobs</u> a year were filled through the exchanges.

The Labour Exchange Act — perfect for swapping jobs...

There's a lot of <u>nasty fiddly detail</u> here — <u>don't panic</u> if you can't remember it all. The <u>easiest way</u> to learn the important bits is by making a timeline of <u>acts</u> and <u>dates</u>. Then make sure you can scribble down the <u>main point</u> of each act — <u>who</u> it was meant to help, and <u>what</u> they got.

Effects of the Liberal Reforms

The Liberals' reforms wouldn't do much good if they couldn't <u>pay</u> for them. They had to get the money through <u>taxes</u> — one reason why some people <u>didn't</u> welcome them with <u>open arms</u>.

Lloyd George wanted to Raise Taxes to pay for reforms

In <u>1909</u> the Liberal Chancellor of the Exchequer Lloyd George decided he'd have to <u>raise taxes</u> to pay for the reforms. He proposed the tax increases in the <u>1909</u> budget. It was designed to tax the rich <u>more heavily</u> than the poor — so it became known as <u>the People's Budget</u>.

- <u>Income tax</u> would go up from 5 pence to 6 pence in the pound.
- There'd be a new <u>super tax</u> of 1s. 2d. in the pound on incomes <u>over £3000</u> per year.
- The inheritance tax — called <u>death duties</u> — would go up.
- Tax on <u>tobacco</u> and <u>spirits</u> would go up.

The Liberals had to call a General Election in 1910

To become <u>law</u> the Budget had to be passed by the House of Commons <u>and</u> the House of Lords.

1) Although <u>the Conservatives</u> were <u>opposed</u> to the Budget, the bill got through the <u>Commons</u>. But it was <u>rejected</u> in the House of <u>Lords</u> where Conservatives held the majority.

2) The Liberals <u>couldn't</u> see any way of getting the bill through Parliament. This was a constitutional crisis — the <u>unelected</u> House of Lords was <u>blocking</u> the will of the <u>elected</u> House of Commons.

3) The Liberals called a <u>general election</u> to make sure they had the British people's support. The <u>only issue</u> of the campaign was the People's Budget.

4) The <u>Liberal Party won</u> the election. They reintroduced the Budget and finally it was passed by the <u>Commons and the Lords</u>.

To prevent such crises the <u>Parliament Act</u> was passed in <u>1911</u>. The Lords were <u>no longer</u> allowed to reject <u>bills on financial issues</u>. They could reject other bills <u>twice</u>.

The People's Budget — taxing the rich to pay the poor...

The fact that the Liberals had to call a <u>general election</u> and <u>change the law</u> about the House of Lords shows what a <u>stir</u> they'd caused. Make sure you know <u>why</u> the Parliament Act of 1911 came about.

Effects of the Liberal Reforms

After the Liberals won the 1910 general election, and the People's Budget was passed, they were free to start tackling Britain's poverty — with <u>arguable success</u>.

The **Liberal Reforms** left some problems **Unsolved...**

1) Hardly any of the new schemes were designed to help the <u>whole population</u>.

2) The <u>National Insurance Act</u> Part One <u>didn't</u> cover the worker's <u>family</u>. Part <u>Two</u> only covered a <u>few</u> industries.

3) The reforms <u>didn't</u> replace the old Poor Law. <u>Workhouses</u> weren't abolished until 1930.

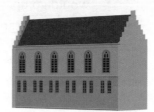

...but **Changed Attitudes** to helping the poor

1) This was the first time that <u>national taxes</u> had been used to help the poor.

2) The state took on <u>responsibility</u> for protecting citizens from <u>extreme hardship</u> in sickness, old age and unemployment for the <u>first time</u>.

3) The schemes were introduced <u>all across the country</u> — they weren't just local affairs.

4) <u>Large numbers</u> of people were covered by some of the schemes — the National Insurance Act Part One covered 10 million workers.

5) The new provisions <u>didn't</u> have the same <u>stigma</u> as the workhouse and because of the new laws fewer people had to rely on the Poor Law system.

6) The number of <u>non-government</u> welfare organisations, e.g. friendly societies, schemes run by churches etc., <u>declined</u>.

The Liberal Reforms really shook things up...

The Reforms were by no means a magical remedy which solved all of Britain's problems — but they did go a <u>long way</u> to changing people's <u>attitudes to poverty</u>. Remember that just a few years earlier the Majority Report from the Royal Commission had recommended leaving the poor to suffer.

Women's Rights in the 1890s

Women in the <u>1890s</u> were treated differently from men. Most women didn't go to school or university, and instead spent their lives raising <u>children</u> and working to <u>run a house</u>.

Women's legal rights **Weren't Equal** — but **Getting Better**

For a long time married women were <u>not protected</u> in law — but several new laws in the 19th century gave them more <u>rights in marriage</u>.

| 1857 | <u>The Matrimonial Clauses Act</u> made it easier for a woman to get a <u>divorce</u> through ordinary law courts. You had to prove your husband had committed <u>adultery</u> and another offence such as <u>cruelty</u> or <u>desertion</u> (leaving you). Before the Act, only <u>Parliament</u> could grant divorces. |

| 1870 | <u>The Married Women's Property Act</u> gave women the right to <u>keep</u> their <u>earnings</u> when they got married. Before the Act it <u>all</u> went to the <u>husband</u> automatically. In <u>1882</u>, a second <u>Married Women's Property Act</u> gave married women the right to keep their <u>property</u> as well. |

| 1886 | <u>The Married Women (Maintenance in Case of Desertion) Act</u> said that a husband who left his wife had to keep <u>paying</u> for her maintenance — i.e. her <u>living expenses</u>.
The <u>Guardianship of Children Act</u> allowed women to be their children's <u>legal guardians</u> if the father died or if the marriage broke up. Being the <u>legal guardian</u> meant having <u>responsibility</u> for any property left to the children as well as seeing they were properly looked after. |

Some **Professions** were **Open to Women**

1) Many working-class women had <u>jobs</u> as well as running the home, e.g. in the <u>textile industry</u>. These jobs tended to be <u>low paid</u> with <u>poor conditions</u>.

2) Middle-class women were less likely to work outside the home. Access to <u>higher education</u> and <u>professional jobs</u> was <u>limited</u>.

3) <u>Queen's College, London</u> was opened to train women <u>teachers</u> in <u>1848</u>.

4) <u>Florence Nightingale</u> established <u>nursing</u> as a respectable job. She set up a <u>training school</u> where women could train to become nurses.

Florence Nightingale

Women's Rights — things could only get better...

Career's advice in the 1890s was pretty straightforward if you were a woman. <u>Teaching</u> and <u>nursing</u> were the two main professions, whilst <u>working-class women</u> tended to work in textile factories as well as raising a family and running the household.

The Campaign for the Vote 1900-1914

The campaign for women's votes wasn't brand new in 1900 — but the campaigns from 1900 to 1914 were more energetic than ever. Some campaigns were peaceful, some weren't...

Women **Couldn't Vote** in national elections

During the 19th century, several reform acts had given more people in Britain the vote — but only men. Most people thought it was perfectly sensible that women didn't have the vote.

1) They thought the public sphere was for men.
   Women should look after the home.

2) Many people believed that women weren't very
   rational and so couldn't make big decisions.

3) Many politicians thought that men needed to be householders
   to get the vote. Only a very few rich women owned houses or
   paid the rent, so it would be a bit odd to give them a vote.

4) If only rich women got the vote they'd probably vote Conservative.
   The Liberals didn't like that idea.

After 1894 married women were allowed to vote for district councils, and to sit on the councils.
But they still couldn't vote in national elections for MPs, or become MPs themselves.

Campaigners for votes for women argued that:

1) Women's rights and opportunities were improving
   — being given the vote was a natural step forward.

2) Women were just as capable as men of making sound decisions.

3) Women had gained the vote in some other countries, e.g. in New Zealand in 1893.

The **Suffragists** were **Moderate** in their protests

1) The suffragists' formal name was the NATIONAL UNION
   OF WOMEN'S SUFFRAGE SOCIETIES (NUWSS).

suffrage = the right to vote

2) They were founded in 1897.
   Their leader was Millicent Fawcett.

3) Their main tactics were persuasion,
   meetings and petitions to Parliament.

You've got to fight for your right — to vote in local elections...

After the four 19th century acts which gave women more legal rights, the next step to equality was
gaining the right to vote — this would give women the chance to affect how Britain was run.
At first most people were against it — list the reasons why people thought women shouldn't vote.

The Campaign for the Vote 1900-1914

The Suffragists had a <u>civilised approach</u> to their campaign,
which some women felt was not getting <u>fast enough results</u>...

The **Suffragettes** were more **Direct**

1) The <u>suffragettes' formal name</u> was the <u>WOMEN'S SOCIAL AND POLITICAL UNION (WSPU)</u>.

2) They were founded by <u>Emmeline Pankhurst</u> in <u>1903</u>, with her daughters <u>Christabel</u> and <u>Sylvia</u>. Emmeline Pankhurst had previously founded the <u>Women's Franchise League (WFL)</u>, which campaigned to get women the vote in <u>local elections</u>.

3) The <u>suffragettes</u> thought the <u>suffragists</u> took things <u>too slowly</u>. They wanted <u>results</u> fast.

4) The suffragettes <u>didn't mind</u> getting <u>arrested</u>. It attracted <u>some sympathy</u> and showed they were <u>serious</u>. In <u>1905</u> Christabel Pankhurst and Annie Kenney heckled Sir Edward Grey, who was speaking at a meeting in Manchester, and ended up <u>in prison</u> for a <u>week</u>.

5) They hoped the Liberal government after <u>1906</u> would be <u>sympathetic</u>. They were encouraged by the <u>1907</u> <u>Qualification of Women Act</u> which let women become county and borough councillors, or mayors. However, in 1908, Asquith, a Liberal, became Prime Minister — he was <u>against</u> votes for women.

After **1912** the protests got **More Extreme**

By <u>1912</u> the Liberal government had accepted the idea of some women voting, and tried to put it into their <u>Plural Voting Bill</u> for Parliament to discuss. But the Speaker <u>refused</u> to let them add it. The suffragettes were furious and protests got far <u>more extreme</u> and violent.

1) Suffragettes <u>chained themselves to railings</u> outside Downing Street and Buckingham Palace.

2) They <u>physically assaulted politicians</u>. The Prime Minister, Asquith, was attacked on a golf course. Suffragettes tried to tear off his clothes, and beat him with dog whips.

3) They <u>destroyed paintings</u> in the National Gallery, and smashed shop windows.

4) Suffragettes <u>made arson attacks</u> on post boxes, churches and railway stations. In 1913, they even <u>bombed</u> the house of Lloyd George, who was <u>fairly sympathetic</u> to votes for women.

5) At the <u>1913</u> Derby at Epsom, a suffragette called <u>Emily Davison</u> threw herself under the feet of the King's horse. She <u>died</u> of her injuries.

<u>Suffragists</u> thought these tactics <u>held</u> the campaign <u>back</u>. The government didn't want to be <u>seen</u> to be <u>giving in</u> to violence. The violence also <u>put off</u> many <u>moderate</u> supporters.

The **Government** dealt with the protests **Harshly**

1) They sent many suffragettes to <u>prison</u>. The suffragettes often went on <u>hunger strike</u>, so the prison authorities force-fed them, but this was <u>dangerous</u> and <u>violent</u>.

2) The so-called "Cat and Mouse" Act was passed in <u>1913</u>. Under this act the authorities could <u>release</u> hunger strikers then <u>rearrest them</u> when they were fit again.

Women's suffrage — I get the -gist...

Try not to get <u>suffragettes</u> and <u>suffragists</u> mixed up. Watch out for questions on whether protests helped win the vote — you'll need to write about all the <u>types</u> of protest, and what <u>effect</u> they had.

The Start of World War One

For <u>Britain</u> the First World War began with the British Expeditionary Force (BEF) going over to Europe to fight the Germans. British people were <u>keen</u> to join up and fight in the war. Nobody imagined it was going to last <u>four years</u>, or take the lives of <u>3 million</u> Allied soldiers.

Britain **Declared War** on Germany on **4 August 1914**

1) <u>Britain</u> was allied to <u>France</u> and <u>Russia</u> by an agreement called the <u>Triple Entente</u>.

2) <u>Germany</u> was allied to the <u>Austro-Hungarian Empire</u> and <u>Italy</u> by an agreement called the <u>Triple Alliance</u>.

3) The Austro-Hungarian Archduke Ferdinand was <u>assassinated</u> by Serbs, in the Bosnian capital Sarajevo on <u>28 June</u>. Austria-Hungary declared <u>war</u> on Serbia. <u>Russia</u> agreed to help Serbia. <u>Germany</u> declared war on <u>Russia</u>, then on Russia's ally <u>France</u>.

4) Germany already had a strategy for invading France — it was called the <u>Schlieffen Plan</u>.

5) The plan was to push down through <u>Belgium</u> and then <u>capture Paris</u>. According to the Schlieffen Plan the Germans should be able to take control of France within <u>weeks</u>.

6) But Belgium was a <u>neutral</u> country — <u>Britain stepped in</u> to help them and declared war on <u>4 August</u>.

Britain sent the **BEF** to help **France** and **Belgium**

1) The BEF sent <u>4 divisions</u> of troops to France. The French Army in the field had <u>70 divisions</u>.

2) The BEF commander was <u>Sir John French</u>.

3) The British and French <u>aim</u> was to stop the Germans from invading or <u>capturing</u> France.

4) The BEF and the French didn't manage to <u>stop</u> the Germans in Belgium, or to stop them <u>invading</u> France.

5) But once the Germans were <u>in France</u>, the BEF and the French fought <u>three major battles</u> at Mons, the river Marne and Ypres (it's pronounced a bit like EEPr), which brought the Germans to a standstill.

The German First Army met British forces at <u>Mons</u> on <u>23 August 1914</u>. The Germans were flummoxed because they <u>didn't expect</u> to see British soldiers. The <u>small</u> British force beat them back — but it wasn't a <u>lasting victory</u> as the French army <u>retreated</u> and the British had to <u>follow</u>.

The Germans needed to cross the <u>Marne</u> to get to Paris. In <u>September 1914</u>, the French managed to beat them <u>back</u> as far as the river <u>Aisne</u>. They were <u>supported</u> by the BEF. The Germans dug <u>trenches</u> to defend their position. It became <u>clear</u> that the war was going to last <u>longer</u> than a few weeks.

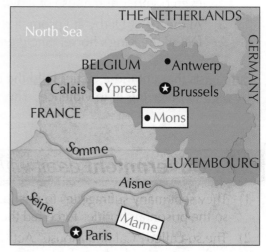

The Germans tried to <u>outflank</u> the Allies by advancing west towards the sea. The Allies tried to <u>block them off</u> — this was known as the '<u>race to the sea</u>'. The armies met at <u>Ypres</u> — they fought through October and November 1914. There were <u>terrible casualties</u>. Half the BEF were wounded and around <u>75 000 were killed</u>.

The ultimate lottery — your country needs you...

Get the <u>order of events</u> in <u>1914</u> clear. Remember — the <u>BEF</u> went to help <u>Belgium</u> and <u>France</u>. <u>Write down</u> what happened at Mons, Marne and Ypres from <u>August</u> to <u>November 1914</u>. Learn it.

Trench Warfare

One of the big reasons why the war was so terrible was the development of <u>trench warfare</u>.

After Ypres the British Army needed More Men

1) <u>Kitchener</u>, the Secretary for War, wanted <u>conscription</u> but <u>Asquith</u>, the Prime Minister, <u>refused</u>.

2) <u>Instead</u> of conscription there was a massive <u>poster campaign</u>, e.g. "<u>Your Country Needs You</u>".

3) By <u>September 1914</u> there were <u>half a million volunteers</u>. Another <u>half million</u> joined by <u>February 1915</u>.

Trench Warfare created Deadlock

1) The generals in charge, including <u>Sir John French</u>, weren't used to <u>this type</u> of fighting. They knew more about the type of battles where everyone met up on a <u>big field</u>, then the cavalry <u>charged in</u>, followed by <u>footsoldiers</u> and backed up with <u>artillery</u>.

2) After the <u>Marne</u> and <u>Ypres</u>, neither side could drive the other back. Both armies <u>dug trenches</u>. By the <u>end of 1914</u> the trenches stretched from the <u>Alps</u> to the <u>North Sea</u>. This line of trenches was called the <u>Western Front</u>.

3) The trenches were <u>easy</u> to <u>defend</u>...

- <u>machine guns</u> mowed down attacks
- <u>heavy guns</u> were behind the trenches
- <u>guards</u> spotted attacks from the other side
- <u>trenches</u> led back from the front line to bring in <u>men</u> and <u>supplies</u>
- trenches were protected by <u>barbed wire</u>

...and <u>difficult</u> to <u>attack</u>.

- artillery was meant to <u>break through</u> the enemy's barbed wire and wear them down to make attacks easier — in practice it just <u>warned</u> the other side an attack was coming
- the land between the trenches was often knee-deep or even waist-deep in mud

4) Even <u>if</u> you made it to the enemy trench in one place, it was hard to <u>hang on</u> to your position because you were <u>surrounded</u> by the enemy's forces in the rest of the trench.

The trenches were a new and unpleasant way to fight...

The battles of 1914 left the British Army desperate for more men to fight in the trenches. Make sure you <u>learn</u> the <u>lists of points</u> about attacking and defending the trenches.

Trench Warfare

Trench warfare was a <u>new type</u> of fighting...

*Life in the trenches was **Hard** and **Dangerous***

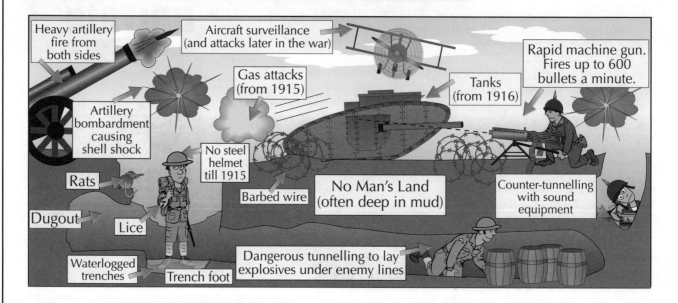

Heavy artillery fire from both sides

Aircraft surveillance (and attacks later in the war)

Rapid machine gun. Fires up to 600 bullets a minute.

Gas attacks (from 1915)

Tanks (from 1916)

Artillery bombardment causing shell shock

No steel helmet till 1915

Rats

No Man's Land (often deep in mud)

Counter-tunnelling with sound equipment

Barbed wire

Dugout

Lice

Dangerous tunnelling to lay explosives under enemy lines

Waterlogged trenches

Trench foot

Each man got paid <u>one shilling</u> a day.

The main rations were <u>bully beef</u> (also called corned beef), <u>jam</u> and <u>tea</u>.

Thousands of lives were lost for **Small Gains**

1) Both sides had plenty of <u>men</u> and plenty of <u>money</u> for ammunition and weapons, so the generals kept sending more and more men '<u>over the top</u>' — even though it didn't achieve any <u>obvious</u> success.

2) The major battles in <u>1915</u> were <u>Neuve Chapelle</u>, <u>Loos</u> and the <u>2nd Battle of Ypres</u>. Thousands of lives were lost but neither side <u>gained</u> much from the battles — the front line <u>hardly moved</u> at all.

3) Sir John French was <u>replaced</u> as commander by <u>Sir Douglas Haig</u>.

Trench warfare — wearing the other side down...

You definitely need to know what the trenches were <u>like</u>. The picture will help you.
Throughout 1915 neither side made much <u>progress</u>, despite thousands of soldiers losing their lives.

New Weapons

New weapons were used in the First World War. Not surprisingly they made a <u>massive difference</u> to the way wars were fought. That's what you've got to learn about.

Aircraft were Developed throughout the war

1) On the Western Front <u>both sides</u> used <u>planes and balloons</u> to find <u>enemy weak points</u> to attack.

2) <u>The Germans</u> used airships called <u>Zeppelins</u> to carry out bombing raids like the <u>May 1915</u> one on London.

3) In <u>1915</u> new planes carried <u>synchronised</u> machine guns which <u>wouldn't</u> shoot the propeller. <u>One man</u> could fly <u>and</u> handle the gun — where before they'd needed <u>two people</u>. Fighter planes <u>escorted bombers</u> on raids, <u>attacked</u> enemy bombers, and <u>fought each other</u>, especially on the Western Front.

4) Both sides developed <u>planes</u> for <u>long-distance</u> bombing raids. The first serious raid on Britain was in <u>May 1917</u> — 71 people were killed at <u>Folkestone</u>. Britain sent bombers into <u>Germany</u> too.

Tanks made it easier to attack on the Ground

The <u>tracks</u> on tanks meant they could go over very <u>rough ground</u>, and plough through <u>barbed wire</u> without problems. The <u>heavily armoured</u> body of the tanks meant ordinary gunfire couldn't stop them. Tanks <u>should</u> have allowed the British army to break the deadlock on the trenches, but it took a while to develop effective tactics, and the early tanks often broke down.

1) The first time tanks were used was at the <u>Battle of the Somme</u> in <u>July 1916</u>. Sir Douglas Haig sent in <u>49 tanks</u>. He could have waited for more, but he decided it was more important to <u>surprise</u> the Germans, and went ahead anyway. The tank division captured <u>2 km</u> of German-held territory but <u>couldn't</u> hold on to it.

2) At <u>Cambrai</u> on the Western Front in <u>November 1917</u>, tanks were used more successfully. Nearly <u>500</u> tanks advanced about <u>6 km</u> into German territory, but <u>again</u> couldn't hold on to their gains.

Poison Gas was a deadly weapon

1) The Germans were the first to use <u>chlorine</u> gas — in the <u>Second Battle of Ypres</u>, <u>April-May 1915</u>. It caused <u>terror</u>, and killed many. The British tried it at the <u>Battle of Loos</u> (<u>September 1915</u>), but the wind blew some of it back on them. Chlorine has the military disadvantage of being <u>highly visible</u>.

2) In <u>December 1915</u> the Germans tried <u>phosgene</u>, which is <u>invisible</u> and <u>deadly</u> but <u>slow-acting</u>. At the battle of Riga, in <u>September 1917</u>, they introduced <u>mustard gas</u>, which causes horrible <u>blisters</u> and <u>internal bleeding</u>.

3) Gas became a standard weapon used by both sides, not a <u>war-winning weapon</u>. Countermeasures like <u>masks</u>, <u>pads</u> and <u>gas helmets</u> meant few British battle losses were due to gas.

The Creeping Barrage became a standard tactic in 1916

1) First used on a large scale by the British at the <u>Battle of the Somme</u> (<u>July-November 1916</u>), the creeping barrage was an <u>advancing curtain of artillery fire</u> preceding the <u>advancing infantry</u>.

2) It was a <u>difficult and dangerous</u> tactic because it depended on precise timing. When the barrage outpaced the infantry, the gap between them allowed the Germans to re-emerge from shelter and man their positions. But when the infantry <u>moved too fast</u>, they ran into their <u>own shellfire</u>.

New technology — it changed warfare for ever...

The development of <u>aeroplanes</u> and <u>tanks</u> as <u>weapons</u> was one of the most important <u>long-term effects</u> of the First World War. Draw a <u>timeline</u> for each weapon, giving <u>dates</u> for the main events.

The Western Front

The Battle of the Somme was a major attack by the British army against the German line.
It led to a <u>staggering loss of life</u> — and had a <u>long-term effect</u> on how the war was <u>remembered</u>.

The **Battle of the Somme** killed *1 million men*

In <u>February 1916</u>, the Germans began an attack on Allied forces around <u>Verdun</u>.
If they captured Verdun, <u>Paris</u> would be open to attack.

By <u>July</u>, 700 000 men were dead. In order to <u>relieve the pressure</u> on Verdun, Haig decided on a <u>major attack</u>.

1) This was the <u>Battle of the Somme</u>. It began on <u>1 July 1916</u>.
2) After a massive <u>artillery bombardment</u>, the soldiers were sent 'over the top' to charge the German trenches.
3) British soldiers were under orders to advance <u>slowly</u>, not run.
4) This gave the Germans time to get ready. The slow-moving British soldiers were an <u>easy target</u>.
5) 57 000 Britons were <u>killed</u> or <u>wounded</u> on the first day alone. 21 000 died in <u>1 hour</u>.
6) The battle dragged on to <u>November</u>. By then over <u>one million</u> soldiers had died.

The Battle of the Somme had **Mixed Results**

1) Despite <u>months of fighting</u> and all the <u>deaths</u>, very little ground was <u>gained</u>. In <u>some places</u> the Allied forces advanced about <u>6 kilometres</u>, in <u>others</u> it was only a <u>few hundred metres</u>.
2) The Germans <u>weren't beaten</u> at the Somme, but they took a <u>severe battering</u>. The battle probably helped to <u>wear them down</u>. This was what Haig wanted — a "<u>war of attrition</u>".
3) Many men in the army were <u>appalled</u> at how many lives were lost. They felt the generals' tactics were <u>wrong</u> — and some started to <u>lose confidence</u> in the officers commanding the war.
4) There was less confidence in the <u>artillery</u> too. They were supposed to <u>destroy</u> the German <u>barbed wire</u> before the attack and didn't manage to do it.

People still **Disagree** on whether the **Tactics** were right

Many people <u>nowadays</u> feel that the tactics used at the Somme and in other battles were <u>wrong</u>. Their <u>picture</u> of the First World War comes from <u>TV, books and films</u> — which often see Haig as a "Butcher". But in fact, it's much <u>more complicated</u> than that. Here are some of the <u>main opinions</u> on <u>both sides</u>:

AGAINST	FOR
• Hundreds of thousands of men were killed under Haig's command.	• Haig's overall strategy was to wear the Germans down, whatever the cost. It's every general's job to win wars, not to save lives.
• Haig could have waited for more tanks, which might have saved many lives.	• Haig couldn't wait for more tanks — he had to relieve the pressure on Verdun, or the whole war might have been lost. He used the tanks he had.
• Once he saw the first day's slaughter he could have changed his tactics.	• By 1918, Haig had learnt to adapt these attacking tactics so that they became highly successful.

The Somme — be sure to give both sides of the story...

The Somme was a <u>disaster</u> — but some people argue it was <u>necessary</u>. If you're going to write about it, you have to give <u>both sides</u> of the argument. Don't miss out the actual <u>facts</u> though.

The War at Home

When the First World War broke out the government had to be sure Britain was <u>ready</u> to cope. They gave themselves <u>special powers</u> by... surprise... getting Parliament to pass a <u>law</u>.

Parliament passed the Defence of the Realm Act

The <u>Defence of the Realm Act</u> (DORA) was passed in <u>August 1914</u>, right at the start of the war. There were <u>two</u> basic things the government was trying to do:

> 1) Make sure the country had <u>enough resources</u> to fight the war.
> 2) Make sure <u>British people</u> were in a <u>fit state</u> to fight and support the war effort.

The law <u>allowed</u> the government to...

- take control of <u>vital industries</u> like coal mining
- take over <u>2.5 million acres of land</u> and <u>buildings</u>
- bring in <u>British Summer Time</u> for more daylight (working) hours
- control <u>drinking hours</u> and the <u>strength of alcohol</u>

- introduce <u>conscription</u>
- <u>stop people talking</u> about the war or spreading rumours
- <u>censor</u> newspapers
- enforce <u>rationing</u>

Thousands Volunteered to fight — but it Wasn't Enough

When war broke out, thousands of men <u>rushed</u> to volunteer for the fighting. They believed the war would be over <u>quickly</u> — 'by Christmas'. They thought it was going to be an <u>adventure</u>, and wanted to be <u>part of it</u>. The enthusiasm <u>didn't last</u>.

By <u>1915</u> the number of <u>casualties</u> was going <u>up</u> — and the number of <u>volunteers</u> was slowing <u>down</u>. On the <u>Western Front</u> so many men were being killed and wounded that there <u>weren't enough</u> volunteers to <u>replace</u> them.

There was also a growing feeling <u>in Britain</u> that it <u>wasn't fair</u> that some men were <u>avoiding</u> military duty.

The Government introduced Conscription in 1916

1) All <u>single men</u> aged between <u>18 and 40</u> had to fight.
2) When there <u>still</u> weren't enough soldiers <u>married men</u> had to join up too.
3) People who didn't <u>believe</u> in fighting were called <u>conscientious objectors</u>. They were treated as <u>criminals</u> and sent to <u>prison</u>. They were seen as <u>traitors</u> because they refused to fight. Some were members of groups like the Quakers, who had <u>religious objections</u> to fighting. Many agreed to carry out non-violent war work, such as driving ambulances.

Women started doing "men's jobs"

I wonder what she's doing now...

I wonder what he's doing now...

Many of the <u>original volunteers</u> came from <u>heavy industries</u> like coal mining. There was a <u>shortage</u> of workers in these industries and without them Britain couldn't <u>supply the army</u>. When <u>conscription</u> started there were even <u>fewer men</u> available to do the <u>vital jobs</u>. <u>Women</u> started taking their places in the <u>pits</u> and <u>factories</u>.

Surviving at home — major changes were needed...

You've <u>got</u> to know all about the <u>Defence of the Realm Act</u>, and <u>conscription</u> — scribble and learn.

Food Shortages

Britain had problems keeping <u>food supplies</u> going in the war. Something needed to be done to make sure nobody starved. The important thing is to learn <u>all three</u> of Lloyd George's tactics.

German U-boats made it hard to Import Food

1) In <u>1914</u> Britain was used to <u>importing</u> quite a lot of food from the <u>United States</u> and countries that were part of the <u>Empire</u>.

2) Germany used <u>U-boats</u> (submarines) to <u>attack shipping</u> all round Britain and made it <u>impossible</u> to import all the food Britain needed to survive.

3) By <u>April 1917</u> Britain only had <u>six weeks'</u> supply of wheat. The Prime Minister, David Lloyd George, took <u>three big steps</u> to solve the food crisis:

1) Navy Convoys protected Merchant Ships

1) Ships travelling <u>alone</u> were <u>easy targets</u> for the U-boats. <u>25%</u> of merchant ships coming into Britain were being <u>sunk</u>.

2) The Navy began a <u>convoy system</u>.   Merchant ships travelled in <u>groups</u> with an escort of <u>Royal Navy</u> ships to protect them.

3) U-boats <u>couldn't attack</u> as easily. With the convoy system <u>less than 1%</u> of ships were sunk.

2) Compulsory Rationing started in 1918

When food rationing started in <u>1917</u> it was <u>voluntary</u>. In <u>1918</u> shortages were still a problem and rationing was made <u>compulsory</u> for <u>beer, butter, sugar</u> and <u>meat</u>.

1) Everyone got <u>rationing coupons</u>. They had to <u>hand them over</u> when they bought <u>beer, butter, sugar</u> and <u>meat</u>. When the week's coupons for, say, <u>sugar</u> ran out, they couldn't buy any more that week.

2) Some people <u>hoarded</u> food, partly because they were afraid it would <u>run out</u>, and partly because of <u>increasing prices</u>. They would sell it on <u>later</u>, creating a '<u>black market</u>' in food.

3) There were <u>shortages</u> of some kinds of food, but <u>no one</u> starved.

4) The government had never been <u>this involved</u> in organising people's daily lives before.

3) Britain Grew more food

1) Farmers were encouraged to use <u>more</u> of their land so they could <u>grow more food</u>.

2) The <u>Women's Land Army</u> was set up in 1917. Women from the Land Army were a <u>big</u> new labour force available to work on the <u>farms</u>.

Food supply — crucial to avoiding a crisis...

How Lloyd George <u>avoided</u> a <u>food supply crisis</u> isn't the most exciting topic in this section — but you've definitely got to know about the three steps he took: <u>convoys</u>, <u>rationing</u> and <u>production</u>.

Attitudes to the War in Britain

There's a <u>dramatic difference</u> between people's <u>cheerful</u> attitude at the beginning of the war and their <u>horror</u> at the waste of life by the end. Make sure you know why attitudes <u>changed</u> so much.

At the *Start* the war looked like an *Adventure*

In <u>1914</u> there was <u>huge enthusiasm</u> for the war. It seems <u>strange</u> now, but nobody at the time <u>knew</u> what it was going to be like. These are <u>some of the things</u> people felt about the war:

Fighting in the war would be an adventure.	It was right to fight for your country when it went to war.	The war would be "over by Christmas". Britain would win easily.

Obviously not <u>everybody</u> thought exactly like this — but a fair few <u>did</u>.

At first people *Didn't Really Know* what was going on

The government <u>deliberately</u> kept people <u>ignorant</u> of what was going on:

1) <u>Letters</u> from soldiers were <u>censored</u>.

2) Reporters <u>weren't allowed</u> to see battles very often.

3) <u>Newspapers</u> were <u>censored</u> from <u>1914</u>.

4) <u>No photographs</u> could be taken which showed <u>dead</u> soldiers.

5) Casualty figures <u>weren't available</u> from the government.

Britain had <u>never</u> before been involved in a war where most of the fighting was done in <u>trenches</u>, or one in which so many people were <u>killed</u>. People away from the front couldn't imagine how <u>terrible</u> the war was.

During the war ordinary people's *Attitudes Changed*

The government <u>couldn't</u> keep the facts about the war <u>secret</u> for ever.
As the war carried on people couldn't help <u>finding out more</u>, and attitudes began to <u>change</u>.

1) During the war <u>1500 civilians</u> were killed in <u>bombing raids</u>. This was a new and <u>terrible danger</u>.

2) There were no <u>obvious</u> successes on the Western Front up until <u>1918</u>.

3) The government could hide the overall <u>casualty figures</u>, but they couldn't hide <u>crippled</u> and <u>blinded</u> veterans who <u>returned</u> to Britain, or keep <u>deaths</u> secret from the <u>families</u> of soldiers.

4) <u>Rationing</u> was difficult, and richer people felt it was a <u>hardship</u>. <u>Taxes</u> had <u>increased</u> to pay for the war. By 1917 most people in Britain were sick of the war, and wanted to see it end.

Britain used *Propaganda* to encourage people to fight

1) <u>Propaganda posters</u> were used to encourage men to sign up — such as the famous poster of Lord Kitchener with the caption "<u>Your Country Needs You</u>".

2) Some propaganda was aimed <u>abroad</u> — in particular to encourage <u>US military involvement</u>.

3) In <u>September 1914</u> the newly formed <u>War Propaganda Bureau</u> asked 25 of Britain's leading writers to aid the war effort. They produced pamphlets such as the <u>Report on Alleged German Outrages</u> (1915), which included shocking accusations of <u>German crimes</u>.

4) The <u>Ministry of Information</u> produced <u>propaganda films</u>, but it's not clear how much public support they generated. The propaganda film *The Battle of the Somme* (<u>1916</u>), made by The British Topical Committee, was so <u>realistic</u>, it could have been seen as anti-war.

5) In <u>June 1917</u>, the government set up a <u>National War Aims Committee</u> to issue propaganda literature and sponsor speeches to improve morale.

Have a propaganda at this...

This page is about people's <u>opinions</u> and <u>attitudes</u> about what happened, as well as the basic facts. Scribble a list of the main reasons why attitudes to the war <u>changed</u> between 1914 and 1917.

The End of the War

The war changed everybody's lives, whether they'd been away <u>fighting</u> or stayed at home. It wasn't easy to get used to <u>normal life</u> again — especially for the soldiers.

The war *Finally Ended* in *November 1918*

1) The USA joined the Allies in <u>April 1917</u> — but at first only sent <u>one division</u>.

2) More Americans were sent during <u>1918</u>. The German commander <u>Ludendorff</u> decided to try <u>one more</u> big attack <u>before</u> there were so many Allied troops that a German victory would be impossible.

3) The Ludendorff Offensive <u>nearly worked</u>, thanks to <u>new tactics</u> in trench warfare — attacking <u>several points</u> along the line at the <u>same time</u>, with a constant artillery bombardment of the enemy as support.

4) The Allies counter-attacked from different sides. <u>Haig</u> began an attack on the German line near <u>Amiens</u> in France on <u>8 August 1918</u>. Hundreds of tanks were sent in and the Germans were pushed back through France <u>towards Germany</u>. The Allied forces <u>could have</u> pushed right through into Germany, but <u>before</u> that happened an <u>armistice</u> (a sort of ceasefire) was signed.

5) The trench warfare had <u>worn Germany down</u>. <u>Mutinies</u>, <u>food shortages</u> and <u>revolution</u> in Germany made it <u>impossible</u> for them to carry on. They <u>asked for</u> the armistice and it was signed on <u>11 Nov</u>.

The *Peace Treaty* was signed at *Versailles* in *June 1919*

1) The terms of <u>The Treaty of Versailles</u> meant:

- Germany had to return land taken from France, Belgium, Poland and others.
- German colonies in Africa were shared between France and Britain.
- Germany had to pay reparations of £6600 million to compensate the Allies for the cost of the war.

2) The <u>main negotiators</u> at Versailles were <u>Lloyd George</u>, <u>Clemenceau</u> the French Prime Minister, and <u>Woodrow Wilson</u> the US President. The <u>French</u> thought the peace treaty should <u>punish</u> Germany. Lloyd George thought it was important to punish Germany, but <u>not</u> to make them <u>bitter</u>. The US President favoured a more <u>lenient approach</u> — America <u>hadn't been as badly affected</u> by the war.

3) The Versailles Treaty <u>embittered</u> and nearly <u>bankrupted</u> Germany. It would be remembered in the future.

The Versailles Treaty — the roots of another war...
Don't forget the final facts about <u>1918</u> and the Versailles Treaty, as well as the effects of the war.

The End of the War

People in Britain thought there could <u>never</u> be another war as bad as the First World War. The <u>mood</u> in Britain immediately after the war was pretty <u>bleak</u>.

The war was known as "the war to end all wars"

1) The government had tried to <u>control information</u> during the war. Even so, people had found out some <u>real</u> facts about the war. Many now felt that <u>politicians</u> and <u>authority figures</u> couldn't always be <u>trusted</u>.

2) Many people <u>came to believe</u> that the generals had been <u>incompetent</u>, and that they <u>didn't care</u> how many lives were lost. This gave people <u>even more reason</u> to stop trusting people in powerful positions.

3) The <u>public school officers</u> in the trenches turned out to be no more competent than the <u>working class soldiers</u>. Some people began to <u>question</u> the way the upper classes dominated society.

4) Soldiers who'd been through the war were even more <u>disillusioned</u> when they returned home. There was <u>unemployment</u> and <u>poverty</u>. They wondered what they had been <u>fighting for</u>.

5) <u>No war</u> in European history had produced so many <u>casualties</u>. It felt as though the loss of <u>huge numbers</u> of young men had changed the <u>balance of society</u>.

6) Many people in Britain were <u>very angry</u> with Germany — they wanted <u>revenge</u>. Because of this many British people <u>supported</u> the harshness of the <u>Versailles Treaty</u>.

There were some Positive Outcomes of the war too

Even though people had many reasons to be <u>disappointed</u> there <u>was</u> a sense of satisfaction that Britain had won.

Attitudes towards <u>women</u> and the <u>poorer</u> members of society generally improved, as the war showed <u>everyone</u> could do something useful if they were given the opportunity.

<u>Lloyd George</u> got <u>re-elected</u> as Prime Minister in <u>December 1918</u>.

The First World War changed people's attitudes in Britain...

Although the Allies <u>won the war</u>, many British people felt in <u>no mood to celebrate</u> — they had lost loved ones, had to endure poverty and hardship, and had been lied to by the government.

Women and the Vote 1914-1928

After the First World War there was a different attitude to the suffrage movement. Partly, the war had made the suffragette violence of 1913 and 1914 seem a bit less serious (p. 201). But there were other reasons too — especially the work women had done for the war effort.

During the war Women did "Men's Jobs"

1) So many men were away fighting in the war that there weren't enough to do vital jobs. The jobs were opened up to women — women were happy to take them, and they proved that they could do them just as well as men.

2) Women worked as: bus conductors, drivers, postal workers, farm labourers and coal deliverers. All these vital jobs kept the country going.

3) They also worked in the munitions factories, and engineering workshops. This work was technical, and directly related to the war effort.

4) Women joined women's branches of the armed forces, and worked as nurses in military hospitals.

By doing work that helped Britain win the war, women proved they were important to public life as well as home life. There was also gratitude towards women for their contribution.

The Other Reasons for giving women the vote were...

1) A shake-up of the voting system was already happening. There was a rule that a man could only vote after living at the same address for 1 year. This needed to be changed to allow soldiers who had been away fighting to vote. If the voting system was going to be changed anyway, it was a chance to include women.

2) People's attitudes to women had changed — and not just because of the war. A lot of people remembered the suffragettes' protests and felt it was unfair that women had been denied full political rights.

3) The suffragettes had called off their campaign at the beginning of the war. Nobody wanted them starting it up again.

Women 30+ got the vote in 1918

1) The Representation of the People Act became law in 1918.

2) Not all women got the vote. The ones who did had to be:

over 30 and a householder	OR	married to a householder

The same act gave all men over 21 the right to vote.

3) Women were also able to become MPs. Constance Markiewicz, a Sinn Fein candidate, was elected in 1918 but didn't take up her seat. The first woman to actually become an MP was Nancy Astor, who got elected in 1919.

4) The vote didn't go to all women over 21 until 1928, when women finally got equal voting rights.

Votes for women — a giant leap for womankind...

The 1918 Representation of the People Act is a big landmark — make sure you know exactly which women got the vote. But just as important, scribble a list of the main reasons why they got it.

Build-up to the General Strike 1918-1926

As women were gaining influence, so were the trade unions — especially after the First World War. They became much more active in trying to get better pay and conditions by holding strikes.

Unions were in a Strong Position after the war

During the First World War (1914–1918), the unions cooperated with the government. Between 1914 and 1918, there were hardly any strikes. Wages in industry were good. Membership of many unions went up. High wages and membership strengthened the unions. After the war there was less pressure to avoid strikes — and disputes over pay began again.

1) The police and railway workers held successful strikes in 1918 and 1919.
2) Total union membership in 1920 was 8.3 million.
3) Two new unions were founded — the Amalgamated Engineering Union in 1920, and the Transport and General Workers' Union in 1921. Both became extremely large and powerful.

There was trouble in the Coal Industry...

During the 1920s there were constant disputes between the coal miners and mine owners, over pay and the length of the working day. These disputes eventually led to the General Strike.

1) During the First World War the coal industry was nationalised — the government took over ownership and control of the mines.
2) In 1919 a Royal Commission was appointed to decide whether to return the mines to private ownership. The Commission recommended that the government should keep the mines. Lloyd George's coalition government wasn't keen and privatised them in 1921.
3) People were beginning to use gas, oil and electricity more than coal. Also mines in Germany and Poland were using efficient modern machinery, which produced more coal more quickly and cheaply. Customers couldn't afford British coal, and the mines became less and less profitable.

...which led to a Strike in the Coal Industry

1) The new private mine owners announced a cut in wages and longer working hours for the miners. The miners refused to accept this and went on strike. Neither side was willing to negotiate.
2) The miners' union was in a triple alliance with the transport workers and railwaymen. When they went on strike they asked for support from these allies. The transport workers and railwaymen thought the miners should have tried harder to negotiate, and refused to join in with the strike on 15th April 1921. This day became known as 'Black Friday'.
3) The strike was a failure — eventually they had to go back to work and accept worse conditions.
4) In 1925 coal sales dropped off. Mine owners announced more wage cuts and longer hours.
5) The miners began negotiations, backed by the Trades Union Congress — a federation of all the unions.
6) On 'Red Friday' in July 1925, the government agreed to pay a subsidy to keep miners' wages at the same level. The subsidy would be paid for nine months.
7) At the same time a Royal Commission — the Samuel Commission — looked into what could be done to sort out the dispute. The Samuel Commission reported in March 1926.

It all started with the miners...

There's a lot here for you to digest — you'll definitely need to know why the coal industry was doing badly and what year the Samuel Commission was appointed.

The General Strike 1926

The General Strike was one of the biggest showdowns between the people and the government in 20th century Britain.

The Samuel Report was Fair but Nobody Liked It

The Samuel Commission said mine owners should reorganise their businesses and introduce modern machinery. That way the mines would be more efficient and profitable. There would be no need to cut wages and increase hours. This suited the miners but not the mine owners.

The Commission also said the subsidy should stop. Miners would have to take a temporary pay cut until the owners had reorganised the mines. The miners weren't pleased with this.

The General Strike began when the Subsidy Ended

1) Neither side accepted the Samuel Report. The mine owners said they would cut wages on 30 April. The miners said they'd strike on 1 May. The owners locked out the workers on 30 April — starting a strike.

2) The Trades Union Congress (TUC) felt that if the miners' wages were reduced, then those of other workers would soon follow. They threatened a strike of all key workers — a general strike — starting on 3 May.

3) Negotiations between the TUC and the government began on 2 May.

4) But the Prime Minister, Stanley Baldwin, pulled out of the negotiations.

The strikers Couldn't Close the Country Down

Thousands of workers joined in with the strike. There were workers from mining, transport, the railways, construction, shipbuilding, printing, electricity and the steel industry.

1) The printers' strike closed down ordinary newspapers, but the TUC and the government each produced their own. The government paper was called the British Gazette, edited by Winston Churchill. It described the strike as violent, disorganised and an attack on the British constitution. The TUC's paper, the British Worker, emphasised the solidarity of the strike, and said the strike was an industrial issue, not an attack on the government. It also attacked Churchill.

2) 100 000 people volunteered for the Organisation for the Maintenance of Supplies. They were mainly students and middle-class men. They kept the buses, trains and London Underground moving.

3) Food supplies were transported in armoured convoys escorted by special constables. In London, Hyde Park was used as a centre for distributing milk. There were no shortages because of the strike.

4) Although the government expected violence, it wasn't that bad. Some buses were attacked in London, and there was minor crowd trouble in Nottingham, Leeds, Edinburgh, Glasgow and Aberdeen.

The government refused to negotiate, but offered a peace plan drawn up by Sir Herbert Samuel. The TUC called off the strike on 12 May, and everyone except the miners gave up. The Prime Minister, Stanley Baldwin, said the end of the strike was "a victory for common sense".

1926 — a striking year in history...

Don't forget that the Russian Revolution was less than a decade old at the time — so talk of a general strike made a lot of people worried there might be a revolution.

Effects of the General Strike

The General Strike is a bit of an odd event — observers from Russia hoped there would be a communist revolution, but couldn't believe how peaceful it was. But it had major effects long-term.

The General Strike Didn't Last Long

The General Strike lasted just nine days before the TUC gave in.
There were several reasons:

1) The government refused to negotiate. They saw the strike as a test of their strength. The TUC realised that the government was never going to back down, so there was no point in carrying on.

2) The government's reaction was so strong that there was a danger of violence if the strike continued — amongst others, Churchill had said "we are at war", and called for armoured cars to protect food convoys.

3) The TUC wasn't keen on the idea of a strike, and weren't well enough organised.

4) The National Sailors' Union and the Firemen's Union didn't want to strike. They went to the High Court to prove they didn't have to. The court said the strike was illegal.

5) Some unions didn't have enough cash to fund their members for long, and the banks wouldn't give them overdrafts. The TUC had already spent £4m out of their strike fund of £12.5m.

6) The TUC thought it would be better to have a definite end to the strike than for it to fizzle out.

7) There were rumours that the government was going to arrest the leaders of the TUC.

8) The Labour Party didn't support the strike — its leader worried it would lose them votes.

The Strike's failure was a Blow to the Unions

1) The miners stayed out on strike for another six months. When they finally gave in and went back to work they had to accept lower wages and longer hours. The strike hadn't really improved anything.

2) The Trades Disputes and Trade Union Act was passed in 1927. The Act made it illegal for a union to join a general strike or a sympathy strike (one where you go on strike to support workers from a different union).

3) The strike cost the TUC about £4 million. Without funds they weren't in a position to threaten new strikes. Membership dropped to about 3.25 million by 1933, so the unions had less income.

4) There was also a general blow to morale. The unions lost confidence and there were very few strikes in the 1930s.

5) But many workers began to realise that the Labour Party was their best hope of changing the system — and in 1929 Labour won the general election.

Learn it in general — and then in detail...

The 1926 General Strike is really important. Scribble a quick date list for these two pages to check you've got all the events straight, then learn the effects of the strike on the unions and Labour.

Revision Summary

Britain in 1928 was a very different place to the Britain of 1890. So many big changes, including a massive, terrible war. Such a big period in British history deserves a big load of practice questions...

1)   What was the name of the institutions run to give the very poor somewhere to live and work?

2)   What are the names of the two men who published reports on poverty in 1889 and 1901?

3)   Which government set up a Royal Commission to look at the Poor Law? What year was it?

4)   How many reports did they write? What were they called?

5)   Who won the general election in 1906?

6)   Name three things children under 16 weren't allowed to do after the Children's Charter in 1908.

7)   What two new ideas did Herbert Samuel come up with to help young offenders?

8)   What was Part One of the National Insurance Act about?

9)   How many people got a minimum wage by 1914?

10)   What was the popular name for Lloyd George's 1909 budget?

11)   Who stopped the 1909 budget from becoming law at the first attempt?

12)   Give two reasons why the Liberal reforms changed attitudes to helping the poor.

13)   Give two possible jobs that a young woman could do in the 1890s.

14)   Give four reasons why some people believed women shouldn't have the vote in the 1890s.

15)   Who were the suffragists? Who was their leader?

16)   Who were the suffragettes? In what ways were they different from the suffragists?

17)   What happened in 1907 to encourage the suffragettes?

18)   What happened in 1912 to make the suffragettes' campaign turn more extreme?

19)   Give four examples of extreme tactics used by the suffragettes.

20)   Who were Britain's allies at the start of the First World War?

21)   What was the Schlieffen Plan? How was it supposed to work?

22)   Give two reasons why trenches were easy to defend, and two reasons why trenches were hard to attack.

23)   Who replaced Sir John French as the British commander in 1915?

24)   Give two things aircraft were used for during the war.

25)   What was the reason for the British attack on the Somme?

26)   Give two reasons why some people say Haig's tactics at the Somme were wrong.

27)   Give two reasons why some people say Haig's tactics at the Somme were right.

28)   Give four things the government was allowed to do by the Defence of the Realm Act 1914.

29)   When was conscription introduced?

30)   What three steps did Lloyd George take to avoid a food supply crisis?

31)   Give three reasons why people's attitudes to the war changed between 1914 and 1918.

32)   Give two of the main points from the Versailles Treaty of 1919.

33)   Give four reasons why some women got the vote after the First World War.

34)   What categories of women got the right to vote in the Representation of the People Act, 1918?

35)   When did women finally get equal voting rights to men? What age did they have to be?

36)   Name the two big new unions set up in 1920 and 1921.

37)   What does "nationalisation" mean?

38)   What did the Royal Commission say the government should do with the coal mines in 1919?

39)   Why did British mines have trouble selling their coal during the 1920s? Give three reasons.

40)   Give three possible reasons why the General Strike didn't last very long.

41)   What sort of strikes were made illegal in the Trades Disputes and Trade Union Act of 1927?

Exam Sources

Study **Sources A to D** below and then answer the questions that follow.

Source A

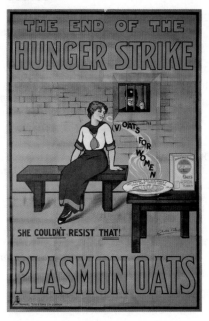

A poster advertising Plasmon Oats, from the early 20th century.

You don't need to answer these questions if you're sitting the AQA exam.

Source B

© Mary Evans Picture Library / Grenville Collins Postcard Collection

A postcard, showing a gardener and baker of the Women's Auxiliary Army Corps during the First World War, circa 1916.

Source C

> Even the outbreak of war could not affect the action of the WSPU, so long as our comrades were in prison and under torture. Since their release, it has been possible to consider what should be the course adopted by the WSPU, in view of the war crisis. It has been decided to save the Union's energies and finances by temporarily suspending our activities.

From the Circular Letter written in August 1914 by Mrs Pankhurst.

Source D

> Jones was found guilty of concealing 480lb of flour, 277lb of sugar, 85lb of bacon and ham, 14lb of split peas, 21 tins of salmon and 221lb of jam and marmalade.
>
> He was fined £600.

Report in a local British newspaper from 1918.

Exam Practice

Changes in British Society 1890-1928

1 Study Source B.
What is the message of this postcard?
Use details of the source and your knowledge to explain your answer.

(6 marks)

2 Study Sources B and D.
Which source do you think gives a more accurate view of British attitudes towards the war effort? Use details of the source and your knowledge to explain your answer.

(9 marks)

3 Study Source A.
Does the message of this poster surprise you?
Use details of the source and your knowledge to explain your answer.

(6 marks)

4 Study Source C.
How useful is this source for understanding Mrs Pankhurst's views on how WWI should affect the Suffragettes' struggle?
Use details of the source and your knowledge to explain your answer.

(7 marks)

5 Study Sources B, C and D.
"The men and women of the UK all acted together and supported each other between 1914 and 1918."
How far do these sources support this statement? Use details of the sources and your knowledge to explain your answer. Remember to identify the sources you use.

(12 marks + 3 marks for SPaG)

Changes in British Society 1890-1928

6 Study Source A.
What can you learn from Source A about the public's attitude towards the Suffragettes' struggle?

(4 marks)

7 Study Source B.
What was the purpose of this postcard?
Use details of the postcard and your knowledge to explain your answer.

(6 marks)

8 Study Sources B and D.
Do these sources support the view that the UK's food supplies were seriously at risk during the First World War? Explain your answer, using the sources and your own knowledge.

(10 marks + 3 marks for SPaG)

Origins of World War I

Study **Source A** and then answer the questions below.

Source A

© Mary Evans Picture Library

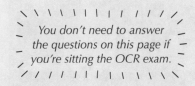

You don't need to answer the questions on this page if you're sitting the OCR exam.

A cartoon entitled "The Great Naval Race", published in a German magazine in 1919.

Origins of World War I

1 (a) In the period up to 1914, the Balkans were known as the 'powder keg of Europe'.
Describe the main international tensions that centred on the area.

(4 marks)

(b) Source A suggests a view about the causes of the First World War.
Do you agree that this was the main cause?
Explain your answer by referring to the purpose of the source, as well as using its content and your knowledge.

(6 marks)

(c) Which of these was the more important reason for Germany's involvement in the First World War:
• Germany's attempts to become an imperial power;
• Germany's alliance with Austria-Hungary?
You must refer to both reasons when explaining your answer.

(10 marks + 3 marks for SPaG)

Origins of World War I

2 (a) Describe one cause of the rivalry between Germany and France in the period up to 1914.

(2 marks)

(b) Briefly explain how tensions in the Balkans led to disagreements between the Great Powers.

(6 marks)

(c) Explain why Britain entered the war in 1914.

(12 marks + 3 marks for SPaG)

The Peace Settlement

Study **Source A** and then answer the questions below.

Source A

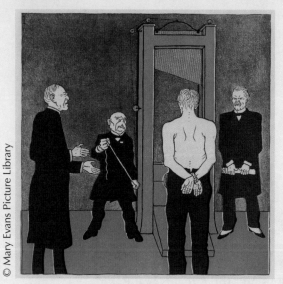

© Mary Evans Picture Library

Cartoon by a German artist, published in 1919.
The man facing the guillotine represents Germany.
The men in black are the leaders of the "Big Three".

The Peace Settlement

1 **(a)** The League of Nations had many different aims.

Describe the main successes of the League of Nations.

(4 marks)

(b) Source A suggests a view about the fairness of the Treaty of Versailles.

Do you agree with this view about the Treaty?

Explain your answer by referring to the purpose of the source, as well as using its content and your knowledge.

(6 marks)

(c) Which of these was the more important reason for the failure of the League of Nations:
  • The harshness of the Treaty of Versailles;
  • The failure of the League of Nations to stand up to aggressive countries?

You must refer to both reasons when explaining your answer.

(10 marks + 3 marks for SPaG)

The Peace Settlement

2 **(a)** Describe one reason why the United States of America did not join
the League of Nations.

(2 marks)

(b) Briefly explain why some people thought the Treaty of Versailles was unfair.

(6 marks)

(c) Explain why there were disagreements at the peace conference held in Paris after the war.

(12 marks + 3 marks for SPaG)

Origins of World War II

Study **Source A** and then answer the questions below.

Source A

© Mary Evans Picture Library/Interfoto

A photograph showing British Prime Minister, Neville Chamberlain, holding the Munich agreement signed with Adolf Hitler, 30th September 1938.

Origins of World War II

1 **(a)** In the years leading up to 1936 Hitler managed to break the terms of the Treaty of Versailles without sparking an international response.
   Describe the main features of Hitler's early successes in breaking the Treaty.

   (4 marks)

   (b) Source A suggests a view about the British attitude to appeasement.

   Do you agree with this view?

   Explain your answer by referring to the purpose of the source, as well as using its content and your knowledge.

   (6 marks)

   (c) Which of these was the more important reason for the success of Germany's aggressive foreign policy in the 1930s:
   • The unwillingness of the British and French to go to war;
   • The existence of large numbers of German speakers outside 1930s Germany?

   You must refer to both reasons when explaining your answer.

   (10 marks + 3 marks for SPaG)

Origins of World War II

2 **(a)** What was the Manchurian Crisis?

   (4 marks)

   (b) Explain how the Depression damaged the League of Nations.

   (6 marks)

   (c) "The USSR was justified in signing a pact with the Nazis, given the actions of the British and French." How far do you agree with this statement? Explain your answer.

   (10 marks + 3 marks for SPaG)

Origins of World War II

3 **(a)** Describe one reason why Hitler was able to get away with sending troops into the Rhineland in 1936.

   (2 marks)

   (b) Briefly explain the key features of the Abyssinian Crisis (1935-36).

   (6 marks)

   (c) Explain why the Depression made a long-term peace less likely.

   (12 marks + 3 marks for SPaG)

Origins of the Cold War

Study **Source A** and then answer the questions below.

Source A

Photograph showing American and Russian troops shaking hands at a bombed bridge on the River Elbe, Germany, 26th April 1945.

Origins of the Cold War

1 **(a)** Describe the policy of the USSR in Eastern Europe after World War 2.

(4 marks)

(b) Source A suggests a view about US-USSR relations in 1945.

Do you agree with this view?

Explain your answer by referring to the purpose of the source, as well as using its content and your knowledge.

(6 marks)

(c) Which of these was more likely to have started a world war:
  • The nuclear arms race between the US and the USSR;
  • The Korean War?

You must refer to both reasons when explaining your answer.

(10 marks + 3 marks for SPaG)

Origins of the Cold War

2 **(a)** Describe one policy of the USA intended to stop communism spreading in Europe.

(2 marks)

(b) Briefly explain how the ideology of the USSR differed from that of the USA at the end of the Second World War (1945).

(6 marks)

(c) Explain why there were tensions over Berlin between 1945 and 1949.

(12 marks + 3 marks for SPaG)

Cold War Crises

Study **Source A** and then answer the questions below.

Source A

Photograph showing the entrance to the
Hotel Capri in Havana in December 1962.
The banner says "Death to the invader".

Cold War Crises

1 **(a)** Describe the main features of the Prague Spring.

(4 marks)

   (b) Source A suggests a view about the cause of the Cuban Missile Crisis.

   Do you agree that this was the main cause?

   Explain your answer by referring to the purpose of the source, as well as using its content
   and your knowledge.

(6 marks)

   (c) Which of these was more damaging for US-USSR relations:
   • The building of the Berlin Wall;
   • The U-2 crisis?

   You must refer to both reasons when explaining your answer.

(10 marks + 3 marks for SPaG)

Cold War Crises

2 **(a)** Describe the deal that ended the Cuban Missile Crisis.

(4 marks)

   (b) Explain why the US was unsuccessful in Vietnam.

(6 marks)

   (c) "Nobody won the Cuban Missile Crisis." How far do you agree with this statement?
   Explain your answer.

(10 marks + 3 marks for SPaG)

End of the Cold War

Study **Source A** and then answer the questions below.

Source A

© Mary Evans Picture Library/Rue des Archives

French poster published in 1980, calling for a boycott of the 1980 Olympic Games in Moscow. The message says "Solidarity with the opponents, workers and people of the USSR".

End of the Cold War

1 (a) Describe how the election of Ronald Reagan affected the Cold War.

(4 marks)

(b) Source A suggests a view about the source of tensions between the USSR and the West.

Do you agree with this view?

Explain your answer by referring to the purpose of the source, as well as using its content and your knowledge.

(6 marks)

(c) Which of these factors was more important in the end of the USSR:
- The economic problems in the USSR;
- The reforms of Gorbachev?

You must refer to both reasons when explaining your answer.

(10 marks + 3 marks for SPaG)

End of the Cold War

2 (a) Describe one reason why détente ended.

(2 marks)

(b) Briefly explain the key features of détente.

(6 marks)

(c) Explain why the Cold War ended.

(12 marks + 3 marks for SPaG)

A New World

Study **Source A** and then answer the question below.

Source A

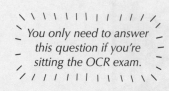

You only need to answer this question if you're sitting the OCR exam.

Photograph showing demonstrators attending a massive peaceful anti-war protest in Berlin, Germany, 29th March 2003.

A New World

1 (a) Describe two reasons why the US invaded Iraq in 2003.

(4 marks)

(b) Study Source A.

What is the message of this placard?

Use details of the cartoon and your knowledge to explain your answer.

(6 marks)

(c) Explain why there were protests against the Iraq War.

(10 marks + 3 marks for SPaG)

Causes and Events of the First World War

Study **Sources A to C** below and then answer the questions that follow.

Source A

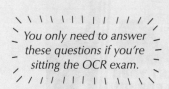

You only need to answer these questions if you're sitting the OCR exam.

Poster published 31st May 1916, to celebrate the Allied victory at the Battle of Jutland.

Source B

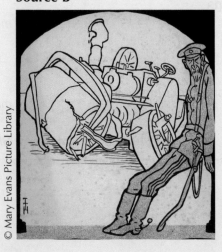

© Mary Evans Picture Library

German cartoon published in 1917, entitled "The Russian 'Steamroller' breaks down".

Source C

> At first the German offensive worked because it took us by surprise and pushed us back. But the vital point is that although it pushed our line back it didn't break it. They just couldn't get through. When they retreated, they didn't have time to get back into their trenches. We had them on the run, as it were. The German prisoners were exhausted and had the look of defeat on their faces.

From the memoirs of George Jameson, a British soldier, who was 100 years old when his memoirs were published in 1993. Jameson served on the Western Front in 1918.

Causes and Events of the First World War

Causes and Events of the First World War

1 (a) Study Source B.

What is the message of this cartoon?

Use the source and your knowledge to explain your answer.

(7 marks)

(b) Study Source A.

Why do you think this poster was published?

Use the source and your knowledge to explain your answer.

(6 marks)

(c) Study Source C.

How far does this source accurately describe events on the Western Front in 1918?

Use the source and your knowledge to explain your answer.

(7 marks)

2 (a) Describe the main tensions in the Balkans leading up to 1914.

(4 marks)

(b) What problems did the generals on the Western Front face?

(6 marks)

(c) The following are reasons why Germany was drawn into war in 1914:

  i) Germany's attempts to become an imperial power;

  ii) Germany's alliance with Austria-Hungary.

Which do you think was more important?

Explain your answer, referring only to (i) and (ii).

(10 marks + 3 marks for SPaG)

Germany: 1918 to 1945

Study **Sources A to D** below and then answer the questions that follow.

Source A

A German cartoon about Ebert's task as the first President of the Weimar Republic, published February 1919.

Source B

Photograph of a German U-boat captain, featuring a compulsory portrait of Adolf Hitler, published in the late 1930s.

Source C

First worker

We work outdoors in all kinds of weather, shovelling dirt for as little as 51 Pfennigs an hour. Then there are deductions that are taken automatically by the state such as 35 Pfennigs for what they ladle out of a large pan and call dinner — more like slop.

Second worker

I'm trained as a printer. In the summer of 1933 I lost my job. I collected the dole until the spring of 1934 — and that was a lot better than what I am doing now. At least I was at home with my family. Now I'm in compulsory labour service with ten days' holiday a year.

From *In Hitler's Germany, Everyday Life in the Third Reich*, by Bernt Englemann, published in 1988. Here Englemann is recalling a conversation he heard on a train in Germany in 1936.

Source D

Stresemann believed Germany's best chance for recovery came from working with other countries. He agreed to various international plans and treaties between 1924 and 1925, and in 1926 Germany became a permanent member of the League of Nations Council. Stresemann won the Nobel Peace Prize for his efforts to make Germany a "normal" nation.

Stresemann's efforts to promote Germany's recovery.

Germany: 1918 to 1945

Germany: 1918 to 1945

1 (a) What does Source D suggest about developments in Germany's international relations between 1923 and 1929?

(4 marks)

(b) Explain the effects of the Munich Putsch on the Nazi Party's tactics in the 1920s.

(6 marks)

(c) How useful is Source A for a historian studying the problems faced by the Weimar Republic in the period 1919-1929?

Use Source A and your knowledge to explain your answer.

(10 marks + 3 marks for SPaG)

Germany: 1918 to 1945

2 Study Source B and then answer both parts of the question below.

(a) Using Source B and your own knowledge describe how Hitler gained support from the German people in the years 1933-39.

(8 marks)

(b) "Propaganda and censorship were the main methods employed by the Nazis to control the German people."

Do you agree? Explain your answer.

(12 marks + 3 marks for SPaG)

Germany: 1918 to 1945

3 (a) Study Source A.

What is the message of this cartoon?

Use the source and your knowledge to explain your answer.

(6 marks)

(b) Study Source B.

Why do you think this photograph was published in the late 1930s?

Use the source and your knowledge to explain your answer.

(7 marks)

(c) Study Source C.

How far does this source prove that most people in Germany were better off under Nazi rule?

Use the source and your knowledge to explain your answer.

(7 marks)

4 (a) Describe the methods used by Stresemann to lead Germany back to recovery.

(4 marks)

(b) Explain why the Nazis persecuted many groups in German society.

(6 marks)

(c) The following are reasons why Hitler was able to consolidate his power in 1933:

    i) the Reichstag fire;

    ii) the Enabling Act of 1933;

    iii) the Night of the Long Knives.

Which do you think was the most important?

Explain your answer, referring only to (i), (ii) and (iii).

(10 marks + 3 marks for SPaG)

Germany: 1918 to 1945

Germany: 1918 to 1945

5 **(a)** What can you learn from Source C about the methods used by the Nazi party to reduce unemployment in Germany from 1933?

(4 marks)

(b) Describe the ways in which the Nazi party tried to influence young people in Germany from 1933 to 1939.

(6 marks)

(c) Explain the effects the Reichstag fire had on Hitler's power in 1933.

(6 marks)

(d) Explain why Germany could be described as a police state from 1933 to 1939.

(6 marks)

6 Explain why the Nazi party's popularity grew in the years 1929-1932.

(6 marks)

7 Was the Versailles Treaty the most serious problem facing the Weimar Republic in the years 1918-23?

Explain your answer.

(12 marks + 3 marks for SPaG)

The USA: 1919 to 1941

Study **Sources A to D** below and then answer the questions that follow.

Source A

Photograph showing the People of New York celebrating the end of Prohibition with beer, 1933.

© Mary Evans Picture Library/ Imagno/ Austrian Archives

Source B

Cartoon published in the USA in 1935.

Source C

I shall continue to regard it as my duty to use whatever means may be necessary to supplement State, local and private agencies for the relief of suffering caused by unemployment. With respect to this question, I have recognized the dangers inherent in the direct giving of relief and have sought the means to provide not mere relief, but the opportunity for useful and remunerative work. We shall, in the process of recovery, seek to move as rapidly as possible from direct relief to publicly supported work and from that to the rapid restoration of private employment.

Part of Franklin Delano Roosevelt's First State of the Union Address, 3rd January 1934.

Source D

Film became a multi-million dollar industry, with huge cinemas built to seat up to 4000 people. And millions of radio sets were sold. By 1929, $850m was spent on sets and parts every year.

Young people enjoyed smoking, dancing and cocktail parties, while church attendance fell and the divorce rate increased. Films, popular songs and paperbacks encouraged new fashions.

Changes to American society in the 1920s.

The USA: 1919 to 1941

The USA: 1919 to 1941

1 **(a)** What does Source D suggest about life in the USA in the 1920s?

(4 marks)

(b) Explain the effects of the policy of Prohibition in the USA.

(6 marks)

(c) How useful is Source A for studying attitudes among the American people towards Prohibition?

Use Source A and your knowledge to explain your answer.

(10 marks + 3 marks for SPaG)

The USA: 1919 to 1941

2 **Study Source B and then answer both parts of the following question.**

(a) Using Source B and your knowledge, describe why many businessmen objected to the New Deal.

(8 marks)

(b) "The Depression was an important factor behind President Hoover losing the 1932 election." Do you agree? Explain your answer.

(12 marks + 3 marks for SPaG)

The USA: 1919 to 1941

3 **(a) Study Source B.**

What is the message of this cartoon?

Use the source and your knowledge to explain your answer.

(4 marks)

(b) Study Source C.

How far does this source prove that Roosevelt's New Deal succeeded in reducing the suffering caused by unemployment?

Use the source and your knowledge to explain your answer.

(6 marks)

4 Explain why the 1920s in the USA was in some ways a decade of intolerance.

(10 marks + 3 marks for SPaG)

Russia: 1905 to 1941

Study **Sources A to D** below and then answer the questions that follow.

Source A

> The New Economic Policy reversed War Communism. Small businesses no longer had to be state-owned — the private owners were allowed to make a profit. Vital industries such as coal, iron, steel and railways stayed in state hands. But experts were brought in on higher salaries, and extra wages were paid for efficiency.

A change in Soviet economic policy.

Source B

'The Last Decisive Battle', a Soviet poster celebrating the 3rd anniversary of the October Revolution, 1920.

Source C

Rex Features

A photograph of Stalin — the two men who had been stood on either side of Stalin have been airbrushed out.

Source D

> We have moved on to the policy of eliminating kulaks as a class. To launch an attack against the kulaks means that we must prepare for it and then strike at the kulaks, strike so hard as to prevent them from rising to their feet again.

From a speech by Stalin in December 1929.

Russia: 1905 to 1941

Russia: 1905 to 1941

1 (a) What does source A suggest about the importance of communism to Bolshevik policies between 1921 and 1924?

(4 marks)

(b) In February-March 1917, the Provisional Government took power in Russia. Explain why it was unable to hold on to it.

(6 marks)

(c) How useful is Source B for studying attitudes towards the civil war?

Use Source B and your knowledge to explain your answer.

(10 marks + 3 marks for SPaG)

Russia: 1905 to 1941

2 Study Source C and then answer both parts of the question below.

(a) Using Source C and your knowledge, describe how Stalin tightened his grip on the Soviet Union in the late 1920s and 1930s.

(8 marks)

(b) "Stalin's agricultural policy from 1929 to 1940 was a disaster."

Do you agree? Explain your answer.

(12 marks + 3 marks for SPaG)

Russia: 1905 to 1941

3 (a) What does Source B tell us about how the Russian leadership felt about the Russian Civil War?

(4 marks)

(b) Explain why Lenin abandoned War Communism in 1921.

(6 marks)

4 Explain how the leadership of the Communist Party changed between 1922 and 1929.

(10 marks + 3 marks for SPaG)

Russia: 1905 to 1941

Russia: 1905 to 1941

5 (a) Study Source B.

What is the message of this poster?
Use the source and your knowledge to explain you answer.

(6 marks)

(b) Study Source C.

How is this source useful as evidence for historians studying Stalin's methods
of controlling the USSR?
Use the source and your knowledge to explain your answer.

(7 marks)

(c) Study Source D.

How far does this source account for the suffering caused by Stalin's agricultural policies?
Use the source and your knowledge to explain your answer.

(7 marks)

6 (a) Describe the main features of Stolypin's economic reforms.

(4 marks)

(b) Explain why the Bolsheviks were successful in seizing power in 1917.

(6 marks)

(c) "The First World War was the main reason the Tsar fell from power."
Do you agree? Explain your answer.

(10 marks + 3 marks for SPaG)

The USA: 1945 to 1975

Study **Sources A to E** below and then answer the questions that follow.

Source A

A photograph showing a civil rights march, 28th August 1963. Over 200 000 protestors gathered on Constitution Avenue in Washington D.C. Martin Luther King is at the front of the crowd.

Source B

A photograph showing USA teammates Tommie Smith and John Carlos giving the 'Black Power' salute as a civil rights protest, at the 1968 Olympics in Mexico.

Source C

I have in my hand 57 cases of individuals who would appear to be either card-carrying members or certainly loyal to the Communist Party, but who nevertheless are still helping to shape our foreign policy. We are not just dealing with spies. We are dealing with a far more sinister type of activity because it permits the enemy to guide and shape our policy.

Senator Joseph McCarthy speaking to a women's club, 1950.

Source D

An anti-Vietnam War poster.

Source E

King shrewdly organized protests in places (Birmingham, Selma) where volatile lawmen were in power, expecting that violence against peaceful demonstrators would promote national revulsion against white racism and elicit popular sympathy for his goals.

A historian writes in 1998 about the tactics of Martin Luther King.

The USA: 1945 to 1975

The USA: 1945 to 1975

1 Study Source B and then answer both parts of the following question.

(a) Using Source B and your knowledge, describe the role of the "Black Power" movement in the civil rights struggle.

(8 marks)

(b) "Martin Luther King was a vital figure in the African Americans' civil rights struggle."

Do you agree? Explain your answer.

(12 marks + 3 marks for SPaG)

The USA: 1945 to 1975

2 (a) Study Source C.

How far does this source prove that communist sympathisers were a serious issue in the USA in the 1950s?

Use the source and your knowledge to explain your answer.

(7 marks)

(b) Study Source E.

To what extent does this show Martin Luther King to be the most effective campaigner in the era of the civil rights struggle?

Use the source and your knowledge to explain your answer.

(7 marks)

(c) Study Source A.

What message would this photograph have sent when published?

Use the source and your knowledge to explain your answer.

(6 marks)

3 (a) Describe the achievements of Cesar Chavez.

(4 marks)

(b) Explain why Native Americans pursued a civil rights campaign in the 1950s and 1960s.

(6 marks)

(c) How successful was the campaign for women's rights in the USA between 1960 and 1975?

(10 marks + 3 marks for SPaG)

The USA: 1945 to 1975

The USA: 1945 to 1975

4 Study Source C.

What can you learn from Source C about McCarthyism?

(4 marks)

5 Study Source D and use your own knowledge.

Why was this poster put up in the USA?

Use details of the source and your own knowledge to explain your answer.

(6 marks)

6 Study Sources A, B and E and use your own knowledge.

Do these sources support the view that non-violent protest was an effective way for African Americans to campaign for greater civil rights?

Explain your answer, using the sources and your own knowledge.

(9 marks)

7 Study Sources D and E.

How useful are Sources D and E as evidence of the effectiveness of American protest movements' methods?

Explain your answer.

(9 marks)

8 Study all the sources and use your own knowledge.

"The United States of America was a divided country between 1945 and 1975."

How far do the sources in this paper support this statement?

Use details from the sources and your own knowledge to explain your answer.

(12 marks + 3 marks for SPaG)

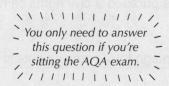

You only need to answer this question if you're sitting the AQA exam.

The USA: 1945 to 1975

9 Study Source D and answer both parts of the following question.

(a) Using Source D and your own knowledge, describe the role of the protest movement in the Vietnam War.

(8 marks)

(b) "The war in Vietnam was lost in America, not in the jungles of south-east Asia."
Do you agree? Explain your answer.

(12 marks + 3 marks for SPaG)

Britain: 1890 to 1928

Study **Sources A to J** and then answer the questions that follow.

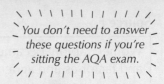
You don't need to answer these questions if you're sitting the AQA exam.

Source A

© Illustrated London News Ltd/Mary Evans Picture Library

Photograph showing a volunteer acting as a guard on a train during the General Strike, 1926.

Source B

SHE. IT IS TIME I GOT OUT OF THIS PLACE. WHERE SHALL I FIND THE KEY?

CONVICTS
AND
LUNATICS
HAVE NO VOTE
FOR
PARLIAMENT

Should all Women be classed with these?

A Suffragette poster from 1920. The woman is saying "It is time I got out of this place. Where shall I find the key?"

Source C

> Gas! Gas! Quick, boys! — An ecstasy of fumbling,
> Fitting the clumsy helmets just in time;
> But someone still was yelling out and stumbling,
> And flound'ring like a man in fire or lime…
> Dim, through the misty panes and thick green light,
> As under a green sea, I saw him drowning.
> In all my dreams, before my helpless sight,
> He plunges at me, guttering, choking, drowning.

An extract from the poem Dulce et Decorum Est by Wilfred Owen, a British soldier, 1917. Owen served in the trenches and was killed November 1918.

Source D

> Together with patience, the nation must be taught to bear losses. No amount of skill on the part of the higher commanders, no training, however good, on the part of officers and men, no superiority, however great, of arms and ammunition, will enable victories to be won without the sacrifice of men's lives.

An extract from a letter sent to the editors of the main British newspapers by Sir Douglas Haig, the senior commander of the British Army, May 1916.

Source E

> At first the German offensive worked because it took us by surprise and pushed us back. But the vital point is that although it pushed our line back it didn't break it. They just couldn't get through. When they retreated, they didn't have time to get back into their trenches. We had them on the run, as it were. The German prisoners were exhausted and had the look of defeat on their faces.

From the memoirs of George Jameson, a British soldier, who was 100 years old when his memoirs were published in 1993. Jameson served on the Western Front in 1918.

Britain: 1890 to 1928

Source F

Women rapidly became indispensable, not only in the nursing and welfare services but in offices and factories and agriculture, changing the whole balance of society in the process. By 1918 that change was reflected in a new Representation of the People Act, by which the vote was extended from seven million to twenty-one million people, including women over the age of 30. Almost as a by-product of the war, Britain became something approaching a full democracy.

A historian writes about the First World War's impact on women, 2002.

Source G

A postcard celebrating David Lloyd George as the man responsible for introducing unemployment insurance (which required people to collect National Insurance stamps).

Source H

It is proved:
• That there were... deliberate and systematically organised massacres of the civil population, accompanied by many isolated murders and other outrages.
• That looting, house burning, and the wanton destruction of property were ordered... by the officers of the German Army...

Extract from the *Report of the Committee on Alleged German Outrages*, produced by the British War Propaganda Bureau, 1915.

Source I

German comment on WWI food shortages in Britain.

Source J

20 000 women filled the Albert Hall, to protest and show their anger at the government's plan to make all householders pay National Insurance contributions of 3d a week for each of the servants in their household.

Report from a British newspaper, November 1911.

Britain: 1890 to 1928

Britain: 1890 to 1928

1 Study Source B.

What is the message of this poster?

Use details of the source and your knowledge to explain your answer

(5 marks)

2 Study Sources B and F.

Which source do you think gives a more accurate view of why some women were given the vote in 1918? Use details of the source and your knowledge to explain your answer.

(8 marks)

3 Study Sources G and J.

Does Source J prove Source G is wrong?

Use details of the source and your knowledge to explain your answer.

(8 marks)

4 Study Source I.

How useful is this source for understanding what life was like for civilians in Britain during WWI? Use details of the source and your knowledge to explain your answer.

(7 marks)

5 Study all the sources.

"Between 1890 and 1918, life changed for the better for the British people."

How far do the sources in this paper support this statement? Use details of the sources and your knowledge to explain your answer. Remember to identify the sources you use.

(12 marks + 3 marks for SPaG)

Britain: 1890 to 1928

6 Study Source D.

What can you learn from Source D about the thoughts and attitudes of Sir Douglas Haig during World War I?

Use details of the source and your knowledge to explain your answer.

(6 marks)

7 Study Source B.

What is the purpose of this poster?

Use details of the source and your knowledge to explain your answer.

(8 marks)

8 Study Sources A and F.

Do these sources support the view that militant action was not the best way to bring about social change in Britain in the early 20th century? Explain your answer.

(9 marks)

9 Study Source H.

Does the message of this extract surprise you?

Use details of the source and your knowledge to explain your answer.

(7 marks)

10 Study Sources C and E.

How useful are Sources C and E as evidence of the experiences of British soldiers on the front line in WWI? Explain your answer.

(10 marks + 3 marks for SPaG)

Answers

Before the answers, a bit of explanation about how History exams are marked.

See also the Exam Skills section at the start of the book.

Answer Schemes in History are Based on Levels

1) We've tried to make these answers as <u>useful</u> and as <u>realistic</u> as possible. But the mark schemes the exam boards use for History are a bit complicated, so what we've done is given answers that should earn <u>good marks</u> in an exam, and then we've tried to show you <u>why</u> they'd deserve those marks.

   Our answers are just examples, though. Answers very different from ours could also get top marks.

2) Just like the exam boards, we've used both 'levels' and 'marks', and just like in the real exam, the higher the level you reach, the more marks you'll get.

3) To reach a higher level, you'll need to give a 'more sophisticated' answer. Exactly what 'sophisticated' means will depend on the type of question but, generally speaking, a more sophisticated answer could:
   - include *more detail*,
   - involve *more background knowledge*,
   - make a *more complex judgement*.

4) You'll see things like **[1, L2]** scattered around in our answers — this means that that bit of the answer has earned <u>1 mark</u>, and that it's at <u>Level 2</u>. You'll see how marks are accumulated as you add 'sophistication'.

Here's an Example...

Here's a sample <u>5-level</u> scheme for a question asking *whether you agree with the ideas in a given source*. The sophistication increases as you 'use the facts' to answer the question you've been asked (see p.2).

- **Level 1**: <u>Brief, general comments</u> made.

  Comments have to be relevant to the topic of the question (obviously), but for Level 1 they don't necessarily have to be 'joined together'.

- **Level 2**: <u>Identifies</u> and/or <u>describes</u> reasons on <u>one side</u> of the statement.

  <u>Identifying</u> or <u>describing</u> something doesn't usually involve lots of detail.

- **Level 3**: <u>Explains</u> <u>one side</u> of statement.

  <u>Explaining</u> something involves more detail than identifying or describing.

- **Level 4**: Explains <u>both sides</u> of statement.

  For this question, why the ideas in the source <u>should</u> be believed, and why the ideas in the source <u>should not</u> be believed.

- **Level 5**: Explains both sides of statement, and <u>evaluates their relative importance</u>.

  This means <u>weighing up</u> the two sides of the argument, and explaining which side you find <u>more convincing</u>. At this level you're genuinely 'using the facts' to come to a conclusion. This is why you could never get Level 5 marks just by listing facts.

Only Things Relevant to the Question can Earn Marks

1) Not all questions have five levels of answer. Generally, the <u>more marks</u> a question is worth, the more sophisticated your answer needs to be to answer the question properly, and the <u>more levels</u> there will be.

2) But to get marks at any level, what you write needs to be <u>relevant</u> to the question. For example, if the question asks you to describe what <u>caused</u> a particular event, you wouldn't get marks for describing things that happened <u>after</u> that event (since they couldn't have <u>caused</u> it).

Remember to Use the Sources

1) Some questions are based on a <u>source</u> (e.g. a piece of writing, a photo, a cartoon).

2) To get higher-level marks for these questions, you <u>will</u> need to refer to the source, but you'll probably also need to use your <u>background knowledge</u>.

This'll all make sense once you start marking your answers...

Answers: Sections 1-2

Some questions also carry extra SPaG marks for spelling, punctuation and grammar. These are given according to the mark scheme immediately below.

Spelling, Punctuation and Grammar (SPaG)

Threshold Grade
- Use of spelling, punctuation and grammar does not make the writing unclear.
- Any mistakes do not stop the reader understanding the points being made.
- Some technical terms are used.
    (Award 1 mark out of a possible 3)

Intermediate Grade
- Use of spelling, punctuation and grammar is generally good.
- Any mistakes are small or few in number.
- Regular use of technical terms.
    (Award 2 marks out of a possible 3)

Higher Grade
- Use of spelling, punctuation and grammar is excellent.
- Few mistakes of any kind.
- Wide selection of technical terms are used.
    (Award 3 marks out of a possible 3)

Section 1

1 a) • By 1914 two main alliances existed [1, L1], the Triple Alliance (consisting of Germany, Austria-Hungary and Italy) and the Triple Entente (Russia, Britain and France) [1, L2].
     • The alliances were formed for security, but by 1914 they were like two huge armies facing each other [1, L2].
     • The countries built up armies and expected help from their allies if attacked, e.g. Austria-Hungary expected German help, and Russia expected French and British help in the event of an attack [1, L3].

   b) • The overlapping pictures and the caption suggest they're united [1, L1].
     • However, the countries had different aims and enemies: Austria-Hungary was interested in gaining territory in the Balkans, while Germany wanted to become a world power. And while Austria-Hungary's enemy was Russia, Germany's enemies were Britain and France [1, L2]. This suggests the unity shown in the source is superficial [1, L2]. In fact, since the Turkish Emperor is shown in the middle of the picture, it may be propaganda [1, L3] celebrating Turkey joining the alliance between Austria-Hungary and Germany [1, L3].
     • The caption (and the fact that this is a postcard) suggests this is a German source, printed for public distribution, and intended to raise confidence in the Kaiser by showing strong alliances. This may explain the exaggerated unity shown [1, L4].

   c) • The assassination set off a chain of events [1, L1], although the arms race had created conditions in which things could quickly escalate [1, L1].
     • The assassination of Archduke Franz Ferdinand by Serbian terrorists who resented Austria-Hungary's annexation of Bosnia set off a chain of events. Austria-Hungary demanded compensation and the right to send troops into Serbia, and took military action after Serbia refused [1, L2]. Russia mobilised its troops to support Serbia, meaning Austria-Hungary (of the Triple Alliance) and Russia (of the Triple Entente) were in direct conflict [1, L2]. Germany then declared war on Russia, while France supported Russia. Germany now launched the Schlieffen Plan to avoid having to fight France and Russia simultaneously, violating Belgian neutrality, and causing Britain to join her allies. The assassination had been the spark which set this off [1, L2].
     • Germany's aim to double the size of its navy challenged Britain's military strength (and her claim to world power) [1, L3]. Britain's response was to launch the Dreadnought class of battleships (which made previous battleships obsolete) and adopt a policy called the Two-Power Standard (meaning the Royal Navy had to be as strong as the next two biggest navies combined), leading to Germany and Britain racing to build ever more powerful ships, and Britain preparing an army ready to send to Europe if needed [1, L3]. So when Germany

violated Belgian territory, Britain was ready to declare war on Germany, which, without the arms race, may not have been possible [1, L3].
     • Both the assassination and the arms race were important, though perhaps neither was the most important reason for the war; in fact, the formation of alliances can be seen as the most important factor [1, L4]. Without the existence of alliances, the war between Austria-Hungary and Serbia might have remained a small war in eastern Europe, and Germany may not have felt compelled to launch the Schlieffen Plan [1, L4]. [+ 3 marks for SPaG]

2 a) • The source shows pictures of the three countries' leaders in three overlapping ovals [1, L1], which are linked by a ribbon showing the message "United In War" [1, L1], suggesting close links between the countries [1, L2]. Its message is that Germany, Austria-Hungary and Turkey were close allies, who would support each other during the war [1, L3].

   b) • The Moroccan Crises involved the great powers squaring up to each other [1, L1].
     • Tension was increased as a result because Germany was forced to back down twice [1, L2]. Also, Britain became increasingly concerned about Germany's naval strength, while public opinion in Germany became increasingly anti-British [1, L2]. Importantly, the crises meant the alliance between Britain and France was made stronger [1, L3], while the first Moroccan Crisis involved cooperation between Britain, France and Russia (with the formation of the Triple Entente following in 1907) [1, L3]. This caused Germany to feel that she was being encircled by her enemies [1, L3].

   c) • The assassination of Archduke Franz Ferdinand triggered WWI [1, L1] — war was to break out within weeks of the killing [1, L1].
     • The assassination of Archduke Franz Ferdinand by a Bosnian Serb terrorist who resented Austria-Hungary's annexation of Bosnia set off a chain of events [1, L2]. Austria-Hungary demanded compensation and the right to send troops into Serbia, and took military action after Serbia refused [1, L2]. Russia mobilised its troops to support Serbia, meaning Austria-Hungary (of the Triple Alliance) and Russia (of the Triple Entente) were in direct conflict [1, L3]. Germany then declared war on Russia, while France supported Russia. Germany now launched the Schlieffen Plan to avoid having to fight France and Russia simultaneously, violating Belgian neutrality, and causing Britain to declare war on Germany [1, L3].
     • However, there were other causes of WWI too. For example, the arms race between Germany and Britain, the attempts by various countries to increase the size of their empires [1, L4], Germany's frustrations in Morocco, and the fact that Russia had been forced to accept Austria-Hungary's annexation of Bosnia all led to increased tensions between the powers [1, L4].
     • But probably the most important reason for the outbreak of war was the existence of two heavily armed alliances which had been making plans of what to do in the event that a war broke out [1, L4]. Without the existence of alliances, the war between Austria-Hungary and Serbia might have remained a small war in eastern Europe, and Germany may not have felt compelled to launch the Schlieffen Plan [1, L5]. [+ 3 marks for SPaG]

Section 2

1 a) • President Wilson came up with the 14 points in January 1918 when the Germans asked for a truce [1, L1].
     • The points emphasised openness in diplomacy and self-determination for different national groups [1, L2]. He also proposed disarmament by all and a League of Nations to settle disputes [1, L2].
     • The aim of these points was to prevent another war breaking out. This is why the points didn't treat Germany as harshly as the British and French wanted [1, L3].

   b) • The source is a photo of a scrapyard containing the skeletons of German warplanes, showing Germany's armed forces were severely damaged [1, L1]. However, although the photo does show many wrecked aircraft, it does not prove that Germany's armed forces were virtually destroyed [1, L2].

Answers: Sections 2-3

- The Versailles Treaty stated that Germany was no longer allowed to have an air force, or any armoured vehicles or submarines [1, L2]. However, the treaty actually allowed Germany to keep an army of 100 000 men and 6 battleships, so the armed forces were still powerful [1, L3].
- The photo may have been an attempt by the German government to generate international sympathy because they wanted to achieve a relaxation of the terms of the Treaty in the 1920s, and so the damage inflicted by the Treaty may be deliberately exaggerated in the photo [1, L3].
- Although Germany's armed forces were not really "virtually destroyed", real damage was done, and the treaty did temporarily reduce Germany's ability to fight another war (although Germany was later able to rearm) [1, L4].

c) • The Versailles Treaty forced Germany to pay reparations to the allies as compensation for the damage caused during the war [1, L1], while it lost huge amounts of territory both in the east and the west [1, L1].
- The justification for the reparations was that Germany was "to blame" for the start of the war (the War Guilt clause) [1, L2]. However, Germany believed that it and its allies were not the only ones responsible [1, L2]. Germans also believed they had suffered as much as any other country, had not been defeated militarily, and were now experiencing an economic crisis brought on by the reparations [1, L2].
- Germany's territorial losses included Alsace and Lorraine, all its colonies, and huge amounts of land in the east, while the Rhineland was made into a demilitarised zone [1, L3]. This meant that many Germans were now living under foreign rule [1, L3], while Germany had been weakened as a country due to the loss of industrial areas [1, L3].
- Both reparations and territorial losses caused huge resentment, but it is difficult to say which was more important. However, the resentment of both arose because the German people felt that their politicians rather than their soldiers had lost the war, and that Germany was being treated unfairly [1, L4]. So resentment of reparations and territorial losses is really just resentment of the humiliation of Germany and the belief that the allies were trying to destroy its economy [1, L4].
[+ 3 marks for SPaG]

2 a) • The source is a photo of a scrapyard containing the skeletons of destroyed German warplanes [1, L1]. This suggests that the German armed forces were devastated [1, L1] as a result of the Treaty of Versailles [1, L2]. The photo may have been evidence that the scrapping was taking place [1, L3].

b) • The Treaty of Versailles punished Germany by making it pay reparations and stripping the country of some of its territories [1, L1].
- As part of the Treaty, Germany was forced to accept blame for the war [1, L2]. To prevent Germany from being able to start future wars, Germany's armed forces were therefore restricted [1, L2] to 100 000 men, and were allowed no armoured vehicles, no submarines, no aircraft and only 6 battleships [1, L3].
- Germany was also stripped of large amounts of territory (for example, Alsace-Lorraine and its overseas colonies), while the Rhineland was made into a demilitarised zone. This meant that Germany was weakened as a country due to the loss of industrial areas, and humiliated in the eyes of its citizens [1, L3].
- Germany was also expected to pay reparations of £6600 million, damaging Germany's ability to recover economically [1, L3].

c) • The Treaty of Versailles was certainly very harsh towards Germany [1, L1], and was unfair enough that its aim of preventing another war was undermined [1, L1].
- The Germans certainly felt the Treaty was unfair, as they had had no say in the negotiations and did not believe that they had actually lost the war [1, L2]. Many people at the time felt the allies were destroying Germany's chances of economic recovery by taking valuable industrial land and making them pay reparations which they could not afford [1, L2]. Even US President Wilson believed that Germany was being punished unjustly, which could possibly end up causing enough anger and resentment to lead to another war [1, L3]. The Treaty resulted perhaps from pressure being put on politicians from the people at home, who wanted revenge on Germany for the War [1, L3].

- France and Belgium probably deserved reparations, as they had only become involved in the war initially because Germany launched the Schlieffen Plan [1, L4]. And Germany was not treated any more harshly than the other defeated countries [1, L4]: all the defeated countries were punished eventually by separate treaties [1, L4].
- I think the Treaty was unfair. I doubt any treaty would have been considered fair by everyone, but by being so harsh, it caused enough resentment and anger that WW2 perhaps became inevitable [1, L5]. [+ 3 marks for SPaG]

Section 3

1 a) • The League encouraged cooperation rather than war as a means of dealing with international disputes [1, L1].
- Where countries did get into disputes, the League warned them about the consequences of aggression, which might include economic sanctions being placed on them [1, L2] (e.g. Italy had sanctions placed on it after it invaded Abyssinia in 1935). The Permanent Court of International Justice could also make decisions on border disputes [1, L2] (helping to settle the border dispute between Germany and Poland over Upper Silesia).
- The League had various peaceful means to settle disputes without fighting, although it did have the ability to send troops in if required. However, in practice it was difficult to find troops, since they had to be supplied by (often reluctant) member countries [1, L3].

b) • The cartoon shows the Big Three leaders as angels, but they are standing on Germany. This shows that the cartoonist felt that, for all their rhetoric of wanting a better world, the League of Nations was designed to keep Germany down [1, L1].
- Some Germans may have felt this because the Big Three (who were the parties most responsible for the Treaty of Versailles) also set up the League [1, L2]. These Germans may have believed that the League was keeping the peace, but only by protecting the settlement that had cost Germany a lot of territory [1, L2].
- In some ways the cartoonist is right, in that the League, which was supposed to act when countries were aggressive, did nothing when France occupied the Ruhr [1, L3]. And Germany had been excluded from the League when it was formed, which must have increased the sense of the Big Three countries imposing their will on them [1, L3].
- In fact, the US never joined the League. This was partly because they did not agree with the Treaty, and associated the League with it. And when the League did take action in a problem involving Germany, it did not simply side against Germany (e.g. during the dispute with Poland over Upper Silesia). The cartoonist is possibly justified in thinking that Clemenceau and Lloyd George would have liked to control Germany. However, in practice the League's approach towards Germany wasn't so one-sided [1, L4].

c) • The League of Nations was certainly weaker than it would have been if the USA had joined [1, L1], but the League's failure to stop Japan when it took Manchuria was a significant failure, making it look weak and irrelevant [1, L1].
- Without US leadership, economic might and military power, the League was unable to use its powers effectively [1, L2]. For example, economic and military sanctions were hard to impose [1, L2], since they could only really work with a powerful nation like the US behind them [1, L2].
- The Manchurian Crisis also weakened the League. It was made to look weak [1, L3] when it produced a report condemning the Japanese invasion of Manchuria but then didn't take action to force the Japanese to leave [1, L3]. In fact, it would have been very difficult for the League to take strong action because it had no army of its own [1, L3].
- Although both reasons played a part in the League's failure, the Manchurian Crisis just served to highlight existing weaknesses [1, L4]. Since some of these weaknesses were due to the failure of the USA to join, this is probably the more important factor [1, L4]. [+ 3 marks for SPaG]

2 a) • The British, French and US leaders are shown as angels with swords [1, L1] standing over a prostrate figure representing Germany [1, L1]. This suggests that the cartoonist is contrasting the Big Three's virtuous-sounding calls for the world to use the League of Nations to settle disputes, with their harsh treatment of Germany, particularly the Treaty of Versailles [1, L2].

Answers: Sections 3-4

- The cartoon also suggests the fear that the League was being set up to control Germany, using force if necessary [1, L3].

b) • The Depression led to countries sorting out their own problems at home, and worrying less about the work of the League of Nations [1, L1].
- The Depression also caused widespread poverty [1, L2], which led to political discontent, and a rise in fascist governments hoping to solve domestic problems by territorial expansion [1, L2].
- So when fascist governments came to power in Japan and Italy [1, L3] and invaded Manchuria and Abyssinia [1, L3], other countries were unwilling to try to solve the disputes because of their own economic weaknesses [1, L3].

c) • Although the League did have many underlying weaknesses right from the start, which made its job very difficult [1, L1], the factors that ultimately caused its downfall were beyond its control [1, L1].
- One of the weaknesses right from the start was the fact that the USA did not join the League [1, L2], meaning the League lacked the economic power necessary to use economic sanctions successfully [1, L3]. This, plus the fact that other countries (e.g. Britain and France) were unwilling to commit troops abroad [1, L2], also meant that the League could not impose solutions to disputes on unwilling countries [1, L3].
- However, there were some early successes in solving international disputes, such as the Germany-Poland border dispute over Upper Silesia in 1921 [1, L4]. And the League also had other aims, such as helping refugees, and it was able to achieve a lot of success in this [1, L4].
- The factor which probably sealed the League's fate, though, was the Depression, and this wasn't a weakness in the organisation [1, L4].
- So, while the League certainly did have weaknesses from the start, these didn't mean it was 'doomed to failure'. It was able to work towards some of its aims successfully, and might have achieved even more success under different circumstances (e.g. no depression) [1, L5]. [+ 3 marks for SPaG]

Section 4

1 a) • Appeasement means giving in to aggressors to maintain peace [1, L1].
- This had been the British policy for several years before the Munich Conference. For example, in 1935, Britain negotiated a naval agreement with Germany that broke the terms of the Versailles Treaty [1, L2]. Then France and Britain both refused to confront Hitler as he took over more and more territories in Europe (e.g. Austria) [1, L2].
- The policy had many supporters (many of whom thought that Hitler was only supporting the legitimate rights of Germans living outside Germany, and that Hitler would make no more territorial claims once these claims were settled), and reached its climax in 1938 when the Sudetenland was handed to Germany at the Munich Conference. The result of this policy was ultimately to make Hitler bolder and bolder in his claims, and eventually make war unavoidable [1, L3].

b) • The source shows Hitler in a smiling crowd within a map of the Sudetenland, along with a caption thanking the Führer [1, L1].
- This suggests the policy was a popular one with the German people [1, L2], although the source could have been produced by the German government itself, and so not a reliable guide [1, L2].
- It is true that the German people considered the Versailles Treaty to be too harsh [1, L3], and so a policy that promised to restore German greatness by taking back territory lost at Versailles may well have been popular [1, L3].
- Although this postcard was probably produced as propaganda, the fact that it draws attention to the taking of the Sudetenland suggests the Nazis thought it would be a popular policy. I think that breaking the Treaty of Versailles and bringing Germans back into Germany's borders would have been very popular [1, L4].

c) • Both Chamberlain's policy of appeasement and the Nazi-Soviet Pact played a role in the start of WWII [1, L1], since they both encouraged Hitler to carry on with his aggressive foreign policy [1, L1].
- The policy of appeasement meant Hitler was able to break terms of the Versailles Treaty without facing serious consequences [1, L2]. When Hitler sent troops into the Rhineland, the troops were under orders to retreat if they met any resistance, but there was none [1, L2].

Encouraged by this lack of reaction, Hitler began to 'grab territory'; however, eventually Britain and France had to react, and so they declared war [1, L2].
- Hitler did not want a two-front war. When Stalin decided to protect the USSR by signing the Nazi-Soviet Pact with Germany, the threat of a war on two fronts was removed [1, L3]. But this same pact also involved Germany and the USSR dividing Poland between them [1, L3]. However, by this time, Britain had made a pact to help Poland in the event of a German attack, and so this invasion actually triggered the start of WWII [1, L3].
- The invasion of Poland that the Nazi-Soviet pact led to was the trigger that immediately preceded the outbreak of war, but I think the policy of appeasement was perhaps a more important underlying cause [1, L4], because not appeasing Hitler may have convinced him to be less ambitious overall [1, L4]. [+ 3 marks for SPaG]

2 a) • The source shows Hitler in a smiling crowd within a map of the Sudetenland [1, L1], along with a caption thanking the Führer [1, L1].
- This suggests Hitler was popular with the German people, and that the German population was supportive of Hitler [1, L2].
- Specifically, this source suggests that Hitler's success in gaining the Sudetenland was popular in Germany and with the Germans in the Sudetenland [1, L3].

b) • Hitler challenged the Versailles Treaty because it was a very unpopular treaty in Germany [1, L1]. It was seen as an unfair "diktat" [1, L2], and the War Guilt Clause, reparations, military restrictions and territorial loss all seemed to be attempts to humiliate Germany [1, L3].
- Hitler also did not believe that anyone would seriously challenge him [1, L2]. The League of Nations had proven itself unable to stand up to a strong power during the Manchurian and Abyssinian Crises [1, L3]. Also, the USA was still following a policy of isolationism, and the British and the French were too preoccupied with the effects of the depression [1, L3].

c) • The policy of appeasement was a mistake, as Hitler wasn't stopped [1, L1] and Britain eventually had to fight the war that appeasement was designed to avoid [1, L1].
- However, there were good reasons why the policy of appeasement must have looked attractive. The British people weren't prepared to support the idea of war in 1938 [1, L2], Britain was suffering from the depression [1, L2], and her armed forces were weak [1, L3]. So appeasement may have been a way to buy time to prepare for war [1, L3].
- But appeasement just encouraged Hitler to continue with his aggressive policies [1, L4]. He was allowed to break the terms of the Versailles Treaty without punishment [1, L4], which ultimately led to the invasion of Poland in September 1939 and the start of WWII [1, L3].
- Although there are arguments for appeasement, it was ultimately a mistake, and did not achieve its objectives of avoiding war [1, L5]. [+ 3 marks for SPaG]

3 a) • Germany challenged the Treaty by bringing in military conscription [1, L1], breaking the terms of the Treaty, which had limited Germany's army to 100 000 men [1, L2].
- Germany also reached a naval agreement with Britain [1, L1]. This agreement implied that Germany had a right to rearm, which broke the Treaty of Versailles. [1, L2]

b) • Britain and France appeased Germany by failing to object to the remilitarisation of the Rhineland in 1936 [1, L1]. If Britain and France had reacted aggressively, Germany may have withdrawn its troops. But France was busy with an election and Britain refused to act [1, L2].
- Germany was also allowed to take over Austria in 1938 [1, L1]. Hitler had wanted 'Anschluss' with Austria, so encouraged Nazi revolt in Austria and threatened invasion. Britain and France did nothing [1, L2].
- They also negotiated the German takeover of the Sudetenland in 1938 [1, L1]. There was a large German population in Sudetenland and Hitler wanted it to become part of Germany. The Munich agreement was produced to avoid war, and gave the Sudetenland to Germany [1, L2].

Answers: Sections 4-5

c) • War broke out in September in 1939 for various reasons. The trigger for war was the German invasion of Poland on 1st September [1, L1], but other factors had brought this invasion about, and they are just as important to consider.
  • One reason was the effects of the depression [1, L1], which meant extremist parties like the Nazis grew more popular [1, L2]. It also meant that other countries were too preoccupied with their own problems to stop aggressive countries like Germany [1, L2].
  • The policy of appeasement was another important factor in the lead-up to war [1, L1]. This meant that Hitler was allowed to continue with his aggressive policies [1, L2], and encouraged him to take each new step, each time thinking he would not be opposed [1, L2].
  • Although the invasion of Poland was the spark that triggered the war, other factors had brought Hitler to power in the first instance [1, L3], and then encouraged him to pursue his aggressive foreign policy [1, L3]. These underlying factors were perhaps more important overall when considering the reasons for the outbreak of war [1, L3]. [+ 3 marks for SPaG]

Section 5

1 a) • The US planned to stop communism spreading by adopting the Marshall Plan and the Truman Doctrine [1, L1].
  • The Marshall Plan promised US aid to European countries to rebuild their economies [1, L2]. This was done as the US believed an impoverished Western Europe would be vulnerable to communism [1, L2].
  • The Truman Doctrine meant that the US would support any nation that was threatened by communist takeover. For example, financial aid was given to Greece and Turkey [1, L3].

  b) • The source shows the delivery of the millionth ton of supplies to West Berlin during the Berlin Airlift [1, L1].
  • The Berlin Airlift was a vital reason behind West Berlin not becoming part of East Germany [1, L2], because this was the only way for supplies to reach West Berlin from the West [1, L2].
  • However, the main effect of the Airlift was not so much the supplies that were taken in, but the determination it showed on the part of the Allies not to let West Berlin become part of East Germany [1, L3]. Even though the Red Army could probably have overrun West Berlin quite quickly, the Airlift showed Stalin the Western Allies were serious about supporting West Berlin, and that for Stalin there was a real risk of war against the West if he had tried to take West Berlin [1, L3].
  • This photo is probably trying to show how successful the Allies were in breaking the blockade, and therefore its futility [1, L4].

  c) • The Berlin Blockade involved the USSR blockading West Berlin in response to the Western Powers taking steps to combine their zones of occupation [1, L1]. The Korean War was a fight between the communist North of Korea, which was allied with China, and the capitalist South, which was aided by a UN force led by the US [1, L1].
  • The Berlin Blockade was an aggressive action by Stalin, who was trying to assert his control in Eastern Germany [1, L2]. Although the USSR didn't use military force, they did cut off the supply lines that ran from West Germany to West Berlin, which was deep in East Germany. They hoped to force the Western powers to give up the city [1, L3]. The Western powers responded by flying in supplies. Although this was not an aggressive action, it did involve non-stop flights over Soviet- controlled East Germany, which clearly heightened tension between the USSR and the Western powers [1, L2].
  • The Korean War was in some ways more likely to cause a world war in that it was a regional war that had dragged in other countries [1, L3]. The UN forces, which were largely made up of US troops, forced the North back to near the Chinese border. This made the Chinese fear a Western invasion, so they became involved in the conflict — this shows how other countries got drawn into the conflict [1, L2]. Chinese success in the war made the US consider attacking China, which would have risked further escalating the war. That Truman refused to attack China and sacked General MacArthur, who backed the plan, shows how dangerous he thought the situation was [1, L3].
  • As the Korean War was an actual conflict there may have been a greater chance of it starting a broader war [1, L4]. However, I think the stakes were higher in Berlin, as Stalin had already made clear how

serious he was about maintaining control in Eastern Europe, and would have seen a rejuvenated Germany as a bigger threat than a united Korea. And while the Chinese intervention was in many ways successful, they lacked atomic weapons. In contrast, the USSR exploded its first A-bomb in 1949, the year the blockade ended [1, L4]. [+ 3 marks for SPaG]

2 a) • An RAF officer is handing over a sack of supplies to a man from Berlin [1, L1], in front of a banner reading "1,000,000 tons" [1, L1]. This shows the success of the airlift in delivering relief to Berliners [1, L2], which in turn suggests a hostile relationship between the West and the USSR [1, L3].

  b) • The USSR blockaded Berlin to cut off West Berlin and therefore gain control of it [1, L1].
  • Stalin had ordered the blockade in protest at the British, French and US plan to combine their zones of occupation in Germany [1, L2]. This new combined zone had a single government and new currency to aid economic recovery. However, Stalin wanted Germany to remain weak [1, L2].
  • The underlying reason was that there were strong ideological differences between the East and West [1, L3]. Communism in the East and capitalism in the West created a 'Cold War' between the USSR and USA, and Stalin was trying to establish a zone of influence in Eastern Europe [1, L3]. The blockade was therefore an attempt to reduce American influence in Europe and bring Berlin under Soviet control [1, L3].

  c) • The Berlin Blockade involved the USSR blockading West Berlin in response to the Western Powers taking steps to combine their zones of occupation [1, L1]. The Korean War was a fight between the communist North of Korea, which was allied with China, and the capitalist South, which was aided by a UN force led by the US [1, L1].
  • The Berlin Blockade was an aggressive action by Stalin, who was trying to assert his control in Eastern Germany [1, L2]. Although the USSR didn't use military force, they did cut off the supply lines that ran from West Germany to West Berlin, which was deep in East Germany. They hoped to force the Western powers to give up the city [1, L3]. The Western powers responded by flying in supplies. Although this was not an aggressive action, it did involve non-stop flights over Soviet controlled East Germany, which clearly heightened tension between the USSR and the Western powers [1, L3].
  • The Korean War was in some ways more likely to cause a world war in that it was a regional war that had dragged in other countries [1, L2]. The UN forces, which were largely made up of US troops, forced the North back to near the Chinese border. This made the Chinese fear a Western invasion, so they became involved in the conflict — this shows how other countries got drawn into the conflict [1, L4]. Chinese success in the war made the US consider attacking China, which would have risked further escalating the war. That Truman refused to attack China and sacked General MacArthur, who backed the plan, shows how dangerous he thought the situation was [1, L4].
  • As the Korean War was an actual conflict there may have been a greater chance of it starting a broader war [1, L4]. However, I think the stakes were higher in Berlin, as Stalin had already made clear how serious he was about maintaining control in Eastern Europe, and would have seen a rejuvenated Germany as a bigger threat than a united Korea. And while the Chinese intervention was in many ways successful, they lacked atomic weapons. In contrast, the USSR exploded its first A-bomb in 1949, the year the blockade ended [1, L5]. [+ 3 marks for SPaG]

3 a) • One way the US planned to stop the spread of communism was by using the Marshall Plan [1, L1]. This plan promised US aid to European countries to help them rebuild their economies. This was done because the US believed impoverished countries were vulnerable to communism [1, L2].
  • Another way the US tried to stop communism was with the Truman Doctrine [1, L1]. The Truman Doctrine showed that the USA would support any nation threatened by a communist takeover. [1, L2]

Answers: Sections 5-6

b) • There were several reasons why the Berlin Wall was built. By 1961, 2.5 million people had left East Germany through West Berlin [1, L1]. The communist government wanted to stop this flow of people [1, L2].
   • Another reason was the 'Cold War' between the USA and the USSR [1, L1]. Communist USSR feared US capitalist influence, and wanted to keep tight control of Eastern Europe by separating it from the West [1, L2].
   • The USSR feared a revived Germany [1, L1]. They preferred to see it weak and to keep it divided into two separate countries. The wall helped them do this [1, L2].

c) • There were several reasons why a 'Cold War' existed between the USA and the USSR by 1955. The most fundamental was the ideological differences between the capitalist system of the USA and the communist system of the USSR [1, L2]. Each country saw the other as a genuine threat to their way of life [1, L2].
   • There had also been a change in leadership of the USA between the Yalta and Potsdam conferences, with Roosevelt being replaced as president by Harry Truman. Firstly, Truman was suspicious of the USSR [1, L1]. Secondly, Stalin thought that he would be able to take advantage of Truman's inexperience [1, L2]. Both factors led to increased tensions between the countries [1, L2].
   • The arms race had also started by 1955, with both countries developing ever more deadly and sophisticated arms [1, L1]. This helped increase suspicion and distrust between the countries [1, L2].
   • All these factors are interlinked. The two opposing systems led to distrust and suspicion, and a desire to take advantage whenever circumstances allowed, creating further distrust [1, L3]. This meant both powers felt the need for sophisticated arms in order to protect themselves [1, L3], which created further distrust, but also ensured both powers were extremely reluctant to challenge the other directly [1, L3]. [+ 3 marks for SPaG]

Section 6

1 a) • After a period of better relations between the USSR and the US, a new cold war was triggered when the USSR invaded Afghanistan [1, L1].
   • This was a period of suspicion and distrust. US President Carter abandoned the SALT 2 treaty, which would have limited the number of nuclear weapons held by the US and USSR. Instead the new US President Reagan began another arms race, with the US developing new missiles and laser weapons [1, L2]. There were also implications for the Olympics, with the US boycotting the Moscow Games of 1980, and the Soviets boycotting the LA Games of 1984 [1, L2].
   • But this new cold war was so expensive that the USSR couldn't afford to keep up, and Soviet living standards were affected dramatically [1, L3].

b) • The source shows graffiti on the Berlin Wall thanking Gorbachev for his role in bringing about the fall of the Berlin Wall. The photograph was taken after the wall 'fell' in 1989 [1, L1].
   • The fall of the Berlin Wall took place while Gorbachev was in charge of the USSR, when he had the most influence over the Warsaw Pact countries [1, L2].
   • Because this piece of graffiti is in English, it is probably intended by the author to be read by an international audience [1, L2].
   • Gorbachev's abandoning of the Brezhnev Doctrine was vital in bringing about the end of the wall. The Brezhnev Doctrine was the guarantee that the USSR would get involved if socialism was threatened in other countries, so scrapping it made it possible for the countries of Eastern Europe to escape from the control of the USSR [1, L3].
   • The fall of the Berlin Wall could also be linked to Gorbachev's policy of 'glasnost', which gave new rights and freedoms to Soviet citizens. This weakened the formerly totalitarian control of the Communist Party in the Soviet Union, and made it far more difficult for states like East Germany to maintain strict controls, as their citizens expected to receive similar freedoms, such as the freedom to travel [1, L3].
   • While a piece of graffiti clearly doesn't count as evidence of the direct impact of Gorbachev's policies, the fact that somebody risked getting into trouble to write it suggests that they had felt inspired at the time by Gorbachev's policies. And this belief among the people that Gorbachev was changing things would itself have made people expect and demand even greater changes, such as the fall of the wall [1, L4].

c) • Economic problems meant that the leadership of the USSR had to risk change [1, L1]. Political change came in the form of greater freedoms for the people of the USSR [1, L1].
   • The Soviet economic system had been inefficient for decades. Living conditions didn't compare favourably with the West, and ordinary citizens began to see how badly the communist system was serving them [1, L2]. The 1979 Afghanistan invasion and the new cold war added to the economic problems [1, L2]. This increased popular discontent, which would be a key factor in the rejection of communism in the USSR, in that it aided the election of Yeltsin [1, L2].
   • Political events also played a role. In 1991, Yeltsin was elected President of Russia and immediately demanded the end of communist domination and the break-up of the USSR [1, L3]. The fact that Yeltsin could have been elected at all was due to new policies established by Gorbachev as part of his policy of glasnost [1, L3]. Old communist leaders feared reform, and a group of hardline communists attempted a military coup to get rid of Gorbachev. Yeltsin rallied the Russian people to resist the coup, and the coup failed. Gorbachev was left with no power and was forced to resign, meaning communism in Russia was dead. It was the people's appetite to defend the political changes that had happened that in the end took power away from Gorbachev and from the hardliners [1, L3].
   • There was a close link between the economic problems and politics in the events leading up to the collapse of Soviet communism. But the economic problems can be seen as the principle cause [1 L4], as it was economic problems which would have caused the broadest discontent with communism, which would have led to people voting for Yeltsin and protesting against the coup [1 L4]. [+ 3 marks for SPaG]

2 a) • The source is a photograph showing a piece of graffiti on the Berlin Wall [1, L1] thanking "Gorby" (i.e. President Gorbachev) [1, L1]. This photo was taken in 1990, the year after communism fell all over Europe [1, L2], and shows that the person thought Gorbachev had played a major role in bringing about the fall of the Berlin Wall [1, L3].

b) • The arms race was too expensive [1, L1]. The USSR spent so much on weapons that living standards fell [1, L2].
   • The USSR got involved in an expensive war in Afghanistan [1, L2]. This war ran from 1979 to 1988 and cost billions of dollars [1, L3].
   • The Soviet government was corrupt, which would have damaged the economy [1, L3], and Soviet agriculture was inefficient, which meant money had to be spent importing food [1, L3].

c) • Solidarity was the first anti-communist trade union of Eastern Europe [1, L1], and played an important role in bringing about the collapse of communism in Europe [1, L1].
   • Solidarity was set up in Poland in 1980 by shipyard workers, led by Lech Walesa, in protest at food price increases. They demanded the right to strike and to be consulted on issues that affected them. By 1981, it had 9 million members, and had become the first ever broad-based anti-communist movement within a communist country [1, L2]. In 1981 they were banned, but continued underground [1, L2]. This set an important precedent for popular resistance in Eastern Europe, as nothing like this had ever been seen before in the communist world [1, L3]. During the 1988 'illegal' strikes, the Polish government were forced to negotiate with Solidarity. A communist authority negotiating and making concessions was previously unheard of in the Eastern Bloc. Therefore Solidarity, and Walesa, became symbols of resistance against communist oppression, giving hope to the rest of Eastern Europe [1, L3].
   • However, Gorbachev also played an important role. His Glasnost and Perestroika policies weakened the Communist Party's totalitarian control in the Soviet Union, making it more difficult for countries like East Germany to uphold old-style Stalinist control [1, L4], so communism began to lose its grip on the Eastern Bloc [1, L4]. He also ended the Brezhnev doctrine and told the UN that Eastern Bloc countries now had a choice — the Soviet Union was no longer going to control them [1, L4].

Answers: Sections 6-8

• The activities of protestors, like Solidarity, set a precedent for resistance. But, without Gorbachev's reforms it seems unlikely that the Eastern Bloc would have collapsed so quickly and with so little bloodshed [1, L5]. [+ 3 marks for SPaG]

3 a) • One reason for the period of détente between the US and USSR was the realisation after the 1962 Cuban Missile Crisis that the world had been brought to the brink of nuclear war [1, L1]. Both sides realised that misunderstandings could lead to a total catastrophe, which led to a warming in relations [1, L2].
• Another reason for détente was that neither country could afford to carry on with the Cold War [1, L1]. The USSR couldn't afford to carry on building up its nuclear arsenal, and the US wanted to improve relations in order to end the costly Vietnam War [1, L2].

b) • In the 1980s, Gorbachev introduced a policy of 'glasnost', meaning new freedom and openness [1, L1]. It meant thousands of political prisoners were released, free speech was encouraged and new rights were given to Soviet citizens [1, L2].
• He also introduced 'perestroika', a policy of economic restructuring, which aimed to reduce party corruption and bureaucracy to make the Soviet economy more efficient [1, L1].
• Both glasnost and perestroika helped to weaken the formerly totalitarian control of the Communist Party. Glasnost even allowed for the beginning of free debate about alternatives to communism. But neither policy managed to deliver prosperity [1, L2].
• Gorbachev also abandoned the Brezhnev doctrine [1, L1], allowing countries in the Eastern Bloc to break away from Soviet control [1, L2].

c) • One reason why the communist leaders in the Soviet Union found it harder to keep control was because the country was in economic difficulties [1, L1]. Their economic system was inefficient, a situation which was made worse by corruption among the leaders of the Communist Party [1, L2].
• The 1979 invasion of Afghanistan also played a role [1, L1]. This expensive and unpopular war made economic problems worse, and triggered a new cold war with the US [1, L2].
• The anti-communist Solidarity movement in Poland caused further problems for the communist leaders [1, L1]. During the 1988 strikes, the Polish government was forced to negotiate with Solidarity — and a communist authority negotiating and making concessions was unheard of [1, L2], so people in the rest of Eastern Europe saw that popular resistance was possible [1, L2].
• Greater economic hardship combined with greater corruption [1, L3], together with Gorbachev's reforms leading to a weakening of government control in the USSR (as well as greater freedom for governments in other Eastern European states) [1, L3], meant that communist leaders now struggled to contain demands for reforms [1, L3]. [+ 3 marks for SPaG]

Section 7

1 a) • The Troubles were a long period of serious violence between Catholics and Protestants in Northern Ireland between 1969 and 1998 [1, L1]. The IRA, a terrorist group, wanted Eire and Northern Ireland to be reunited, while the loyalist UVF and UDA wanted Northern Ireland to remain a part of the UK [1, L1]. The IRA used terrorist tactics to try to wear down the British government in the hope that they would abandon Northern Ireland [1, L1]. For example, they were responsible for killing British soldiers and bombing commercial targets, and they even tried to assassinate Margaret Thatcher in 1984 [1, L2].

b) • The source shows a mural painted on the side of a house in the Shankill Road area of Belfast [1, L1], and consists of a UVF (Ulster Volunteer Force) badge surrounded by gunmen in balaclavas [1, L1]. It shows that Catholics and Protestants were divided, since the UVF is a Protestant, "loyalist" group [1, L2]. The picture tells us that the UVF was committed to an armed struggle to defend their position, and that the dispute between the communities was a violent one [1, L3].
• The UVF wanted Northern Ireland to remain separate from the Republic of Ireland. It therefore opposed paramilitary groups such as the IRA who wanted to see Northern Ireland united with the (mainly

Catholic) Republic [1, L4]. This mural is probably making a statement that that area is a strongly Protestant one, and it is probably seeking to both reassure Protestants and intimidate Catholics [1, L4].

c) • The PLO and Al-Qaeda have both used similar methods [1, L1], since both have in the past made use of terrorist tactics [1, L2]. However, the PLO has now officially given up on violent tactics and tries to achieve its aims through more peaceful means [1, L2].
• Al-Qaeda is a terrorist organisation. It aims to bring about a unified Muslim nation, and uses violence to achieve this. In fact, the organisation's leader, Osama bin Laden, has said that it is the duty of every Muslim to kill Americans [1, L3]. The organisation has carried out many terrorist attacks, such as the bombing of Khobar Towers in Saudi Arabia in 1996, the US Embassy bombings in East Africa in 1998, and the Bali nightclub bombings in 2002. The most spectacular attack was the September 11th attack on New York in 2001 [1, L3].
• The PLO has used terrorist tactics in the past, such as those used in the Coastal Road Massacre in 1978, when 38 Israelis were killed [1, L4]. However, it also wanted to become accepted by governments as the representative of the Palestinian people [1, L4], something it achieved when it recognised Israel's right to exist in peace [1, L4].
• Whatever methods the PLO and Al-Qaeda use, they both share the broader ambition of exerting pressure on governments, and so are similar to a certain extent [1, L5]. But while Al-Qaeda continues to use terror, the PLO has moved away from these tactics and uses political means to achieve its aims, meaning that their tactics in recent years have actually been quite different [1, L5]. [+ 3 marks for SPaG]

Section 8

1 a) • The cartoon shows a soldier asleep in a trench, being attacked by a snake. The snake represents the danger of gas attacks, which could strike at any time [1, L1]. More specifically, the snake represents gas attacks from Germany, and the message of the cartoon is that German tactics were evil and cowardly, and therefore that Germans themselves were evil [1, L2]. The purpose of the cartoon is probably to show the Germans had to be defeated, no matter what the cost [1, L3].
• The cartoon was published in a book devised by the UK War Department, and is clearly anti-German propaganda, probably to make sure people were behind the war effort [1, L4], since the loss of life and the lack of progress must have been clear to the people back in the UK [1, L4]. In fact, it was at about this time that footage of the appalling conditions of the Battle of the Somme was shown in the UK, and the public had become openly critical of the generals fighting the war, and so the government may have been trying to show the country that the war had to be fought, even if it was unpopular [1, L5].

b) • The source shows that at least some British soldiers had measures to protect themselves against gas attacks [1, L1], which were used for the first time against the British in 1915 [1, L2].
• However, the source does not prove that all British soldiers had been issued with anti-gas equipment [1, L3]. And although the trench shown in the background is well protected with sandbags [1, L4], other trenches may not have been [1, L5].
• The photograph also does not demonstrate anything about whether or not the British had effective offensive weapons and tactics with which to attack the Germans [1, L5].
• Although the picture shows that new defensive measures were being taken to help defeat the Germans, the picture was probably published for its propaganda value, and so is of limited use when trying to evaluate honestly how well equipped the British were [1, L5].

c) • This source describes the first day of the Battle of the Somme as a success, when it was actually a major disaster for the British [1, L1]. Haig gives the impression that everything is proceeding according to his plan [1, L1]. However, after a huge artillery bombardment, British soldiers were ordered 'over the top' and told to advance slowly to take the German trenches. This resulted in 57 000 Britons killed or wounded on the first day alone [1, L2].
• But it perhaps isn't surprising that Haig claimed success. It is possibly true that some objectives were being achieved, and that Germans were surrendering [1, L3]. And this probably did seem the most important thing to Haig, since his aim was to win the war, not to save lives, and he probably saw this loss of life as worth it if it helped win an

Answers: Sections 8-9

important battle [1, L3]. Haig also had reasons to emphasise the positive. He was in charge of the British attack, and would not have wanted to be seen as failing [1, L4].
  - So while this report is not really an accurate account of all the horrors of the battle, it is possible that, from Haig's perspective, things might have been progressing positively at that early stage [1, L4].

2 a) • The Schlieffen Plan was Germany's plan for war. The plan aimed to attack and defeat France through Belgium [1, L1], before Russia was ready and mobilised [1, L1]. The Germans could then turn back and defeat the Russians [1, L1]. The aim was to avoid having to fight a war on two fronts, a real possibility given the alliances in Europe [1, L1].

  b) • The Schlieffen plan failed because Germany could not defeat France as quickly as the plan demanded [1, L1].
  - Firstly, Belgium refused to let the German army through to attack France [1, L2]. This meant German forces had to fight their way through Belgium, which delayed them, and gave the French (and the Russians) time to prepare their defences [1, L3].
  - The Russians also mobilised for war far more quickly than the Germans had anticipated [1, L2]. This meant that Germany had to send troops to fight the Russians, instead of pushing into France [1, L3].
  - This was made worse because the troops that remained in the west also had to fight the British, since Britain had signed a treaty with Belgium to protect it as a neutral country (although the Germans hadn't expected the British to honour the treaty) [1, L3].

  c) • Trench warfare was awful, and the tactics used at the Somme certainly seemed brutal [1, L1]. On the first morning of the Battle of the Somme, 57 000 Britons were killed or wounded, all under the leadership of Sir Douglas Haig [1, L1].
  - Haig seems to have made many mistakes during the battle [1, L2]. He refused to change his tactics despite the first day's horrific losses [1, L3] (even though these tactics had already failed in other battles). It has also been claimed that Haig could have waited for more tanks, which could have reduced British losses [1, L2]. He was apparently oblivious to the loss of life, believing that the British attacks at the Somme had to carry on regardless of loss of life [1, L3]. So there are reasons to think the title is deserved.
  - However, Haig had to relieve the pressure on Verdun or the whole war might have been lost — the Battle of the Somme was Haig's attempt to do this. In Haig's eyes, almost any cost was probably worth paying [1, L4], and he may have felt there was little time to develop new tactics or equipment [1, L4]. It can also be argued that the loss of German lives (though at the expense of British lives) did turn out to be significant in the eventual winning of the war, since some of Germany's best troops were killed at the Somme and couldn't be replaced [1, L4].
  - On balance, I do not think that Haig deserves the title 'Butcher of the Somme'. It wasn't just his tactics that caused the huge loss of life, but many different factors combined. It is also possible that, whoever had been in charge, the outcome would have been the same, given the weaponry, terrain and tactical alternatives in 1916 [1, L5]. [+ 3 marks for SPaG]

Section 9

1 a) • Source B suggests that many people didn't like the new Weimar Republic and didn't want it to succeed [1, L1]. They blamed the Weimar leaders for losing the war and for signing the Treaty of Versailles [1, L2].
  - Many people also believed that they had not actually been militarily defeated in WWI, but had been betrayed [1, L1]. This led to a belief that the Weimar government was not legitimate and potentially to rebellions against the government [1, L2].

  b) • The government faced an economic crisis [1, L1], since Germany was required to pay reparations as part of the Versailles Treaty [1, L1].
  - The Versailles Treaty was hated by the German people, meaning the government was unpopular because the Weimar leaders had signed it. The Weimar Republic faced opposition from extremist groups [1, L2], who tried to overthrow the government through riots and rebellions

(e.g. the Kapp Putsch of 1920) [1, L2].
  - The Weimar constitution also weakened the government [1, L3], as its proportional representation electoral system meant there were so many parties in parliament that laws were difficult to pass [1, L3].

  c) • A woman is burning money instead of coal during the 1923 hyperinflation crisis [1, L1]. This shows how little the money was worth [1, L1].
  - The source is a photograph that illustrates how bad hyperinflation was, and may have been published to try to gain sympathy for Germany [1, L2]. But that does not mean that the picture is not genuine — we know, for example, that money lost its value so quickly that people had to be paid twice a day [1, L2]. In fact, it is perfectly believable that the German mark had become virtually worthless, not even worth as much as the coal this lady would normally burn [1, L2].
  - The source is useful in illustrating just how desperate people had become [1, L3]. If having as much money as this woman did not mean you could buy coal to burn, then it would also mean you would not be able to buy other necessities, such as food [1, L3]. This is not a situation that can continue forever, so the picture shows not just the effects of hyperinflation for this woman, but also how it must have created instability in the country as a whole [1, L3].
  - We do not know the circumstances of this individual woman [1, L4]. However, given what we do know about hyperinflation at that time, this woman's experience may well have been fairly typical, which would make this a useful source for studying hyperinflation [1, L4]. [+ 3 marks for SPaG]

2 a) • The source describes how Nazi propaganda was to become part of everyday life in schools [1, L1] in an attempt to indoctrinate German children with Nazi beliefs and values [1, L1].
  - Teachers were also encouraged to join the Nazi Teachers' Association [1, L2], and children were told to report any teachers who didn't use Nazi teaching methods [1, L2]. This helped censor what German children were being taught and sent the message that the Nazi way was the right way [1, L2].
  - The Nazis also created youth groups such as the Hitler Youth [1, L3]. These groups aimed to train boys to be soldiers and girls to be wives and mothers [1, L3]. Like the method in the source, these groups aimed to create Nazi loyalty from a young age, so the Nazis would remain strong [1, L3].

  b) • The Depression caused widespread unemployment, meaning the German people experienced poverty and suffering in the 1920s and 1930s [1, L1]. During the Depression, the Weimar government kept changing and was unable to solve Germany's economic problems [1, L1].
  - The German people also felt the Treaty of Versailles had humiliated Germany [1, L1]. So the people saw the government as generally weak and ineffective [1, L2], and began to look to other, less mainstream parties for a solution to the country's problems [1, L3].
  - The Nazis capitalised on this situation by using propaganda effectively [1, L2] to emphasise the strong leadership that Hitler would provide [1, L3].
  - The Nazis were also helped by disunity among the other parties [1, L4]. The Nazis, although the largest party in the Reichstag, never had a majority, and so the other parties could have kept Hitler out of power [1, L4].
  - The Nazis also gained votes from those people who shared the party's anti-Semitism and hatred of communism, which was nothing to do with the Depression [1, L4].
  - So the Depression played a part in Hitler's rise to power, but there were other factors too [1, L5]. The Nazi Party exploited this using sophisticated propaganda techniques, and grew in popularity until eventually they were the largest party in the Reichstag, leading to Hitler being appointed Chancellor [1, L5]. [+ 3 marks for SPaG]

250

Answers: Sections 9-10

3 a) • Nazi methods of control included the use of forceful means such as the SS and Gestapo [1, L1], and peaceful means such as propaganda and censorship [1, L1].
   • The Nazis took over the media, controlling radio broadcasts and using films and posters to spread their messages [1, L2]. Books and newspapers were also censored so that no anti-Nazi material was published [1, L2]. These methods were used to try and control how German people thought. Germans were bombarded with pro-Nazi messages, and anything anti-Nazi was banned [1, L3].
   • The SS (a military-style police force) and the Gestapo (the secret police) were used to intimidate people, and concentration camps were set up [1, L2]. People were also encouraged to report anyone showing disloyalty [1, L3]. This created an atmosphere of fear and suspicion, which made it harder for people to undermine the Nazi message [1, L3].

b) • The Depression caused mass unemployment, which the Nazis had promised to solve. They did this in various ways [1, L1]. For example, Hitler created jobs through public works programmes [1, L1]. These were often "infrastructure" projects, such as the building of the Autobahns [1, L2]. They created huge numbers of jobs, although many were poorly paid and the conditions were tough [1, L3].
   • The Four Year Plan of 1936 was also geared towards preparing Germany for war, and also had an effect on unemployment [1, L2]. The aim was to make Germany self-sufficient in preparation for war, so importing foreign goods was discouraged. This meant that industrial production had to increase, and this boosted employment, as well as Germany's productivity [1, L3].
   • Although the unemployment figures did fall under the Nazis, not all of the falls were due to more jobs being created [1, L3]. Jewish people were eliminated from the economy and women pressured to stay out of paid work, so their unemployment wasn't counted in the statistics, leading to "invisible unemployment" [1, L3].
   • So while the Nazis did have some success in reducing unemployment [1, L4], the extent of this success was exaggerated by their fiddling of the statistics [1, L4]. And some of the Nazis' success in reducing unemployment led to other problems [1, L4]. Many of the jobs were very low paid and involved working in bad conditions, for example. But the most extreme knock-on effect was that many of the jobs were created as a result of the country preparing itself for the war it eventually fought, which makes it hard to say that the Nazis' battle against unemployment was a genuine success [1, L4].
   [+ 3 marks for SPaG]

4 a) • The source shows a woman burning money, which tells us that money had become virtually worthless [1, L1]. It was probably published to highlight the scale of the economic crisis [1, L2], and how people are suffering [1, L2].
   • It may have been published as a form of protest, to show that things could not be allowed to continue as they were [1, L3].
   • The photograph may be part of a demand that a leader be appointed who would be able to deal with the economic situation [1, L4], and unless this happened, things could become even worse [1, L4].
   • This would fit in with the timing of the photograph's publication, since Gustav Stresemann was appointed chancellor in mid-1923, and introduced a new currency, the Rentenmark, later that year [1, L5].

b) • This "Strength through Joy" poster shows the Nazi ideal of the German family — pure, united, happy, hardworking and Aryan [1, L1]. It suggests a man's role is to work, shown by the man carrying a tool, and that a woman's role is to look after children, shown by the woman's arm around the child [1, L1].
   • The poster implies that the Nazi way of life will bring happiness to a family, and make Germany stronger in the process [1, L2].
   • This poster is typical of the propaganda used by the Nazis at this time [1, L3], to encourage the belief that the Nazi policies are positive for Germany, and that people should continue to support the party and take part in the various Nazi organisations [1, L4], all of which would make the Nazis' grip on power even stronger [1, L5].

c) • The source describes how the Hitler salute was used in schools. This suggests teachers and the young were loyal to the Nazi party [1, L1].

• However, it also says that this has been ordered by the government, which would not say anything about people's genuine loyalty [1, L2].
• This kind of scheme was typical of the ways Hitler tried to influence the German people from an early age [1, L3], and so there are reasons to doubt whether it says anything at all about the success of the Nazis in winning the support of the people [1, L4].
• The Nazis even controlled the media, so the report itself could have been placed by the Nazis [1, L5].
• Having said this, the Nazis were undoubtedly popular, as they rose to power basically by democratic means [1, L5].
• So while the text does not prove that the Nazis had won the support of the German people, the fact that they had reached a position of power from which they could order such actions in schools does say something about the level of support for the Nazis in Germany [1, L5].

5 a) • The Weimar Constitution meant that Germany was a democratic republic [1, L1]. A President was elected every 7 years, who was also head of the army and chose who was Chancellor [1, L1]. There were two houses in the parliament, the Reichstag and the Reichsrat, and the Reichsrat could delay any laws passed by the Reichstag. The Reichstag was elected by proportional representation [1, L2]. This meant the number of seats won by a party was worked out as a proportion of the number of votes they won in the election. This resulted in there being many small parties in the Reichstag, with no one party able to dominate [1, L2].

b) • Stresemann brought stability by making changes to help the economy and by improving international relations [1, L1].
   • For example, he helped to end the Ruhr crisis by telling workers to go back to work [1, L2]. He also introduced a new currency, the Rentenmark [1, L2]. Both these measures helped to make the currency and country more stable [1, L3].
   • In 1924 he also accepted the Dawes Plan, which meant Germany was lent US money to pay reparations, which also gave a financial boost to aid Germany's recovery [1, L2]. This stability may not have been possible without Stresemann improving international relations, as the recovery depended heavily on money from the US [1, L3].

c) • In the Munich Putsch, the Nazis attempted to seize power by force [1, L1]. They failed and the Nazi Party was banned, and Hitler jailed for 9 months [1, L1]. After the Putsch, the Nazis realised they couldn't achieve power through force alone, which led to a change in the party's tactics [1, L2].
   • By the mid-1920s the economy improved under Stresemann, which weakened the hand of the extremist parties such as the Nazis [1, L2], meaning the circumstances were now very different from before, and the idea of overturning the government by coup seemed impossible [1, L2].
   • On his release, Hitler therefore decided to use the democratic system to win support [1, L3]. The Party was reorganised on a national basis, and sophisticated propaganda methods developed and used [1, L3]. After the Great Depression hit Germany, the Nazi party appealed to the German population by promising them prosperity and an end to unemployment [1, L1], and these policies helped to increase the number of Nazi party members [1, L1]. By 1932, the Nazis were the largest party in the Reichstag and Hitler was appointed Chancellor in 1933 [1, L3]. [+ 3 marks for SPaG]

Section 10

1 a) • The source shows an assembly line at a Ford motor factory, used for the mass production of cars [1, L1]. This was a new manufacturing method that allowed industries to make products more quickly and efficiently, as each worker masters one part of the production process [1, L1].
   • The source suggests this new method helped create the boom. Improved efficiency meant production levels rose and costs fell, so products became more affordable for people. Employment then increased as demand increased, and so employment and demand increased further still [1, L2]. This increased demand was not just in the car industry; other industries benefited too. This all helped create the boom of the 1920s [1, L2].

Answers: Section 10

b) • In 1917, the government introduced a literacy test [1, L1] for immigrants entering the USA, which would have the effect of controlling the number of people entering the country, especially from non-English speaking countries [1, L2].
  • The US government reduced immigration by introducing a quota system in 1921 [1, L1], limiting annual immigration, and ending the open-door policy in which almost anyone was allowed into the US [1, L2].
  • In 1924, this quota system was replaced by the National Origins Act [1, L1], which discriminated against immigrants from Southern and Eastern Europe, and Asia [1, L2].

c) • The source implies the boom benefited all Americans [1, L1], through a better standard of living and more job security [1, L1]. Certainly many people did benefit, unemployment was low, and consumer goods were more available and accessible, so the comments are fair to an extent [1, L2].
  • But the source doesn't tell the whole story — poverty was actually widespread and wealth unevenly distributed [1, L2]. The gap between the rich and the poor was big, and under 5% of the wealth was owned by the poorest 60% [1, L3]. Also, workers in older industries didn't benefit from the boom [1, L3]. The coal industry suffered as cars, and oil, began to take over from railways. Agriculture suffered badly too, causing rural poverty as many farmers struggled to pay their mortgages, losing their farms [1, L4].
  • The source is a speech by Hoover from his election campaign in 1928. His party was hoping to be re-elected [1, L2], and so he was probably exaggerating the extent of the benefits from the boom to win favour [1, L3]. The source is more useful for telling us about Hoover's election message, than about the boom's effects on the lives of ordinary people [1, L4]. [+ 3 marks for SPaG]

2 a) • The source shows Roosevelt in a boat, and instead of pulling a man from the sea of 'depression' to the safety of the 'national recovery' boat, he's reluctantly pushing him back, while saying it's the Supreme Court's fault [1, L1]. This suggests that the Supreme Court opposed Roosevelt's attempt to bring national recovery through the New Deal [1, L1].
  • Many of the court's judges decided the New Deal interfered too much in people's lives [1, L2]. This led to them declaring some measures unconstitutional and so illegal, which is why the cartoon is called 'the illegal act' [1, L2].
  • Republicans were also against the New Deal, claiming the New Deal made people too dependent on government help [1, L2].
  • There were other opponents of the New Deal. Unlike the judges, some felt the New Deal didn't go far enough to help people [1, L3]. For example, Huey Long set up the 'Share Our Wealth' plan, in which he wanted to tax the rich and give money to the poor [1, L3], while Dr Francis Townsend wanted a plan to give a $200 per month pension to every American over 60, provided they spent it within the month [1, L3].

b) • The New Deal aimed to solve the problems of the depression by giving short-term relief to the needy [1, L1], restoring the economy's stability [1, L1], and introducing long-term reforms to social security and working conditions [1, L1].
  • Individuals received help in several ways. Emergency aid, such as dole payments and soup kitchens, was given to those in need [1, L2], while loans were provided for people whose homes were in danger of being repossessed [1, L2]. A minimum wage was also established [1, L2].
  • The banking crisis was solved by the introduction of the Emergency Banking Act, which helped restore confidence in the banks [1, L3], and so people began to deposit their money again, improving the economy's stability [1, L3].
  • And in 1935 the second New Deal introduced the basic elements of a welfare state [1, L3], giving workers pensions and unemployment benefits, although provision lagged behind countries such as Britain and Germany [1, L3].
  • The New Deal did have some short-term success in bringing about an improvement in ordinary people's lives and in restoring a degree of self-confidence in the US [1, L4]. However, it did not manage to reduce unemployment to pre-depression levels. It was only the start of

WWII that really saw unemployment fall permanently, and a longer-term recovery [1, L5]. [+ 3 marks for SPaG]

3 a) • In the 1920s many people had more money to spend on leisure, which resulted, for example, in a massive increase in the number of cinemas and radio stations [1, L1]. Manners and morals were also changing, with smoking and dancing becoming more popular [1, L1], and church attendance falling [1, L1]. Women were also gaining more independence, thanks to better educational and employment opportunities [1, L1].

b) • Temperance movements, which were often Christian and tended to be popular in rural areas, had campaigned for prohibition since the 19th century [1, L1]. They believed alcohol led to violence, immoral behaviour and family breakdown [1, L2].
  • This attitude was shared by many in the middle class, who felt alcohol was responsible for the criminal behaviour among immigrants and the working class [1, L2]. Similarly, many businessmen felt that alcohol made workers unreliable [1, L3].
  • There was also a belief that prohibition was a patriotic policy, since many of the breweries were owned by German immigrants [1, L2], the very people that the Americans had just been fighting in WWI [1, L3].

c) • From 1920 to 1933, the American government tried unsuccessfully to enforce Prohibition [1, L1]. Although some people supported the ban, a lot of people didn't and Prohibition led to a growing trade in illegal alcohol and organised crime [1, L1].
  • Prohibition was difficult to enforce because it led to so many people becoming involved in illegal activities, such as the manufacturing of illegal liquor (moonshine), or the redistilling of industrial alcohol [1, L2]. Also, a large number of illegal bars (speakeasies) opened to sell alcohol that had been obtained illegally [1, L3].
  • Gangsterism also made it hard to enforce Prohibition as the trade in illegal alcohol was very lucrative, and many gangs became involved in its supply [1, L1]. During Prohibition, the gangster Al Capone was making $60 million a year from alcohol [1, L2], which suggests that there was both a huge market for illegal liquor and that the police were failing to enforce the law effectively [1, L3].
  • The enforcement of Prohibition was also undermined by the corruption of people who were meant to enforce it [1, L1]. Some policemen and judges accepted bribes in return for turning a blind eye to illegal activity, and a few policemen got involved in the illegal production of alcohol [1, L2].
  • Although Prohibition lasted for over ten years, the sheer demand for alcohol, the scale of illegal activity and the corruption of judges and policemen meant that Prohibition was impossible to enforce [1, L4]. [+ 3 marks for SPaG]

4 a) • The source shows a Ford motor factory assembly line, used for the mass production of cars [1, L1]. This was a new manufacturing method that allowed industries to make products more quickly and efficiently [1, L2].
  • The source suggests life in 1920s USA was a time of innovation, with new manufacturing methods being used to create products affordable to ordinary Americans [1, L3]. This led to a boom, with increased employment and increased demand for goods [1, L4], even those goods (e.g. Ford Cars) that had previously been available only to the rich [1, L4].
  • But the photo was taken in 1929, when the good times were coming to an end. The photo may have been taken to bolster confidence in Ford's profitability, and to boost share prices when they were falling [1, L5].

b) • The cartoon shows Roosevelt starting to pull a man from the sea of 'depression' to the safety of a boat, the 'national recovery', but then says he must push the man back, blaming the Supreme Court [1, L1]. This shows that Roosevelt was trying to pull the American economy and Americans out of the depression [1, L2].
  • The cartoon was published to highlight the Supreme Court's opposition to Roosevelt's New Deal [1, L2]. The Supreme Court had declared that some of the New Deal's measures were unconstitutional, and so this is why the cartoon is called "The Illegal Act" [1, L3].

Answers: Sections 10-11

- The artist is showing his/her disapproval of the Court's decision, implying that, without this help, people will 'drown in the depression' [1, L4]. Since the cartoon was published in 1935, the year of the Supreme Court's decision on the New Deal, this is possibly an attempt to sway the opinion of the public and of politicians [1, L4], to allow Roosevelt to put more Democrats on the Supreme Court to make sure this wasn't a problem in the future [1, L5].

c) • The source implies the boom benefited all Americans, through a better standard of living and more job security [1, L1]. Certainly many people did benefit, unemployment was low and consumer goods were more available and accessible [1, L3], so the comments are fair to an extent [1, L2].
- But the source doesn't tell the whole story — poverty was actually widespread and wealth unevenly distributed [1, L4]. The gap between the rich and the poor was big, and under 5% of the wealth was owned by the poorest 60%. Also, workers in older industries didn't benefit from the boom. The coal industry suffered as cars, which run on oil, began to take over from railways. Agriculture suffered badly too, causing rural poverty as many farmers struggled to pay their mortgages, losing their farms [1, L4].
- The source is a speech by Hoover from his election campaign in 1928. His party was hoping to be re-elected and so he probably exaggerates the extent of the benefits from the boom to win favour [1, L5]. The source is possibly more useful for telling us about Hoover's election message, than about the boom's effects on the lives of ordinary people [1, L5].

5 a) • One source of opposition to the New Deal was the Supreme Court [1, L1]. The Court ruled in 1935 that some New Deal measures were unconstitutional [1, L2]. The Court may also have opposed the New Deal because many of the judges were Republicans, who claimed the New Deal interfered too much in people's lives, and made people too dependent on government help [1, L2].
- But there were other opponents of the New Deal. Unlike the judges, some felt the New Deal didn't go far enough to help people. For example, Huey Long and Dr Francis Townsend, who both wanted to give increased help to America's poor [1, L2].

b) • During the boom, share prices had been high due to the success of the economy, but these became unrealistically high, and eventually fell sharply when investors lost confidence [1, L1].
- The price of shares had become unrealistically high when investors, seeing how much money could be made in a rising stock market, started to buy shares on credit, believing they could make a quick profit by selling them when their value rose [1, L2].
- But by 1927 there was a downturn in demand [1, L2]. Companies had been making more goods than people could actually buy. This led to staff losing their jobs, and the unemployment meant there were fewer people to buy goods than before [1, L3]. Investors saw what was happening and began to sell their shares, leading to a fall in share prices, which led to more and more people selling. Eventually by October 1929 there was panic and the value of shares crashed as everyone tried to sell [1, L3], and no measures to restore confidence were successful [1, L3].

c) • The Depression caused terrible poverty in America [1, L1]. People lost savings and faced homelessness; some of the homeless built shanty towns to live in [1, L2]. The lack of money to buy food led to malnourishment [1, L1], and many had to rely on charity to survive [1, L2].
- The Depression also greatly affected agriculture. Product prices fell so much that it cost farmers more to produce goods than they got from selling them. Many farmers were bankrupted [1, L1], and either evicted from their farms or forced to become tenants, losing their independence [1, L2].
- Companies collapsed, meaning that unemployment rose sharply [1, L1]. Many farm labourers joined the ranks of the unemployed too. Many people had to migrate to find work, while the wages of many people who did have jobs fell [1, L2].
- All this left people demoralised [1, L1]. Some fathers abandoned their families to look for work, marriages were delayed, and the birth rate fell [1, L2]. [+ 3 marks for SPaG]

6 a) • Taxes were reduced [1, L1], so people had more money to spend [1, L2].
- Hoover tried to boost the economy by suspending war debts payments from European countries for one year [1, L1] in order to stimulate international trade and increase demand for American goods [1, L2].
- He tried to boost employment [1, L1], through the expansion of public works and by trying to persuade industrialists to maintain jobs and wage rates [1, L2].
- He set up the Reconstruction Finance Corporation [1, L1], which provided loans to help firms through the depression [1, L2].

b) • The Wall Street Crash was an important cause of the depression as it directly led to the bankruptcy of many banks [1, L1]. And as a result of the crash, those banks that didn't go bankrupt began to call in their loans and severely reduced their lending, which then caused many firms to collapse [1, L2].
- However, there were other causes of the depression too, such as the underlying state of the economy at the time [1, L1]. For example, there was overproduction in industry. This meant that stock piled up, production fell, and staff were dismissed [1, L2]. There was also an unequal distribution of wealth, meaning that profits from the 1920s boom were not shared out as widely as they might have been. This meant that many people simply couldn't afford to buy the goods made by industry [1, L3].
- The above factors are interlinked. The banking crisis was caused by speculators who had borrowed money to buy shares, often at inflated prices [1, L1]. But when demand fell as a result of the underlying economic problems, investors began to sell their shares, causing share prices to fall, and causing investors to lose huge amounts of money [1, L2]. When share prices fell further in the panic that followed, more money was lost. And since many of the investors losing money were the banks themselves, the effects on the economy were disastrous [1, L3].
- It is likely that long-term weakness in the economy would have led to a recession at some point [1, L4]. However, the Wall Street Crash and the banking crisis that followed probably ensured that the recession turned into a depression [1, L4]. It is probably fairer to say that the main cause of the depression was actually the unregulated speculation [1, L4] that led to the Crash and the banking crisis in the first instance [1, L4]. [+ 3 marks for SPaG]

Section 11

1 a) • The source shows Lenin sweeping away the ruling classes [1, L1]. Lenin does this on behalf of the working class, shown by his flat cap [1, L1]. The source suggests the Bolsheviks were the main force behind the revolution of 1917 [1, L2]. The fact that Lenin is stood on top of the world suggests this revolution in Russia was just the start of a wider communist revolution [1, L2].

b) • The Bolsheviks won the civil war because of the brilliant leadership of Trotsky and the unity of the Red forces [1, L1], compared to the divisions of the White forces [1, L1]. The White army consisted of many groups, a long way apart, and all with different aims and purposes [1, L2]. This made attacks difficult to coordinate, and some groups didn't want to work together because of their political differences. This benefited the Red Army as they were able to fight the White armies one by one, rather than fighting on several fronts at once [1, L2].
- The Red Army was also well organised, supported and supplied. War communism was introduced, which was a strict and ruthless system that geared the whole country towards providing for the war effort [1, L3]. Also the communists, though only controlling a small part of the country, had control of the main cities, communications systems and railways, which made organising and supplying the Red Army easier [1, L3].

c) • The source describes the complete breakdown of law and order in Russia in September 1917 [1, L1], as well as the widespread mutiny of the armed forces [1, L1]. The source is useful in giving a first-hand account of the situation in September 1917 just before the revolution [1, L2], and describes how the Provisional Government had lost control of Russia [1, L2]. The source describes there being 'no law and order', and in fact after the failure of the Russian offensive against the Germans in July 1917, there was widespread rioting and mutiny against the government [1, L3].

Answers: Section 11

• But the source is only useful for telling us about the situation in Russia at that time and gives us no information on why the Bolsheviks were actually successful in taking power [1, L2]. It's clear the government had lost control, which would have helped the Bolsheviks' attempts to take over [1, L3]. But they also succeeded for reasons such as Lenin's leadership giving them a good sense of direction, the Red Army and their clear plan of how to seize power [1, L3].

• Also, this source is an eyewitness account written in 1922, by which time the Bolsheviks had won the civil war. So it's possible this account may be exaggerating the extent of the chaos in 1917 [1, L4], in order to justify the way in which the Bolsheviks seized power by force [1, L4]. [+ 3 marks for SPaG]

2 a) • The source shows a happy Stalin, together with a group of equally happy workers, next to a new hydroelectric complex [1, L1], part of his plan to modernise Soviet heavy industry [1, L1].

• The Soviet government replaced the relatively relaxed New Economic Policy (NEP) with state planning for industry [1, L2]. The Gosplan commission set targets for industrial production, with Five-Year plans drawn up containing production targets for heavy industries such as coal, oil and electricity [1, L2], and whilst the first plan's targets weren't met, production saw remarkable growth and output almost doubled by the end of the 1930s. The source is a painting showing one such achievement, a modern hydroelectric complex, built to produce more electricity [1, L3].

• But, these achievements were at the expense of Soviet workers [1, L2], who faced long working hours, poor living conditions and low wages. Also, much of the work was done in forced labour camps by criminals and political prisoners [1, L3]. The source does not show this side of things, but it is probably a piece of propaganda aimed at glorifying the achievements of the Stalinist policy of State planning [1, L3].

b) • In the 1930s, Stalin increasingly controlled all information available to the Russian people, aiming to shape and control their beliefs so his rule might be more readily accepted [1, L1]. Writers, journalists, historians, artists and teachers were forced to portray Stalin as Lenin's chosen heir, and to glorify his ideas and policies [1, L1]. His opponents were portrayed negatively or ignored, and alternative ideas suppressed [1, L1].

• But, whilst propaganda was an important part of Stalin's strategy, it does not completely explain how he was able to become a dictator. Another reason was his control of the Communist Party [1, L2]. Many party members were personally loyal to him, because they relied on him for career advancement. This then enabled him to carry out other strategies, e.g. controlling information and the purges [1, L3].

• The terror and purges were another reason [1, L2]. They began with the murder of Kirov, a popular head of the party, in 1934. Stalin used this as an excuse to root out any remaining enemies and increase his control of the party [1, L3]. Show trials were used to persuade people that Stalin was a great leader surrounded by evil conspirators, and that opposition was futile. The purges also spread to ordinary people and the armed forces [1, L3].

• The 1936 constitution also contributed [1, L2]. Many government posts were made subject to popular election, but this increased Stalin's power as only Communist Party members were allowed to stand, and his control meant he could select who was a candidate [1, L3].

• Propaganda did play a part in Stalin becoming a dictator, as it was used to reinforce and justify the Communist Party's use of terror. This terror made people too afraid to oppose him openly, and propaganda told them what they had to say in order to survive the terror [1, L4]. But it was Stalin's total control of the Communist Party which enabled him both to carry out the terror, and to create the propaganda to justify it [1, L5]. [+ 3 marks for SPaG]

3 a) • The Soviet government aimed to modernise industry in the 1930s by replacing the New Economic Policy (NEP) with state planning [1, L1] and the introduction of productivity targets via Gosplan [1, L1].

• The Gosplan commission was established to set targets for industrial production. The Five-Year plans set targets for all basic industrial factories and workers in heavy industries, e.g. oil and electricity [1, L2]. Whilst the first plan's targets weren't met, production saw remarkable

growth and output almost doubled by the end of the 1930s [1, L3].

• But, these achievements were at the expense of Soviet workers [1, L2], who faced long working hours, poor living conditions and low wages. Also, much of the work was done in forced labour camps by criminals and political prisoners [1, L3]. Different methods were used to motivate and encourage workers [1, L2]. For example, bonuses were paid to any workers who exceeded their production targets, and propaganda was used to encourage workers to work harder [1, L3].

b) • At the time of the revolution, Russian agriculture wasn't sufficiently productive [1, L1]. Stalin's solution was collectivisation, where all land was pooled into large, collective farms. Peasants would work together to produce food, which was sold at a fixed price to the Soviet government [1, L1].

• One way in which collectivisation was successful was that modern farming methods and technology were introduced into Russian agriculture [1, L2]. But this was unpopular with peasants, who resisted the change, feeling it would destroy their traditional way of life [1, L3].

• Collectivisation also ended the exploitation of peasants by greedy landlords and kulaks [1, L2]. However, the cost was high. Because Stalin blamed kulaks for some peasants refusing to collectivise, he ruthlessly persecuted them, killing many [1, L3].

• Collectivisation did increase agricultural production in the long term [1, L2], but between 1929 and 1933 production decreased, leading to widespread famine in 1932-33 which killed 5 million people [1, L3].

• Although collectivisation did modernise Russian agriculture and did lead to the increased productivity [1, L4] necessary to supply the industrialisation programme of the Five-Year Plans [1, L4], it was achieved at a terrible price [1, L4]. In addition, it could be argued that collectivisation merely replaced the exploitation of peasants by landowners with the exploitation of peasants by the government [1, L4]. [+ 3 marks for SPaG]

4 a) • The source shows Lenin sweeping away royalists and capitalists [1, L1], on behalf of the working class (shown by the flat cap) [1, L1]. The source's message is that Lenin was making the world a cleaner, more pleasant place by removing the 'polluting' royalty and capitalists [1, L2]. It also hints at this being part of a wider revolution [1, L3], shown by the fact that Lenin is sweeping ruling classes from the whole world [1, L4]. The picture shows Lenin as a force for good for working classes everywhere [1, L5].

b) • The source shows a happy Stalin, together with a group of equally happy workers, next to a new hydroelectric complex [1, L1], showing the success of his plan to modernise Soviet heavy industry [1, L2]. The painting is clearly propaganda aimed at glorifying the achievements of the Stalinist state planning [1, L2], and to show people who were proud and happy with their country's development [1, L3].

• The painting was published in 1935, two years after the Second Five-Year Plan started [1, L4]. These plans had increased production but at the price of misery and low living standards for workers [1, L5]. This picture aims to offer an encouraging vision of the beneficial end results, to try and motivate workers to keep working hard [1, L5].

c) • The source describes the complete breakdown of law and order, and widespread mutiny of the armed forces in September 1917 [1, L1]. The source is useful in providing a first-hand account of the situation and to describe how the Provisional Government had lost control. But it doesn't prove this was the key reason why the revolution succeeded [1, L2].

• There were many other reasons for the Bolsheviks' success, such as Lenin's strong leadership, which gave them a clear sense of direction, and a clear plan for how to seize power [1, L3]. The Bolsheviks' Red Army also played a big part in their ability to seize power [1, L4].

• Still, the source does suggest the country was in disarray, which must have been to the advantage of the Bolsheviks [1, L5], but it does not prove that this was the main reason for the Bolsheviks' success.

• By the time the source was written in 1922, the Bolsheviks had won the civil war [1, L5]. So it's therefore possible the account may be exaggerating the extent of the chaos in 1917 in order to justify the way in which the Bolsheviks seized power by force [1, L5].

254

Answers: Sections 11-12

5 a) • Thousands of sailors were unhappy with War Communism, the famine and the terror [1, L1], so they mutinied and seized Kronstadt naval base near Petrograd [1, L1]. Lenin was worried that dissent would spread when the Kronstadt sailors left the base, so he ordered Trotsky and the Red Army to crush them [1, L2]. The Kronstadt sailors were defeated and the base was captured in a brutal battle [1, L2].

b) • The NEP was a replacement for War Communism in 1921 [1, L1]. It meant that peasants no longer had to hand over all their produce for the war effort [1, L1].
• It allowed peasants to set up their own businesses [1, L1], paying tax on any profits [1, L1].
• Large industries remained in state hands [1, L2], although experts were paid a higher level of wages in order to run them efficiently [1, L2].

c) • War Communism was the economic policy followed by the Bolsheviks during the civil war (1918-21), to ensure the Red Army was well supplied with food and equipment [1, L1]. The state took over the management of all factories and farms, all private trade was banned, and crops were forcibly taken from the peasants [1, L2]. All adults had to work except pregnant women and the sick, and industrial workers weren't allowed to strike or be absent from work [1, L2].
• The result of these policies was famine and decline. From 1920 there were food shortages, there was famine from 1921, and over 7 million people died of hunger [1, L3]. Money became worthless and workers were paid in food and fuel instead [1, L2]. However, because of the food shortages, there wasn't enough food to go around, so workers left the cities. This caused industry to decline [1, L2].
• Opposition was dealt with ruthlessly [1, L1]. The Cheka (secret police) hunted down any enemies of the state [1, L2], and people were either shot or taken to forced labour camps. The same fate awaited any peasants who refused to hand over food to the Red Army [1, L3].
• Whilst this created a climate of fear and terror, it was the policy to put all production under state control that had the most horrific consequences: a famine that cost millions of Russian lives [1, L3]. [+ 3 marks for SPaG]

Section 12

1 a) • The source shows a civil rights march on Washington DC in August 1963 [1, L1]. This is an example of the kind of non-violent protest [1, L2] that was used to gain public support and put pressure on the government in the civil rights struggle [1, L2]. Other forms of non-violent protest included bus boycotts, sit-ins and freedom rides [1, L3].
• Not all protest was non-violent, though [1, L1]. For example, the Black Panther Party mounted armed patrols [1, L2] to protect people from police violence, the SNCC passed resolutions at its conference calling for a black militia (an armed force) [1, L2], and there were also riots in many inner-city areas [1, L3].

b) • Non-violent protest was a very effective way for African-American civil rights campaigners to achieve their aims [1, L1]. Many laws and attitudes changed as a result of the civil rights campaigns, in which non-violent protest played a major part [1, L1].
• Non-violent tactics, especially if they provoked a violent reaction, were able to generate a great deal of sympathy for the campaign's goals [1, L2]. For example, in Birmingham, Alabama in 1963, peaceful demonstrators were met by police with fire hoses, truncheons and police dogs [1, L3], and during the Freedom Summer of 1964, the murder of three student volunteers led to a great deal of publicity [1, L3].
• The Montgomery bus boycott was also a non-violent protest [1, L2]. This boycott eventually led to a landmark ruling in the Supreme Court against bus segregation laws. This shows that non-violent protest could lead directly to changes in the law [1, L3].
• A key figure in the civil rights struggle was Martin Luther King, who was in favour of non-violent protest to achieve his aims [1, L2]. He was able to generate huge amounts of support for the civil rights cause, with some of the marches he led being attended by hundreds of thousands of people, of all races [1, L3]. In 1964, he was awarded the Nobel Peace Prize, international recognition of the importance of the cause and the morality of the tactics he used [1, L3].
• This does not mean that every civil rights campaigner favoured

non-violent tactics. Members of the Black Panther Party went on armed patrols, claiming to be defending African Americans, and a Black Power conference called for an African-American militia to be set up [1, L4]. But non-violent protest does seem to have been the method that achieved the greatest results, possibly because it was able to generate sympathy among Americans of all races, without provoking a backlash from white Americans (as often happened with violent protests) [1, L5]. [+ 3 marks for SPaG]

2 a) • Martin Luther King was a campaigner for civil rights for African Americans in the USA. This poster claims that he is a communist [1, L1]. It has been put up next to a highway, where it will be seen by many people [1, L2] on the route of a civil rights march that King was leading [1, L2].
• In 1965, the USA was involved in an ideological struggle with the (communist) Soviet Union [1, L3]. The aim of this poster was therefore to show that King was sympathetic to the views of the Soviet Union [1, L4], and therefore undermine support among the public for King and his campaign [1, L4]. It might even have been intended to show King was some kind of 'traitor', which could have caused some of his supporters to abandon the campaign or become critical of King [1, L5].

b) • President Kennedy is making a speech about equal rights in the USA. He is saying that he would like all races to be treated equally [1, L1], but that at that time they were not [1, L2].
• In the early part of his presidency, Kennedy gave only limited support to the African-American civil rights campaign, as he did not wish to alienate Southern white voters [1, L3]. However, in this speech he is very clear that he wants the USA to be a land of equal rights. This would have been very important for the president to say, as it sets a precedent that others may well follow [1, L4]. So this speech shows that President Kennedy was willing to back the civil rights campaign at a time before some important civil rights bills had been passed. This certainly makes his contribution an important one [1, L5].
• However, the source doesn't tell us whether Kennedy did any more than just talk about equal rights. It also doesn't show how his contribution compares with that of other politicians [1, L5], such as President Johnson, who was president when some of the more important civil rights acts were passed into law [1, L5].

c) • This photograph shows a civil rights sit-in by three people in a crowded store in Mississippi in 1963 [1, L1]. Two of the protestors are white, and one of them is black [1, L1]. This shows that there were people of all races who supported the campaign for African-American civil rights [1, L2].
• It also sends a message that they are determined to campaign peacefully, since their protest was taking the form of a sit-in [1, L3], and it looks like they are being provoked by some of the people in the crowd (the man on the left looks like he is pouring something over one of the protesters) [1, L3]. This perhaps sends the message that the civil rights campaigners are actually behaving very reasonably and respectably, implying that their campaign is also reasonable and respectable [1, L4].

3 a) • The 1965 Immigration Act amended the existing system of quotas controlling the number of people of different ethnicities that could enter the USA [1, L1].
• The new Act used different categories to determine who should be allowed to enter the USA [1, L1]. These categories included kinship relations and occupation [1, L2].
• The effect of the Act was to increase immigration from Latin America and Asia [1, L2].

b) • The protest at Wounded Knee in 1973 aimed to secure better conditions for Native Americans [1, L1]. The village of Wounded Knee was seized at gunpoint by people protesting against corruption in the running of a reservation [1, L2]. The choice of Wounded Knee was symbolic [1, L2] because it was the site of an 1890 massacre of Native Americans by the Army [1, L3]. After a long siege, during which two people were killed, the issues that had led to the siege were settled by negotiation [1, L3], which was a significant triumph for the American Indian Movement (AIM) [1, L3].

Answers: Section 12

c) • Presidents Johnson and Nixon, and Rosa Parks all made significant contributions in the struggle for civil rights in the USA [1, L1]. The two presidents were in a position of great power, and so their contributions would clearly be significant, while the contribution of Rosa Parks attracted a great deal of attention, and led to a successful campaign against segregation [1, L1].
   • Rosa Parks made her mark when she refused to give up her seat on an Alabama bus to a white man, and was arrested [1, L2]. Her treatment led to a bus boycott [1, L3]. This peaceful protest led to a legal challenge of the law, and the Supreme Court eventually decided that segregation laws on buses were unconstitutional [1, L4].
   • President Johnson was in power when the Civil Rights Act of 1964 and the Voting Rights Act of 1965 were passed into law, both of which were very important [1, L2]. He also introduced a preferential hiring policy that aimed to change the under-representation of African Americans in various areas of employment [1, L3].
   • President Nixon also made an important contribution, since he introduced a programme which guaranteed a proportion of government contracts would be awarded to businesses owned by ethnic minorities [1, L3], a policy that was controversial at the time [1, L4].
   • Although all three people made contributions in the civil rights struggle, I don't think that they can all be considered equally important. I believe that Rosa Parks made the bravest and most inspirational mark. She was a member of a disadvantaged group herself, and made her protest at a time when the civil rights struggle was still seen by many people as an undeserving cause [1, L5].
   [+ 3 marks for SPaG]

4 • This photograph shows a civil rights sit-in by three people in a crowded store in Mississippi in 1963. It shows that there were people of different races supporting the campaign for African-American civil rights [1, L1], since the male and female protester in the foreground are white, and the other female protester is black [1, L1].
   • It shows that civil rights protests could be peaceful, since their protest is taking the form of a sit-in [1, L3], although it looks like they are being provoked by some of the people in the crowd (the man on the left looks like he is pouring something over one of the protesters) [1, L2], which suggests that the campaign aroused angry opposition [1, L3].

5 • At first glance, the message of the poster is quite surprising; it accuses Martin Luther King of being a communist, even though he wasn't [1, L1]. In 1965, most Americans were terrified of the threat of communism [1, L3], so by labelling King as a communist, the poster aims to make any of his sympathisers think twice about supporting him [1, L4].
   • The poster is also surprising because it is a very underhand tactic. [1, L1]. Today, it would be unacceptable to libel someone so publicly on a poster [1, L1].
   • However, in some respects, the poster is unsurprising. Some people were so against the civil rights movement they were willing to murder civil rights supporters [1, L1], so it is unsurprising that they tried to discredit King in any way they could [1, L2].

6 • The African-American civil rights campaign achieved many of its aims, in that many of the laws that discriminated against African Americans were changed [1, L1]. Non-violent protest was a vital tactic during this struggle, although this does not mean that changes happened without violence [1, L1].
   • Source A shows a civil rights march that took place in 1963. Some of the marchers have brought their children, showing that the likely intention was for this to be a peaceful march [1, L2]. Source B shows a sit-in, another peaceful form of protest. However, it looks as though all of the protestors have had something poured over them, which shows that even non-violent protests could generate violent reactions [1, L2].
   • Source D shows President Kennedy describing how "it ought to be possible" for Americans to attend public institutions "without having to be backed up by troops", or to register to vote "without interference or fear of reprisal". He also says that, at the time, this was not the case [1, L2]. This shows that violence had been used during the campaign

for African-American civil rights, though Kennedy is clearly talking about violence against those being discriminated against [1, L3].
   • So the sources do not support the view that the African-American civil rights campaign achieved its aims without violence [1, L3]. However, they do not show that campaigners intended to use violence themselves [1, L3].

7 • Both these sources date from the period of the civil rights struggle in the USA, in which Martin Luther King was a prominent figure [1, L1]. They both show scenes from marches that Martin Luther King took part in [1, L1], and so they say something about the tactics favoured by Martin Luther King [1, L2].
   • The fact that King took part in marches gives a clue as to his beliefs. Source A shows some of the marchers have brought their children [1, L1], which shows that this is probably intended to be a peaceful protest, suggesting King favoured non-violent action [1, L2].
   • Source C suggests that King was a communist, something that would not have been popular with Americans at the time, given that the country was involved in an ideological struggle with the (communist) Soviet Union [1, L3]. This means that King is unlikely to have put up the poster himself — it is much more likely to have been put up by people wishing to discredit King [1, L2]. So, this is unlikely to be a very good indication of King's political beliefs [1, L3].

8 • Martin Luther King was a leader in the black civil rights movement, and organised protests such as the Montgomery bus boycott, which eventually led to a landmark ruling in the Supreme Court against bus segregation laws [1, L1]. Sources A and C show that King had a considerable following, and considerable opposition. For example, Source A shows a march on Washington that King took part in, and it is clear that there are a considerable number of people there [1, L2]. In fact, this march was attended by hundreds of thousands of people, and the "I Have a Dream" speech that King made has become iconic.
   • Source C on the other hand shows that his campaign had attracted enemies with the means to erect this giant poster, which shows he was a figure worth trying to discredit [1, L3].
   • Source D shows part of one of President Kennedy's addresses to the American People. Kennedy was the leader of the USA at a crucial point in the civil rights struggle, and he is speaking out against the inequality that existed in the country [1, L1]. He contrasts his vision of a country where people are treated equally with the reality of the USA in 1963 [1, L2]. This would have been very important for the president to say, as it sets a precedent that others may well follow, at a time before some of the more effective civil rights bills had become law [1, L3].
   • The sources show that both Kennedy and King were very high profile figures able to command the respect and following of many people [1, L2]. While the sources show that King was an active member of the campaign and that his enemies tried to smear him [1, L3], they also show that Kennedy was in a unique position to influence the American people, due to the access to radio and television that he had as President [1, L4].
   • On balance, I think that Martin Luther King probably was the most influential figure in the civil rights struggle when it came to convincing people that the cause was right [1, L1], although other people were in a better position to actually change the law [1, L4]. The fact that King was assassinated also perhaps shows his significance, while after his death King was to become a martyr for the civil rights cause, meaning his influence continued [1, L4].
   [+ 3 marks for SPaG]

Answers: Section 13

Section 13

1 • This postcard shows two members of the Women's Auxiliary Army Corps [1, L1], showing how women helped the war effort [1, L2]. The postcard is appealing to people's sense of patriotism [1, L3], and is trying to get other women to help the war effort as well [1, L3], as shown by the patriotic caption "Doing Their Bit" [1, L4]. Since so many men had gone off to fight, there was a shortage of labour, and so women were needed to carry out a lot of jobs that men would traditionally have done [1, L5].

2 • Source B shows two members of the Women's Auxiliary Army Corps helping the war effort [1, L1], whereas Source D describes how one man was found guilty of hoarding food, which was illegal at the time [1, L1].
  • Source D should be a reliable source, in that it is a factual account of the result of a court case, and does not contain any opinions that may be biased one way or another [1, L2]. Source B, on the other hand, is trying to persuade women to help the war effort, and so is trying to present a particular image of people "doing their bit", and so the message needs to be treated almost as if it were propaganda [1, L2].
  • However, it is certainly true that women "did their bit". The women in the postcard are shown helping to keep the country supplied with food, but women worked in all kinds of industries, such as farming, engineering and manufacturing [1, L3]. Many of these jobs were directly related to the war effort [1, L4].
  • Source D describes how a man has been found guilty of the crime of hoarding food. Although some people did hoard food after rationing began in 1917 [1, L4], it never led to a situation where people were in danger of starving [1, L5].
  • Overall, I think Source B provides a more accurate view of British attitudes towards the war effort. We know that millions of people did "do their bit", as large numbers of men fought in the armed forces and large numbers of women joined the WAAC or took up work usually done by men in order to keep the country moving. There were people who did not act as the government would have liked (e.g. those who hoarded food), but not in big enough numbers that the war effort was derailed [1, L5].

3 • At first glance, the message of the poster is quite surprising, as it is using hunger strikes, a very unpleasant topic, in order to try and sell a breakfast cereal [1, L1]. The idea is to show that Plasmon Oats are so delicious that not even someone on hunger strike could resist them [1, L1].
  • Times were very different in the early 20th century, and this advert probably did seem less offensive then [1, L2]. Certainly the company who made the advert would not have expected a hostile reception from the public. In fact they would probably have been fairly confident that this would reflect the public mood [1, L3].
  • Given that the Suffragettes' tactics were often extremely militant, and that many people (including the Prime Minister) genuinely thought that women should not be allowed to vote [1, L4], the Suffragettes could easily have been very unpopular and acceptable targets for an advert like this, making the message seem less surprising than it seems at first [1, L5].

4 • The source describes how the Suffragettes' campaign was to be suspended because of the war [1, L1]. This is a very useful source for understanding Mrs Pankhurst's view on how to conduct the Suffragettes' struggle during the war [1, L1], since it was written by Mrs Pankhurst herself [1, L2], and dates from the month that war broke out [1, L2].
  • The extract is taken from a letter that was probably sent to members of the WSPU, and so represents the policy of the group [1, L3]. Since Mrs Pankhurst was an important member of this group, the official policy of the group may well coincide with her own personal view [1, L3]. However, it does use the words 'our', which suggests that she might be presenting the result of a discussion between several people that she did not personally agree with [1, L4].

5 • During the war, women performed different roles in society than they would have been used to [1, L1]. Because so many men were away fighting the war, there was a shortage of labour at home [1, L1], and so women performed a lot of jobs that would normally have been done by men [1, L2], such as those in munitions factories and engineering workshops, and on farms [1, L3]. This shows that men and women generally did work together to help the country fight the war [1, L3].
  • Source B shows members of the Women's Auxiliary Army Corps (WAAC) working as a gardener and a baker [1, L4], while Source C shows how the WSPU suspended its activities for the duration of the war, given that the country was in crisis [1, L4].
  • However, despite the fact that most people did work together for the common good, the sources show that not all men and women acted together and supported each other [1, L5]. In fact, there were some people who took advantage of the circumstances [1, L5]. For example, after compulsory food rationing was introduced in 1918, some people hoarded food, as is shown in Source D, sometimes so that they could resell it for a profit later [1, L5].
  • So although the sources do seem to suggest that the country did pull together during the crisis of the war, they also show that there were certainly some who tried to take advantage of the circumstances for their own ends [1, L5]. So the statement is largely, but not exclusively, true [1, L5]. [+ 3 marks for SPaG]

6 • The source shows that women's hunger strikes were being used to try and sell a breakfast cereal. The poster is saying that Plasmon Oats were so delicious that not even someone on hunger strike, a very extreme method of protest, could resist them [1, L1].
  • The idea that Suffragettes were acceptable targets for such an advert suggests the company had little sympathy or respect for the Suffragettes' cause or for the Suffragettes themselves [1, L2].
  • The company must have believed this attitude would also have reflected the overall public mood too [1, L3], and so we can probably learn that the Suffragettes were unpopular or were not taken seriously [1, L3].

7 • The postcard shows two members of the Women's Auxiliary Army Corps [1, L1].
  • The message was that women were taking on jobs traditionally done by men at a time when many men were away fighting [1, L2]. The idea was to show that they were playing their part in the war effort, a message which is reinforced by the caption "Doing Their Bit" [1, L2].
  • The purpose of the source is to generate a sense of patriotism amongst British women [1, L3] and to persuade other women to join the war effort and "do their bit" for their country [1, L3]. The aim was to try and solve the labour shortage facing Britain in 1916, when so many men were away in the army [1, L3].

8 • The UK did not have plentiful supplies of food during WWI. In fact, compulsory rationing was introduced in 1918 [1, L1]. One of the problems was that German U-boats sinking merchant shipping made it difficult for the UK to import food [1, L1], meaning that Britain had to grow more of its own food [1, L1].
  • Source B shows a postcard trying to help recruit women for service in the Women's Auxiliary Army Corps [1, L2]. The photo shows a gardener and a baker, both of whom would have been helping keep the country supplied with food. This supports the view that the country was trying to grow more of its own food [1, L2], which in turn suggests that food from overseas was not in plentiful supply [1, L2].
  • Source D shows how someone was convicted of hoarding food, which again suggests that there was not enough food for everyone to purchase and store large supplies [1, L2].
  • However, neither source shows how precarious (or not) the position was [1, L3]. In fact, although there were shortages of some kinds of food, no one starved [1, L3]. So the sources show that resources were being carefully managed, but not that there was a serious risk of the country running out [1, L3]. [+ 3 marks for SPaG]

Answers: 219-20

Practice Assessment

Page 219: Origins of World War I

1 a) • One reason for tension was the disagreements between Austria-Hungary and Serbia [1, L1]. Austria-Hungary had areas with a large Serbian population, which many Serbians hoped would become part of a larger Serbia [1, L2].
   • Another reason came in 1908, when Austria-Hungary annexed Bosnia and Herzegovina. This angered the Russians as they felt that Austria-Hungary was breaking an agreement with them [1, L2]. Russia allied itself with Serbia, as a fellow Slavic country, and due to its rivalry with Austria-Hungary. This was serious as Austria-Hungary was a member of the Triple Alliance and Russia was a member of the Triple Entente. This meant that arguments between them over the Balkans could, and did, lead to wider conflict [1, L3].

b) • The source suggests the Anglo-German naval race would lead to war and death [1, L1]. In some ways the source is correct, as the naval race did contribute to the tensions that led to World War One [1, L2]. Germany attempted to double the size of its navy between 1900 and 1914, a direct challenge to Britain's naval superiority, which led to rivalry between them [1, L2].
   • However, the two opposed alliances were probably a more important cause, as the conflict started in the Balkans [1, L3]. Germany's alliance with Austria-Hungary led it to declare war on Russia, which had mobilised to defend Serbia [1, L3].
   • The cartoon isn't biased as it portrays both countries as heading on a course of mutual destruction, and so is more anti-war than pro-German. But while not biased, it only warns against possible war with Britain. In fact Britain was the last of the major European powers to enter the war [1, L4].

c) • Both reasons played a part in Germany's involvement in the First World War. Germany became a rival of Britain's because it was jealous of its empire [1, L1], and it was in support of Austria-Hungary that Germany entered the war [1, L1].
   • To gain a large empire, Germany needed to challenge Britain's naval superiority [1, L2]. Between 1900 and 1914 Germany attempted to double the size of its navy. This increased tensions with Britain, which reacted by building more (and better) warships of her own [1, L2]. Germany's imperial ambitions also led to tensions with France. In 1905 and 1911 Germany unsuccessfully tried to force the French to give them influence and control in Morocco [1, L2].
   • But the spark that set off WW1 was a crisis in the Balkans. Germany was allied with Austria-Hungary, and so tied into its struggles in the 'powder keg of Europe' [1, L3]. Allying with Austria-Hungary increased Germany's chance of war as it was involved in a struggle with Slav nationalists who were supported by Serbia, who were backed by Russia [1, L3]. In 1908, Germany had shown its willingness to anger Russia in favour of Austria-Hungary over the 1908 annexation of Bosnia and Herzegovina. This would have made war with Russia more likely [1, L3].
   • While Germany's alliance with Austria-Hungary was the immediate reason for Germany's declaration of war with Russia, it was Germany's desire for a larger empire that was one of the main reasons it was an enemy of both Britain and France in 1914 [1, L4]. The tensions between Germany and Britain and France would have been a big reason to make the alliance with Austria-Hungary stronger and of a clearer military nature, to make sure Germany had allies against them when war came [1, L4] [+ 3 marks for SPaG].

2 a) • There was tension between Germany and France over Alsace and Lorraine [1, L1]. The French had lost the area in the Franco-Prussian war in 1871, and had prepared Plan 17 to recapture it [1, L2].

b) • There was tension in the Balkans between Austria-Hungary and Serbia [1, L1]. Austria-Hungary had a large Serbian population in its lands and wanted to keep them as part of their empire. Serbia wanted these Serbs to join its country, which would require Austria-Hungary to lose part of its territory [1, L2]. This led to tensions between Russia and Austria-Hungary [1, L1]. Russia allied itself with Serbia, as a fellow

Slavic country [1, L2]. Because Russia and Austria-Hungary were in rival alliances their disagreements led to wider troubles [1, L1]. When the Archduke Franz Ferdinand was assassinated by a Serbian nationalist, Austria-Hungary demanded the right to send troops into Serbia, and when they were refused they shelled Belgrade. The Russians mobilised to defend Serbia, which led to the two alliances declaring war against each other [1, L2].

c) • Britain declared war when Germany sent troops through neutral Belgium [1, L1] to attack France [1, L2]. Britain had agreed to protect Belgium, and so ordered Germany to withdraw. When Germany refused, Britain declared war [1, L2].
   • But Britain also declared war partly because it was a member of the Triple Entente, along with Russia and France [1, L1]. Although neither the Triple Entente nor the Triple Alliance (of Germany, Austria-Hungary and Italy) was intended as a military alliance, the tensions they created meant countries soon wanted strong armed forces [1, L2]. So when Russia and France went to war, Britain was quickly drawn into war too [1, L2].
   • Another of Britain's reasons for entering the war was its rivalry with Germany [1, L1]. Germany had challenged Britain's naval superiority by building up its navy [1, L2]. Britain, as an island with a large overseas empire, felt threatened by Germany's naval expansion [1, L2].
   • So although Germany's invasion of Belgium was the immediate cause of Britain entering the war in 1914 [1, L3], it seems likely that Britain was likely to end up at war eventually anyway because of its membership of the Triple Entente and its long-term rivalry with Germany [1, L3]. Britain's defence of Belgium was only the spark that sent Britain to war, and perhaps not as important as some of the other underlying reasons [1, L3] [+ 3 marks for SPaG].

Page 220: The Peace Settlement

1 a) • One of the League's main early successes was stopping international conflicts [1, L1]. The League resolved disputes such as those between Germany and Poland over Upper Silesia, and the dispute over the Aaland Islands between Finland and Sweden [1, L2].
   • The League also had some success in its aim to improve people's living and working conditions [1, L2], by carrying out important campaigns against problems like slavery, and against diseases such as leprosy, plague and malaria [1, L3].

b) • The source suggests the Treaty aimed to destroy Germany [1, L1]. In some ways the source is correct, since the Treaty aimed at reducing German military and economic strength [1, L2]. It was ordered to pay £6600 million in reparations, which was not due to be paid off until the 1980s [1, L2].
   • However, Germany had invaded France, which had led to millions of deaths and the devastation of a large part of France and Belgium. The French suffered the worst of the Big Three, as the war had been fought on their territory and they wanted to make sure Germany would not be strong enough to fight again [1, L3]. Also, Germany had turned down the chance of a peace based on the 14 points in 1918, so they should have expected the settlement to be tougher than that would have been [1, L3].
   • The source is arguing from a German perspective that the settlement was too harsh, but doesn't take into account the suffering that had taken place caused by the war, which Germany was largely responsible for [1, L4].

c) • Unhappiness with the Treaty of Versailles meant Germany would seek to challenge the settlement when they got the chance [1, L1]. Also, the League of Nations failed to stand up to aggressive countries like Japan, which meant other countries weren't afraid of it [1, L1].
   • The Treaty's harshness, which left Germany with a huge reparations bill and a loss of much of its territory, meant they in particular didn't feel any commitment to the world order the League was trying to protect [1, L2].

Answers: 220-1

- In 1931, the League faced its biggest challenge when the Japanese used the excuse of disturbances in Mukden to launch an invasion of Manchuria. The League sent Lord Lytton, who said Japan was the aggressor, but the League did nothing [1, L2]. This showed the world that the League was unprepared to step in to fight aggression, which gave confidence to leaders like Mussolini, who launched his invasion of Abyssinia, confident that the League would do nothing [1, L2].
- The Treaty failed to create a peaceful Europe in which Germany felt no need to seek to improve its lot through conflict [1, L3]. However, if the League had stood up to aggression, it might have discouraged other countries from being so aggressive [1, L3]. Also, it could have come within the powers of a more active League of Nations to organise the restructuring of the Versailles settlement, and to stand up for the defeated powers when the victors threatened them, as the League failed to do when the French occupied the Ruhr, and as the Americans did with the Dawes plan [1, L3].
- This suggests that the League's failure to stand up to aggression was the more important reason, as it was within its power to take these decisions and failed to do so [1, L4]. However, the Treaty's harshness was one of the main reasons why the USA didn't join the League of Nations, and that greatly reduced its ability and willingness to get involved in international disputes [1, L4] [+ 3 marks for SPaG].

2 a) • The US didn't join the League of Nations as many Americans thought that being in the League would get them involved in wars that had little to do with them [1, L1]. They feared that this would be expensive. Seeking to avoid this became known as isolationism [1, L2].

 b) • The Germans thought the Treaty was unfair because it was harsh and they hadn't had any say in it [1, L1]. The Treaty was called a 'Diktat', as they'd had no choice but to sign it, and it was a source of anger in Germany [1, L2].
 - Many thought it was unfair because the reparations bill was too high [1, L1]. Germany was given a reparations bill of £6600 million, and it would have taken them until the 1980s to pay it off [1, L2].
 - Also, Germany was forced to accept that it was responsible for the war [1, L1]. This came in the form of Article 231, and was rejected by the Germans as they didn't accept they were solely responsible for starting the war [1, L2].

 c) • There were disagreements at the conference because Britain and France wanted to punish Germany, whereas America wanted to be fairer [1, L1]. Britain and France had suffered more than America and so had more reason to be angry with Germany [1, L1]. France was more concerned with making sure Germany was too weak to fight again, whereas America wanted to be fairer to stop wars happening again [1, L1].
 - France and Britain were particularly keen to make Germany take the blame for the war, so they refused to let the Germans take part in the talks [1, L2]. This led to Article 231, which stated it was Germany and its allies who were wholly responsible for the war [1, L2].
 - France wanted to punish Germany more than America did because it had suffered more in terms of casualties, but also because much of the war took place on French soil [1, L2]. The US suffered a lot less than France and Britain, and so were more concerned with creating a fairer and more open Europe, as expressed in President Wilson's 14 points [1, L2].
 - France shared a border with Germany and wanted to make sure that Germany was kept militarily and economically too weak to threaten France again [1, L2]. America was more concerned with avoiding wars again, and as its 14 points show, wanted free sea movement and free trade for all nations. It was more concerned with making economies grow than restricting the German economy [1, L2].
 - The arguments on how much to punish Germany, and whether a weakened Germany was necessary for a secure Europe, would have been influenced by how much the countries, and its voters, had suffered during the war [1, L3]. The desire to punish and to weaken Germany were linked, given that punishing them economically with huge reparations would have stopped it strengthening its economy and its military. Without the desire to punish severely, the US was less likely to want to weaken it militarily and economically [1, L3]. In the end it would have been the experience of the war which was the most

important factor, as the French leader Clemenceau, who wanted to be the harshest on Germany, was criticised by many French people for not being harsh enough. In contrast, it wasn't accepted in the US as it was felt to be too harsh [1, L3] [+ 3 marks for SPaG].

Page 221: Origins of World War II

1 a) • Hitler broke the Treaty by putting troops back in the Rhineland [1, L1], using a treaty between Russia and France as an excuse, claiming it meant Germany was threatened and needed troops on its borders [1, L2].
 - He also built up the German military, against the terms of the Treaty, by reintroducing conscription [1, L2]. Although Britain protested, in 1935 they agreed that Germany could rearm by signing a naval agreement which accepted Germany would build its navy past the Treaty's limits [1, L3].

 b) • The source suggests the policy of appeasement was popular and supported by the British people [1, L1]. In some ways the source is correct. Many British felt the Treaty of Versailles had been too harsh on Germany, and that it should be allowed to rebuild its power [1, L2]. Also, no one in Britain wanted another war in 1938 [1, L2].
 - The source is a British photograph, showing Chamberlain waving the Munich agreement in front of a happy crowd, which aims to reassure the British people that his negotiations had brought about "peace for our time" [1, L3]. However, whilst Chamberlain appears to be proudly holding up the agreement, the source doesn't provide good proof that he held the same attitude towards appeasement as the British people [1, L4]. Britain's economy and armed forces were weak, so it's possible Chamberlain gave in to Hitler, not to avoid war, but instead to buy more time to prepare [1, L4].

 c) • Both reasons played a part in the success of Germany's aggressive foreign policy. France and Britain's desire to avoid war meant they let Hitler get away with aggression against other countries [1, L1]. An opportunity to stand up to Germany was missed when Hitler reintroduced conscription, which broke the Treaty of Versailles [1, L2].
 - The large number of German speakers living in areas outside Germany's borders gave Germany an excuse to try to take those areas [1, L1]. Many Germans lived in the Sudeten area of Czechoslovakia. These groups' existence gave Germany an excuse for aggression [1, L2]. The Nazis organised demonstrations in the Sudetenland complaining against discrimination, which allowed it to seem like Germany was only defending Germans when it took the Sudetenland [1, L2].
 - The presence of Nazi Germans in other countries gave the Nazis the tools to create disorder abroad [1, L3], and the Treaty's perceived unfairness made appeasement more popular as a way to a fairer settlement [1, L3]. But it was the desire to avoid war that meant that no one stood up to Germany when it was threatening the Sudetenland or Austria, and no direct action was taken when Germany invaded Czechoslovakia itself [1, L3].
 - France and Britain struggled through the Depression and had suffered terribly through World War One. It seems likely that these experiences of their own would be more important in their thinking than the fate of Germans outside Germany [1, L4]. At the same time, the presence of Germans in other countries was a reason for Britain and France not standing up to Nazi aggression and made the aggression easier in the first place. But the fact that Britain and France hadn't reacted to acts of aggression from countries other than Germany, for example when Mussolini invaded Abyssinia, suggests that it was the unwillingness to fight that secured the success of Hitler's aggressive foreign policy [1, L4] [+ 3 marks for SPaG].

2 a) • The Manchurian Crisis was caused by the Japanese invading Mukden and the rest of Manchuria in 1931 [1, L1]. They claimed they were putting down a disturbance [1, L1]. But the League of Nations sent Lord Lytton to investigate, and his report said that the Japanese had been wrong [1, L1]. However, the League failed to stand up to Japanese aggression, showing the world it was weak [1, L1].

Answers: 221-2

b) • The Depression damaged the League of Nations by making the powerful countries less able to afford military action [1, L1]. France and Britain were both badly hit [1, L2], and in the absence of the US, they were the ones who carried the most responsibility for enforcing the League's decisions, but weren't strong enough [1, L3].
• The Depression also made the League's work harder by causing poverty [1, L2], which led to the rise of a number of extreme right-wing leaders, such as Hitler, who people hoped would bring stability [1, L3].
• The Depression also played a part in certain conflicts. For example, the Manchurian crisis was sparked off because Japan attempted to cover the damage done to its economy with military expansion [1, L3].

c) • The USSR was disappointed at how France and Britain hadn't stood up to Germany [1, L1]. The USSR and Germany signed a pact agreeing not to attack each other [1, L1].
• The USSR feared a German attack [1, L2], as Germany had recently annexed Austria and taken much of Czechoslovakia [1, L3]. But the USSR also agreed to split up Poland with the Germans, which suggests that their aims may not have solely been to gain security [1, L3].
• However, the USSR had also made a pact with France against Hitler in 1935 [1, L2]. This showed the USSR recognised the threat that Hitler posed [1, L4]. But, the French had not stood up to Germany when the Germans threatened war on Czechoslovakia to take the Sudetenland, or when they had annexed Austria [1, L4]. This would have frightened the USSR and suggested that they'd need to make arrangements of their own with Germany as they couldn't rely on France [1, L4].
• So in some ways, the USSR was justified in signing the pact. The USSR knew Hitler couldn't be trusted and, because of appeasement, realised they couldn't depend on Britain and France to resist any further attempts by Germany to expand [1, L5] [+ 3 marks for SPaG].

3 a) • Hitler was able to get away with sending troops into the Rhineland, as Britain and France didn't want to get involved in a conflict [1, L1]. The French were in the middle of an election campaign, which meant that no one was prepared to start a war [1, L2].

b) • In October 1935, Mussolini sent troops with heavy artillery and tanks to invade Abyssinia [1, L1]. Mussolini wanted to make Italy a great empire again and Abyssinia was well placed to add to Italy's lands in Africa. He had also seen Japan get away with the Manchurian invasion, despite threats from the League of Nations [1, L2].
• The Abyssinian leader appealed directly to the League for help [1, L1]. The League imposed economic sanctions, but delayed banning oil exports in case the USA didn't support them [1, L2].
• But, Britain and France didn't close the Suez Canal to Italian ships [1, L1]. This meant supplies could still get through despite the imposed sanctions, and by May 1936 Italy had conquered all of Abyssinia [1, L2].

c) • The Depression caused poverty [1, L1], which led to the rise of a number of extreme right-wing leaders, such as Hitler, who people hoped would bring stability [1, L2]. Some of these leaders planned to solve domestic problems through territorial expansion, which made conflicts between countries more likely [1, L2].
• The Depression also damaged the economies of those in the League of Nations [1, L1], making the powerful countries less able to afford military action [1, L2]. France and Britain were both badly hit, and in the absence of the US were the ones who carried the most responsibility for enforcing the League's decisions, but weren't strong enough [1, L2].
• The Depression also played a part in certain conflicts [1, L1]. For example, the Manchurian crisis was sparked off because Japan attempted to cover the damage done to its economy with military expansion [1, L2]. When the League of Nations failed to confront the Japanese aggression, its weaknesses were seen by dictators like Hitler and Mussolini, meaning it was just a matter of time before it was challenged again [1, L2].
• All these reasons played a part in making long-term peace less likely. The Depression weakened the League, but it already had weaknesses, as without US help it found it hard to enforce sanctions [1, L3]. Also, the weaknesses were only really exposed due to conflicts such as the Manchurian crisis, and the rise of extreme right-wing leaders, caused in part by the Depression [1, L3]. It was this exposure that

encouraged dictators like Hitler and Mussolini, making conflict a greater possibility. However, it is probable that no organisation could have stopped aggressive leaders like Hitler peacefully [1, L3] [+ 3 marks for SPaG].

Page 222: Origins of the Cold War

1 a) • Communist USSR wanted to control Eastern Europe [1, L1]. The Red Army occupied Eastern Europe after World War 2 and Stalin installed pro-Soviet puppet governments in countries such as Poland and Hungary [1, L2]. Free speech was suppressed and non-communist parties banned [1, L2]. Even communist parties were controlled by the Cominform, so they consisted solely of Russian-style communists [1, L3].

b) • The source suggests the US and USSR had a good, friendly relationship in 1945 [1, L1]. It is true that they had been allies during the Second World War [1, L2]. Also, in February 1945, the USSR leader Stalin, US President Roosevelt and British Prime Minister Winston Churchill met at the Yalta Conference to make plans as to what they wanted to happen after the war, which shows there was cooperation between the two [1, L2].
• However, the situation changed after Yalta. Leadership changes in the US and Britain, as well as Stalin's expansion westwards into the Baltic states, led to mistrust between the "big three" [1, L3]. Then, after the war, the capitalist US and communist USSR became rivals [1, L3].
• The photograph shows Russian and US soldiers shaking hands. It is clearly a publicity shot, aiming to celebrate the end of the war being near, and the fact that the allies had successfully defeated Germany. But whilst it shows the US and USSR had been united against a common enemy, their differing ideologies would actually cause huge problems and tensions in the years to come [1, L4].

c) • The nuclear arms race began when the US and USSR became rivals after WWII [1, L1]. Both countries felt threatened by each other and so wanted to be the strongest superpower, with the most powerful weapons [1, L2]. In 1945, the US dropped two atom bombs on Japan. They were incredibly powerful and killed thousands of civilians. The US had attempted to keep the atom bomb a secret from the USSR. For four years, the US was the world's only nuclear power [1, L2]. But in 1949, the USSR exploded their own atom bomb. This was followed by the US developing the even more powerful hydrogen bomb in 1952. The USSR had their own by 1955. This made them even more afraid and mistrustful of each other, as they both had hugely powerful weapons at their disposal [1, L2].
• The Korean War was a war between North and South Korea, in which the US intervened, on behalf of the UN [1, L1]. The war began when communist North Korea went to war with South Korea to try and reunite the country. This was seen as a direct challenge from communism to the West [1, L3]. The UN ordered an immediate attack on North Korea, and by September 1950, UN forces drove the North Koreans back. President Truman gave General MacArthur, the UN commander, permission to invade North Korea. This worried China, who feared invasion from the West. So in October 1950, China joined the North Koreans in an attack which drove the UN forces back [1, L3]. MacArthur wanted to attack China, Truman disagreed, and MacArthur was sacked after an argument. Truman wanted peace and in 1953, a ceasefire was agreed [1, L3].
• Both reasons made a world war a real possibility. But the arms race actually created a 'Cold War' (rather than a 'hot war') between the US and USSR. They realised the destructive power of their atomic weapons was so great that using them would be catastrophic, not just for them, but the whole world [1, L4]. The Korean war posed a greater threat of world war, as fighting was already happening. If matters had escalated (e.g. after China entered the war) the world might have faced a global war [1, L4] [+ 3 marks for SPaG].

2 a) • The US tried to stop communism spreading through the Marshall Plan, which promised aid to European countries to rebuild their economies [1, L1]. The USA believed that if Europe remained weak, then it might be vulnerable to communism [1, L2].

Answers: 222-4

b) • The USSR was communist, whilst the USA was capitalist. This meant the USSR believed in having a one-party-state [1, L1], while the US valued a democracy with free elections [1, L2].
  • Communism meant state control of agriculture and industry [1, L1]. In contrast, the US valued private enterprise and believed anyone could, and should be able to, work their way to the top to be wealthy and successful [1, L2].
  • Also, the USSR wanted to control Eastern Europe, and aimed at communism spreading worldwide [1, L1]. But this made the US fearful, as they saw it as a threat to their democracy, and also to the growth of their capitalist economy [1, L2].

c) • Berlin had been divided at Potsdam in August 1945. The four zones of occupied Berlin were split between France, Britain, the US and USSR [1, L1]. Berlin was in Eastern Germany, which was controlled by the USSR. This caused tension when the USA and USSR became rivals after World War Two, due to their ideological differences [1, L2]. Communism in the East and capitalism in the West created a 'Cold War' between the USSR and US, and an "iron curtain" began to divide the West from the Soviet Union [1, L2].
  • In 1948, the USSR blockaded Berlin in opposition to the West [1, L1]. Stalin had ordered the blockade in protest at the British, French and US plan to combine their Berlin zones [1, L2]. This new combined zone would have a single government and new currency to aid economic recovery. Stalin didn't like this, as he wanted to keep Germany weak [1, L2]. He was trying to establish a zone of influence in Eastern Europe [1, L1]. He wanted to push the allies out of West Berlin, so the USSR could get rid of a symbolic outpost of the West within communist territory [1, L2]. The US, especially, wanted to demonstrate its resolve in standing up to communism [1, L2].
  • The main reason why tensions existed were the ideological differences between the West and the USSR. The capitalist US and communist USSR were fearful of each other, and both wanted to be the biggest superpower [1, L3]. Whilst the blockade did add to tensions, it served more to highlight the tensions that already existed, and it acted as a way of both sides trying to exert power [1, L3]. Despite Stalin's claims, the blockade was really an attempt to push the West out of Berlin, as part of USSR plans to expand its zone of influence. The West's response of the Berlin airlift showed their determination in not allowing this to happen [1, L3] [+ 3 marks for SPaG].

Page 223: Cold War Crises

1 a) • Czechoslovakians tried to make their country more free [1, L1]. In 1968, Dubcek tried to bring in greater freedom for Czechoslovakians, such as free elections and the right to travel to the West [1, L2]. To reassure the USSR, Dubcek promised not to take Czechoslovakia out of the Warsaw Pact [1, L2]. But the USSR wasn't prepared to let Czechoslovakia weaken communism in Eastern Europe, so they sent 500 000 troops in. This led to Brezhnev announcing that the USSR would intervene in any country where socialism was threatened; this was known as the Brezhnev Doctrine [1, L3].

 b) • The Cubans were worried about the US invading [1, L1]. The US had supported attempts to overthrow Fidel Castro [1, L2] and backed the Bay of Pigs invasion, which was carried out by Cuban rebels, but was aided by the CIA [1, L2]. This led to the Cuban Missile Crisis, as it was the threat of US invasion that led Castro to ask the USSR for military assistance [1, L3]. But it was the presence of the USSR's nuclear missiles on Cuba, only about a hundred miles from American soil, which made disputes between the USA and Cuba into the potential cause of a nuclear war [1, L3].
  • The banner was up in Cuba and would probably have been taken down if it had expressed a different viewpoint. However, that doesn't mean fears of an American invasion were inaccurate or not justified [1, L4].

 c) • The Berlin Wall surrounded West Berlin [1, L1]. It had been built to stop people from East Germany crossing to the West and was a tightening of the USSR's grip on the people of Eastern Europe [1, L2].
  • The U-2 crisis was where the USSR shot down a US spy plane [1, L1]. The crisis was an embarrassment for the US, as President Eisenhower was shown to have lied about the spy plane [1, L2]. He had denied the plane was a spy plane, but the USSR was able to produce the pilot, who had survived, and the wreckage as evidence [1, L2].

• The building of the Berlin Wall was a bad moment for US-USSR relations. It led to President Kennedy making his speech in which he declared a commitment to protect West Berlin [1, L3]. However, Berlin had already been split in two, and the tensions were in no way as serious as those that had taken place in 1948 [1, L3]. Perhaps the U-2 crisis was more serious as it disrupted talks between the nations: Khrushchev left talks in Paris with the US when Eisenhower refused to apologise [1, L3].
• The building of the Berlin Wall was historically more important as it affected far more people and stopped the flood of people, 2½ million between 1949 and 1961, crossing from East to West Germany [1, L4]. But the dispute over the U-2 crisis was more directly between the two powers and led to diplomatic confrontation, with Khrushchev abandoning talks in Paris, suggesting a serious chill in relations [1, L4] [+ 3 marks for SPaG].

2 a) • The Cuban Missile Crisis was ended when Khrushchev agreed to order his ships to return to the USSR [1, L1]. He also agreed to remove the missiles from Cuba [1, L1]. In exchange, the US agreed to lift the naval blockade [1, L1]. The US also promised not to invade Cuba [1, L1].

 b) • The US was unsuccessful as the Vietcong were very skilful soldiers [1, L1], who avoided open conflict and mainly used sudden attacks and ambushes [1, L2]. Also, the US wasn't used to jungle warfare [1, L2].
  • US public opinion turned against the war due to the high casualties, with around 14 000 US soldiers killed in 1968, and due to the terrible images broadcast on television [1, L3]. This led to the US pulling its troops out of Vietnam [1, L3]. Also, the North Vietnamese won the support of many in the south as they treated them well, whereas US bombing was responsible for the deaths of many civilians [1, L3].

 c) • The Cuban Missile Crisis nearly brought about nuclear war [1, L1]. Both the US and USSR had to back down [1, L1]. The USSR was forced to remove its nuclear weapons from Cuba [1, L2]. It also had to turn its ships around and send them away [1, L2].
  • The Americans got what they wanted — the removal of the nuclear missiles from an island so close to their border, which is why they had threatened to invade. This suggests that the crisis was a victory for the US [1, L3].
  • US pressure had forced the USSR to remove its weapons from Cuba and turn its ships around. This suggests the USSR was defeated [1, L3]. But, the USSR got the USA to promise not to invade Cuba, which was the threat that had first made Cuba request US military assistance [1, L4]. The USSR also got other concessions from the USA, in particular the removal of US nuclear weapons from Turkey, on the USSR's border [1, L4]. That this was kept secret suggests America might have viewed the concession of removing their weapons from Turkey as a defeat [1, L4].
  • In the end it seems that both sides recognised that the crisis had come too close to nuclear war to seem a victory for either side. To stop such disagreements becoming dangerous again there was a direct phone line put in place between the Kremlin and the White House [1, L5] [+ 3 marks for SPaG].

Page 224: End of the Cold War

1 a) • The election of Ronald Reagan helped end détente [1, L1]. He was a dedicated anti-communist [1, L2], who described the USSR as an "evil empire" [1, L2]. He restarted the arms race with the USSR. Under his leadership the US developed new weapons, such as the medium-range Cruise and Pershing missiles, and started the Star Wars programme, which aimed to develop laser weapons able to shoot down missiles [1, L3].

 b) • The poster is comparing the USSR to a prison camp [1, L1]. The source is correct in that the USSR was less free than the West, and didn't have elections or a free press [1, L2]. The communist government had a firm grip on the USSR [1, L2]. The differences in ideology, with the USSR being a one-party state and the US a democracy, were important in creating tension between the two nations [1, L3]. The source claims that the Olympics should be boycotted because of the USSR's lack of freedom, as the US did in fact do in 1980 [1, L3]. However, the US had other more pressing reasons for its

Answers: 224-7

boycott, such as the USSR invasion of Afghanistan [1, L4].

c) • The USSR struggled due to an economic crisis caused by the Cold War [1, L1]. Their involvement in the 1980s arms race was too expensive [1, L2], and living standards dropped because so much money was spent on weapons [1, L2]. The communist government was unable to give Soviet people the same high living standards as the West, causing discontent, which ultimately played a part in the end of the USSR [1, L2].
• Gorbachev also played an important role. His policies helped Eastern Europe break away from communist control [1, L1]. He brought in new policies of openness. These allowed for the election of those opposed to Gorbachev and communism in general [1, L2]. His policies were the more immediate cause of the end of the USSR. His abandoning of the Brezhnev Doctrine led to the loss of control over countries like Hungary and East Germany [1, L3], while some parts of the Soviet Union demanded independence, especially the Baltic republics [1, L3].
• However, it was the problems with economics that would have affected the citizens of the USSR, and USSR-controlled Europe, more strongly [1, L4]. If the economy had been sound, with higher living standards and low corruption, then people would have been less likely to use the freedoms given to them by Gorbachev to protest or attempt to break away from the USSR [1, L4] [+ 3 marks for SPaG].

2 a) • Détente ended because of the Soviet invasion of Afghanistan [1, L1]. This led the US to withdraw from the SALT 2 arms limitation treaty, and to boycott the Moscow Olympics [1, L2].

b) • Détente was a period when the US and USSR tried to get along better [1, L1]. The USSR was struggling to pay for its military spending. Also, the US withdrew from Vietnam and tried to get on better with the communist world [1, L2]. Both countries tried to cut down on their numbers of weapons [1, L1]. In 1972 the two superpowers signed the SALT 1 agreement, which put limits on their numbers of nuclear weapons [1, L2].
• They also reached an agreement on the European borders [1, L1]. They agreed to the Helsinki Accords, which recognised the postwar borders, including the split of Germany [1, L2].

c) • The Cold War ended because Gorbachev changed the USSR's foreign policy [1, L1]. He abandoned the Brezhnev Doctrine, and told the UN the countries of Eastern Europe now had a choice; the USSR would no longer control them [1, L2]. This meant the USSR wouldn't intervene if countries in Eastern Europe stopped being communist [1, L2].
• Gorbachev also brought in elections [1, L1]. New policies allowed the election of those opposed to Gorbachev and communism in general [1, L2]. Poland held free elections in 1989, where a new non-communist government came into power, and communism began to fall all over Eastern Europe [1, L2].
• The Cold War also ended as the USSR couldn't afford to match US military spending [1, L1]. The cost of the arms race had reduced living standards in the USSR, which caused discontent [1, L2]. This forced the USSR to seek friendlier relations rather than competition [1, L2].
• The most important immediate reason for the end of the Cold War was the collapse of the Soviet Union's control of Eastern Europe [1, L3], followed by its own collapse [1, L3]. But this was brought about by the combination of economic problems and political liberalisation [1, L3] [+ 3 marks for SPaG].

Page 225: A New World

1 a) • The US invaded Iraq because Iraq hadn't met the conditions of the 1991 ceasefire [1, L1], and it believed that Iraq had been developing weapons of mass destruction (WMD) [1, L1].
• The US thought that Iraq was harbouring and protecting terrorists [1, L1], and was therefore a threat to the US [1, L2].

b) • The placard is protesting against the Iraq War [1, L1], and is a parody recruitment poster. The source suggests the Iraq war was about oil [1, L2], the message being that Americans only wanted to invade Iraq to secure oil [1, L3]. The placard suggests lives are being wasted to achieve this, as it refers to blood for oil [1, L4]. However, as the

poster is for a demonstration, it is clearly anti-war and doesn't take into account the other reasons for US involvement in Iraq [1, L4]. The US claimed their involvement was based on fears about the presence of weapons of mass destruction (WMD) and Iraq's failure to comply with Resolution 1441 [1, L5].

c) • There were protests against the Iraq War because some people felt the US had ulterior motives for invading Iraq [1, L1], while others thought there were better ways to deal with the situation [1, L1].
• Another reason was that the US didn't get the UN's support [1, L2]. The UN had passed Resolution 1441 to try and force Iraq to give up its weapons. Iraq failed to comply, but many people thought the resolution didn't authorise war, and so the US should have got the UN's support before invading [1, L3]. Also, some people thought the US was using the issue of WMD and links to Al-Qaeda to cover over its main interest in Iraqi oil [1, L2]. The doubts about WMD and Al-Qaeda were proved correct [1, L1], as there was no evidence of strong links between Saddam Hussein's regime and Al-Qaeda, and no evidence of WMD [1, L3].
• There were other concerns about Western nations invading Iraq. Some people were concerned there were echoes of colonialism [1, L3], as Iraq had been ruled by the British as a League of Nations mandate [1, L3]. Others felt uncomfortable with the mainly Christian nations invading the mainly Muslim Iraq [1, L3] [+ 3 marks for SPaG].

Pages 226-227: Causes and Events of the First World War

1 a) • The cartoon shows a broken-down steamroller and an exhausted Russian soldier [1, L1]. The cartoon is mocking the idea, held by many in the years before the war and at its start, that the Russian army would 'roll' into Europe and crush Germany [1, L1]. In fact in 1917, the year this cartoon was published, Russia had given up fighting following the Bolshevik Revolution [1, L2], and signed the Treaty of Brest-Litovsk, which required Russia to give up large sections of its old empire [1, L2].
• This is a German cartoon, so it is probably meant as propaganda [1, L3] to encourage Germans to think that the forces they were supposed to fear weren't as strong as was imagined [1, L4]. This would have been an important message, as 1917 had seen the start of the US's involvement in the war — a major source of concern for Germany [1, L5].

b) • The poster celebrates Britain's 'victory' in the Battle of Jutland [1, L1]. The Germans had left the battle first, which the British considered a victory for them [1, L2]. However in the clash of around 250 ships, the British had lost more ships — 14 to the Germans' 11 — and the German ships and firepower had seemed stronger [1, L2].
• This is a propaganda poster, encouraging people to remember the encounter as a victory [1, L3]. The poster links this 'victory' to more clear-cut triumphs in the past, as can be seen by the old-fashioned sailing ships in the top half of the poster [1, L4]. At the time, no one would have known that this would be the last major sea battle of the war, and so the British probably also wanted to increase confidence in the Royal Navy, and to keep up morale [1, L5].

c) • This source describes the events on the Western Front in 1918, with the Germans launching a huge attack which was successful at first, but which was eventually beaten back [1, L1]. It was written by somebody who was there in the trenches, and so it gives an idea of what it was like to be there at the time [1, L2].
• The source does have limitations. It was published around 75 years after the events it describes and so relies on old memories [1, L4]. And as it was written by someone who was involved in the fighting, he was only telling what happened on one small part of the front [1, L5].
• However, the source does accurately describe the kind of events that took place during the Ludendorff Offensive in March 1918, when Germany tried one massive attack to win the war before the Americans were ready to send their troops into battle [1, L3]. Initial successes were followed by demoralising defeats, after which you would expect the German troops to be exhausted and look defeated, as Germany itself was heading to an exhausted defeat [1, L5].

- As the source is correct in at least some of its details, there is no reason to suspect that it is misleading. However, it should be treated with caution, as it's a record of events a long time before the source was published, and it is based on personal memories that would need to be checked against other people's from the time [1, L5].

2 a) • There were nationalist groups in many of the countries that the Ottoman Empire had controlled, causing instability [1, L1].
   • As the Ottomans were forced out, there was increasing tension between Austria-Hungary and Serbia, since Austria-Hungary had areas with a large Serbian population, and many Serbians hoped they would become part of a larger Serbia [1, L2].
   • One flashpoint between Austria-Hungary and Serbia came in 1908, when Austria-Hungary annexed Bosnia and Herzegovina [1, L1]. This angered the Russians, as they felt Austria-Hungary was breaking an agreement. This was serious as Austria-Hungary was a member of the Triple Alliance, and Russia was a member of the Triple Entente. This meant that arguments between them over the Balkans could, and did, lead to wider conflict [1, L2].

   b) • The development of trench warfare, and the use of new technology, made attacks far more difficult [1, L1], since they tended to favour the defenders [1, L2]. There was also thick mud in no-man's land, making quick attacks even more difficult as soldiers and vehicles became bogged down [1, L3]. This would have made things difficult for generals expected to achieve rapid victories [1, L3].
   • The generals were also commanding massive armies, far bigger than anyone had commanded before [1, L2]. And because these armies were largely made up, at least at first, of inexperienced conscripts, they would have been harder to command than the generals were used to [1, L3].

   c) • Germany became a rival of Britain's because it was jealous of Britain's empire [1, L1]. To gain a large empire itself, Germany needed to challenge Britain's naval superiority, which made Britain worried [1, L2]. Between 1900 and 1914 Germany attempted to double the size of its navy, increasing tensions with Britain, which reacted by building more (and better) warships of her own [1, L3].
   • Germany's imperial ambitions also led to rivalry with France. In 1905 and 1911 Germany unsuccessfully tried to force the French to give them influence and control in Morocco. [1, L3].
   • But the spark that set off WWI was a crisis in the Balkans [1, L1]. Germany was allied with Austria-Hungary, and therefore tied into its struggles in the 'powder keg of Europe' [1, L2]. Allying with Austria-Hungary increased Germany's chance of being drawn into a war, as Austria-Hungary was involved in a struggle with Slav nationalists who were supported by Serbia, which was in turn backed by Russia [1, L4].
   • In 1908, Germany had shown its willingness to anger Russia in favour of Austria-Hungary over the annexation of Bosnia and Herzegovina [1, L4]. This would have made war with Russia more likely — and in fact, it was against Russia that Germany first declared war [1, L4].
   • While Germany's alliance with Austria-Hungary was the immediate reason for Germany's declaration of war with Russia, it was Germany's desire for a larger empire that was more responsible for drawing it into a war, as it was this that made it an enemy of both Britain and France by 1914. This tension between Germany and Britain and France would have led to a strengthening of Germany's alliance with Austria-Hungary, and also to this alliance becoming more military in character, to make sure that Germany had allies against Britain and France when war came [1, L5] [+ 3 marks for SPaG].

Pages 228-230: Germany: 1918 to 1945

1 a) • The source says that Germany began to work with other countries to help its recovery [1, L1], suggesting that Germany, through Stresemann, was cooperating more with foreign countries and trying to deal with problems peacefully [1, L2].
   • This effort was recognised by other countries [1, L1], as is shown by Germany being allowed to become a permanent member of the League of Nations and through Stresemann being awarded the Nobel Peace Prize [1, L2].

   b) • In the Munich Putsch, the Nazis attempted to seize power by force and failed [1, L1]. This led to the Nazi Party reinventing itself and using different tactics to try to gain power [1, L1].
   • After Hitler's release from prison, the Nazis realised they couldn't achieve power through force alone, and so changed their tactics [1, L2], deciding to use the democratic system to gain control instead [1, L3]. The Party was reorganised on a national basis [1, L2], and sophisticated propaganda methods developed and used to try and gain support [1, L3].

   c) • Source A is a German cartoon showing Ebert rowing a boat through a stormy sea towards the safety of the island in front of him [1, L1]. This shows that Ebert and the Weimar Republic faced great difficulties [1, L1].
   • The source is useful because it shows how Ebert's task was seen in Germany at the time he was in power [1, L2]. The cartoonist is making the point that Germany was facing real difficulties, although there was hope in the distance [1, L3].
   • However, the source gives no details about the actual problems faced by the Weimar Republic [1, L2], and so we cannot tell which particular economic or political problems the cartoonist is commenting on [1, L2]. It also doesn't show how people felt about Ebert's efforts to deal with the problems [1, L3], although the boat is at least being steered in the right direction, which is a clue [1, L3].
   • So although the source is useful for studying attitudes in Germany at the time [1, L4], it is of little use for studying the details of the problems it is commenting on [1, L4] [+ 3 marks for SPaG].

2 a) • The photograph shows a senior member of the armed forces who has a picture of Hitler on the wall of his cabin [1, L1]. This is an example of how propaganda was used by the Nazis to increase support among the German people [1, L1].
   • This photo was perhaps trying to persuade the German people that Hitler was a strong and authoritative leader [1, L2], who had the support of the armed forces [1, L3]. This would be one of many Nazi messages carried in the German media as Hitler attempted to infiltrate all aspects of German people's lives (including those in the armed forces) [1, L2].
   • This photograph also shows Hitler defying the Versailles Treaty [1, L2], which was much hated by the German people [1, L2]. The treaty banned Germany from having submarines, but this picture suggests that Hitler had made Germany's armed forces, and therefore Germany itself, strong again. This rearmament provided jobs for the German people, and aided Germany's recovery from the Depression. It also boosted German pride, after the humiliation of the Treaty of Versailles [1, L3].

   b) • Propaganda was used to spread Nazi ideas and beliefs [1, L1]. The Nazis took over the media [1, L1], controlling radio broadcasts, and using films and posters to spread their messages [1, L2]. Books and newspapers were censored so that no anti-Nazi material was published [1, L1], and all artists, writers, journalists and musicians had to register with the Ministry of Public Enlightenment and Propaganda [1, L2]. The aim was to try and control how German people thought [1, L2]. Nazi propaganda was also taught in schools, and subjects like history were rewritten to fit in with Nazi beliefs, in order to indoctrinate young people with Nazi ideas and to establish loyalty to the Nazis from a very young age [1, L3].
   • However, the Nazis controlled the German people in other ways. They created a climate of fear in Germany with the SS and the Gestapo. These were police-style organisations that sought out and arrested anyone who opposed the Nazis. Those arrested might be put into one of the new concentration camps [1, L3]. This meant German people were intimidated into only being positive about the Nazi beliefs and regime. The SS in particular were feared for their cruelty [1, L3].
   • To monitor the population effectively, local wardens were employed to make sure Germans were loyal to the Nazis, and people were encouraged to report anyone who expressed opposition, so people felt unable to express anti-Nazi views even around friends and family, in case they were informed on and arrested [1, L3].
   • Propaganda and censorship did play a huge role in the way the Nazis controlled the German people, and they recognised its importance in training young people to be the Nazis of the future [1, L4]. However,

it was the use of the secret police that had the biggest impact on controlling the people, as it created such a climate of fear that people were too afraid to express any negativity about the Nazis and their regime, for fear that their own family and friends would report them [1, L5] [+ 3 marks for SPaG].

3 a) • The cartoon shows Ebert rowing a boat through a stormy sea [1, L1]. He's got to get through this stormy sea to reach the safety of the island in front of him [1, L1], so the message is partly that as the first President of the Weimar Republic, he faces a difficult task to steer Germany to safety and stability [1, L2].
• The cartoon acknowledges that the Weimar Republic faces many difficult challenges, represented by the stormy sea [1, L3]. These partly resulted from the fact that it was set up after Germany was defeated in WWI, which led directly to many of the difficulties Ebert now had to overcome (e.g. the reparations Germany was forced to pay) [1, L4]. However, the message of the cartoon seems to be that Ebert is steering the boat in the right direction, and so it is basically a vote of confidence in him [1, L5].

b) • The photograph shows a senior member of the armed forces who has a picture of Hitler on the wall of his cabin. The photo was probably published as propaganda [1, L1].
• The photo was perhaps trying to persuade the German people that Hitler was a strong and authoritative leader [1, L2] who had the support of the armed forces [1, L2].
• This cartoon was published in the late 1930s, after Hitler had begun rearming the German military [1, L3], and so it may have aimed to show that Hitler was defying the much-hated Versailles Treaty, which banned Germany from having submarines [1, L3].
• This message that Germany was militarily strong with a strong leader may have been aiming to reassure the German public [1, L4] at a time of increasing tension in Europe in the run-up to WWII [1, L4].

c) • The source says one man was given a job through the compulsory labour service, rather than being on the dole [1, L1]. However, the man says he was actually better off on the dole than doing this job, while the other man talks about having low wages and poor working conditions [1, L2].
• The Nazis gave work to 6 million unemployed people. But as the source describes, some people considered the kinds of jobs they were offered under the Nazis as actually worse than having no job at all [1, L3]. The second worker clearly feels overqualified for the work he is doing, while the first worker complains that he is forced to buy terrible food at quite a high price. There were also no longer any trade unions, so workers couldn't campaign for better conditions [1, L4].
• The extract was written by someone who actually lived in Nazi Germany, and so it should give a reliable insight into how things actually were then and how people felt [1, L5].
• Overall, the source doesn't prove most Germans were better off. In fact, the opinions of these two are actually negative towards these jobs [1, L5]. It also only tells us about the employment situation, and so doesn't give any other information about people's lives in Nazi Germany [1, L5].

4 a) • Stresemann urged workers in the Ruhr to return to work [1, L1]. He also introduced a new Rentenmark to make the currency more stable [1, L1], and accepted the Dawes plan [1, L1], which meant the US would lend money to Germany, so that they were able to pay reparations [1, L2].

b) • The Nazis believed Aryans were the 'master race' [1, L1] and that people of other ethnicities were inferior [1, L2]. The Nazis wanted a German population of only 'pure' Aryan people who fitted in their idealised, unified society [1, L3], and wanted to eliminate those who didn't fit, for example people of other races or those who held different beliefs [1, L3].
• The Nazis especially persecuted the Jews as they blamed them for the problems in German society [1, L2]. Hitler claimed it was their fault that Germany had lost World War 1, which was the root of Germany's problems [1, L3].

c) • Hitler consolidated his power in various ways in the years preceding 1934 [1, L1].
• The Reichstag fire was used to remove communist opposition [1, L1], while during the Night of Long Knives, Hitler removed opposition from within his own party [1, L2]. The Enabling Act established Hitler as a dictator, giving him power to rule as he chose [1, L2].
• The Reichstag fire happened just before the 1933 election. Hitler claimed it had been started by a communist, and used this to whip up fear and opposition against the communists. Many communists were arrested in this period. Hitler was also able to obtain emergency powers to deal with the situation, and used these to intimidate communist voters [1, L3]. For these reasons, Hitler and the Nazis were able to win more seats in the 1933 election and consolidate their power in the Reichstag [1, L3].
• The communists still won 81 seats in the 1933 election, so Hitler declared them illegal. This meant he had enough support to bring in an Enabling Bill, which let him govern for four years without parliament [1, L4]. This made all other parties illegal, and meant that Hitler was now able to make his own laws, meaning he was almost in full control of Germany [1, L4].
• However, Hitler still had rivals within his own party, in particular Ernst Röhm, who controlled the SA. During the Night of the Long Knives, Hitler had several hundred people killed, including Röhm, and so any potential opposition had been stamped out [1, L4].
• The three factors were all important, but consolidated power in different ways. The Reichstag fire and the Enabling Act were important in consolidating the Nazis' power. However, it was the Night of the Long Knives that concentrated power in Hitler's hands alone. Overall, I think the Enabling Act was the most important factor, as it made the previously vital institution of parliament more or less irrelevant [1, L5] [+ 3 marks for SPaG].

5 a) • The source tells us the Nazis forced people to work, for example through compulsory labour services [1, L1]. These jobs gave workers low wages, bad food and poor working conditions [1, L2], and people sometimes did jobs they were overqualified for [1, L2]. The source shows how one worker would have preferred to collect the dole, while another describes tough work in poor conditions [1, L3].

b) • The Nazis tried to influence young people through controlling education [1, L1]. Schools taught Nazi propaganda and subjects were rewritten to fit in with Nazi beliefs, such as anti-Semitism. Young people were therefore indoctrinated with these beliefs [1, L1].
• Teachers were encouraged to join the Nazi Teachers' Association and trained in Nazi methods [1, L1]. Children were told to report anyone who didn't use these methods, which aimed to instil the belief that the Nazi way was the right way [1, L2].
• The Nazis also created groups like the League of German Maidens and the Hitler Youth [1, L1], where boys were trained to be soldiers and girls to be wives and mothers, with the aim of establishing loyalty in people from a very young age [1, L2].

c) • Hitler was able to strengthen his power in the Reichstag as a result of the fire [1, L1]. This is because, by blaming a communist for having started the fire, he was able to whip up opposition to communists generally, and then start a mass arrest of communists [1, L2].
• Hitler was also given emergency powers to deal with the situation [1, L2] and used these powers to intimidate communist voters [1, L3], allowing the Nazis to increase their share of the vote in the election that followed shortly after [1, L3].
• A few weeks later, but still in an atmosphere where communists were distrusted because of the Reichstag fire, Hitler declared the communist party illegal, giving him enough support in parliament to pass the Enabling Act, effectively making Hitler a dictator [1, L3].

d) • The Nazis created a climate of fear in Germany through the use of the SS and the Gestapo, police-style organisations [1, L1]. They sought out and arrested anyone who opposed the Nazis [1, L2], meaning the German people were intimidated into only being positive about the Nazi regime, with the SS in particular being feared for their cruelty [1, L3].
• Local wardens were employed to make sure Germans were loyal to the Nazis [1, L2], and people were encouraged to report anyone who was disloyal [1, L3].

• Those arrested could be placed in concentration camps, which were used to hold political prisoners or anyone considered dangerous. This again made people afraid to voice their opposition [1, L3].

6 • The depression caused the Nazis' popularity to rise [1, L1]. During the depression the Weimar government kept changing, but none managed to solve the economic crisis [1, L2], so extremist groups like the Nazis became more popular, as people looked for strong leadership [1, L3].

• Hitler promised the Nazis would make Germany great again and bring back prosperity, which appealed to many of those who were suffering. This meant Nazi membership and popularity grew [1, L3].

• A change of tactics also helped. After the Munich Putsch, Hitler realised the Nazis couldn't gain power through force alone, and decided instead to try and gain control through the democratic system [1, L1]. He reorganised the party and developed sophisticated propaganda techniques. This new strategy was successful and their popularity grew, as people then saw them as a viable choice to lead the country [1, L3].

7 • The Versailles Treaty was a major cause of the Republic's problems, since it created massive discontent amongst the people [1, L1]. Many Germans denied they'd lost the war, and did not feel that they alone were responsible for starting it. They therefore hated the government for signing the treaty that punished Germany so harshly and that blamed Germany alone for causing the war through the 'War-Guilt Clause' [1, L1].

• As part of the Treaty, Germany had to pay reparations. In 1923, when they defaulted on payments, the French took up occupation of the Ruhr to take resources instead [1, L2]. Germany ordered workers there to stop working, devastating German industry, leading to an economic crisis and hyperinflation. The mark lost its value and people lost savings [1, L3].

• But the Weimar Republic also had weaknesses in its constitution, which caused political problems [1, L2]. Proportional representation was used to elect members of the Reichstag. This led to lots of political parties being represented, which made it hard for the governments to pass laws, and made them look ineffective [1, L3].

• The government also had to deal with riots and rebellions. For example, in the 1920 Kapp Putsch, rebels led by Wolfgang Kapp took over Berlin to form another government [1, L3]. The Weimar government had to put down these rebellions and punish the rebels, but this was hard to do as many judges sympathised with people like Kapp [1, L3].

• The Versailles Treaty did create huge problems for the Weimar Republic [1, L4], and it ultimately led to further problems like the economic crisis [1, L4]. But weaknesses in the constitution were the main reason for the problems. The coalition governments were too weak and ineffective to solve any problems [1, L4], fuelling people's dissatisfaction, and leading to riots and rebellions [1, L4] [+ 3 marks for SPaG].

Pages 231-232: The USA: 1919 to 1941

1 a) • Source D shows that the 1920s were a time of great social change [1, L2], with things like dancing and cocktail parties becoming much more popular, and church attendance falling [1, L1]. It was also a time when people had a lot of money to spend [1, L2] on activities such as going to the cinema, and on consumer goods such as radios [1, L2].

b) • Prohibition led to a growing trade in illegal alcohol [1, L1] and also to an increase in organised crime [1, L1].

• Prohibition led to many people manufacturing their own, illegal liquor (moonshine) [1, L2]. A large number of illegal bars (speakeasies) also opened to sell the alcohol that had been obtained illegally [1, L2].

• The trade in illegal alcohol was very lucrative, and many gangs became involved [1, L3]. This led to a wave of murders and other crimes (e.g. corruption), as gangs competed against each other for business [1, L3].

c) • The picture shows Americans in a crowded bar toasting the end of Prohibition with beer [1, L1]. It suggests the reaction of Americans to the end of Prohibition was very positive [1, L1].

• But this only shows the reaction of a very small number of people [1, L2] at the end of the Prohibition era [1, L2]. It does not show people's attitudes before or immediately after Prohibition's introduction, and it does not show the reaction of people who were not happy that Prohibition had ended (who would not be in a bar) [1, L2].

• Attitudes towards Prohibition may well have changed after it was introduced [1, L3] due to the negative effects it had on American society (e.g. it led to increases in crime and corruption) [1, L3], and so this photo should not be used to gauge earlier attitudes towards Prohibition [1, L3]. [+ 3 marks for SPaG]

• Also, the photo is quite possibly staged [1, L4]. This means it may not be a typical reaction [1, L4] [+ 3 marks for SPaG].

2 a) • The New Deal was unpopular with many big businesses [1, L1]. The cartoon shows two businessmen complaining about how the New Deal is ruining the country (even though the headlines show that the profits of many businesses are actually rising) [1, L1].

• There are various reasons why many businessmen might have objected to the New Deal. Rich businessmen might have objected because the rich had to pay more tax to pay for some of the New Deal's measures [1, L2]. Many businessmen claimed that these higher taxes discouraged people from working harder and creating more wealth and jobs [1, L3].

• Businessmen also raised objections that the New Deal allowed trade unions into the workplace [1, L2], which may well have been seen as interference in their business affairs [1, L3].

• Some people also objected to measures that were quite 'socialist' and 'un-American' in character (e.g. direct relief for the unemployed), which they felt made people too dependent on government aid to get by rather than relying on their own efforts [1, L2]. Many businessmen (who were likely to hold capitalist views) are likely to have objected to these measures [1, L3].

b) • The Depression almost certainly cost Hoover the 1932 election [1, L1]. He was making efforts to try to solve the problems of the Depression, but his approach did not focus on helping individual Americans [1, L1]. Franklin Roosevelt (FDR) promised a new and energetic approach and the New Deal, and he was swept to power in the election [1, L1].

• President Hoover's policies to deal with the Depression included an expansion of public works, a Home Loans Act to help people pay their mortgages, and financial help for businesses through the Reconstruction Finance Corporation [1, L2].

• However, Hoover's policies were mainly based around the belief that 'rugged individualism' was the key to solving the problems of the Depression. This meant that, instead of providing individuals with financial aid, he saw the government's job as being to create the conditions in which individuals could work themselves out of poverty [1, L2]. He also refused to pay bonuses to WWI veterans in the 'Bonus Army' protests of 1932, and sent in the police and army to break up their camps. This all made Hoover very unpopular with voters [1, L2].

• Hoover's policy of imposing high tariffs on imported foreign goods, and the tariffs imposed by other countries in retaliation, were perhaps even making problems worse [1, L2].

• FDR promised a very different approach. His New Deal included a promise of direct relief for individuals [1, L3], as well as of recovery and reform for industry [1, L3]. His energetic campaign must also have made it look like the country's problems would be handled with a real sense of urgency [1, L3].

• The Depression was a big factor in the 1932 election. Even if Hoover's approach would have solved the problems eventually, Roosevelt promised individual Americans more immediate help [1, L4], and this must have given him a huge advantage [1, L5] [+ 3 marks for SPaG].

3 a) • The cartoon shows two businessmen complaining about the New Deal, even though the headlines show that the profits of many businesses are

Answers: 231-5

actually rising [1, L1]. This shows that the New Deal was unpopular with many big businesses [1, L2], but that (in the cartoonist's view) the businessmen's views are mistaken and the New Deal is not actually ruining the country [1, L3].
- The cartoon shows the businessmen as fat and well-dressed, and complaining about a plan that was designed to help people who were desperately poor as a result of the Depression, so it is showing businessmen as unsympathetic characters [1, L4].

b) • The source shows that FDR wanted to reduce the suffering of the unemployed by providing direct relief initially [1, L1], and then by creating more jobs [1, L2]. The source does not show whether the policies were successful though [1, L3].
- In the short term, emergency relief was provided to reduce the most immediate suffering, with the government paying for soup kitchens and dole payments [1, L4]. Eventually, the New Deal did create jobs [1, L4], though not as many as were needed [1, L5].

4 • The 1920s saw the Ku Klux Klan, a racist group, gain new popularity [1, L1]. The group was opposed to African Americans being given equal rights [1, L2], and used violence and intimidation to achieve its aims [1, L2].
- There were also racist laws, such as the 'Jim Crow Laws' that discriminated against African Americans [1, L1]. For example, some African Americans were effectively barred from voting in elections [1, L2].
- Segregation was another practice allowed by the law [1, L1]. This meant that whites and African Americans had to use separate facilities, such as schools, buses, parks and theatres [1, L2]. Although the facilities were supposed to be 'separate but equal', the ones provided for African Americans were usually much worse [1, L2].
- During this period, immigrants were also discriminated against during the 'Red Scare' [1, L1], when over 4000 people were deported [1, L2]. [+ 3 marks for SPaG].

Pages 233-235: Russia: 1905 to 1941

1 a) • The Bolsheviks abandoned strict communism [1, L1]. Lenin was pragmatic and could see War Communism was damaging Russia, and that they needed to slow the rate of reform to allow Russia to recover [1, L2]. The Bolsheviks were more concerned with holding on to power than enforcing their communist principles [1, L1]. Rebellions such as the Kronstadt Mutiny had shown that if the Bolsheviks wanted to keep power, they'd have to compromise, at least in the short term [1, L2].

b) • The Provisional Government was only ever meant to be temporary [1, L1], but it soon found itself hit by an economic crisis [1, L1]. Inflation meant that prices were ten times higher in 1917 than in 1914, making the country more unstable [1, L3].
- The Provisional Government was also undermined by the activities of the Soviets [1, L2]. The Petrograd Soviet issued 'Order Number 1', which said soldiers shouldn't obey the Provisional Government if the Soviet disagreed, undermining the Provisional Government's authority [1, L3].
- The Provisional Government inherited a Russia in near chaos, due to economic crisis and food shortages. But it was the Provisional Government's failure to get out of the war — the main cause of Russia's problems — that was perhaps the biggest cause of its unpopularity and its eventual overthrow [1, L3].

c) • The source shows a Red Army soldier fighting a caricature capitalist [1, L1]. The source is limited, as it is clearly Bolshevik propaganda [1, L1]. But it does show how the Bolsheviks wanted the war to be perceived [1, L2]. Since many Russians chose to side with the Reds, and the Bolsheviks went on to win the war, many people do seem to have felt sympathy for the Bolshevik cause [1, L2].
- However, the source does not show how those who supported the Whites felt [1, L2], or how the many ordinary people who didn't like, but went along with, Bolshevik rule felt [1, L4].
- The source is useful in that it shows how people felt the Red Army was defending Russia from foreign threats, which is understandable, since the Whites were backed by a range of foreign powers surrounding Bolshevik Russia [1, L3].

- The poster is also useful in showing how supporters of the Bolsheviks may have seen this moment as the "dawn" of a new age for Russia, as the poster has a large rising sun for a background [1, L3]. Perhaps the final battle is meant to involve the Red Army surging through Poland to join up with communists elsewhere to carry out a world revolution [1, L3].
- The poster is most useful for showing how the Reds would have gained support for various patriotic reasons (as defenders of Russia) as well as for political reasons (defending and spreading revolution) [1, L4] [+ 3 marks for SPaG].

2 a) • This source shows how photos were doctored under Stalin [1, L1]. Stalin also purged those he disagreed with out of the party [1, L1].
- Not only does this source show how Stalin tried to remove from sight those he wanted forgotten, it also shows how Stalin tried to make himself look more important, since in this photo he is left standing on his own in the middle of the picture [1, L2]. In fact, the official history of the October Revolution was rewritten to give Stalin a more important role than the relatively minor one he'd had in the real events [1, L3].
- Much of Stalin's power was based on fear [1, L2]. Stalin's control of the party was secured with a series of purges, which eventually included various organisations and 'non-political' people [1, L2]. Stalin used the NKVD, the secret police, to imprison or execute anyone suspected of disloyalty [1, L3]. No one, not even Stalin's wife, was safe if Stalin doubted them [1, L3].

b) • The policy was a failure in the sense that food production actually fell [1, L1]. Part of the problem was the resistance from farmers [1, L2], who burnt their crops and destroyed their livestock rather than have the communists take them. This meant that a programme designed to increase food production actually led to famine [1, L2]. The policy was devastating for those whom Stalin blamed for its failure, the kulaks, or rich farmers [1, L1].
- An estimated 3 million people who had previously been involved in food production were killed during collectivisation [1, L2].
- However, from some perspectives collectivisation was a success — for example, by 1939, 99% of farm land had been collectivised [1, L3]. Collectivisation was also a success in that it put communism into practice in the countryside [1, L1], since party officials ran things on behalf of the state, rather than leave things to rich farmers or landlords [1, L3]. And collectivisation strengthened the Communist Party's control of the countryside, since the Communist Party gained the kind of hold over rural areas that previously they had only had in the cities [1, L3].
- From the point of view of most ordinary Russians in the countryside Stalin's agricultural policy was a disaster. It destroyed their way of life, forced them into conflict with the government, and led to the deaths of millions, and famine and shortages for others [1, L4].
- However, Stalin appeared indifferent to the suffering of his people. The fact that collectivisation was completed, and that the Communist Party tightened its grip on the rural areas of Russia, would have meant him considering collectivisation a success [1, L5]. And the fact that the communists were now feared in the countryside may also have been a sign of success for Stalin, rather than a sign of failure [1, L5] [+ 3 marks for SPaG].

3 a) • The poster shows a Red Army soldier defending Russia by fighting off a caricature capitalist [1, L1], suggesting the Russian leadership believed the civil war had struck a decisive blow against capitalism [1, L2].
- The soldier is stood on top of the world, which suggests this revolution is intended to spread to other countries [1, L1]. The poster also has a rising sun for a background, suggesting the "dawn" of a new age for Russia and Europe [1, L3].

b) • War Communism damaged the Russian economy, and the Bolsheviks faced unrest [1, L1].
- War Communism led to workers leaving the towns and cities in search of food in the countryside. This led to a decline in industry [1, L2]. The Bolsheviks wanted industry to be strong and Russia to develop so that they could prove that communism could work [1, L3].

Answers: 233-5

- War Communism may also have been scrapped to help end revolts against the Bolsheviks [1, L2]. The fact that the Kronstadt sailors mutinied was particularly worrying, as they had been supporters of the communists in 1917. It showed that the Bolsheviks were perhaps losing support due to their policies [1, L3].
- Although the policy of War Communism can be seen as important during wartime to guarantee supplies to the Red Army, Lenin may have felt it was less necessary after the war had been won [1, L2].

4
- In 1922 Lenin had a stroke, and lost control of the Communists [1, L1].
- Communist Party policy was taken over by Zinoviev, Kamenev and Stalin [1, L2].
- Stalin joined with Zinoviev and Kamenev to force Trotsky out [1, L1]. Zinoviev and Kamenev were on the left wing of the party with Trotsky [1, L1], but they joined together with Stalin in order to stop Trotsky taking over — Trotsky was seen as arrogant and had made many enemies [1, L2].
- Stalin then forced Zinoviev and Kamenev out [1, L1]. Stalin supported the New Economic Policy against the leftist Zinoviev and Kamenev, who wanted fast economic modernisation, and used the issue to force them out of the Party [1, L2].
- By 1929 Stalin had defeated all his rivals and assumed total control of the Communist Party [1, L1]. He achieved this by switching support to fast economic modernisation [1, L2], which allowed him to get rid of his former allies on the right such as Bukharin and Rykov who had supported the New Economic Policy [1, L2] [+ 3 marks for SPaG].

5 a)
- The poster shows a Red Army soldier fighting a caricature capitalist [1, L1]. They appear to be fighting for the whole globe, showing how important their conflict is [1, L1].
- The poster shows that the Red Army is driving the capitalist away and defending Russia [1, L2]. The fact that it is 'the last decisive battle' may mean that the poster is arguing that the communists will be able to drive into Europe, and help spread the revolution there [1, L3].
- The poster gives both a patriotic message (the soldier is defending Russia) and a political message (the soldier could be seen as driving capitalism out of Europe) [1, L4]. The poster both calls on people to defend Russia, and gives them a hopeful message for the future, which is emphasised by the rising sun bringing in a "new dawn" [1, L5].

b)
- The source is a doctored photo [1, L1], showing how Stalin tried to control the media [1, L1]. Stalin not only purged those he disagreed with from the party, but also removed them from the history books, as this photo shows [1, L2].
- The source is useful as not only does it show how Stalin tried to remove from sight those he wanted forgotten, it also shows how he tried to make himself look more important, since in this photo he is left standing on his own in the middle of the picture [1, L3]. In fact, the official history of the October Revolution was rewritten to give Stalin a more important role than the relatively minor one he'd had in the real events [1, L3].
- Disinformation was a key part of Stalin's rule of terror, since people could be removed from history. But Stalin's use of terror to control the party also involved a series of purges, which eventually included various other organisations and 'non-political' people [1, L4]. Stalin also used the NKVD, the secret police, to imprison or execute anyone suspected of disloyalty. No one was safe if Stalin doubted them. However, the photo does not show Stalin's use of these kinds of tactics [1, L4].

c)
- The source is from a speech by Stalin where he talks of eliminating the kulaks [1, L1]. It shows he wanted to do as much damage to them as possible [1, L2]. The kulaks were the richer peasants who were often quite influential in farming villages. An estimated 3 million kulaks were killed as a result of Stalin's actions [1, L2].
- However, there were other problems in agriculture. Some farmers were against the communists and collectivisation, perhaps for political reasons or perhaps because collectivisation disrupted their more traditional way of life [1, L4]. So some farmers preferred to burn their crops and destroy their animals rather than hand them over during collectivisation [1, L3]. This helped to create food shortages and starvation [1, L4].
- But the source does show how indifferent to the fate of ordinary Russians Stalin was, suggesting that much of the suffering of both kulaks and others was either deliberately inflicted or a matter of indifference [1, L5].

6 a)
- Stolypin ended the control of the mir over how land was distributed [1, L1]. The mir were local councils that controlled peasant villages [1, L2].
- Hard-working peasants could now rent or buy their own land for themselves, and were given help by special Peasant Banks [1, L1]. These better-off peasants were known as kulaks [1, L2].

b)
- The Provisional Government was weak [1, L1], and the Bolsheviks were ruthless and opportunistic in their pursuit of power [1, L2].
- The Bolsheviks had a military force (the Red Guard) under their control [1, L2]. They had also benefited when General Kornilov attempted to seize power, since to stop him, the Provisional Government had given weapons to the Bolsheviks and the Petrograd Soviet. These would later be used when the Bolsheviks made their own grab for power [1, L3].
- The Provisional Government had failed to deal with the big problems Russia was facing — a breakdown in law and order, famine and Russia's continued participation in the war. This made the Provisional Government unpopular, and meant more people supported the actions of the Bolsheviks [1, L3].
- The Bolsheviks were well organized. Leon Trotsky did detailed planning for the seizure of power, which helped the Bolsheviks take power quickly in Petrograd by gaining control of key buildings [1, L3].

c)
- The war certainly caused huge difficulties for the Tsar [1, L1]. However, he had already faced disruption in 1905, well before the war [1, L1].
- The Tsar took personal command of the army in 1915. This made the Tsar unpopular because it meant his wife was left in power. She was also unpopular, and was felt to be too heavily influenced by the "holy man" Rasputin, undermining the Tsar's authority [1, L2].
- The war caused high inflation, and food and fuel shortages. These led to demonstrations and riots in the capital city. When troops refused to fire on protesters but instead started to desert, it became clear that the Tsar had lost control. It was these problems which sparked the revolution, and these did result directly from the war [1, L3].
- After 1905, the Tsar had allowed a parliament to be set up. But he had repeatedly forced out parties critical of his rule. This meant that people's concerns had not been addressed, and the Tsar was still the most important figure who could be blamed when things went wrong [1, L3].
- The fact that there had been a near revolution in 1905 shows that there were deeper, longer-term problems in Russia that weren't directly a product of the war [1, L3]. For example, people wanted more power to affect their own lives. Conditions were still very hard for industrial workers in towns and cities, so workers in Petrograd formed the Petrograd Soviet, which ended up sparking the revolution through their protests [1, L4].
- There was also tension between peasants and those who had grown rich through agricultural reforms — the kulaks. When the Russian Revolution did occur there was violence between these groups [1, L4].
- The hunger and discontent with the war were probably the most important reasons for the Tsar's fall [1, L5]. They would also lead to the unpopularity, and eventual overthrow, of the Provisional Government that followed [1, L5] [+ 3 marks for SPaG].

Answers: 236-8

Pages 236-238: The USA: 1945 to 1975

1 a) • The photograph shows two black American athletes giving a "Black Power" salute at the 1968 Olympics. This protest was part of their campaign for civil rights for African Americans in the USA [1, L1], and an event that would have been seen by millions of people [1, L1].
   • "Black Power" was a slogan made popular by the civil rights campaigner Stokely Carmichael [1, L2], who had been chairman of the SNCC (Student Nonviolent Coordinating Committee) [1, L2]. "Black Power" involved a militant and extreme approach to civil rights [1, L2], contrasting strongly with the non-violent approach of Martin Luther King [1, L3]. For example, a Black Power conference had called for a separate African-American nation, and an African-American militia (an armed group of private citizens) [1, L3].
   • The protest in the picture and these more extreme "Black Power" beliefs, would have been controversial among some civil rights campaigners, since this more extreme approach may have made people feel less sympathetic towards their cause [1, L3].

b) • Martin Luther King was a key activist in African Americans' struggle for civil rights [1, L1]. He favoured peaceful protests, such as marches, sit-ins and freedom rides [1, L1], believing that they were more likely to win sympathy from people than violent methods [1, L1].
   • Among the many protests that Martin Luther King helped organise was the Montgomery bus boycott. This was a key event in the civil rights struggle, as it led to a successful legal challenge against segregation, and showed that a peaceful approach could achieve results [1, L2].
   • Other King protests included mass marches, with around 250 000 people attending the 1963 march on Washington [1, L2], showing the level of support that the campaign had won [1, L2].
   • This does not mean that King was the only important figure in the civil rights struggle [1, L3]. Many other people made significant contributions too, such as Rosa Parks, and Presidents Kennedy and Johnson [1, L3]. And King's approach was not popular with everyone [1, L3], with some people becoming frustrated with the non-violent approach [1, L3].
   • But King was a vital campaigner. After his assassination, he was seen as a kind of martyr figure, and there were riots in many major cities [1, L5]. A Civil Rights Bill was passed shortly after [1, L4] [+ 3 marks for SPaG].

2 a) • This extract shows McCarthy's claim that there were communist sympathisers in influential positions in the USA, but it does not prove that he is correct [1, L1]. He claims to have a list of names of these communist sympathisers [1, L2], but there is no evidence in the source to suggest that they did have communist beliefs, or that they would try to influence American policy in a way that was not in America's best interests [1, L3]. The source really just shows McCarthy's personal views [1, L4].
   • This does not mean that American communist sympathisers were not a problem at all for the USA at this time. Julius and Ethel Rosenberg were executed for passing atomic secrets to the Soviets in 1953, for example [1, L5]. And many people, including the director of the FBI, did actually believe that there were American 'subversives' in influential positions [1, L5]. However, Source C does not on its own establish that communist sympathisers were a serious issue in the USA in the 1950s [1, L5].

b) • This extract shows that its author believes King was an effective campaigner [1, L1]. He praises King, saying that he chose the locations for his protests "shrewdly", in a way that would "elicit popular sympathy for his goals" [1, L2].
   • King certainly did attract a large and sympathetic following, as is clear from the number of people attending some of his protests. For example, the march on Washington in 1963 was a mass event [1, L3], and the size of the crowds was certainly a factor in its effectiveness [1, L3].
   • However, this extract does not prove that King was the most effective campaigner in the civil rights struggle, since it does not compare the contributions of other campaigners, such as Malcolm X or Stokely Carmichael [1, L4].

• Although it is only one person's opinion, the extract is taken from a book written long after the events it is describing, so the author would have had an overview of which events and people were most significant in the civil rights struggle [1, L5]. For this reason, I think the source is useful for gaining an insight into the civil rights struggle, but it does not establish that King was the most effective campaigner of that era [1, L5].

c) • This photograph shows a civil rights march in Washington in August 1963. It shows Martin Luther King in front of a massive crowd campaigning for greater civil rights for African Americans in the USA [1, L1]. This photograph would have shown the level of support the campaign had [1, L2], and that King was an influential figure in the campaign and could attract a huge following [1, L2].
   • As well as showing the overall popularity of the campaign, since many of the faces in the crowd are white, it would have shown that this campaign was supported by a broad cross-section of society [1, L3].
   • The photo also shows the march to be peaceful and orderly, suggesting that the protesters (and therefore perhaps also the cause itself) are respectable [1, L4]. This may have been an especially powerful message, given that a peaceful protest earlier that year in Birmingham, Alabama was met by police with fire hoses, truncheons and police dogs [1, L5].

3 a) • Cesar Chavez was the grandson of Mexican immigrants into the USA, and he was an important figure in the struggle for better conditions for American workers [1, L1]. He formed the United Farm Workers union in 1962 [1, L2], and campaigned for greater rights and better conditions for migrant workers, and at one stage called for Americans to boycott grapes to protest against poor working conditions [1, L1]. His campaign raised awareness of the unfair treatment of Hispanic Americans [1, L2].

b) • In the 1950s, the American government adopted a policy aimed at ending the special recognition and status that had previously been granted to Native American tribes [1, L1]. The aim of the new 'termination' policy was to completely assimilate Native Americans into the wider population [1, L2]. This required 'terminated' Native American tribes to pay more taxes than previously, which led to them selling land and mineral rights, and leaving them financially less well off than before [1, L3].
   • The Native Americans' civil rights campaign addressed other issues too. Some Native Americans were subjected to police harassment [1, L2], while the campaign later pushed for better living standards [1, L3] and greater recognition of the tribes' rights under earlier treaties [1, L3].

c) • The campaign for women's rights achieved much greater levels of equality between men and women by 1975 than had existed before [1, L1]. There were changes in many fields, including employment [1, L2] and education [1, L2].
   • Paying women less for doing the same job [1, L3], and discriminating on the basis of sex while recruiting someone for a job, both became illegal [1, L3]. The law also changed to force educational establishments to provide equal facilities and opportunities for both sexes [1, L3].
   • However, there were also frustrations. Although employers now had to pay men and women the same for doing the same job, employers could easily get round this law by using different job titles [1, L4]. And while workplace discrimination based on sex was illegal, little was done to enforce this law [1, L4].
   • So the position of women had certainly improved by 1975, to a large extent due to those campaigning for women's rights [1, L5]. But other factors had also contributed, such as the introduction of the contraceptive pill, which made it easier for women to put off having children while they established themselves in a career [1, L4] [+ 3 marks for SPaG].

4
- In 1950, Senator Joseph McCarthy thought that there were communists working in the US government [1, L1]. The extract shows that McCarthy considered all communists (even American citizens) to be the 'enemy', since their first loyalty would be "to the Communist Party" [1, L3]. He felt that this was a serious danger to the USA [1, L2], because that would mean the 'enemy' were actually helping to shape US policies [1, L3].

5
- This poster was put up by people protesting against American involvement in the Vietnam War. It is trying to convince the government to withdraw American troops [1, L1].
- The poster shows a character who represents the USA 'wanting out' of the Vietnam War [1, L2]. He is wearing bandages over various wounds, and this is supposed to show that the USA has suffered badly during the war [1, L2].
- The figure is looking pleadingly at passers-by, as if begging them to support the policy of troop withdrawal [1, L3]. This poster, which is a parody of a WWI military recruitment poster, was put up to gain support for troop withdrawal at a time when students were protesting increasingly strongly against a war [1, L3] being fought for a cause that many people did not believe in [1, L3].

6
- These sources show that non-violent protest was an effective way for African-American civil rights campaigners to try and achieve their aims [1, L1]. Many laws and attitudes changed as a result of the civil rights campaigns, in which non-violent protest played a major part [1, L1].
- Source A shows a civil rights march in Washington in August 1963. It shows Martin Luther King in front of a massive crowd campaigning for greater civil rights for African Americans in the USA [1, L2]. King was in favour of non-violent protest to achieve his aims, and so this photo shows the level of support both for the campaign and for King's approach [1, L2].
- Source E says that King "shrewdly" organised protests where he could have expected a violent reaction from the authorities which would "elicit popular sympathy" for his goals [1, L3]. This suggests that King's tactics had worked out as he had anticipated. And because the extract was written so long after the events it is describing, the historian author perhaps has a clearer view of the success or failure of particular tactics than someone writing at the time these events actually happened [1, L3].
- Source B shows a different form of protest, a "Black Power" salute at the 1968 Olympics. Although the Black Power movement was generally more militant and held more extreme views than Martin Luther King, this salute is a non-violent form of protest [1, L2], and would have been widely seen because of the popularity of the Olympics. However, there is no way to judge the effectiveness of this protest [1, L2].
- I think the sources do support the view that non-violent protest was an effective way to campaign — the tactic was popular at the time, and the historian seems to consider them successful, although it should be remembered that Source E shows only one person's opinion [1, L3].

7
- Source E describes methods used by Martin Luther King, a campaigner for African-American civil rights [1, L1]. It was written some time after the events it describes took place, but this means the author had time to assess the effectiveness of the tactics it describes [1, L1].
- Source E is a historian's judgement of the tactics used by Martin Luther King. It suggests that the non-violent approach used by King produced a violent response, and therefore elicited sympathy for King's goals [1, L2]. So it is commenting fairly directly on the effectiveness of King's campaign [1, L2].
- Source D shows a poster urging people to support the withdrawal of US troops from Vietnam, so this shows another method used by a different protest group [1, L1].
- On its own, Source D cannot say much about the effectiveness of the campaign against the Vietnam War [1, L2]. The source is only really useful in telling us that there were some people against the war, who tried to rally further support against it [1, L2].

- Although Source E is only one person's interpretation of events, the author is a historian who has researched the period, making it more credible and authoritative than some accounts [1, L3]. And because the author explains not just what results the campaign achieved, but how it achieved those results, it is especially useful [1, L3].

8
- All the sources show, or refer to, some form of protest. There are protests in support of civil rights for African Americans, protests against American involvement in the Vietnam war, and in Source C a 'protest' against Americans holding particular views [1, L1]. These are all protests by Americans against Americans, and so suggest that the country was divided in many ways in the years between 1945 and 1975 [1, L1].
- Source C shows Senator McCarthy's claim that some Americans working for the government held communist beliefs, and would therefore betray the USA because they had a greater loyalty to communism than the USA [1, L2]. However, this is one man's opinion, and Senator McCarthy never proved his allegations [1, L2]. There was certainly a great deal of anti-communist feeling at the time, but McCarthy eventually lost popularity both with the general public and with his colleagues in the US Senate. I do not therefore think this source shows evidence of a divided country [1, L3].
- Source A shows a large group of people campaigning against laws that discriminated against African Americans [1, L2]. These laws had led to a great deal of violence, including riots and assassinations. Source E shows that people enforcing the USA's laws were prepared to use violence against their fellow citizens [1, L3], while the Black Power movement, represented by Source B, even called for a separate African-American nation. These all suggest that there were serious divisions in the USA at that time [1, L3].
- Source D represents the campaign against the Vietnam War [1, L2]. This had been a source of disagreement for many years, with clashes between protesters and the police in 1968, and deaths in 1970 when National Guardsmen opened fire on student anti-war protesters [1, L3].
- Importantly, all the situations represented by the sources have moved on over the years, with unpopular laws and policies eventually having to change [1, L4]. I think this all shows the USA was divided, but was able to overcome its divisions to find answers to problems [1, L4] [+ 3 marks for SPaG].

9 a)
- Source D shows a poster urging people to support the withdrawal of US troops from Vietnam [1, L1]. The poster's aim was to turn people against the war [1, L2] and gain more support for the protest movement [1, L2].
- As the war dragged on and casualties rose, posters like Source D and high-profile protests against the war became more common [1, L2]. In October 1967, 50 000 people marched on the Pentagon during 'Stop the Draft Week' to protest against the draft (conscription) [1, L2]. Further protests, such as in Chicago in 1968 (during the Democratic Convention) and in Washington DC in 1971 by the Vietnam Veterans Against the War, encouraged a greater anti-war feeling [1, L3].
- The protest movement began to lower the morale of the troops in Vietnam as the soldiers questioned why they were fighting [1, L3]. It also increased pessimism about the Vietnam War in America and made both President Johnson and President Nixon look for a way to end the war quickly [1, L3].

b)
- The failures of the US military in the jungles of south-east Asia certainly contributed to the USA's defeat in the Vietnam War, but the loss of public support back home in America made it impossible to win the war [1, L1].
- The US struggled to fight against the highly developed guerrilla tactics used by the Vietcong. The Vietcong skilfully used surprise attacks, traps and tunnels to inflict casualties on the US soldiers [1, L2]. The US military also found it difficult to make progress against the Vietcong because even when they had driven them out of an area they could not stop them from returning [1, L2]. On top of this, many of the US soldiers were very young and often only served for a year, so they found it hard to defeat their more experienced enemy [1, L2].
- As the US military struggled, public opinion in the US was rapidly turning against the Vietnam War. The anti-war protest movement

Answers: 236-41

encouraged more and more people to campaign against the conflict, and this started to undermine the soldiers' morale [1, L4].

- In particular, media coverage of the Tet Offensive had a negative impact on US public opinion [1, L2]. US TV audiences saw footage of the Vietcong attacks on the American Embassy in Saigon, which seemed to prove that the Vietcong were very strong and the US military was a long way from defeating them [1, L2]. The Tet Offensive caused many people to lose faith in the US's ability to win the war [1, L3].
- The Tet Offensive turned out to be a massive military defeat for the Vietcong, but it had convinced many Americans to demand a peaceful end to the war [1, L3]. Richard Nixon promised that he would bring 'peace with honour' to Vietnam, and this helped him to be elected president in 1968 [1, L2]. Nixon began to withdraw troops, but the public was outraged when he tried to escalate the war with attacks on Cambodia and Laos in order to force peace talks with North Vietnam. By this point, most Americans were sick of the war and Congress cut its funding, forcing Nixon to back down and ultimately agree to a peace deal in 1973 [1, L3].
- The US military struggled to fight against the Vietcong, but in the end the war was lost at home. This can be shown by the Tet Offensive, which was a military defeat for the Vietcong, but made many Americans believe that the war could not be won. This led to demands for a peaceful end to the war, the withdrawal of US troops, and Congress cutting the war's funding — effectively forcing Nixon to agree to the peace deal in 1973 [1, L5] [+ 3 marks for SPaG].

Pages 239-241: Britain: 1890 to 1928

1   • This poster shows a woman wanting to escape from a cage she is trapped in, alongside convicts and 'lunatics' [1, L1]. From the caption in the centre of the poster, we can see the cage represents the situation of women, convicts and 'lunatics' not being allowed to vote [1, L2].
   • The poster is trying to convince people that women should not be grouped alongside these other categories of people, and should be 'freed' to vote as they like [1, L3]. The woman is dressed in academic robes to show that women were just as mentally capable as men [1, L4]. This is important since many people justified not allowing women to vote by saying that women were too irrational and therefore incapable of making sensible decisions [1, L5].

2   • Source B is a Suffragette poster showing a woman trying to escape from a cage that she is locked up in, alongside convicts and lunatics. It is saying that women should be given the vote for moral reasons (i.e. because women are morally equal to (and no less capable than) men and so it would be <u>unfair</u> not to give them the vote) [1, L1].
   • Source F describes how women were given the vote "almost as a by-product of the war", as if women were given the vote more for practical reasons than moral reasons (i.e. because women were now so indispensable in society, it would be <u>politically difficult</u> to deny them the vote, though not necessarily unfair) [1, L1].
   • Source B was produced before women were actually given the vote [1, L2], and so the makers were not in a position to know why women were eventually given this right [1, L3]. It gives us a good insight into the authors' beliefs, but cannot describe events that were yet to happen [1, L4].
   • Source F was written fairly recently, and so the author would have had a good perspective to judge why some women got the vote in 1918. However, this is still just one person's opinion [1, L3].
   • In reality, women were given the vote for a mixture of moral and practical reasons. Attitudes towards women had certainly been changed by the war. There was a sense of gratitude towards women for what they had done, and a feeling that it would be unfair to deny them full political rights, meaning the view suggested by Source B did have some bearing on the decision [1, L5]. But as Source F states, the whole balance of society was different after the war, and this made for some very practical reasons for giving women the vote (although only women over 30 were given the vote in 1918) [1, L5].

3   • Both sources are about the introduction of National Insurance (NI). Source G praises David Lloyd George for introducing it, while Source J describes a protest against it. But Source J doesn't necessarily prove Source G wrong — they just show two different opinions on the subject, most likely from two groups of people who would be affected by it differently [1, L1].
   • Source J is a newspaper article about women protesting against the introduction of National Insurance [1, L2]. The source suggests they resented householders having to pay contributions of 3d for each of their servants [1, L3].
   • Source G is a postcard celebrating the introduction of NI [1, L2]. It includes a picture of David Lloyd George, which takes up most of the postcard, suggesting the purpose of the postcard was more to gain votes for Lloyd George and his party than to celebrate the extra protection for the working class [1, L3].
   • National Insurance was always likely to be more popular with people receiving the benefits than with those having to pay for it, and this is basically what the sources show [1, L4]. Source J describes the protest of some of those expected to pay [1, L5], while Source G shows a postcard aimed at popularising Lloyd George with those who may expect to receive the benefits. Therefore Source J does not prove Source G wrong [1, L5].

4   • The source shows food shortages in Britain, with a stereotypical British man and a corpse-like symbol of famine looking at empty shop windows [1, L1]. However, the cartoon was produced in Germany during World War I and so almost certainly is propaganda [1, L1].
   • The German artist who drew the cartoon would not have been in a position to know the situation in Britain in detail [1, L2], but would have known that German U-boats were sinking a lot of British merchant shipping, and would perhaps have believed that there were food shortages in Britain as a result [1, L3]. So there is a small element of truth, although very exaggerated [1, L3].
   • The cartoon is of very little use in understanding the true situation in Britain because the cartoonist had such a strong propaganda motive for depicting the British as starving [1, L4], especially given that the Germans were suffering severe food shortages themselves [1, L5].

5   • Between 1890 and 1918, the British government brought in many measures to improve living conditions for the people [1, L1]. But British people suffered greatly during WWI [1, L1].
   • At the start of the 20th century, the government tried to improve living conditions for the country's poor [1, L2]. Source G shows David Lloyd George, who was the Liberal Prime Minister who brought in the National Insurance Act of 1911 [1, L3]. This Act meant that people were entitled to sick pay when they were too ill to work, and workers in some trades would also be entitled to unemployment benefit if they lost their job. Other Acts aimed to improve conditions for children and the elderly [1, L4]. Source F also shows how women were given the vote in 1918, although Source B suggests that it was a struggle for women before they were given this right [1, L4].
   • However, this period also saw the British people fighting the First World War [1, L3]. This was obviously a time of great suffering for the soldiers who went to war, as Sources C and D suggest [1, L5]. But it also involved hardship for people at home. Source I shows that the Germans were hoping to cause food shortages for the British [1, L5], and they were actually successful enough that rationing had to be introduced [1, L5].
   • The sources do suggest that the British people probably were better off overall in 1918 than in 1890 [1, L5]. However, the sources also show that this was not a period during which conditions steadily improved, as life was made extremely harsh as a result of the war [1, L5] [+ 3 marks for SPaG].

Answers: 239-41

6
- Sir Douglas Haig, the senior commander of the British Army during WWI, believed in 1916 that the war would continue to kill large numbers of soldiers [1, L1], since he says that "the nation must be taught to bear losses" [1, L2].
- He thought this loss of life was inevitable [1, L2], and that "no training" and "no superiority [...] of arms and ammunition" would allow the war to be won without the country suffering these deaths [1, L3].
- He also thought it was important that the public understood that many more soldiers would die [1, L3], since he is asking British newspapers to explain that there was no way to win the war without the "sacrifice of men's lives" [1, L3].

7
- This poster shows a woman in academic robes [1, L1] wanting to escape from a cage in which she is trapped, alongside convicts and 'lunatics' [1, L1]. From the caption in the centre of the poster [1, L2], we can see that the cage represents the situation of women, convicts and 'lunatics' not being allowed to vote [1, L2].
- The poster is trying to convince people that women should not be grouped alongside these other categories of people [1, L3], and should be 'freed' to vote as they like [1, L3]. The woman's academic robes are supposed to show that women were just as mentally capable as men [1, L2], which is important since many people justified not allowing women to vote by saying that women were too irrational and therefore incapable of making sensible decisions [1, L3].

8
- Strikes and violent protests were not the most effective way to bring about social change in Britain in the early 20th century [1, L1]. Source A shows a photograph taken during the General Strike of 1926, which did not achieve its aims [1, L1], while Source F shows that women were not given the vote as a direct result of confrontation with the government or protests [1, L1].
- The General Strike of 1926 could not exert as much pressure on the government as the strikers wanted because the government was able to "keep the country moving" [1, L2]. For example, the government was able to recruit volunteers to keep vital services such as the buses, trains and London Underground running. Source A shows one such volunteer worker on the trains [1, L2].
- Source F describes how women were eventually given the vote. However, it describes how this was not the result of direct protest, but of changing attitudes in society as a result of women's contribution to the war effort [1, L2]. This contribution had "changed the whole balance of society" in a way that helped persuade the government to extend the vote to all women over the age of 30 [1, L2].
- These sources do support the view that strikes and protests were not the best way to bring about social change in Britain in this period, but they do not prove it [1, L3]. One isolated picture of a volunteer working on a train could easily be an example of propaganda, and therefore proves little, while Source F is merely one person's opinion [1, L3].

9
- This message does not surprise me, since the British government produced a great deal of propaganda during the war [1, L1]. This extract makes the Germans look evil and barbaric [1, L1].
- This report was probably written to help justify the war to the British people [1, L2], so that they would think the war needs to be fought and would be willing to "get behind" the war effort [1, L3]. The extract mentions "organised massacres of the civil population", which might make people think the Germans had to be defeated, at almost any cost [1, L3].
- The British produced various types of propaganda aimed both at the British people (e.g. to get men to sign up for the army) and governments overseas (e.g. to encourage the United States to become involved in the war) [1, L4]. With this report, the government might have been trying to convince people to accept drastic wartime measures (either measures already introduced, such as those in the Defence of the Realm Act, or those that might be necessary in the future, such as conscription, rationing or censorship) [1, L5].

10
- Both sources are useful, since they were written by people who had served in the trenches [1, L1]. However, Source C is a poem, and so not every word should be taken absolutely literally [1, L1]. And Source E was written a long time after the events they are describing, when the author was a very old man [1, L1].
- Source C emphasises the horror of the battlefield and was written during the war [1, L2], and so it probably reflects the feelings the author had at that time [1, L2]. Source E is a more positive account of heroic determination, but there is a risk after such a long time that the author's actual memories may have faded, which could mean he is placing too great a focus on his positive experiences [1, L2]. This does not necessarily mean the account is inaccurate, but it is noticeable that none of the inevitable suffering of the battle is described [1, L2].
- Both sources are useful, but in different ways. The poem is perhaps best used for understanding how it felt to be a soldier at the front [1, L3], rather than as a literal description of what the physical environment was like there [1, L3]. Source E is still an eyewitness account and so is certainly useful, but it feels more 'remote' from the events that it is describing, and does not seem to show the full experience of a British soldier during a battle [1, L3] [+ 3 marks for SPaG].

Acknowledgements

The publisher would like to thank the following:

Rex Features for permission to use the images on pages 80, 113, 188, 223, 233 and 236.
Mary Evans Picture Library for permission to use the images on pages 9, 24, 30, 41, 49, 62, 92, 113, 130, 138, 164, 169, 217, 219, 220, 221, 224, 226, 228, 231, 236, 239 and 240.
Getty Images for permission to use the images on pages 120, 134, 169 and 225.

Page 14   *Source B — J F Aylett, The Cold War and After, Hodder Arnold, 1996.*
           Reproduced by permission of Edward Arnold (Publishers) Ltd.

           Source C — © Associated Newspapers Ltd

Page 72   *Source A — 'Thank you Gorby', graffiti on the Berlin Wall, 1990 (b/w photo)*
           by Berlin, Germany/ © H.P. Stiebing/ The Bridgeman Art Library

Page 138   *Source B — Reproduced With Permission of Punch Ltd., www.punch.co.uk*

Page 164   *Source B — Stalin at the hydro-electric complex at Ryon in the Caucasus Mountains, 1935,*
           reproduction of the original in 'Soviet Painting', 1939 (colour litho) by Toidze, Irakli
           Moiseievich (1902-p.1941)
           Private Collection / Archives Charmet/ The Bridgeman Art Library

Page 188   *Source A — The March on Washington: Freedom Walkers, 28th August 1963*
           (b/w photo) by Herz, Nat (1920-64)
           Private Collection / Barbara Singer / The Bridgeman Art Library

Page 217   *Source A — 'The End of the Hunger Strike', poster advertising Plasmon Oats,*
           early 20th century (litho) by Reed, Anita (20th century) (after)
           Private Collection / The Stapleton Collection / The Bridgeman Art Library

Page 222   *Source A — American and Soviet troops shake hands at a bombed bridge on the Elbe, near Torgau,*
           26th April 1954 (b/w photo) by American Photographer, (20th century) / © SZ Photo
           The Bridgeman Art Library

Page 226   *Source A — Battle of Jutland, 31st May 1916, poster celebrating Allied victory (litho)*
           © Imperial War Museum, London, UK / The Bridgeman Art Library

Page 228   *Source B — The cabin of a German U-boat captain, featuring a compulsory portrait of Adolf Hitler*
           (b/w photo) by German Photographer (20th Century) / © SZ Photo
           The Bridgeman Art Library

Page 231   *Source B — 'Boo-hoo the New Deal is ruining the Country',*
           cartoon of the effects of Franklin Roosevelt's (1882-1945) economic policies,
           1936 (litho) by American School, (20th century)
           Private Collection / Peter Newark American Pictures / The Bridgeman Art Library

Page 233   *Source B — 'The Last Decisive Battle', Soviet poster celebrating the 3rd Anniversary of the October*
           Revolution,
           1920 (colour litho) by Russian School, (20th century)
           Private Collection / Barbara Singer / The Bridgeman Art Library

Page 236   *Source D — 'I Want Out', anti-Vietnam War poster (colour litho) by American School, (20th century)*
           Private Collection / Peter Newark American Pictures / The Bridgeman Art Library

           Source E — from "Grand Expectations: The United States, 1945-1974" by Patterson James (1997).
           By Permission of Oxford University Press, Inc

Page 239   *Source B — 'Convicts and Lunatics Have No Vote for Parliament. Should all women be classed with these?',*
           Suffragette propaganda poster, c.1910 (litho) by Harding Andrews, Emily J. (fl.1910)
           Fawcett Library, London, UK / The Bridgeman Art Library

Page 240   *Source F — from "The First World War: Very Short Introductions" by Howard Michael (2002).*
           By Permission of Oxford University Press, Inc

Index

Index

Index

Index

Make sure you're not missing out on another superb CGP revision book that might just save your life...

...order your **free** catalogue today.

CGP customer service is second to none

We work very hard to despatch all orders the **same day** we receive them, and our success rate is currently 99.9%. We send all orders by **overnight courier** or **First Class** post.
If you ring us today you should get your catalogue or book tomorrow. Irresistible, surely?

- Phone: 0870 750 1252   (Mon-Fri, 8.30am to 5.30pm)
- Fax: 0870 750 1292
- e-mail: orders@cgpbooks.co.uk
- Post: CGP Orders, Broughton-in-Furness, Cumbria, LA20 6BN
- Website: www.cgpbooks.co.uk

...or you can ask at any good bookshop.